Unfinished Business

Unfinished Business

South Africa, Apartheid and Truth

TERRY BELL

with

DUMISA BUHLE NTSEBEZA

VERSO

London • New York

This edition published by Verso 2003
© Terry Bell 2003

First published in South Africa in 2001 by RedWorks
for and on behalf of Understanding Our Past
© Terry Bell 2001

1 3 5 7 9 10 8 6 4 2

Verso
UK: 6 Meard Street, London W1F 0EG
USA: 180 Varick Street, New York, NY 10014–4606
www.versobooks.com

Verso is the imprint of New Left Books

ISBN 1–85984–545–2

British Library Cataloguing in Publication Data
Bell, Terry
    Unfinished business: South Africa, apartheid and truth
    1. Apartheid 2. Civil rights – South Africa 3. Political
    crimes and offenses – Investigation – South Africa 4. South
    Africa – Politics and government – 1994–
    I. Title II. Ntsebeza, Dumisa Buhle
    323.1'1968

ISBN 1859845452

Library of Congress Cataloging-in-Publication Data
A catalog record for this book is available from the Library of Congress

Typeset in 10/12pt Dante by
SetSystems Ltd, Saffron Walden, Essex
Printed in the UK by Bath Press

To those who sought and who continue to
seek a clearer understanding of the past in
order to build a better future for all

Contents

File Three: From cul-de-sac to compromise

Acknowledgements

This book has taken much longer – and involved help from many more people than was first envisaged. Reminiscences, anecdotes, scraps of documents or whole bundles came our way. Occasionally there were only a few hours to take down notes from massive files. Quantity and quality bore no relation. One small tip-off could provide a vital key as easily as a file of documents.

But a few names stand out, among those who did not request to remain anonymous. None more so than that of Jan-Ake Kjellenberg, the Swedish TRC investigator. Others who must be singled out for special mention are Lungisile Ntsebeza, Tom Newnham, Sampie Terreblanche, Hugh Lewin, Piers Pigou and Sadie Forman, who gave so unstintingly of their time. The hospitality and help of Hans and Gertie Strydom was especially appreciated. Special thanks must also go to the staff of both the National Library in Pretoria and in Cape Town and to various Cape Town city libraries for their help.

In alphabetical order, thanks are also extended to: Eric Abraham, Aversion Project Group, Howard Barrell, Michael Bell, Paul Bell, Debbie Budlender, Geoff Budlender, Colin Bundy, Colin Chiles, Jeremy Cronin, Colin Darch, Cedric de Beer, Ethel de Keyser, Eugene de Kock, Rick de Satge, Rory Doepel, Clive Emdon, Don Foster, Bennie Gool, Bantubonke Holomisa, Mkhuseli Jack, Riaz Jawoodeen, Sheila Lapinsky, Leslie London, Wilson Magadla, Sherry McLean-Schoon, Pamela Mntonintshi, Meshack Mochele, Glenn Moss, Mvelaphanda Holdings, Mxolisi Mgxashe, Aida Parker, Jill Pointer, *Private Eye* (London), André Proctor, Neville Rubin, James Sanders, Laura Schultz, Ronald Segal, Ray Simons, Yasmin Sooka, Spain's Africa Austral support group, Helen Suzman, Mike Terry, Amy Thornton, Peter Thuynsma, Peter and Louise Vale, Jeremy Veary, Ginny Volbrecht, Ann Wolfe, David Wolfe. Conversations over the years with comrades including Amin Cajee and the late Eli Maroko, Eli Weinberg and Jack Simons enriched my understanding.

Of course, without Dumisa Ntsebeza and the research undertaken by my partner, Barbara, this book would never have emerged. Thanks also to the contributions of our children, Ceiren and Brendan, and to Ahmed Rajab and the Africa Analysis team for the support they have given.

Last – and by no means least – mention must be made of the editing skills of Bryan Rostron, of his thoughtful advice and good humour, which were invaluable in determining the final result.

Terry Bell
London, 2002

Abbreviations

AB	Afrikaner Broederbond
ANC	African National Congress
Apla	Azanian People's Liberation Army
ARM	African Resistance Movement
ASB	Afrikaner Studentebond (Afrikaner Students' Union)
AWB	Afrikaner Weerstandsbeweging (Afrikaner Resistance Movement)
Azapo	Azanian People's Organisation
BC	Black Consciousness
BLA	Black Lawyers' Association
BOSS	Bureau of State Security
BSAP	British South African Police
CCB	Civil Cooperation Bureau
Codesa	Convention for a Democratic South Africa
COSAS	Congress of South African Students
Cosatu	Congress of South African Trade Unions
CUSA	Congress of Unions of South Africa
DCC	Directorate of Covert Collection
DMI	Department of Military Intelligence
DONS	Department of National Security
DRC	Dutch Reformed Church
EDA	Environmental Development Agency
ERT	Educational Research Trust
FNLA	Frente Nacional de Libertação de Angola (National Front for the Liberation of Angola)
Frelimo	Frente de Libertação de Moçambique (Mozambique Liberation Front)
HNP	Herstigte Nasionale Party (Reconstituted National Party)

IDAF	International Defence and Aid Fund
Idasa	Institute for a Democratic Alternative
IFP	Inkatha Freedom Party
IUEF	International University Exchange Fund
KIK	Kordinerende Intelligensie Komitee (Coordinating Intelligence Committee)
MK	Umkhonto we Sizwe: 'Spear of the Nation', the armed wing of the ANC
MNR	Mozambique National Resistance
MPLA	Movimento Popular de Libertação de Angola (Popular Movement for the Liberation of Angola)
Nadel	National Association of Democratic Lawyers
NIA	National Intelligence Agency
NP	National Party
NSMS	National Security Management System
NUSAS	National Union of South African Students
OB	Ossewa Brandwag (Oxwagon Guard)
PAC	Pan Africanist Congress
Pirsa	Psychological Institute of the Republic of South Africa
Priwelpro	Prisoners' Welfare Programme
Puflsa	People's United Front for the Liberation of South Africa
PST	Prisoners' Support Trust
RAU	Rand Afrikaans University
RI	Republican Intelligence
SACP	South African Communist Party
Sactu	South African Congress of Trade Unions
SAPET	South African Prisoners' Education Trust
SASO	South African Students' Organisation
SSC	State Security Council
SSD	Students for Social Democracy
SWAPO	South-West Africa People's Organisation
TRC	Truth and Reconciliation Commission
Trewits	Teenrewolusionre Inligtingtaakspan (Counter-Revolutionary Information Task Team)
UDM	United Democratic Movement
UNITA	União Nacional para a Independencia Total de Angola (National Union for the Total Independence of Angola)
WUS	World University Service
ZANU	Zimbabwe African National Union
ZAPU	Zimbabwe African People's Union

Introduction

To a burst of media frenzy, the first of a series of class action legal claims against banks and companies that profited from apartheid was launched on 17 June 2002. The claims were triggered by the publication in South Africa of the first edition of this book. Although the concentration was on the billions of dollars in potential damages to be claimed, the cases also opened up again the whole question of what the system of apartheid was all about, how it was run, by whom and to whose benefit. Also how the negotiated settlement of the apartheid impasse came about. These are vital questions concerning the unfinished business of South Africa.

And there is a huge amount of unfinished business relating to the country's apartheid past. Failure to deal with it leaves South Africa crippled in many ways. Corruption and pockets of poisonous racism remain embedded deep within our society. Many of apartheid's most senior agents – within the army, the police, the secret services and the civil service – remain in place. Some, as this book demonstrates, were even drafted in after the fall of apartheid, to conduct investigations into their former colleagues. There are also thousands of compromised individuals, many in prominent positions, whose still secret betrayals and abuses leave them open to blackmail and manipulation.

It is generally agreed that the past must be confronted in order to have any real hope of an open and democratic future. Yet how much have we really confronted the apartheid past?

In the following chapters I endeavour to provide a series of interrelated images of the past. These are constructed from shards and fragments of fact uncovered or reappraised in more than three years of research. Some of these were tragically sad or dramatic; others mundane, yet horrifying – and often grotesque.

Many people, both in South Africa and abroad, hoped that the Truth and Reconciliation Commission (TRC) established in 1996 would uncover this hidden history. It is a widely propagated myth that it did so. But most of the thirty-three-year mandate of the TRC was ignored. Behind a façade of time constraints and managerial shortcomings, some intended investigations never proceeded, others were bungled. Were truth and justice sacrificed to an idealistic concept of reconciliation?

Most importantly, no serious examination was made of the system that gave rise to some of the most horrific racist social engineering of modern times. Instead, there was a concentration on a proportion of the individual victims who came forward and on the immediate torturers, killers and persecutors. This narrowly focused litany of bloodshed and brutality often obscured more than it revealed. Apartheid was presented as a caricature summed up by police assassin and torturer Jeff Benzien demonstrating his 'wet bag' torture technique during his application for amnesty.

After 1960 and the banning of organisations advocating votes for all, and the criminalisation of anti-apartheid opposition, apartheid was categorised by the United Nations General Assembly as a crime against humanity. Many of the specific maintenance programmes of the apartheid state, from death squads to attempts to manipulate, psychologically and chemically, whole populations, stem from this era. Yet the TRC signally failed to get to grips with this vital period of apartheid.

All of the frequently bizarre schemes hatched by various secret entities established then were aimed at promoting a concept that hinged on the geographic separation of ethnic groups. The cornerstone of this policy was the 'homeland' of Transkei. When its launch into independence in 1976 failed, the vision – the hope – of promoting apartheid as a viable and acceptable option, vanished. Those in charge of, and those benefiting from, the system then desperately sought a way out of their impasse. As they did so, they relied on the brute maintenance of the status quo.

These are three separate facets of the modern apartheid past and they are represented by the three sections or files in this book.

The first deals with the early years, giving a unique glimpse at the origins of some of the secret projects which came to light through the TRC hearings and the trial in 2001 and 2002 of chemical and biological warfare specialist, Wouter Basson. It also examines in some detail the effective brain of apartheid, the Afrikaner Broederbond. This secret society to which every president, prime minister, senior parliamentarian, military and police officer belonged, together with most senior church and education leaders, was the primary think tank of the system and the major influence on policy. It was never investigated by the TRC. Nor were any of its officials called to account.

The second file deals with Transkei and introduces the story of Dumisa Ntsebeza, the second most senior black officer of the TRC. It charts his personal journey from naïve Christian student from a small rural village, to anti-apartheid activist, from torture victim to political prisoner, teacher, human rights lawyer and, finally, titular head of the investigations unit of the TRC. It deals, for the first time in detail, with some of the murderous activities of the South African security forces and their surrogates in Transkei.

The third file is devoted primarily to the bloodiest decade of apartheid, the 1980s, the circumstances leading up to the compromise of the negotiated settlement and the creation of the TRC. It provides, I hope, some insight into how it was not only possible, but perhaps inevitable, that the ANC and the renamed 'party of apartheid', the New National Party, could form an alliance. In particular, it deals with the attempt by hidden hands from the past to derail the TRC by crudely fabricating evidence to implicate Dumisa Ntsebeza in a massacre. This is a classic example of the dangers of not fully exposing the past and rooting out those criminals who still remain in positions of power. For the first time, this dramatic story is told in full.

There is now a strong move to close the door on the past, to pretend that all is not just forgiven, but forgotten; to bury many aspects of our recent history. In April 2003, after years of struggling to obtain TRC documents illegally seized and held by the National Intelligence Agency, the NIA finally relented and agreed to release the documents. But the agency did so at the same time that the justice ministry gazetted a renewable regulation exempting the NIA from having to declare what documents it holds. This declaration is a requirement for all public and private bodies under South Africa's Promotion of Access to Information Act. What the regulation means is that any government department wishing to keep secret any records, only has to transfer those records to the NIA where a 'classification and declassification committee' may rule them 'sensitive' or 'secret'.

All of this contributes toward the attempt to draw a bland screen of moral equivalence over South Africa's recent history. F.W. de Klerk who had, for more than twenty years, helped to oversee a political and security apparatus that emotionally, intellectually and physically crippled millions of people continues to be put on a par with Nelson Mandela, who spent twenty-seven years in prison for opposing such practices. This is just one high profile instance of the rewriting of history. The practice has had an army of collaborators, especially within politics and the media, both in South Africa and abroad.

In November 1993, for example, as Nelson Mandela and F.W. de Klerk made their separate ways to Oslo to collect a jointly awarded Nobel peace prize, De Klerk was legally implicated in a massacre. There was no outcry. Hardly anyone knew that the last apartheid president had admitted ordering a cross-border attack by a state hit squad that had seen five school students shot dead while they slept.

Dumisa Ntsebeza was the lawyer supporting the families of the murdered students and I kept in close touch with him at the time. He provided me with all the documentation: De Klerk, on his way to collect the peace prize, was cited as a defendant in the Transkei supreme court in a civil action for murder brought by the parents of the five children who had been killed at his admitted behest. It struck me as a dramatic exposé. As a journalist, I sent it to newspapers in every capital that De Klerk would be visiting as well as to local media. It was not published.

I was enraged. Fergal Keane, the BBC correspondent in South Africa at the time, expressed no surprise. His analysis was simple: 'Who wants to bugger up a fairy tale?' Which was what the South African story was rapidly turning into: a fairy tale, a myth. Here was the 'political miracle' of so many newspaper headlines. This fairy tale, however, has had the effect of severing the moral moorings of our history. Because it amounted to the promotion of amnesia, and denying of the essence of the past, it also means denying what exists in the present and what effect this might have on the future.

Later, and again without attendant publicity, Mandela intervened and persuaded De Klerk to offer compensation to the families of the murdered students in exchange for dropping the case. De Klerk ordered the payment of a large sum of state money to pay for the funerals and legal costs of the families and to compensate loss. A convenient blanket of silence fell over the massacre. Except that Sigqibo Mpendulo, father of twin boys butchered by the death squad, would not let the matter rest. He became one of the first claimants in the class action lawsuits lodged in New York in 2002 and made it clear that he wanted the murder of his children to be seen not as an isolated or aberrant act, but as a logical extension of a system that made victims of millions of people. Full details about this shameful episode are revealed here for the first time.

So too are details of the 'ANC escape route' to Botswana that was operated for six years by the police. It was largely financed by money stolen from anti-apartheid donations from around the world.

I and my researcher and partner Barbara also discovered how the police managed to establish the main anti-apartheid trust funds in South Africa in 1976. Details are given here for the first time, together with the fact that the trustee, the professor of fine arts at the liberal University of the Witwatersrand, who, in 2002, was living in Spain, was a security police agent. We also discovered that the post-apartheid deputy head of Military Intelligence, Horace William Doncaster, was none other than the chief of the apartheid military's secret DCC (Directorate of Covert Collection) unit, which organised murder and mayhem throughout southern Africa. He has never explained or apologised for that role and never appeared before the TRC. Two weeks after the publication in South Africa of the first edition of this book, he was given an 'employer-induced retrenchment package'. In short, he was paid off: given a lump sum payment, guaranteed a large pension and allowed quietly to slip off into early retirement.

Details of the life and times of the longest-serving apartheid Military Intelligence agent in Mozambique are also revealed here for the first time. This agent, who remains a suspect in the assassination of Swedish Prime Minister Olof Palme, drew his last military pay cheque in February 1997. Despite supposedly being on bail in Mozambique on charges of espionage and arson, he settled quietly in Cape Town in 2001.

These are just some of the facts revealed in this book. I have tried to interpret and explain them, but all too often they speak for themselves. The undeniable reality is that many of the principal perpetrators of apartheid were not only never called to account, they remain in positions of power.

This book seeks to probe where – for whatever reason – the TRC failed or feared to tread. It also looks quite closely at the way in which the negotiated settlement in South Africa came about, who was involved and how they acted. This should give readers some understanding of current political developments in South Africa and of the possible motivations of some of the leading players.

But with so much unfinished business still outstanding, one is entitled to ask how long South Africa's 'political miracle' will last.

T.B.
Cape Town, 2003

FILE ONE

A crime against humanity

Not everything that is faced can be changed, but nothing can be changed until it is faced.

– James Baldwin

1

The paper Auschwitz

As the prospect of a democratic transition in South Africa drew close, tons of files, microfilm, audio and computer tapes and disks were shredded, wiped and incinerated. In little more than six months in 1993, while the political parties of the apartheid state negotiated with the representatives of the liberation movements, some forty-four metric tons of records from the headquarters of the National Intelligence Service alone were destroyed. There was so much material that state incinerators could not cope: the furnaces of private companies such as the steelmaker Iscor also had to be used. Into these flames disappeared the last echoes of the voices of thousands of victims. It was a paper Auschwitz, an attempt to eradicate all evidence of the nightmare memories of the tortured and the living dead, to obliterate all trace of those victims whose physical remains lay scattered countrywide in unmarked graves.

Into the flames too went the files of the frightened ones, their craven acceptances of compromise and collaboration etched in dry officialese, but still sweating fear from every syllable. There were also the records of the venal individuals whose greed had driven them to verbal betrayal and beyond. The pasts of thousands of part-time whisperers of secrets and betrayers of trust were turned to ashes. Who and what they talked about, to whom and why, was either vaporised in the furnaces, or shredded to strips, then sold by the kilogram to companies such as Nampak and Sappi to be pulped. A new eco-friendly generation would pen its own secrets on the recycled remains of much of a nation's memory.

This was not the first time that the facilities of private companies had been made available to a state keen to purge the national memory of surviving evidence of the past. Such disposals were, of course, purely business transactions, with no questions asked. This was the nature of the relationship of South African business to the state. It enabled business representatives later to appear before the TRC, to plead ignorance of gross human rights abuses, and even to deny that they had in any sense profited from a system which had, at the very least, guaranteed for decades a cheap and malleable labour force.

Evidence of the destruction of archives surfaced in 1991 at the Convention for a Democratic South Africa (Codesa) forum where government and anti-apartheid representatives eventually agreed their compromise for a transition to a non-racial parliamentary democracy. Inquiries about the taped talks in 1988 between then President P.W. Botha and Nelson Mandela were made at the Codesa talks in the barn-like World Trade Centre building alongside Johannesburg's international airport at Kempton Park. They drew the response that the NIS had destroyed the tapes. This brought immediate demands, especially from anti-apartheid representatives, to halt the destruction of state records, to keep the national archive reasonably intact.

However, there was relatively little protest. For it was not only the governing National Party (NP) leadership and the generals, brigadiers, colonels and foot soldiers in various arms of the security apparatus that the destruction served. There were also the various informers and collaborators in business and civil society as well as within the various anti-apartheid structures for whom the burning and shredding of files promised an end to fears of discovery. Among the negotiators on both sides at the historic Codesa talks were individuals whose future careers depended on records of the past being lost.

But, given the delicate nature of the compromise being sought, legal form must, where possible, be followed. High-handed and obviously unilateral destruction could create problems with the unfolding process. So, while the talks about transition continued, President Frederik Willem – 'F.W.' – de Klerk, as head of government, instructed his office to secure a state legal opinion on the issue of destroying files deemed 'secret'.

This was duly delivered. It decreed that documents labelled in this manner could not be archives. Seven days later, the National Intelligence Service also procured a legal opinion, which it subsequently quoted to justify the mass destruction of records. It confirmed the one obtained by De Klerk's office and added that tape recordings, because they were not written documents, were also not archives. Anything not described as an archive could be destroyed. Legal form had been followed.

At the time, there was no popular outcry about this bureaucratic action. Only a few individuals saw what it could mean. Brian Currin, of the anti-apartheid lawyers' group Lawyers for Human Rights, launched a supreme court action to have the state legal opinions ruled invalid. He lost. It was a battle hardly noticed as the to and fro at Kempton Park continued, along with bellicose and much-publicised threats from the essentially small and fragmented white Right. Also, as a corollary of the talks, there were investigations, formal commissions of inquiry into secret projects and into what the media, encouraged by politicians, referred to as 'Third Force' violence.

The term implied – as it was meant to – that there existed, outside the armed forces of the apartheid state and those of the anti-apartheid movements, another force bent on destabilising the move towards a negotiated settlement. It was this shadowy force that was said to be responsible for arming, training and transporting various gangs and for promoting violent attacks by impis (regiments) of the ethnically based Inkatha Freedom Party (IFP). These attacks resulted in several massacres, the most notorious the killing in June 1992 of forty-five men, women and children in the township of Boipatong, east of Johannesburg.

But whether at Boipatong or anywhere else, there was no Third Force. The units in action were still those of the apartheid state, some of them operating relatively independently, but still within official parameters. This was widely suspected within the anti-apartheid movement, especially in the light of the evidence already made public. By the time the Codesa talks started in 1991, the blanket of secrecy covering the vast complex of repression built up over decades had begun to lift slightly. For while files had been and were being destroyed, human memory remained. It was often fallible and self-serving, but memory could pinpoint physical traces of the end results of orders conveyed through a carefully constructed, secretive, hierarchy. Later, in the wake of the political transition, it would often be a matter of digging for bones in unmarked graves on what were to become known as South Africa's killing fields and death farms.

A corner of this blanket of secrecy had been lifted in 1989 by one man, a black death squad member who had dared to indulge in the freelance killing of a white farmer, Jan Hendrik Lourens. He had expected to get away with it, as he had for so many officially sanctioned murders. But Butana Almond

Nofemela was tried and sentenced to death. On death row he was visited by his death squad commanders who reproached him for having killed a white man and suggested he should 'take the pain'. Their arrogance was not out of place or character; they had little doubt that Nofemela would take that walk down the cold, polished corridor of Pretoria Central Prison's death row and up the forty steps leading to the gallows door at the end. There, like so many hundreds before him, he would end his life, perhaps in the company of up to six others, dangling by his neck from a rope, his lolling tongue and bulging eyes obscured by a white cloth bag.

But Butana Nofemela had no intention of taking that last lethal walk. When it became obvious, just hours before his date with the gallows, that he was not going to be spirited away by his mentors, his execution faked, Butana Nofemela played the last card he had: he got his message out beyond the prison walls and the security establishment. That he could do so was a sign of the times, of the fact that the repressive state had been forced to loosen its grip. Even a year or two earlier the confession that he had taken part in one of the most brutal of then recorded assassinations would have been unlikely to reach beyond the confines of death row. Even if it had, there would have been few to listen, and none who could stay his appointment with the hangman.

In November 1989, change was in the air. The government, forced into a corner by a rising tide of mass resistance and international condemnation, was trying desperately to distance itself from the more loathsome aspects of repression as a prelude to negotiations. In this atmosphere, the anti-apartheid Lawyers for Human Rights had links even into death row. Their contact there was a sentenced anti-apartheid fighter, Sibusiso Masuku. It was to him that Nofemela turned. He told how he had been part of an official death squad which, in November 1981, had hacked to death the human rights lawyer Griffiths Mxenge in a darkened field. Masuku relayed the information to a researcher for the Lawyers for Human Rights. The voice of Butana Almond Nofemela was heard and amplified by popular outrage. His execution was stayed.

This testimony exposed for the first time the existence of state-sponsored death squads. It also gave details of one of the most important death-squad bases, the farm Vlakplaas ('Farm on the Plain'), which nestles beside a gravel road in a crescent of hills on the banks of the Hennops river, just 30 km outside the administrative capital, Pretoria. Nofemela's testimony triggered an apparently full confession from a grudge-bearing mass murderer and former commander of Vlakplaas, Dirk Coetzee, who had been sacked by the police. Nofemela named him and his successor at Vlakplaas, Colonel Eugene de Kock. It focused the mind of Captain Coetzee. Aware of the changes taking place and concerned about his own future, he had been toying with the idea of giving information about state-sponsored terror to the ANC, the organisation he correctly perceived as being the government after any democratic election. Besides, he had little hope of resurrecting his career with the old order even if it did survive. He was reduced to seeking out odd jobs, a far cry from his murderous days at Vlakplaas.

With the help of journalist Jacques Pauw of the anti-apartheid newspaper *Vrye Weekblad*, Dirk Coetzee fled into exile. Coetzee not only confirmed Nofemela's testimony, but added much more detail to a horrifying story of mass murder, kidnapping, torture and the disposal of bodies, of bombing, gunrunning and the fomenting of violence. This had all been done, he admitted, in the name of a declared Christian state that guaranteed immunity from prosecution or retribution.

By confessing, Coetzee betrayed the fundamental principle professed by the foot soldiers of the apartheid state: absolute loyalty. In an essentially racist environment, the racism of apartheid's paid killers was often paternalistic, tempered by an ingrained ideological conviction that they were part of a nobler cause, dedicated to the betterment of all humanity. They saw themselves as hard men doing a tough but necessary job. In this brutal milieu, skin colour or background did not define the most despised individuals – the traitors, the turncoats, the 'askaris'. Dirk Coetzee became a white askari.

Efforts to counter and confuse Coetzee's evidence failed, as did attempts to assassinate him. But, in the process, ANC lawyer Bheki Mlangeni had his brains blown out by booby-trapped headphones meant for the white askari. It was tragic testimony to the efficiency of the international postal service: the booby-trapped headphones and a Walkman tape player were sent to Coetzee at a post office box address in Zambia. To allay suspicion, the sender's name was given as Bheki Mlangeni, with whom Coetzee had been in contact. The return address was Mlangeni's home in the Soweto township, west of Johannesburg.

By the time the parcel arrived in Zambia, Coetzee had left. Uncollected, the lethal package was returned to South Africa in February of 1991 and opened by Mlangeni, who put on the headphones, turned on the tape and was killed instantly. This death again raised fears about 'Third Force' activities. De Klerk and other government ministers repeated their assertions that activities such as those reportedly carried out by a police unit based at Vlakplaas were aberrations, vile and disgusting acts that had nothing to do with the policies and practices of the government. A Third Force, determined to plunge into anarchy the careful settlement process established by men and women of good faith on both sides of the apartheid divide, must be responsible.

This explanation was never taken fully at face value by ANC negotiators, but many were prepared to extend the benefit of doubt. In any event, they were aware that they had, within their own armed ranks, dissident elements who saw the unfolding process as a sellout and who, certainly in the case of the Pan Africanist Congress (PAC) armed wing, Apla (Azanian People's Liberation Army), were prepared to continue 'the struggle'. The same, they assumed, applied with De Klerk and the National Party. As evidence, there were the khaki-clad, sidearm-wearing members of the Afrikaner Resistance Movement (Afrikaner Weerstandsbeweging: AWB) who continued to threaten dire consequences if the 'traitor' De Klerk continued to 'sell out the Afrikaner people'.

The blurring of the distinction between pro- and anti-apartheid was well under way, equating anti-apartheid resister with military or police assassin. New boundaries were drawn: the moral high ground belonged to those who supported the process toward a negotiated settlement. Those who, for whatever reason, opposed or were critical of it were the opponents of progress and harbingers of anarchy. De Klerk and Mandela together epitomised the ranks of the great and the good. However, Mandela made clear that De Klerk's position depended very much on being given the benefit of the doubt.

At the time, De Klerk's supporters were vociferous in pointing out that their man had acted promptly on the information supplied by Nofemela and Coetzee. He had appointed one of his attorneys general, Tim McNally, to investigate the allegations of state-sponsored death squads. McNally found the allegations baseless. Death squads did not exist. The fact that his finding was made without having interviewed either Nofemela or Coetzee weakened its impact, but it did serve to muddy the waters.

Demands for a formal and more thorough investigation persisted, so De Klerk appointed a commission of inquiry. It was headed by a notable judge, Louis Harms, and was instructed to investigate the allegations made about Vlakplaas and death squads. Few commentators remarked that the terms of reference for the commission were so circumscribed as to ensure an extremely shallow trawl. They also failed to note that Judge Harms was not only of the old order, but was also no criminal specialist. His field was patent and copyright law. The man chosen to lead the evidence for Harms about the existence of death squads was the same Tim McNally who had, only months earlier, decreed that they did not exist. Such was the nature of the South African compromise.

Before this farcical inquiry got under way the generals most closely associated with Vlakplaas, Krappies Engelbrecht and Ronnie van der Westhuizen, together with Colonel Hermanus du Plessis, briefed the then Vlakplaas commander, Eugene de Kock. De Kock, in his turn, coached his men on the testimony they were to give to the commission. As a further precaution, he and one of his men burned all the operational and financial records kept at Vlakplaas.

They need not have bothered; Louis Harms duly found the allegations of Nofemela and Coetzee to be 'without foundation'. State-sponsored death squads, he reaffirmed, simply did not exist, and certainly not at Vlakplaas. There the matter might have rested, but for the fact that the exposure of Vlakplaas had dislocated old relations and sown new doubts and anxieties. One askari, Brian Ngqulunga, started to crack under the strain and was thought to be trying to contact the ANC to 'tell them the truth'. General Engelbrecht gave a simple instruction: 'He must be shut up.' He was. On Friday, 20 July 1990, Brian Ngqulunga was beaten, shot to death and buried in a grave on the rocky hill overlooking Vlakplaas.

Despite, often because of, the Harms commission there were also demands for further, independent, investigations. Under pressure, De Klerk relented and appointed another commission of inquiry into the ongoing violence of the time. It was headed by a known liberal judge, Richard Goldstone, and did at least uncover some evidence of security force 'dirty tricks'. De Klerk professed horrified surprise and retired twenty-three generals and other senior officers on full pension. At the same time yet another askari, Joe Mamasela, decided that the best way to spare himself the fate of Brian Ngqulunga might be to spill the beans about Vlakplaas. He was prepared not only to confess to the forty-four murders he had committed, but also to reveal everything he had learned in more than a decade as a death squad member. Urgent action had to be taken. The generals and other branches of the police severed all links with Vlakplaas. The military did the same. De Kock and Vlakplaas would be sacrificed.

The records at Vlakplaas had already been incinerated, but there were myriad ties throughout the security establishment. So, while dismissing any involvement in human rights abuses, and stating that records of national importance would be retained, the government ordered perhaps the greatest destruction of records in the country's history. At the same time, it kept at least some of the clandestine death squads, including the Vlakplaas unit, in operational readiness. The parallel government continued, the open face one of sophistication and hard-nosed charm at the multi-party negotiations at Kempton Park, the hidden one still at work beneath the surface, authorising and ordering surveillance, raids, detentions, murders and massacres.

Occasionally, as when Judge Richard Goldstone's investigators blundered into the headquarters of one of the military's prime covert operations head-

quarters, the Directorate of Covert Collection (DCC), in November 1992, there
were signs of official anxiety, but never of panic. There was no need to panic,
since there existed consensus among the negotiators at Codesa that the process
should remain on track. Even after the massacre at Boipatong on 17 June,
when the ANC had walked out of the Codesa talks, talks about talks continued
behind the scenes. But it was a fraught time for those who had pinned their
hopes and futures on the process.

Goldstone's investigators had surprised themselves as much as anyone else
when they walked into the large open-plan headquarters that occupied the
whole first floor of an office block in the plush Pretoria suburb of Lynwood
Ridge. The office, in the Momentum Mews Building, was filled with rows of
filing cabinets and blinking computer screens. It was a discovery which could
have revealed much of the who, what and why of recent brutal history. It was
also feared in several quarters that disclosure might sink what was already
being widely described, despite the evident problems, as a miracle in the
making at the Codesa talks.

The Goldstone investigators had stumbled over a major component of the
motor and memory of repression. South Africa, certainly in the last decade of
apartheid rule, had been a military, not a police-run state. Yet until what
became known as the 'Goldstone raid' there had never been a whisper of a
unit bearing the title DCC, let alone the fact that it housed tens of thousands
of files.

Secure in its secrecy, the DCC had not apparently destroyed the records of
deeds done, operations running, authorisations given and payments made, or
the lists of named assassins, blackmailers, collaborators and 'targets'. Lawyer
Torie Pretorius headed the unit that found the DCC headquarters. He
telephoned Richard Goldstone to report that the unit was inside what was
apparently a major clandestine department of Military Intelligence. What
should they do? Goldstone realised the importance of the find, but he also
knew the delicate state of play. He was not about to rock any boats or cause
undue disturbance.

Since the investigation which had led Pretorius and his unit to the DCC
headquarters concerned only a former policeman and freelance assassin, Ferdi
Barnard, Richard Goldstone restricted inquiries to that subject. 'I had no doubt
that our presence would not be tolerated for very long,' he noted later.
Adopting a nice, legalistic response, he decreed that the powers given to him
by the De Klerk government did not allow 'a fishing expedition'. It would, he
felt, have been 'a misuse of those powers and could have been interdicted by
a court'.

So Torie Pretorius requested any files the DCC might hold relating to Ferdi Barnard. Three files were produced and transferred to Goldstone's office. The filing cabinets and the computer disks in the DCC office were left untouched and unexamined. They promptly disappeared. 'I don't know what happened to them,' Goldstone noted blithely several years later.

But in tracing professional killer Ferdi Barnard to the DCC the Goldstone unit revealed that Military Intelligence had been conducting clandestine anti-ANC activities. De Klerk promptly announced that all clandestine units and actions had been wound up. He lied, but the word quickly spread among the existing units: an era was coming to an end and the politicians were preparing to sacrifice the rank and file. It was time to ensure maximum personal gain before being cut adrift or exposed and sacrificed.

Against this background the talks at Kempton Park resumed. What had become obvious was that some mechanism would have to be created to deal with the secret horrors of the past. Victims were clamouring for redress; enough was by then publicly admitted of the tortures, killings, poisonings and letter and car bombs. Besides, such directly physical and personalised violence was an issue on which all sides at the Codesa talks could agree.

The National Party and its rightwing fragments accused the ANC and PAC of bombings, and the shooting of police and collaborators. The anti-apartheid movements, for their part, pointed to the evidence of torture and mass slaughter by the state apparatus. The identification of the brutality of the oppressor with the violence of the resister was complete. It became the main driving force behind the demand to establish some form of quasi-judicial forum where such accusations could be aired. The issue of the system itself, the forced removals of millions of people, the institutionalised racism that created vast areas of disease, desperation and death, receded into the background. So did the landmine maimings and the slaughter and destabilisation which had wreaked such havoc in neighbouring states.

Knowledge of those years of bloody abuses conjured up what became an improvised addendum to the final, transitional constitution agreed by the multi-party negotiators. Sometimes referred to as the 'post-amble', this addition made provision for a Truth and Reconciliation Commission (TRC). It would provide a mechanism to establish the truth with the object of reconciling the past with the present.

In what was deemed to be the spirit of reconciliation, in 1996 the TRC enlisted among its staff members drawn from the existing security establishment. Several other matters, including a civil action against President F.W. de Klerk for complicity in mass murder, would be quietly settled in advance. The action in the Transkei Supreme Court, and the manner of its burying, is dealt with in File 2. The outcome was that no beauty, terrible or otherwise, was born; like the new 'rainbow nation', the TRC was destined to wear the grubby swaddling clothes of compromise.

2

The roots of a crime

One problem with facing the past is defining where to start. To begin at the beginning is always difficult, if not impossible, for the complex legacies of the past are inextricably bound up with the present and nourish the shoots of the future. So it was with apartheid.

This Afrikaans word, which was to enter so many languages, dripping with emotive nuances, emerged firmly into English in 1948, when South Africa's National Party began its forty-six years of parliamentary and racist dominance. In that time there were many upheavals and many dates that stand out, but none more sharply than 1960 and 1976. These were the years which, arguably, marked the birth of the final, often lethal and criminal stage of apartheid and the death knell of a system whose terminal throes carried on for a decade and gave rise to the horrific personalised violence that became the focus of the TRC.

But the roots of this peculiar form of oppression and racial domination reach back to the age of slavery. They are also embedded in the era of industrial development, as well as in the South Africa Act of 1909, the historic compromise between Briton and Boer that entrenched racial dominance in South Africa. When the National Party assumed parliamentary control of South Africa in 1948, it had only to refine and further codify a practice of racial discrimination that already existed. Yet while the intentions of the new government were clearly racist and discriminatory, there still seemed to be some prospect for evolutionary change; many believed that a civil rights movement could rise to challenge and change policies based on race.

The banning of the Communist Party of South Africa (CPSA) in 1950, an action broadly welcomed by the Western allies as the Cold War developed, also hardly seemed a worse abrogation of human rights than the persecution of suspected communists in the United States. In many eyes, South Africa was a civil rights issue much like the one evolving across the Atlantic. However mistaken this view, it was widely held and underlay the 'defiance of unjust laws' campaign launched in 1952 by the main anti-apartheid organisation, the African National Congress. It also underpinned the calls for a 'national convention', and was certainly a strong consideration when a 'Congress of the People' was called under the ANC banner in 1956. This congress adopted a Freedom Charter with a preamble that began: 'We the people of South Africa declare for all our country and the world to know that South Africa belongs to all who live in it . . .'

Gross human rights violations, even in those earlier years, were the norm. The system of racial segregation and exploitation provided enormous financial benefits, particularly to the gold-mining companies and commercial farms that formed the backbone of South Africa's economy. It was also justified on the basis of the Christian Bible and sanctified by the Dutch Reformed Church. Systematic, usually unthinking, abuse was a way of life for almost every South African family officially classified 'white'. Almost every white family, irrespective of status or wealth, was an employer of domestic labour within the blanket culture of apartheid.

Even the poverty alleviation schemes of the Dutch Reformed churches made provision, as one of the essentials of white life, for a 'maid's allowance'. This meant that the small number of white families who could not cope economically, despite the advantages of apartheid, would still have the bare necessities: electricity, running water, a roof over their heads and a servant. On the farms, the situation was even more clearcut: there was, again almost without exception, a simple feudal relationship, with whole families variously exploited.

On a much grander scale, this same system provided the mines, the coal delivery companies and the white town and city councils with their armies of unskilled labour. Theirs was the muscle necessary to wield pickaxe and shovel or to carry out the dirty and often backbreaking work necessary to ensure efficient services to white towns and suburbs. There was the collection of toilet buckets – 'night soil' – and coal delivery in the 1950s and 1960s, before water-borne sewage and electric cookers became standard. Then there was the daily collection of household refuse, always at a run to keep up with the garbage truck driven, by law, by a white man.

Like the miners who toiled under the eyes of white supervisors in Stygian blackness, deep beneath the Earth's surface, digging out rock in dust-laden labyrinths, these delivery and removal men returned, at the end of each shift, to their hostels. Stark, utilitarian structures of brick and concrete or even wood and corrugated iron, these single-sex barracks stacked men, like so many living chattels, on shelves three deep around the walls. Rations calculated to provide sufficient nourishment at the cheapest cost were provided and often cooked on open fires on the floor between the tiered slabs which served as each individual's living quarters.

These appalling conditions, the meagre rations and even more meagre wages were not required by law; they were a simple outgrowth of racism and the demand for greater profits. All were in place before 1960 and remained in place. But there was a difference after 1960. The prospect of reform – the chance, however remote, of negotiating a way out of the impasse of institutionalised segregation – disappeared in that year. A series of dramatic events hastened the refining of the system of racial exclusivity until all channels for reform were blocked and a brutally clear line, defended by a vast apparatus of repression, was drawn.

By the end of 1960, that line was clearly in place: there could no longer be any blurring of the distinction between beneficiaries and victims. Behind a façade of parliamentary democracy, the white community was corralled, cushioned by affluence and the trappings of power. This community would supervise, police and commandeer the social, economic and political fabric of the nation while the majority of the population, which supplied the bulk of that same nation's labour, became the object of a grand design steered by a coterie of lobbyists, academics and ideologues.

It was a system that relied, in political terms, almost as much on the existence of a loyal opposition as it did on a massive, complex and brutal security apparatus. For this was no common tyranny. The fascist epithet so widely and loosely applied to it merely helped to obscure the fact that apartheid South Africa was a parliamentary democracy, but a racially exclusive one. As such, democratic forms, if not norms, were almost always followed, but from 1960 they were rigidly effected within constitutionally determined racial ghettos.

The series of events that marked the birth of this new era are well known. First, British Conservative Prime Minister Harold Macmillan, on a visit to Cape Town in February 1960, famously announced that 'the wind of change' was sweeping through Africa. It was a polite warning that the racial oligarchy on Africa's southern tip was becoming an embarrassment even to its friends.

However, it was another date in 1960, the 21st of March, that, more than any other, marks not just the start of apartheid's final, brutish phase, but also the beginning of its end. On that day, several thousand residents of a township south of Johannesburg joined a protest against the pass laws which restricted the movement of blacks. It was organised by the Pan Africanist Congress outside the local police station. A policeman lost his nerve and opened fire. The crowd fled as the police surrounding the station fired, reloaded and fired again. After only minutes, sixty-nine people lay dead. Most of them had been shot in the back.

What made Sharpeville dramatically different from other, similar, massacres in the past was not only the period and the historical context. It was the presence of Ian Berry, a young photographer from the East Rand town of Benoni. As the screams of fear and pain merged with the sound of gunfire, he fell to the ground – and kept on taking pictures. When the firing abated, he was still there, still working.

Those pictures shocked a world that was starting to take a greater interest in a changing continent. The mass-circulation *Daily Mirror* in Britain produced a front page that carried a single photograph of the Sharpeville massacre. Yet, even as the one day of official butchery took place, there was already a much more significant rebellion under way in the north-eastern corner of the Transkei, the 'homeland' earmarked as the territorial cornerstone of the apartheid policy.

That rebellion, by the Mpondo people, was against the very traditional authorities with which the apartheid government had hoped to build their segregationist dream. There was little publicity about the mass resistance, the boycotts and the horsemen of the Intaba movement who displayed a high level of discipline and organisation. Nor was there much reportage of the killings that accompanied the suppression of a remarkably democratic movement. It was this uprising, much more than the shootings at Sharpeville, that caused the apartheid planners to hastily revise their schemes for separate development.

But on an international level it was Sharpeville, more than any other single event, that took the South African government and its apartheid policy beyond the bounds of international acceptability. For the more aware observers, the farce of a marathon treason trial of anti-apartheid activists that began in 1956 and finally collapsed in March 1961 underlined the lost prospect of constitutional change.

The international condemnation, especially over Sharpeville, both angered and frightened the South African political establishment and its supporters. It also worried investors and the business community both internally and abroad.

Business was not bound by the ruling ideology. Even Afrikaner business, which owed much of its success to assistance from the political machine, showed itself to be wholly pragmatic. It began to press for some, at least cosmetic, changes.

At the same time, it mounted a major propaganda effort in support of the apartheid dispensation, and to campaign against a universal franchise, fearing that it might lead to further liberalisation, trade union rights, and demands for better pay and conditions. The South Africa Foundation brought together the doyens of English and Afrikaner business, Harry Oppenheimer and Anton Rupert. What it sought from the government was some official window-dressing, as it conveyed to the world the best possible 'non-political' image of the apartheid system from which its members profited.

But the Dutch-born prime minister, Hendrik Frensch Verwoerd, a devout member of the Afrikaner Broederbond (Brotherhood) secret society, paid little heed to outside advice, having established his own coterie of advisers. A brilliant academic with a ruthless streak of ambition and a consuming interest in behavioural psychology, he was also certain of the rightness and essential reasonableness of his cause. The world outside simply did not understand. He would package the arguments for these doubters, and present within South Africa a glowing example of the brave new world his vision offered. In the meantime, pragmatic politician that he was, he rallied his constituency to the banner of the noble defence of the Afrikaner as underdog.

It was a simplistic message that struck home. Many Afrikaners, their insularity tinged with paranoia, saw outsiders' condemnation of their country and government, this slide into disrepute and even infamy, as evidence of a monstrous conspiracy. In the context of the Cold War this could be related to the battle between God-fearing West and godless East; the age-old fight of good against evil, of noble individualism against suffocating totalitarianism. Never mind that such beliefs were riddled with contradictions. They were fervently held to.

Rebellion by ignorant black hordes, goaded on by an international communist conspiracy encouraged by liberals whose moral laxity disabled them from understanding the real threat, could not be tolerated. The military, convinced by its own crude propaganda, and mindful of the Mpondo rebellion, noted officially that Sharpeville constituted the start of a planned mass uprising. This had to be nipped in the bud. So on 8 April 1960 Hendrik Verwoerd announced that both the African National Congress and the Pan Africanist Congress were outlawed. The last open voices of majority protest were silenced.

David Beresford Pratt, a proud and eccentric liberal and a trout farmer in the Magaliesberg hills west of Johannesburg, was appalled by both the shootings at Sharpeville and the banning of the political organisations that stood for the disenfranchised and oppressed mass of the population. He resolved to make his own dramatic protest, to introduce an element of justice into an increasingly unjust equation. On the morning of Saturday 9 April, Pratt set off from his farm to Johannesburg for the opening of the Rand Easter Show, an annual agricultural exposition which had grown into South Africa's most prestigious trade and industry fair and was to be officially opened by the prime minister. In his righthand trouser pocket was a small .22 calibre pistol. As a farmer, Pratt had access to the members' stand on the south side of the arena in which the traditional parade of cattle and the award of ribbons was held.

He had no fixed plan and took a seat at the back of the stand, immediately behind the VIP enclosure. Verwoerd, with bodyguard in tow, took his seat near the edge of the enclosure after doing the honours among the cattle and their proud owners in the arena. A motorcycle high-wire act was scheduled to begin. As thousands of spectators waited and watched in the blazing afternoon sun or under the shade of the covered stands, David Pratt calmly stood and walked down the concrete steps toward the VIP enclosure, his right hand in his pocket. As he drew level with Verwoerd, he turned, drew out the gun and, reaching across the bodyguard, fired at almost point-blank range into Verwoerd's head. The bodyguard, spattered with blood, fainted, and Pratt loosed off a second shot before stunned officials, including Johannesburg's mayor Alex Gorshel, grabbed him and wrestled him to the ground.

Verwoerd and his bloodied bodyguard were rushed to hospital, Pratt to a police cell. After being declared insane, thus obviating the need for a trial, David Pratt allegedly went on to commit a freakish suicide in the psychiatric hospital where he was held. He reportedly tied two sheets to posts of his bed, inserted his head and then somersaulted over and over again until he managed to strangle himself.

Verwoerd recovered, but the experience changed his entire perception of himself and his role. Whereas before he had privately scoffed at the religious interpretations of the Afrikaner ideal, he now became convinced that divine intervention existed and that he had become 'a hand of God'. The bullet scar high on his right cheek, which he frequently caressed with his fingertips, was the sign. The single-mindedness for which he was renowned would be replaced by a fanatical conviction that he was right in whatever he decided.

Sometimes Verwoerd made cynical capital of his self-proclaimed miraculous escape. (The surgeons admitted he had been lucky, as the wounds could easily have proved fatal. Many of his enemies muttered under their breath that only a fool would use low-velocity, soft-nosed .22 bullets for an assassination attempt – especially, some said, against a skull so obviously thick as Verwoerd's.) At a rally in the staunchly Afrikaner stronghold of Bloemfontein, for example, the freshly recovered Verwoerd was called on to release a dove as a symbol of Afrikaner freedom. He cradled the snow-white fantail in his outstretched hands before dramatically flinging his arms apart. The bird, without so much as a flutter, fell dead at his feet.

Yet the stunned audience had no need to worry about any ominous symbolism. The answer was soon provided: the bird, overcome by the magnetism and power radiating from Verwoerd, had given up its life rather than leave him. That, at any event, was the officially encouraged explanation, carried without a hint of irony by the Afrikaans media.

Professor Sampie Terreblanche, then a dedicated supporter of both Verwoerd and the National Party, was in the Bloemfontein stadium that day. He had a more prosaic explanation: Verwoerd, with an intensely nervous disposition, tended to manifest this physically by clenching his hands. Terreblanche remembered that, as he was about to release the dove, Verwoerd's outstretched hands were characteristically tightly clasped. 'The poor bird just had the life crushed out of it,' he said. It was not an opinion he voiced in 1960. To do so would have been politically and professionally suicidal. A new era was dawning.

Verwoerd may not himself have believed the story of his mystical attraction for the bird, but conveying the message was vital; any explanation that served the greater good was for the best. God worked in mysterious ways. But by underlining the possibility of divinity, or at least intervention from on high, Verwoerd's position was reinforced and his role as national leader and guide made easier.

Such promotion was essential for one who had been selected by the God he had mocked in his youth. His role, after all, was to carve a new path to the future, not only for the Afrikaner but for all the people of South Africa. That path would stand out as a shining example to a world teetering on the edge of anarchy, threatened by moral decay and miscegenation. To save his country he would have to use the most modern, scientific methods and technology – and often have to labour in secret.

The task was nothing less than moulding South Africa and all who lived in it into what he saw as a preordained configuration. It would balance the ideological needs of a deeply ingrained racism with the demands of both the traditional and the emerging industrial sectors for labour which, because of the country's demographics, would have largely to be black. It was on these terms that the elaborate 'homelands' policy was refined, with the lessons of the Mpondo rebellion learned. At a practical level, it was an attempt to bridge the demands of the farmers and small contractors for cheap unskilled labour and those of emerging Afrikaner and established 'English' big business for a more skilled and settled workforce. Both tendencies were represented among the elite who were members of the Afrikaner Broederbond (AB).

Fragmenting of the black population was justified by a highly selective interpretation and sometimes wholesale revision of history, coupled with the legacy of language differences. Rather than encourage the rationalisation of the two main vernaculars – Nguni and Sotho – a process that was already organically under way in the urban areas, the policy was to widen the divisions. There could be one 'white nation', but there would be nine 'black nations', each segregated in its own homeland.

Pockets of land comprising some 13 per cent of South Africa's area – and which had been set aside since 1913 as 'native reserves' – would serve the territorial purpose. Nationality would be determined, where necessary, by paternal descent. This was the initial design of what became known as 'grand apartheid'. The Transkei, in the south-eastern corner of the country, would be its flagship.

Although Hendrik Verwoerd was to go down in history as the architect of apartheid, he was merely its most aggressive public exponent. Every aspect of the system from its basic outlines to demands that Afrikaans be taught to black students, came from the Broederbond. It was the real hidden power in the land. But the TRC did not interrogate even its own AB commissioners, Wynand Malan and Chris de Jager, about the role of the secret society. There was certainly talk about asking the AB whether it would cooperate in providing information, and several commissioners thought this approach had been made and refused. In fact, it never happened. This was perhaps the worst oversight of the TRC process.

3

The nerve centre of apartheid

The Afrikaner Broederbond made the nature of the apartheid administration unique. Most of the country's leading government members, the generals, judges and senior police officers, along with many Church and education officials, operated on the deeply secret level of the AB. This multi-layered web of patronage, manipulation and deceit covered the entire country, ensnaring, rewarding or repressing. In all the years of National Party government, few if any policy decisions taken by any cabinet were not first approved by the executive of the AB – if they were not Broederbond policies in the first place.

An account of who and what the AB was and how it operated is therefore essential for a real understanding of the dynamics of apartheid. For the AB was central to the development, maintenance and eventual revision of the system. Just how much power it wielded was summed up at a major secret meeting in 1968. Speaking at the fiftieth anniversary celebrations of the organisation, one of its surviving founder-members, Henning Klopper, noted:

> Since the Afrikaner Broederbond got into its stride it has given the country its governments. It has given the country every prime minister since 1948 . . . Our nation depends on the Broederbond . . . Show me a greater force on the whole continent of Africa. Show me a greater force on earth, even in your so-called civilised nations. We support the state, we support the church, we support every big movement born of the nation. We make our contribution unobtrusively. We carry it through and so we have brought our nation to where it is today.

There was only a small measure of hyperbole in Klopper's lengthy address, which was larded with references to God and Christianity. Nor was Brother Klopper alone in his assessment of the AB's power and influence. Its chairman at the time, Piet Meyer, also head of the South African Broadcasting Corporation, made crystal-clear the role of what he described as 'brotherhood in action'. The essence lay in 'defining problems facing the volk [people], solving them, and giving uniform policies to all the public bodies on which Broeders [Brothers] serve'. For Meyer, who as the 787th recruit to the organisation was known as Broeder number 787, the AB had undertaken a 'divine mission' which covered every aspect of the life of the volk.

His and other stirring speeches in the name of assisting divine destiny received unanimous applause from an audience which included Broeder number 3737, Balthazar Johannes ('John') Vorster, the then prime minister and successor to Verwoerd. It is not known whether Vorster's feared security police chief, Hendrik Johannes ('Lang Hendrik' – Tall Hendrik) van den Bergh, who was inducted as Broeder number 6745, was present or whether he had more pressing matters to attend to.

The AB had come a long way from its founding in 1918, but its development over half a century had followed what, with hindsight, seems a logical trajectory. It began when three young Afrikaans-speaking men met on a hillside outside Johannesburg in April 1918. Railway workers, they were living in what seemed to be a foreign city in their own country, a place that used their labour but rejected their language, a constant reminder of the defeat of the Boers by Britain in the war of 1899 to 1902.

Like so many Afrikaners before and since, they had been raised on an intellectual diet of myth and potted history which pitted heroic Boer against perfidious Briton in a struggle that impacted on the cosmos itself. They saw the Afrikaners as players in the unfolding of the Book of Revelation, upholding the light of Christian civilisation against an advancing wall of darkness, promoted by the Beast himself. It was God's will that the 'Afrikaner nation', in reality a recent amalgam of Dutch, French, German, Scots, Indonesian, Malay and African ancestry, linked by language and a narrow Calvinism, had been placed on the southern tip of the African continent. His will should be done.

This concept of serving God and the Afrikaner nation with fearsome loyalty was the driving motivation behind Afrikaner nationalism. Over the years, and in particular in the decades following the outbreak of World War Two, it was preached in hundreds of churches every week, invariably by ministers who were members of the Broederbond. It was the crutch and rationale for a community linked by language and religion and kept in thrall to the status quo by the material benefits of the crude fortress into which their fear had driven them.

Their world-view was that of the laager, the defensive circle of wagons which protected the community against marauders in the days of the Voortrekkers, the pioneer Afrikaans-speaking colonists of South Africa's interior. From such a strong position, raids into the hostile territories beyond would be led by heroic soldiers, but directed by far-sighted, tough, and essentially benevolent leaders. The soldier-hero icon was everywhere. It ratified the broad acceptance of the cult of the leader, an acceptance that AB-inspired educational theory would later try to mould into a permanent feature of 'white' youth in general and Afrikaner youth in particular. It certainly provided much of the inspiration for many starry-eyed young men who volunteered to fight 'on the border' or to join one or other of the state's security divisions.

But in 1918, when Henning Klopper, Danie du Plessis and H.W. van der Merwe sat on a sunny hillside and discussed the need to form a club for Afrikaners, they talked only of a refuge for those who wished to preserve and strengthen their language and culture. To them, Afrikaans and the Afrikaner seemed in danger of being swallowed up by the alien morass in a city dominated by 'the English'. They took their idea to their spiritual adviser, the Reverend Johannes Naude, who welcomed it enthusiastically.

So in August 1918, in the front room of the house in which Danie du Plessis was staying, eighteen young men, eleven of them working on the railways and six of them policemen, met to consider the proposal that they form the Young South Africa (Jong Suid Afrika) cultural association. It would act collectively to defend the Afrikaner and 'return him to his rightful place in South Africa'. The organisation would be open to all men who subscribed to this aim; recruits would proudly wear their membership buttons on their lapels.

This was the formal start of the Afrikaner Broederbond. But it was an era of economic difficulty and competition for jobs, during which many Afrikaners began to Anglicise their names and adopt the English language. Times were hard for the Afrikaner. Broederbond buttons became a source of derision in the workplace, and members felt marked out for discrimination. By early 1921, still with fewer than fifty members in that single Johannesburg branch, there were demands that the AB go underground and become a secret society. By then its composition had changed. Although open to all, efforts to recruit the artisans and manual workers who made up the bulk of urban Afrikaners failed. Instead it was teachers, ministers of religion and civil servants who were attracted to join.

Within three years, emergent Afrikaner professionals, the white-collar urban elite, dominated the organisation. At a meeting on 26 August 1921 the calls to transform the AB into a secret society for the advancement of Afrikaners were put to the vote and carried. At the same meeting, a second branch came into being, and six months later a third. By 1930 there were 512 members in 23 branches, and five years later 80 branches around the country catered for 1,395 members.

By then the AB had begun to transform itself into a series of think tanks and to plot the course, outlined in 1934, for the eventual takeover of political power. This included a detailed proposal for the residential segregation of 'racial' groups. It was the blueprint for apartheid. Like any organisation, the AB contained within it the seeds of bureaucracy and elitism. Nurtured by secrecy, these germinated into a virulent strain of autocracy which, in the 1930s, found a ready resonance in the fascist ideas emanating from Europe. Leading Broeders such as Hendrik Verwoerd and Nico Diederichs, a future finance minister, travelled to and studied in Nazi Germany and were impressed by much of what they heard and saw.

The Nazi Party, in a show of solidarity, sent specialists to assist the AB in restructuring the organisation along the lines of the tight cell system that remained in place until at least 1992. In that year the Broederbond formally closed down, to re-emerge as the Afrikaner Bond (Afrikaner Union), which claimed to be an open society that admitted women as members. But although it remains an influential force within the National Party, it and its political wing were, by the time of South Africa's second non-racial election in 1999, marginalised politically. The new AB's role in the election seemed primarily to consist of prodding the former president, F.W. de Klerk, to come out of retirement to support Marthinus van Schalkwyk, a former Military Intelligence officer and leader of the renamed New National Party (NNP).

By then the AB was a shadow of its former self. Links between members remained, but seemingly more in the form of an 'old boys' club'. The core seemed still to be part of the NNP, but other members – either on instructions from the organisation or at their own volition – had joined other political parties where some now held senior positions. The two Broederbond TRC commissioners, Wynand Malan and Chris de Jager, epitomise this. Malan became one of three leaders of the liberal Democratic Party, De Jager an MP of the rightwing and racist Conservative Party and, briefly, a member of the paramilitary AWB. Former cabinet minister, Broeder and NP general secretary Roelf Meyer co-founded the United Democratic Movement (UDM) with General Bantubonke Holomisa, a former 'homeland' military ruler and former ANC deputy minister.

This diversity in Broederbond political allegiance mirrors a similar fragmentation among the volk in whose name and for whose declared benefit the huge exercise in racial social engineering had taken place. But while the once monolithic structure of the AB seemed by 1999 to be fragmented beyond all hope of unity, a core remained. It still maintains contacts across an elite spectrum of South African society and is now represented in all political parties. Its secrecy also remains intact. The official role of the new Bond is still the preservation of Afrikaans language and culture. But it also remains the custodian of more than eighty years of records that include the original drafts and rationale for most of the policies of the apartheid years. No attempt has ever been made to attach or investigate these records.

All that is known of the Broederbond and the extent of the power it wielded until so recently comes from interviews with individual former members and from the two occasions in more than seventy years of secret existence that the security of the AB was breached. The first was in 1963, when a conscience-stricken churchman and Broeder of twenty-two years decided that he could no longer support apartheid or the organisation that effectively planned and ran the system. As a Christian, he had come to the conclusion that there was no biblical justification for apartheid. But, as a man of the cloth and the son of the Dutch Reformed Church (DRC) minister who had enthusiastically pro-moted the AB in 1918, Beyers Naude faced a major crisis of conscience. He had made a solemn commitment, reinforced, as always in the earlier years, by blood-curdling ritual and oaths to a vengeful Old Testament God. An intellec-tual conviction about the sanctity of a holy oath as much as the superstitious fear of brimstone and damnation for treachery to God and nation tended to ensure silence even from those Broeders who left the AB.

The difference with Naude was that while he still felt bound by that same code of honour and set of religious convictions, he found a way around these constraints: he sought spiritual advice from a fellow minister and Afrikaner, Albert Geyser. Geyser was the first South African DRC minister to take public issue with apartheid. A leading theologian, he had been commissioned by his Church to research and explain to an increasingly hostile world Christian community the biblical justification for the apartheid system. He began confidently enough, but then stumbled. He reached the opposite conclusion, and was tried and convicted of heresy. It was to Albert Geyser that Naude went, taking with him the documents accumulated over years and which were necessary to explain his dilemma. These he left in the care of his adviser. They were not to be passed on to anyone else. Nor were they. But Geyser painstakingly photographed each page before handing the documents back.

Not having been a member of the AB, although having twice been asked to join, Geyser was not bound by any oath. He developed the film and then contacted a journalist he knew, Charles Bloomberg, and handed over the negatives. Years later, Bloomberg recalled that he could not at first believe what he had been given. For Naude was not just any Broeder, he was the secretary of the central city cell in the administrative capital, Pretoria. Of all the nearly 500 AB cells around the country at that time, this was perhaps the most important single unit in the organisation in terms of its members' influence and the information that flowed through it. The revelations in the mass-circulation *Sunday Times* by Bloomberg and his colleague, Hennie Serfontein, caused a major stir. They also caused the security police to ensure that, from then on, there was always at least one agent working as a journalist on that newspaper.

As the *Sunday Times* released, in exposé after exposé, the information obtained indirectly from Naude, pressure mounted on the government to institute an inquiry. The entire edifice of the racially exclusive parliamentary democracy had been threatened by evidence that a secret cabal was making the real decisions about the future of the country, while parliament was used as a rubber stamp. But it was nearly a year before Prime Minister Verwoerd, Broeder number 1596, finally announced a commission of inquiry.

It was headed by a supreme court judge, D.H. Botha, who was not an AB member. But, said Verwoerd, the inquiry would not target only the AB. It would also investigate the Freemasons and the Sons of England, a tiny pro-English society, and would ascertain whether any of these organisations posed a threat to subvert the state. All evidence would be heard in camera. The terms of reference alone meant that the Broederbond was bound to be absolved. It was, in effect, the state power and could hardly be guilty of subverting itself, even if it was instead subverting every concept of liberal parliamentary democracy. In any event, the two justice ministry officials who assisted Judge Botha, the one leading evidence and the other acting as secretary to the commission, were both Broeders, although this was not known at the time. The form was followed; the substance predetermined.

Such information only emerged more than a decade later, when the AB was locked in another of its periodic and bitter internal feuds. The traditionalists and the modernisers – referred to by Afrikaans commentators as the verkrampte (literally cramped) and verligte (enlightened) wings of Afrikaner nationalism – were staging a protracted battle for supremacy in the wake of the mass student uprisings of June 1976. These had been triggered by the enforced introduction of Afrikaans as a medium of instruction in black schools, a policy insisted on by the AB traditionalists. Once again the *Sunday Times* was chosen as the vehicle to publish quantities of documents and verbal information about the activities of a secret organisation now grown even more powerful. By 1977 it had 12,000 members organised into 810 cells and, as with previous governments, the cabinet was effectively an AB cell.

The evidence leaked to journalists Ivor Wilkins and Hans Strydom provided the greatest-ever breach in the security of the AB. Above all, it produced thousands of names that gave an accurate – and frightening – glimpse of the power wielded by the cabal. Though it caused a furore at the time, few outside the AB itself realised the full import of what these journalists had done, and fewer still were aware that the initial leaks and the subsequent information obtained by Strydom in particular were symptoms of strife in the AB. At the time there was a desperate attempt by the modernisers, who tended to represent big business interests, to wrest control from the traditionalists who still saw their constituency as the farmers and Afrikaner workers, such as those organised into the hardline segregationist Mynwerkersunie (Mineworkers' Union).

The modernisers wished gradually to dispense with what they perceived as the unworkable system of traditional apartheid while continuing to control society. The traditionalists saw this option as suicidal. They remained convinced that they could bend social, economic and material reality to the demands of an ideology of racial exclusivity that could not be altered at will since it was divinely ordained.

Overlapping with this battle was another bitter struggle for control of the government between the then defence minister, P.W. Botha, and Prime Minister John Vorster and his designated successor, the Broederbond traditionalist Connie Mulder. This internecine political bloodletting finally resulted in a breach in Afrikaner nationalist ranks with the formation in 1982 of the Conservative Party, led by Mulder. Botha, while remaining a member of the AB, tried to operate at one remove from the organisation, relying more on his own power base within the military, where most of the senior officers were also Broeders.

The AB under leading moderniser Pieter de Lange, a Rand Afrikaans University (RAU) professor, was able to purge its ranks of the traditionalists who had joined Mulder in the Conservative Party. The organisation was then re-established by the simple expedient, used twice in the past, of calling for all members to renew their memberships and retake their vows. All members who rejoined retained their original numbers and the membership numbering system continued unbroken.

By the late 1980s the numbering system had gone beyond 20,000, and it is known that some 15,000 new members were recruited after 1960, when the

AB had 5,760 members active in 409 cells. It is also known that some 200 members left at the time of the first major rift between the modernisers and traditionalists. That was in 1969, when Albert Hertzog, a former minister of the quaintly named Posts and Telegraphs Department, left to form the Herstigte Nasionale Party (Reconstituted National Party – HNP). Hertzog had been instrumental in bringing the segregationist Mineworkers' Union into the nationalist fold and headed a faction within the AB known as the Afrikaner Orde (Afrikaner Order).

The Afrikaner Orde was based only in Pretoria, and never had more than 400 members, who clung tenaciously to the traditional twin anchors of Afrikaner nationalism: a vengeful Old Testament God and a brief history dripping with symbolism and peopled by rugged folk heroes. But such subjective commitments, however ferociously held to, made for frail moorings in a modern, more rational, world. They amounted to a throwback to another age, to the beliefs of the nineteenth century. Apart from those members on the traditionalist fringes, most of the AB realised that those clinging to such beliefs would be condemned to the futile endeavour to turn back the wheel of history until it either crushed them or they fled in horror and disgust.

The future of Afrikaner nationalism in such circumstances was grim indeed. Unity remained the fundamental creed. This struggle to marry the contradictory values of an essentially feudal past with the requirements of modern industry drove much of the political bloodletting within the AB. It amounted to a futile and often desperate effort to find a scientific underpinning for apartheid which would leave the traditional anchors in place, although in modified form. When circumstances turned the argument critical, small numbers of Broeders would break away, sometimes to emerge in the form of a purist political sect.

Such was the origin of the HNP and of the Conservative Party. In the case of the latter, however, the fight was more bitter and the split deeper. Yet for all the animosity, it is unlikely that more than 500 members left the AB in the 1982 split. Some, such as Mulder, were prominent, and their departure certainly weakened the Broederbond, but it remained the most powerful political body within the apartheid state. Not being part of government, but permeating all layers of the governing elite, it was simultaneously isolated from, and part of, the control mechanisms of the state. In separate cells, its members discussed and planned, while its ultra-secret watchdog committees collated information and drafted policy suggestions. These were forwarded to the executive that ruled on their implementation and passed them on to parliament when legislation was necessary.

A classic example of how this system operated was with television, a medium that had fascinated Verwoerd. In the 1970s it was one of the issues that divided the AB traditionalists – for whom TV was 'a work of the devil' – from the modernisers who were exerting the pressure within the AB for the introduction of a television service.

Amid the ideological and moral tub-thumping, there was a more prosaic reason for this growing pressure: a number of AB worthies had financial stakes in an embryonic television hire company, Teljoy. This company became South Africa's leading television and VCR rental organisation, with significant interests in cellular telephony. Political modernity had again found its justification in the marketplace.

The charade that followed was a classic of its kind. John Vorster appointed an official commission of inquiry into whether and when South Africa should introduce television. It was chaired by Broeder 787, Piet Meyer, who was simultaneously head of the national broadcaster, the SABC, and of the Broederbond. Eight of its other eleven members also belonged to the AB, while a ninth was a National Party senator. But the twelve commission members merely constituted the public face of the process. As soon as the inquiry was announced, the Broederbond notified its cells and canvassed the opinions that would really matter.

An overwhelming majority of the cabal supported the introduction of television, provided that 'effective control' was exercised to 'the advantage of our nation and country'. The chairman of the commission, as chairman of the AB, also assured members that the Broederbond executive would first discuss the draft report before it was tabled in parliament. This was duly done, the report went on to the cabinet – and parliament approved a South African television service.

Throughout the apartheid era, this tightly knit and secretive cabal remained the collective brain of apartheid, the source of many of the ideological twists and turns that the system engendered. Members of the brotherhood – politicians in some cases, academics in others – were the first to open secret talks with the imprisoned and exiled leadership of the ANC. And it was Brothers who also encouraged, almost simultaneously, the 'Iron Fist' crackdown on the anti-apartheid opposition that triggered waves of secret slaughter.

This nerve centre of the apartheid system, possessing no formal authority and therefore at one remove from the state machine, could still have been probed and exposed by the TRC. There were and are physical traces of all its activities in the paper and computer synapses tying it to government, to the senior levels of the state bureaucracy, and so on down to the commanders in the field and the operations and operatives they ran. It was the carefully considered plans, the studies and theories of the Broederbond, which underlay that massive exercise in social landscaping, the creation and ethnic cleansing of 'group areas'. This resulted in millions of men, women and children being dumped, like so much human garbage, on barren stretches of the rural outback.

Overgrown graves, some of them indicated by simple wooden crosses which have not yet rotted away, or by painted stones, mark the sites of countless premature deaths in places like Dimbaza or Weenan or Morsgat. The silent accusation from these burial grounds of the discarded rings louder than words. It was never really heard at the TRC. Nor were the actions flowing from the education policies designed to cripple the minds and talents of generations of students. These were all carefully considered schemas mapped out by the Afrikaner Broederbond and fed into a system manipulated and often run by AB members. Yet the records of the AB remained intact; its motto, 'Our strength lies in secrecy', was rigorously followed. This ensured that, unlike state records, its history – the history of the system called apartheid – was never under threat of disclosure.

Within its secret conclaves, however, many bruising ideological and tactical battles were fought. From time to time a few very senior brothers in powerful positions aspired to dominate the collective will of the AB elite. None tried harder than Hendrik Verwoerd, once he became convinced of the divine inspiration of his mission. He saw himself as a moderniser, but drew the bulk of his most dedicated support from the traditionalist wing. He was also well aware that his position as head of the government and the National Party relied more on electoral popularity than it did on the support of his peers, many of whom regarded him as intolerably arrogant. He might find it necessary to appeal over the heads of the cabinet, the party, and even the AB, to rally public opinion behind him.

But in order to create a brave new world according to his view of AB doctrine, Verwoerd knew a secure and stable environment would be needed. This might require the use of people and methods that he might personally find distasteful and even dangerous, but on this he was prepared to gamble. It was the start of that aspect of the secret state that became a law unto itself; a corrupt and bloody machine that, in its final decade and more, judged no scheme too squalid or depraved that aimed to prop up a disintegrating ideology.

4

Genesis of the secret projects

The manipulation of ideas, thought and feeling underlay all that Hendrik Verwoerd planned to do. Certainly from the early 1960s he and several close cronies worked to manage in detail what they recognised to be the complex motivations of individuals, groups and society as a whole. Verwoerd believed devoutly that mass communication was the key. If this could be controlled, it could unlock the way to the greater future he imagined he might create, not just for South Africa, but for the world.

So the search was on for means whereby the value systems of entire populations could be moulded. In this respect, he was deeply concerned about the possible impact of television. He recognised, and probably over-estimated, the potential influence of the visual media in influencing opinions and attitudes. But since he was convinced that it was possible to condition whole populations and to modify attitudes, values and behaviour, his concentration on film and television was logical. Yet, then as now, television consumed vast quantities of programme material, millions of sound and image bites, over which no single entity or individual had control. This was unacceptable to the apartheid politicians. So the Dutch Reformed Church-driven campaign – itself a reflection of Broederbond fears – to keep South Africa free from the increasingly widespread electronic curse of polyglot multiculturalism was given active government support.

At the same time Verwoerd realised that, in a world of mass communication, South Africa could not remain indefinitely isolated from the television age. Neighbouring countries were already broadcasting images and messages that reached across the borders; the intrusion could only increase. There were crude lines of defence in censorship, but these were both time consuming and inefficient. What was needed was a clear line of attack. The medium should be used, subtly and unobtrusively. All that this might require was technical innovation, and maybe an element of luck.

One of the people he turned to for help was a fellow psychologist and Broederbond member, Frederik Willem Blignaut, head of the psychology department at the University of South Africa in Pretoria. Unknown to the university administration, Blignaut established the Kommunikasie Navorsingskomitee (KNK – Communication Research Committee). He was also instrumental in setting up, in 1962, the Psychological Institute of the Republic of South Africa (Pirsa), an exclusively 'white' organisation, as opposed to the internationally recognised Psychological Association which had no colour bar to membership.

There has been no public acknowledgement of the work undertaken by the KNK, which appears to have gone to elaborate lengths to preserve its secrecy, even recruiting staff from Europe. One such recruit was Josef Paul Maria Joannes Heylen, a Flemish-speaking Belgian who arrived in South Africa on 26 November 1964. When he arrived he had already been granted a permit as a permanent resident by the South African Department of Internal Affairs. Yet Heylen's Belgian passport, issued in June of that year, revealed that he had travelled in Poland for nearly two weeks in July and had returned to Belgium via East Germany. Given the paranoid anti-communism practised by the South African authorities, this should have brought an instant ban.

Instead he was appointed secretary of the KNK, although he was in theory employed by the government's National Film Board as a film researcher and carried a Film Board identity card. But he had no background in film, or any formal qualifications as a researcher in the field. As a Flemish-speaker, he could understand Afrikaans, and he had the advantage of not being linked to any of the AB factions. He was also grateful to Blignaut and Verwoerd for a job that allowed him eventual membership of Pirsa, despite his lack of academic qualifications.

Heylen admitted playing a part in the experiments dictated by Verwoerd's great dream of subliminally influencing the population. Although by 1964 there was already a body of literature on subliminal advertising, primarily relating to research done in the United States, Blignaut and his team carried out a series of experiments in Pretoria cinemas in 1965. One of these involved the insertion of single 'advertising' frames in movie film, the theory being that the 'flicker' of the advertisement would be too fast to be consciously noticed by the audience, but that its message would be subconsciously absorbed. The experiment was simple: for months, the sales of the soft drinks Coca-Cola and Fanta were monitored in several cinemas during the interval before a main feature, and a profile drawn up giving an average consumption for each cinema.

Subliminal advertisements for one or other drink were then inserted in films shown before the intervals, and consumption monitored again. If the subliminal advertising worked, the KNK should be able to predict increases in the consumption of one or other drink as buying habits were conditioned. This would open the way to exploitation heaven. But the subliminal messages had no apparent effect. This was a blow both to Blignaut and to Verwoerd. It also goes to explain why television only came to South Africa in 1976, and then only after considerable pressure from within the Broederbond. It was John Vorster – like Verwoerd, a conscientious AB member and part of its traditionalist wing – who finally okayed the establishment of the country's first television service, mentioning neither the purist view that television was the work of the devil, nor the increasing pressure in its favour from the modernisers and from the Teljoy shareholders.

By this time, Heylen had left South Africa for New Zealand, where he established a high-profile market research company and ingratiated himself with various politicians including the Labour Party prime minister Bill Rowling. In 1979, in the wake of the 'secret projects' scandal that toppled John Vorster and his security chief, Heylen fled New Zealand, leaving behind a trunkful of documents, some of them relating to his time in South Africa. Some of the information gleaned from him and from the documents, including a claimed government scheme for the mass sterilisation of black men, seemed so outrageous at the time that it was not taken seriously. During TRC hearings and in early 2000, however, with the trial of South Africa's chemical and biological warfare expert, Dr Wouter Basson, the fragments provided by Heylen finally slotted into place in the terrible jigsaw of South Africa's past.

But TV did not top Verwoerd's agenda. His priority was to resolve the contradictions between the ideological need for racial separation and the demands of an industrialising economy for skilled and settled labour. He was confident he could do so; television might help. All he required was time, and a stable environment in which to pursue his divine mission. With instability an ever-present threat, he decided in 1961 that he needed a hard man for the hard job of ensuring the security of the state in the new era. His choice for the post was John Vorster, at the time a very junior deputy minister of education, arts, science, welfare and pensions.

The choice was a calculated gamble. Vorster had his own loyal network of followers from his days as a wartime internee, and the justice portfolio would provide him with a stronger power base. This was one of the reasons that Pieter Willem 'P.W.' Botha preceded Vorster into the prime minister's office in Pretoria's Union Buildings in the afternoon of 23 July 1961. Botha and Vorster, both deputy ministers, were known to share an intense mutual dislike, as well as the trait of ruthless ambition.

Botha was a failed law student who, at the age of twenty, had become a full-time organiser for the National Party. This was the party which, in 1942, expelled Vorster and other members who refused to resign from the paramilitary and openly neo-Nazi Ossewa Brandwag (OB – Oxwagon Guard). The OB, founded in 1939 as a 'cultural organisation', had quickly developed into a political rival to the NP leadership. A bitter struggle ensued, and Botha knew on which side his bread was buttered, launching a vitriolic public attack on the OB in 1941. He played a part in the expulsions from the NP, and helped to discipline the upstart OB general.

By displaying a capacity for hard work and exceptional organisational skills, Botha had overcome evident feelings of inadequacy. Even in those early years, he had forged a reputation as a man of action and was, above all, a party loyalist. Vorster, on the other hand, was arrogantly self-assured, an honours law student and practising lawyer who saw himself in the late 1930s as the future Führer of South Africa.

So Botha received the more senior portfolio of housing while also taking on responsibility for 'Community Development and Coloured Affairs'. Vorster became the minister of justice, police and prisons. Within five years it was to become one of the most powerful political posts in the land. This caused considerable disquiet in government circles and probably led, in March 1966, to Verwoerd appointing Botha to the powerful position of defence minister. It was one of Verwoerd's last appointments before he was killed.

While there is no independent confirmation of Vorster's later claim that he told Verwoerd he would take the job only if he could 'deal with the threat of subversion and revolution in my own way', the demand would have been fully in character. It would also have been what Verwoerd wanted, expected, and possibly feared. It is also probably true that Vorster informed the thinly smiling Verwoerd that he intended 'fighting communism' without reference to 'the Queensberry rules', and that this architect of apartheid told Vorster that he was free to do what he had to, within limits that were never defined.

Before John Vorster and P.W. Botha could take over their new ministerial posts, Verwoerd decided on a snap election as a vote of confidence in himself and his policies. He had already secured a republican mandate – South Africa had become a republic on 31 May 1961 – but he had also walked out of the still British-dominated Commonwealth. Though this act was applauded by Vorster as having 'rescued the nation's pride', there were others, even within government, who feared that the breach might harm trade and the flow of investment. Their fears were misplaced, as were concerns that English-speaking whites would desert the country following the severing of their supposed emotional umbilical cord. The good life proved a stronger tie, and the election was a resounding victory for Verwoerd and the National Party.

It was also seen as a vote of approval for the harsh measures taken in 1960 against anti-apartheid opponents, including the banning of the ANC and PAC and the declaration of a state of emergency for five months which resulted in the arrest and detention of hundreds of opponents. But opposition had not been obliterated. Somehow the underground Communist Party had got wind of the clampdown, and several senior ANC and SACP members had evaded the police net and fled abroad. They began to set up bases in exile and announced that a phase of 'armed struggle' had begun.

In those days, the information the police had about individual opponents and opposition groups was scant and often contradictory. Internal security was in need of an urgent overhaul, and Vorster was given the mandate to do what was necessary. He had clear ideas of what that meant, and he had the man to act as chief of staff: Hendrik Johannes – 'H.J.' – van den Bergh, a fellow former wartime internee, and by then a brigadier and head of the police criminal investigation department.

When John Vorster approached 'H.J.' van den Bergh in 1962 to become chief of the police Security Branch, he resumed a relationship begun nearly twenty years earlier. That was in 1943, when Vorster, already a lawyer and the youngest 'chief general' of the outlawed OB, was Camp Leader of the Koffiefontein internment centre in the western Free State province. It was here that suspected members of the paramilitary pro-Nazi underground were held by Jan Smuts's pro-British government. Van den Bergh, a lanky and athletic former police sergeant who towered head and shoulders over most of his colleagues, was Vorster's counter-intelligence chief at the time. His job was to seek out and expose the government agents sent in to spy on the up to 600 internees.

It was in this dusty former mine compound, with its corrugated iron huts set on concrete slabs and watched over by machine-gun nests in wooden watchtowers, that Vorster and Van den Bergh first discussed many of the plans which they were to put into practice twenty years later. To help them in this task was an intensely loyal core of former police internees who, like Van den Bergh, had lost their jobs when detained. Then Nazi Germany had been defeated and they were released, regarded as traitors by the pro-Allied faction of white South Africa and as the lunatic fringe by many Afrikaner nationalists. They found work wherever they could. Van den Bergh, for example, laboured as a clerk in the Johannesburg offices of the Institute for Architects.

But their fortunes changed in 1948. The National Party, which was allied with the small Afrikaner Party to which the OB men belonged, won the general election. Van den Bergh, on behalf of the League of Former Internees and Political Prisoners (Bond van Ge-interneerdes en Politieke Gevangenes) of which Internee 2229/42 B.J. Vorster was a leading member, successfully petitioned the new government. All the OB police who had been interned and discharged were readmitted to the police force without loss of rank or benefits.

By 1949 Van den Bergh was a lieutenant. When, as a brigadier, Vorster offered him the security job in 1962, Van den Bergh at once advised disbanding and replacing the 'hopelessly antiquated' existing Special Branch. He would bring in 'men we know and can trust'. The 'hard men' of Koffiefontein became the core of a new, tough and efficient security force. This was the first of three priorities. The others were to create a network of undercover agents and to recruit infiltrators from the black community who could be sent abroad to join the ANC in exile.

From these beginnings would spring a formidable security network which Van den Bergh hoped to make the most powerful entity in the land, more powerful even than the Broederbond. It would be an all-seeing, all-knowing agency that would select the right people for the right jobs and not only set the course for the ship of state but steer it too, in splendid anonymity.

To establish the undercover network, he retained Colonel Att Spengler, one of the 'old guard' Special Branch. As head of the Johannesburg Security Branch, he had been the senior security police officer at Sharpeville on 21 March 1960 and had faced down the storm of criticism following the massacre. Spengler had not opposed the government in World War Two and had not belonged to the OB, but this background suited Van den Bergh's purposes.

The public story was that Spengler had had a major row with the new order in the Security Branch, and so had been shunted off to a desk job in some backwater to while away his time until retirement. In fact he was sent to recruit, initially within the police force, the first of the undercover agents who were to start Republican Intelligence (RI), a clandestine unit that would work in tandem with the SB. His initial target was young English-speaking white policemen. Those recruited were given discharges from the police force and cover stories to explain this. With funding no problem, Spengler set up a private detective agency in Johannesburg through which some of his recruits passed and others stayed. Some went on to set up or work in other front companies, or were placed in jobs in both the private and public sectors.

Van den Bergh, in the meantime, rebuilt the 'sharp end' of Security Branch around his handpicked core. They would handle day-to-day operations, including interrogation. To be more proficient, they required training, and who better to provide this than the French secret service, with their copious experience in the brutal and bitter Algerian independence war? The French were happy to oblige. As the TRC discovered, Van den Bergh, the sadistic Theunis Jacobus 'Rooi Rus' (Red Russian) Swanepoel and a group which later specialised in interrogation and torture travelled to France. Contact was also made with other intelligence agencies; in particular, the Central Intelligence Agency of the United States gave advice, and some training. This smartened up the previous South African police torture methods, which had consisted mostly of straightforward beatings. Solitary confinement, sleep deprivation with shifts of interrogators, and the use of electric shocks became more prevalent.

Once he had begun to establish and provide training for his SB core, and Att Spengler had begun to recruit for Republican Intelligence, Van den Bergh decided to embark on an ambitious recruitment drive among journalists. It was a gamble, but worth taking. He and Vorster took up the issue with a sceptical Verwoerd. The prime minister had been a journalist and the editor of the Afrikaans-language *Transvaaler* newspaper. He was convinced that journalists recruited either as full-time agents or part-time informers would be unreliable. The mere fact of their recruitment, he told Van den Bergh, would be 'too good a story' not to be broken. According to one account, he bet the security chief a case of wine that before twelve journalists had been brought into the pay of RI, at least one of them would rush into print to reveal all. Van den Bergh won the bet. Within months he had nearly twenty journalists on the RI payroll, although few knew at that stage that they were part of a wholly new security service.

Verwoerd gave his blessing for Vorster and Van den Bergh's plans. He knew that the new spy service would tend to duplicate what the military was already doing, although its focus was mainly outside the country, but it would provide additional eyes and ears both at home and abroad. Instead of a somewhat casual service with little clear idea of aims and objectives, there would be another, hopefully more efficient, service which would marshal the services of analysts, propagandists and other specialists. It would also offer a useful counterweight to Military Intelligence, as well as a means of weighing the value and veracity of information.

An added attraction of the new service was that it promised to be cost-effective, thanks to some proposals advanced by the new security chief. Van den Bergh knew that the Nazi SS, which he had admired, had been an almost entirely self-funding operation, and this may have decided him to do the same with Republican Intelligence. There is no hard evidence that this was the motivation, but several of the front companies did indeed prosper. Agents who worked in 'outside' jobs were also paid only a 'top-up' fee, which made them cheaper to employ. Journalists would draw their salaries from their employers and then receive perhaps a third or a half as much again from Republican Intelligence, together with any expenses related to RI work.

A number of black recruits were lured into the service through bribery and the promise of immunity for serious criminal offences. They were given special training on a farm, Rietvlei (Reed marsh), near Pretoria. This was the forerunner of the askari operation that was to feature so prominently during the TRC hearings more than thirty years later. Att Spengler, again, was in charge. It was his task to ensure that each recruit was sufficiently conditioned, compromised or beholden to the unit, as well as being competent to spy.

The training appears to have been brutal, and to have brutalised whoever underwent it. Lessons from these early days were passed on over the years, refined, and finally used with considerable success to turn men not only into traitors to causes they might once passionately have served, but into seemingly conscienceless mass killers. Here was a practical example of the blunting of human emotion that had fascinated Verwoerd as a student. As solitary confinement, detention laws, tight state control and virtual immunity from prosecution for torturers came more and more into play, South Africa developed into a useful laboratory for Western torture and interrogation techniques. Over the years there were routine exchanges of information with Chile and Argentina during their bloody military dictatorships, and with Taiwan as well as France and the US. Military interrogators, however, appear to have received much of their training from Italy.

But in the early years there were no formal death squads. Official killings were largely random acts. Some police squads, usually murder and robbery divisions, would sometimes short-circuit the justice system by shooting a suspect, often described in subsequent police statements as a 'notorious' or 'well-known' criminal. Security Branch interrogators would also occasionally, sometimes by accident, sometimes in a blind rage, and now and then by deliberate design, kill political opponents in their custody. Sometimes, as in the case of trade unionist Looksmart Solwandle Ngudle, the first person to die in detention, there may have been an experimental element.

Ngudle had been interrogated for days on end in an office at the SB's Compol building headquarters in Pretoria in 1963. According to one of his interrogators, a wiry and foul-mouthed junior officer called Terreblanche, Looksmart had been hung briefly from a hat rack in the interrogation room when he could no longer stand. 'Then we gave him the wire and sent him back to his cell,' Terreblanche noted months after the detainee had died. 'And we told him we would be back for some more the next day.' Looksmart Solwandle Ngudle was found dead in the morning, hanging from the bars of his cell window by the length of wire that Terreblanche had given him.

There were also apparent mistakes, such as the killing, in 1964, of Babla Saloojee, the Johannesburg anti-apartheid activist, who fell to his death from the seventh-storey window of an interrogation room in The Greys building which housed the SB headquarters in Johannesburg. His interrogators, among them Theunis 'Rooi Rus' Swanepoel, claimed that Saloojee had jumped out of the window in an apparently frantic attempt to escape. The trajectory of the body made nonsense of the claim, but it also seems certain that the interrogation squad did not intend to kill their suspect. At least, not then, when he had not yet given them the information they sought.

As in numerous subsequent cases, no police were ever prosecuted. The interrogators stuck to their story: the slightly built Saloojee had managed to struggle past three burly SB men, leap onto the window sill and jump out of the open window. This he had performed head-first, and less than an arm's length from the wall of the building. The case is one of the many that were not investigated by the TRC, but it seems most likely that, as part of their procedures, one or more of his interrogators held Saloojee by the ankles and dangled him out of the window. There could have been a kick in fear or anger; perhaps the policemen simply lost their grip. At any rate, Babla Saloojee fell onto the concrete parapet below, his body so mangled that signs of physical torture were difficult to distinguish from the damage sustained in his fall. The new security police broom was sweeping a bloody course across the country. 'Rooi Rus' Swanepoel played a prominent role until he retired three decades later, to emerge in 1994 as a parliamentary candidate for the Conservative Party, which H.J. van den Bergh had also joined.

But such deaths in detention had to be justified. In the first place, because South Africa remained committed to the norms of parliamentary democracy, the forms of justice had to be observed. Sloppy, badly managed killings made this difficult. There were propaganda problems for the government, and efficiency was not to be impaired. Van den Bergh had no qualms about killing and torture, but he prided himself on his efficiency. One did not kill someone who could provide information or be otherwise put to use.

However, there were often times when it became necessary to eliminate one or another individual for whatever reason, and such actions needed to be organised and controlled – assassination is a professional business. So Van den Bergh established his own death squad. It was probably in place by 1966 or 1967 and, according to one account, initially comprised five killers who were referred to as the 'Z squad'. This may have been a play on the mythical 'Q' squad, an appellation given to the spies who gave evidence in the 1964 trial of South African Communist Party chairman Bram Fischer and others charged with membership of an unlawful organisation. Van den Bergh invented the term so as to add a touch of glamour to a sordid business.

There had been no need for such window-dressing in 1963 when the entire leadership of the armed wing of the ANC, Umkhonto we Sizwe (MK), were arrested at Lilliesleaf Farm in Rivonia, north of Johannesburg. A well-placed spy, who is still unknown, gave information that a major gathering of the anti-apartheid underground was about to take place in Johannesburg. The information was quite detailed, even down to the fact that one of the participants would be 'travelling from Cape Town in disguise'. This was Denis Goldberg. But another informer, senior MK member Bruno Mtolo, had visited the farm and gave a description, which enabled the police to identify it. In July, the police swooped. So began more than twenty years of incarceration for the MK high command that included Nelson Mandela. It was a major blow against the anti-apartheid movement, and a massive propaganda boost for Van den Bergh and his new security establishment.

He scored another propaganda coup in the 'Fischer trial'. Gerard Gunther Ludi, a journalist on the liberal *Rand Daily Mail* newspaper and a member of the SACP, declared himself in court to be 'secret agent QO18', a warrant officer in the security police. He was one of the first successful blackmail victims of RI, having agreed to spy and give evidence in exchange for immunity under the country's notorious Immorality Act. This forbade, as the police coyly put it, 'illicit carnal knowledge' across the colour bar. Ludi had been having an affair with a young woman classified as 'Indian' and would have faced a public trial and possible six-month prison term.

Police Constable Klaus Schroeder, who had spent months with headphones glued to his ears, monitoring every grunt, groan and verbal indiscretion in a flat occupied by an SACP district committee member, emerged as 'Secret Agent QO43'. His tape recordings provided a wealth of information about the SACP, from names and addresses, to hopes, plans, fears and fantasies. They also gave Van den Bergh the final straw of blackmail which broke the back of Petrus Arnoldus Bernardus – 'Piet' – Beyleveld, the central committee member of the SACP who turned state's evidence.

The subsequent trial had all the hallmarks of Van den Bergh: high drama, a recanting senior communist, secret agents, but not a single mention of Van den Bergh or of Republican Intelligence. Throughout, the proceedings were observed from the back of the courtroom by one of Van den Bergh's protégés, Johan Coetzee. The image of a ruthlessly efficient secret agency, which lurked everywhere, countering the 'Red menace' and its 'liberalistic' fellow travellers, was reinforced.

This image, together with a propaganda barrage which successfully painted liberal opponents of the apartheid order as depraved and immoral, had been carefully orchestrated months earlier during one of Van den Bergh's first major security crackdowns. In the process, he was also able to defuse much of the criticism about a wave of detentions early in July 1964. The international outcry over hundreds of people being held in solitary confinement amid allegations of torture was severely muted by his handling of a case involving the planting of a bomb at the Johannesburg railway station on Friday, 24 July, which killed an elderly woman and seriously injured a child.

The 'station bomb' was catapulted instantly into the annals of official infamy. Spin doctors went straight to work, manipulating, distorting, and milking the event for every ounce of propaganda value. The tale was amended still further in later years, adjusted in step with what was perceived as the prevailing public mood. According to John Vorster, when he was interviewed in 1976, John Harris of the African Resistance Movement planted the bomb. The ARM, he added, was 'a communist organisation financed by Bram Fischer'. It was in fact an organisation of liberals, supporters and members of the non-racial Liberal Party and a couple of Trotskyists who were members of the tiny underground Socialist League. Enraged by the closing down in 1960 of all constitutional avenues to change, these largely university-based oppositionists had embarked on a campaign of non-lethal sabotage to put pressure on the government. Most of them were dedicated anti-communists.

According to government mythology, promoted by Vorster in his 1976 interview, John Harris, a member of the Liberal Party, had been arrested after Van den Bergh had staged a brainstorming session with a group of his detectives and they had deduced that Harris was their man. Van den Bergh himself was also later to claim that he had 'intuitively' come up with the name before even visiting the scene of the bomb blast. The truth is both sadder and more vicious. The police knew well in advance that the bomb had been planted on the station concourse by 'the ARM' because they had received telephone calls to warn them. Both Harris and a woman associate had made calls, both to the police and to newspapers. This fact could not be denied.

What could also not be denied was that John Harris, a popular history teacher at a local private college, was a known advocate of non-violent resistance. He and other leading members of the ARM, including the few revolutionary socialists such as Michael Wade and Roman Eisenstein, subscribed to the view that symbolic sabotage was the way forward. They felt it would act as a catalyst to show the masses that resistance was still possible despite the draconian onslaught from the state. The bomb – plastic bags filled with petrol packed around a relatively small amount of explosive – was obviously designed to provide the maximum pyrotechnic display with the minimum likelihood of damage.

The day after his arrest, and when he had been so severely beaten that his jaw was broken in three places, John Harris was able, in Pretoria local prison, to whisper to another detainee what had happened. He was puzzled. He had been taken to the scene of the blast, but the bomb, he said, had exploded under a bench where people were sitting. This was not where he had placed it. He had put it in the middle of the concourse to make it as obvious as possible. There had also been warnings telephoned to the police and to newspapers to clear the concourse. This version of events was independently supported in a statement made in Zambia in 1965 by the woman who assisted John Harris in his final protest.

This interpretation did not suit Van den Bergh. He was keen to project an image that would justify the brutal state crackdown, the detentions without trial and the tortures routinely denied. This could only be done if he, the government and the apartheid order could be assumed to be defending civilisation against ruthless terror.

For popular consumption, John Harris should be portrayed in this light; for legal purposes, he should be shown to have had a clear intention to kill and maim. This would guarantee a murder conviction and the death penalty. Van den Bergh achieved both. In publicity terms, he used his friends in the media; in court, he underlined this message with the evidence of John Lloyd, journalist and recanting ARM member who had been closely involved with John Harris. Coached by the police, as all state witnesses were, Lloyd told the court that Harris had expressed the intention to kill. According to this testimony, John Harris had stated that it would be 'tactically advisable' if 'a few lives were taken'.

John Harris denied ever having made such a statement. Mr Justice Joseph Ludorf dismissed the denial, accepted Lloyd's evidence and sentenced John Harris to death. What neither the courts nor the public were aware of at the time was that John Lloyd, in his original statement to the police, had also not alleged that John Harris had said any such thing. Thirty years later, the sworn statement of John Nesbitt Lloyd emerged, having escaped the shredders and the furnaces. In it he mentions that John Harris argued for an explosion in a public place to shock the white community. It would also underline that the ARM was not 'broken up'. On the issue of lives in danger, Lloyd's statement adds: 'He then said innocent people had been killed by bombs during the war and that it was a risk everyone would have to take.'

This was a far cry from the statement made in court. Having made it, and while John Harris started his last few months on death row in Pretoria Central Prison, John Lloyd, together with another recanting ARM member, Adrian Leftwich, was allowed to migrate to England. Leftwich, a central figure in the ARM, had confessed weepingly in court that he had had to give away his colleagues in order to save himself from the death sentence. It revealed something of the pressures used by Van den Bergh and his men. Leftwich's information resulted in sentences ranging up to fifteen years in jail for ARM members. But the evidence of Adrian Leftwich was factual. It was damage he could not undo even had he wished to. John Lloyd, however, had provided the one piece of evidence that might tip the scale from life to death for John Harris. Harris's legal team certainly felt so. A recantation, from the relative safety of exile, would trigger massive publicity and could result in a commutation of the death sentence. Harris's family, a close friend and the legal team all petitioned Lloyd to speak out. He refused. On the morning of 1 April 1965 John Harris walked to the gallows singing the anthem of the United States freedom marchers, 'We shall overcome'. The hangman, after he retired, told journalist David O'Sullivan that John Harris 'sang even as he dropped'. This ensured the banning of the song in South Africa.

The TRC ruled that it could not investigate the matter through an amnesty application on behalf of John Harris. No provision had been made for granting amnesties to those already dead, and no one else was prepared to raise the issue – certainly not J.J. Viktor, the sadist who had 'practised drop-kicks' on the jaw of John Harris and who had severely beaten other ARM detainees, with the full knowledge and consent of Van den Bergh. Journalist Hugh Lewin recalled being slumped in a chair, his face swollen and bruised, when Van den Bergh looked into the room shortly after his brutal underling had left. Tweed-suited, the light glinting on his steel-rimmed spectacles, he noted, quite jovially, 'pleased to see you're cooperating', and sauntered out.

The recent discovery of the original sworn statement of John Lloyd answered some questions, but raised many more. After relocating to England, where he eventually became a lawyer – a barrister – in Exeter, Lloyd maintained that he had only made a statement to the police six days after he was detained on 23 July. He lied. The issue was further confused in a private letter written from Bristol on 21 October 1966. Explaining to a friend the claimed sequence of events around the station bomb, Lloyd noted: 'It still puzzles me that I was left unquestioned in the Germiston police cells until 10 am on the Monday.' However, Hugh Lewin saw him in an interrogation room on the day of the bomb blast.

Lloyd's letter also notes that on the Monday, three days after the bomb, he had to 'go through this draft statement and fill in the places where [John Harris] was involved'. But the sworn statement is clearly dated 24 July 1964, the day of the bomb blast. It is, however, timed at both 12.45 pm and at 12.15 pm, or some four hours before the bomb exploded. John Lloyd subsequently maintained that the Afrikaans-speaking policeman who took the statement made the elementary error of confusing 'am' with 'pm'. The statement, he said, was actually completed after midnight on the day that John Harris was arrested. As evidence of this, he pointed to the fact that the eleventh page of the 13-page document states: 'the next time I saw him [John Harris] was at "The Grays" [Security Branch headquarters] on Friday evening 24.7.1964'.

Since John Harris was only arrested at 11 pm that night it is unlikely that the statement could have been completed in little more or less than an hour. This is especially so because the statement is of the conventional post-interrogation variety: it starts with date and place of birth and progresses through school and work records before coming to anything concerning the ARM. This was the standard form for statements after detainees had either broken down or otherwise agreed to talk: first the hard current information would be noted, often acted on. Then, once all the pertinent political information had been extracted, the confessing detainee would be seated opposite a policeman for the lengthy process of writing a formal sworn statement. Handwritten by the policeman, or by the detainee at the prompting of the policeman, it would then be taken away to be checked, perhaps amended, and finally typed, generally on cream government-issue foolscap sheets. The completed draft would be signed by the detainee, dated and witnessed by at least one policeman.

It is possible that an initial post-interrogation statement was amended to include reference to John Harris's arrest. Perhaps this was done on the Monday. John Lloyd has denied this. However, sufficient doubt existed about his statement, and the role he played in the trial, conviction and hanging of John Harris, for him to be dropped, amid considerable public outcry, as a prospective parliamentary candidate for the British Labour Party in the 1996 election.

The Lloyd statement, R.O. 17. 806/7/64, certainly could not answer two personal questions from John Harris's widow Ann and his son David, who were driven from South Africa in 1966 by a vindictive campaign of official harassment. One was answered in the new millennium when a priest and former prison chaplain in Pretoria informed a relative that John Harris had been cremated, and that his ashes had been kept for years in an urn on the desk of 'a senior police officer'. After years of badgering, the priest was able to secure the ashes and had buried them in a local cemetery under a simple concrete slab bearing the name John Harris. This information enabled the family to plan a commemoration in 2002 at which the last wish of John Harris could be carried out and the words 'a true patriot' inscribed on his simple tombstone. But they have never been able to discover what became of the last three letters written by John Harris on the eve of his execution, one to Ann and two to David.

There are also questions of wider importance and outside of the personal realm. They concern the way the security apparatus acted, and how far it interfered with events and created propaganda. What is known is that Van den Bergh and the SB had close links with the Railway Police at the Johannesburg station. These had been reinforced during the police hunt for the underground ANC and SACP leadership, which had culminated in the Rivonia trial. As a consequence, the head of the Railway Police on the station had a direct line to Van den Bergh. So it is feasible that the telephoned warning about a bomb on the station concourse was relayed straight to the head of the SB, who by that stage may have been expecting just such a call. Van den Bergh, for his part, had a direct line, not just to the ministry of police, but to John Vorster himself.

Several questions then arise: was a decision taken at the top to allow the bomb to explode on the station? Was the suitcase moved after the warning was given? If so, who moved it and who decided where it should be placed? The police did not issue a general warning, but did they clear their own personnel from the station, apparently for a 'briefing'? There is certainly evidence to indicate that the 'station bomb' may have been one of the earlier – and successful – attempts to manipulate events for political ends. Perhaps the questions will never be fully answered. To the security services at the time, the facts did not matter: the message sent out was just what they wanted and needed. The later addition of supposed communist involvement was merely an embellishment. It suited the needs of the time, much as the invention of a 'Q' branch had added an aura of Flemingesque glamour to an episode of voyeurism, blackmail and manipulation.

*

The 'Z squad', on the other hand, was very much an in joke. It was, in fact, never mentioned publicly, but the term carried with it the menace its founder intended. Nobody was safe from this squad; it was the avenging sword wielded from on high to dispatch, with cool efficiency, enemies, traitors and those who simply refused to get out of the way. The actions of the squad spelled finality; they were the 'end of the line' and received the end of the alphabet as their unofficial designation.

Little is known of the original squad and how it grew or where and when other, similar, units were set up. What is known is that the squad operated not only in South Africa but also in any country where it was felt necessary to invoke its lethal services. It was the forerunner of Vlakplaas and the murderous Civil Cooperation Bureau, whose brutal behaviour featured so centrally at TRC hearings. It was almost certainly responsible for the murder of journalist and spy Keith Wallace in London in 1969.

Wallace was one of the clutch of journalists recruited by Van den Bergh's security apparatus in the early years of Republican Intelligence. Like a number of the journalists who came to work with the various security agencies over the years, he was drawn in by the offer of exclusive stories with which he built a name for himself as an investigative writer. He was also one of the journalists who became a full-time paid agent. As such, he was given special training and assigned a number with an 'R' prefix. Most of the earlier recruits fell into this category, and some are today senior journalists working in various media both in South Africa and abroad.

Another group of journalists operated as 'reliable sources'. Some merely traded information on an informal basis; others provided information and acted as news conduits for the security services, but were not formally employed, although many received occasional 'expenses'. The doyenne of this group was the Johannesburg-based former newspaper columnist, Aida Parker, who died in February 2003. She spent a substantial part of her inherited wealth on what she saw as furthering her ideological aims. A friend of both Hendrik Verwoerd and P.W. Botha, she never made any secret of her sympathies. Her Aida Parker newsletter, still available in 2002 on subscription, was established as an official operation of Military Intelligence.

The journalists listed on the head office register of the security branch in 1994, and named in 1997 as agents by a senior SB officer, deny their own involvement, but readily point to Parker as an agent. Some also name newspapermen Tony Stirling and Neil Hooper, as well as broadcaster Christo Kritzinger, as agents. This is an echo of the finger-pointing confessions of anti-apartheid detainees during the years of repression. Pressed for names of 'ringleaders' and activists, these detainees usually gave those of allies, colleagues and comrades who were already safely out of the country. In the radically changed circumstances of today, it is the suspected agents and collaborators who are under pressure and the dead who receive the blame. Stirling, Hooper and Kritzinger all died after the democratic transition, but before the TRC process was completed in 1997.

One of the named security police agents who pointed the finger in this way was Chris Olckers, who, like Aida Parker, never made any secret of his rightwing sympathies. Like Parker, he also claims never to have been paid. 'I supported the government. I supported the police. They did not have to pay me,' he said. His ideological commitment does, however, seem to have paid off. He forsook his newspaper career in the early 1990s and emerged briefly as the media spokesman for the prisons department before dropping out of public sight. But by 1999 Olckers had become a uniformed brigadier and the head of one of the country's biggest prison complexes at Baviaanspoort, outside Pretoria.

Keith Wallace was the first known journalist recruit to express doubts about his activities and to threaten to expose them. At the time, he worked for the British *Daily Mail* newspaper, and so had access to an ideal outlet for his disclosures. But Keith Wallace only got as far as mentioning his threat to Van den Bergh. In circumstances that still beg explanation, he was found dead at the bottom of a ventilation shaft of his Kensington apartment block. It was a singular lesson to all agents who might contemplate coming in publicly from the cold: the vengeance of Van den Bergh could reach everywhere.

This was something Van den Bergh made viciously clear on only one recorded occasion. It was in 1978, and there was a major power struggle going on within the Broederbond and the National Party. John Vorster and, with him, Van den Bergh were fighting for their political lives in an attack spearheaded by defence minister P.W. Botha. It used the English-language newspapers as the battlefield in what became perhaps the world's first coup by media. Publicly dubbed the 'Info scandal', or 'Muldergate', since it effectively sidelined Vorster's clear successor, information minister Connie Mulder, in favour of Botha, it involved leaked information about the use and misuse of millions of rands of secret funds.

On the way to toppling Vorster and Van den Bergh, the scandal produced the Erasmus Commission, a three-man inquiry headed by supreme court judge Rudolph Erasmus. Van den Bergh was called to appear before it to give details of the clandestine operations of the security establishment. He was furious when the summons arrived and made it amply clear that he disapproved of the commission. But he obeyed the summons and took his seat at the hearing in camera.

When he spoke, it was with a faint, almost sneering, smile and a voice which seemed to ooze across the room. Only his eyes, narrowed behind the thin-rimmed spectacles, betrayed any trace of cold anger. His suit and tie immaculate, he leaned back in his chair, fixed his gaze on the three men opposite, and proceeded in a calm voice to deliver a warning made all the more chilling because it betrayed no sign of emotion: 'I really want to tell you . . . that I can do the impossible. I have enough men to commit murder if I tell them . . . to kill. I do not care who the prey is, or how important they are. These are the type of men that I have. And if I want to do something like that to protect the security of the state, nobody would stop me. I would stop at nothing.'

He prefaced the warning by noting that Erasmus and his fellow commissioners, 'for the sake of the South African government', would be 'compelled to omit' these comments from their final report. He was right. The final report merely stated that Van den Bergh had admitted 'being in charge of a formidable network of agents whose qualities he described in sinister terms'. The full text of what he said became available only years later.

This was the only open admission by Van den Bergh that the massive apparatus he had put in place contained assassins. Even poor prison conditions, let alone torture, had been routinely denied by the security establishment. The pretence, the façade, had at all times to be preserved; such was the professional code of conduct. Friends in the media helped to a large degree to ensure this. So H.J. – the 'Tall Man' – said no more. Yet it was he who had instituted the first of the country's death squads and had authorised their bloodletting at home and abroad.

When he was forced into retirement, another casualty of the 'Info scandal', his legacy remained. There were spy networks and specialist divisions ranging from bomb-making and poison manufacture to the killer detachments, two of which were later to become the central feature of hearings at the TRC. They were the linear descendants of the secret research facilities established by Verwoerd and about which so many questions still remain. But then, many questions also remain about the death of Verwoerd and the Vorster ascendancy.

5

The Vorster years

Murder and probable blackmail elevated Balthazar Johannes 'John' Vorster to the prime ministership of South Africa in September 1966. Even after Hendrik Verwoerd was stabbed to death on the floor of parliament, Vorster was not the front runner for the highest political post in the land. That status belonged to Barend Johannes 'Ben' Schoeman, leader of the House of Assembly, minister of transport and Transvaal provincial leader of the National Party. He seemed assured of accession to parliamentary and party leadership. But Ben Schoeman suddenly, and to the fury of his supporters, retired from the race, leaving the way open for the only other contender, John Vorster, who was backed by the hardline traditionalists of the National Party.

Afrikaans journalist Beaumont Schoeman briefly interviewed Ben Schoeman in his office on the day before the election, only minutes after the minister had told his agent that he would withdraw. According to the journalist, Schoeman's eyes 'were red and it seemed as if he had been crying'. The minister said he had decided to withdraw because of 'gossip, even about my wife'. He would not elaborate and later promised that all would be revealed in a book he was going to write. The book was never written.

Schoeman's withdrawal left a bitter taste in the mouths of many within senior apartheid circles. More than thiry years later, there were still dark mutterings about the manner of Vorster's rise to power. There were even half-serious calls for the TRC to investigate the murder of Verwoerd. This is not surprising, for the killing and the events surrounding it are as murky as much of the secret history of repression. But even the conspiracy theorists have not really had their day with the murder of Hendrik Verwoerd, because the entire case was presented as a simple fait accompli. Dimitri Tsafendas, a parliamentary messenger of mixed African and Greek parentage, fatally stabbed Verwoerd on 6 September 1966. Tsafendas was clinically insane. He was committed to be detained at the state's pleasure.

Seldom is anything so straightforward. It certainly was not in the case of the killing of Verwoerd. The facts, where they are available, make for fascinating and confusing study, and some of them emerged for the first time during TRC investigations. In the first place, there is the enigma of Tsafendas himself. Born in Mozambique of Greek and African parentage, he was classified 'coloured' by the rules of the apartheid state. A seafarer with a gift for languages – he spoke eight or nine – and a history of psychiatric problems, he had also once been a member of the Communist Party of South Africa. He was therefore disqualified on the grounds of race, political background and mental state from working on the floor of the South African parliament.

Yet Tsafendas was employed as a temporary messenger and given security clearance. This has given plenty of ammunition to conspiracy theorists, many of them within the AB and the National Party. What also has to be weighed, however, is the fact that, for all the fearsome reputation of the security police in general and Hendrik van den Bergh in particular, security precautions around parliament at the time were extremely sloppy. In any case, according to his former landlady and to other messengers who worked with him, Tsafendas showed no untoward signs of emotional disorder, violence or depression.

Shortly before 2 pm on the afternoon of 6 September 1966, Tsafendas took up a position inside the parliamentary chamber as the traditional bells rang to summon members to the session. Hendrik Verwoerd arrived early. He took his seat on the front benches, placing his papers on the desk before him. The public galleries were already packed. Word had gone out that Verwoerd might be making some major announcement. While the bells rang on, the uniformed messenger moved up beside the prime minister, pulled out a long-bladed knife and stabbed downwards. Verwoerd jerked backwards in his seat, his mouth open in a silent cry, before slumping forward.

Still the blood-stained dagger rose and fell. Not till it was plunging downward for the fifth time was Tsafendas wrestled to the ground. The House was in uproar, only those nearest Verwoerd aware at first of what had happened. One of these parliamentarians was P.W. Botha, the recently appointed defence minister. His features warped with rage, he charged across the floor. Shaking his finger at the face of Helen Suzman, the best-known member of the small Progressive Federal Party, he bellowed in Afrikaans: 'It's you who did this. It's all you liberals. You incite people. Now we will get you. We will get the lot of you.'

Suzman was horrified, but after Botha's thuggery she was soon confronted with the other aspect of the apartheid establishment: suave, sophisticated manipulation. For years she had been on friendly terms with the Speaker of parliament, H.J. Klopper, one of the founder-members of the Broederbond. A hardline conservative, he was also a shrewd tactician, and had always gone out of his way to allow her room to speak. In Suzman's own words, he gave her 'more speaking time than ten other MPs together'. She was surprised, but should not have been, for Klopper knew the propaganda value of an opposition voice in parliament, no matter how distasteful he found it. He arranged a meeting between Suzman and Botha, and a grudging half-apology was finally extracted from the belligerent defence minister. Suzman never again spoke to or greeted Botha on a personal basis, but she accepted the apology on an official level, and continued in parliament under the apparently benign chairmanship of Klopper.

The assassin had by then long disappeared from public view. Explanations about his condition and treatment were provided by the police to the news media. Just six weeks after Tsafendas had killed Verwoerd, Judge Andries Beyers, judge president of the Cape Province, heard testimony from government psychiatrists whose expertise and qualifications are still moot, and ruled that Dimitri Tsafendas was mad and therefore unfit to stand trial. 'I could as little try a man who has not at least the makings of a rational mind as I could try a dog or an inert implement. He is a meaningless creature,' said the learned judge. Tsafendas, it was said, suffered under the delusion that a giant tapeworm had infested him and had given him instructions to kill Verwoerd.

But the story was a myth. Transcripts of the lengthy interrogations of Tsafendas not made public at the time, reveal that Tsafendas only mentioned a tapeworm in passing. Responding to a question about his medical history, he said he had suffered from tapeworm infestations. Throughout many hours of interrogation, first by H.J. van den Bergh and a Brigadier Joubert and later by police commissioner and AB member 8125 General J.M. Keevy, Captain Nic Basson and a Major Beeslaar, it is the sole mention. Yet the demon tapeworm story was common currency within days of the assassination. In fact, the transcript records that Tsafendas told Van den Bergh he had killed Verwoerd 'because I didn't agree with him'.

Van den Bergh, however, seemed more interested in knowing if Tsafendas had discussed killing Verwoerd with anyone else. He also seemed keen to establish that the assassin had known that Verwoerd was scheduled to make an important statement and that he had decided to kill him before he made it. A senior detective from Europe who studied the transcripts in early 1999 concluded that 'this was a very strange interrogation'. It posed more questions than it gave answers. While the facts fed for public consumption through a manipulated media presented the case as open and shut, among the Afrikaner political elite it was seen as far murkier and probably sinister, an impression which added to the powerful mythology surrounding Van den Bergh in particular.

Although declared mentally ill, Tsafendas was not placed in a psychiatric institution. Instead he became the first of several political prisoners who were to spend protracted time on death row – in his case a cell in the condemned section of Pretoria Central Prison, alongside the gallows where the wails, prayers, hymn singing and silences of the condemned were punctuated by the frequent thud of the gallows traps. On this conveyor belt, up to seven men at a time met their deaths behind the door at the end of the corridor, which was home for twenty-three years to Dimitri Tsafendas. Isolated in this purgatory, abused regularly by warders, he represented the living dead. It was a tactic that would have driven any man mad who wasn't mad already.

In 1989, when the hangings stopped, Dimitri Tsafendas was moved to another prison. Only after South Africa's democratic transition in 1994, at the age of seventy-five, did he finally enter a psychiatric ward. By then, there was little argument that he was as barking mad as Judge Beyers had assumed twenty-eight years earlier.

Verwoerd, of course, never made that final speech and no record of it remains. The blood-soaked papers presumed to have included a crucial announcement about the future of the apartheid state were cleared away and disappeared. Because there were no copies, this probably over-zealous disposal stoked paranoia among some of Verwoerd's closest confidants. According to the secretary of Verwoerd's secret research committee, Paul Heylen, the speech was to have heralded a major departure from orthodox apartheid. Verwoerd was under international pressure caused both by the excesses perpetrated to institute and maintain apartheid and by South Africa's support for the white minority that had declared independence in Rhodesia (Zimbabwe). He had decided to change tack. The British government had apparently made it clear – as they were again to do when Vorster took over – that they saw the resolution of apartheid as necessary for the resolution of the Rhodesian problem.

The region proximate to the land of institutional apartheid was also in flux. Portugal was making heavy weather of dealing with nationalist guerrillas in the colonies of Angola and Mozambique. Guerrilla activity had begun in Rhodesia. No blind traditionalist, Verwoerd had already by then attempted to adapt the segregationist dream to the reality of an emerging modern industrial state. It was he who had encouraged immigration from Europe and he who had forged closer links with the English-speaking whites. Both policies had caused strains within the Broederbond. In the first place, most of the immigrants were not Calvinists, and most chose English as their first language if they did not already speak it. The traditionalists, led by the dogmatic Albert Hertzog and his Afrikaner Orde faction of the AB, feared that this, combined with closer contact with 'the English', would eventually swamp Afrikaans and the Afrikaner. But they were not strong enough to challenge Verwoerd when, as they saw it, he strayed from the chosen path.

Verwoerd had commissioned his secret communications research unit to investigate just what the electorate would accept under his stewardship. He also toyed with various notions that might combine apartheid with an element of non-racialism – a system which he hoped would satisfy both the integrationists and his segregationist ideals. According to Heylen, Verwoerd decided on the model of a federal South Africa, with a non-racial state along the eastern seaboard comprising essentially the province of Natal and the KwaZulu 'homeland'. The interior and the Cape Province would continue to follow the rules of apartheid in this 'confederation of national states'. By Heylen's account, this was the concept that was scheduled to be floated on that fateful afternoon in parliament. The traditionalists were certainly concerned that their purist vision of apartheid was about to be modified. It was in the hope of averting this that they threw their weight, after the murder of Verwoerd, behind the candidate with the most hardline and racist image: John Vorster.

But the same realities which had so taxed Verwoerd's imagination confronted his successor, and Vorster too began to tinker with the system in an effort to placate the limited demands of local big business and international investors; he too found it necessary to play factions off against one another and to keep secrets even from his closest collaborator, Hendrik van den Bergh. He may even have harboured some fears about his obviously ambitious security chief.

Van den Bergh had, with Vorster's approval, tried to assume control of the entire state security apparatus. This was the reason for the formation in 1969 of the Bureau of State Security, with its apt acronym, BOSS. But BOSS never became the super state security service; it remained essentially a security police organisation. The military intelligence budget had been cut, but the military continued to pursue its own, largely external, agendas. Although the existence of BOSS made for rather more collaboration, the two wings of the security apparatus continued to regard one another with often outright hostility and to make unilateral decisions. Because Van den Bergh had Vorster's ear he was in a much stronger position than his military counterparts, so it was he who – without consulting the military – committed police units to fighting the guerillas in the Rhodesian bush war. This included the promise of helicopters, which the police did not have and the military had to supply.

But Vorster was aware of the shortcomings of police information-gathering, contacts and analysis. As prime minister, he almost certainly learned that the military – and his old antagonist, defence minister P.W. Botha – had achieved considerable penetration in Africa. Botha, after all, had to consult with Vorster in 1969 when he and his MI (Military Intelligence) chief, Colonel Fritz Loots, also a known Broederbond member, wanted to provide logistical and training support to the Biafran side in the bitter Nigerian civil war. The assessment of the military was that the Biafrans could not win, but that support for them could forge close links with those African states supporting the breakaway state in Nigeria. It also strengthened the argument for 'constellations of states' on ethnic lines. Zambia, where the exiled ANC had established its headquarters, was one of the supporting states; Tanzania another, together with Gabon and Côte d'Ivoire, which Botha seems to have visited by then.

Loots, who went on to become the head of special forces, and as such was responsible for the murder of Namibian guerrilla suspects and prisoners of war, argued that such intervention could also help forge closer ties with France. The French, he pointed out, were the main covert suppliers to the Biafrans. Vorster was impressed. He agreed to the sending of a training team, headed by Jan Breytenbach, who a year later was to found South Africa's notorious Reconnaissance Commando Unit. With Breytenbach went tons of arms and munitions. But Botha did not tell Van den Bergh.

Whether it was through French security or the CIA that Van den Bergh came to hear of the Biafra venture is immaterial. When he did hear, he was furious. This slight came immediately after his failed attempt to take control of the entire security apparatus. He had been stymied both from within the police force and by the military. BOSS, he resolved, would have to extend its operations and take over what it could. He and Vorster also mended their bridges. The result was the 'détente' policy credited to Vorster, with Van den Bergh playing the covert contact role developed by Loots.

This was, in many ways, an extension of the close and publicised contact established with Lesotho's chief minister, Chief Leabua Jonathan. On 10

January 1967 Vorster had entertained him to lunch at the Mount Nelson hotel in Cape Town, where he had stressed his doctrine of 'mutual respect and non-interference in another's domestic affairs'. Despite his image as a hardliner and his obvious attraction to the fundamentally anti-democratic philosophy of fascism, John Vorster was a pragmatist. He had wanted the top political job, he had got it and he intended keeping it, even at the cost of a few compromises along the way. After all, Verwoerd himself had made concessions. But these Vorster introduced skillfully into the political arena, carefully marginalising the increasingly bitter AB traditionalists around Albert Hertzog.

And all the time he tried desperately to encourage a settlement between Rhodesia and Britain. The object should be to establish a string of friendly African states, which would allow the apartheid experiment to continue. Those who were indebted tended to make the most reliable allies. So Rhodesia received military aid and troops and Jonathan, when faced with the prospect of losing an election, was helped into office by Vorster's security forces. Vorster determined to divide the countries of the African continent in two: those whose fear of Soviet or some form of 'communist' takeover might incline them to work with him, and those who would have no truck with the apartheid state.

This 'outward-looking' policy would win African allies well beyond the overly dependent and wretchedly poor Malawi of President Hastings Kamuzu Banda. But Vorster's major overt success in Africa – with President Kenneth Kaunda of Zambia – came at a cost of blood and betrayal and was to rack up further bitterness within the military. In an event little publicised even thirty years later, Vorster and Van den Bergh apparently sabotaged an important military operation on the altar of their diplomatic ambition. The military had taken over the training of Lozi dissidents from the former Barotseland Protectorate of Northern Rhodesia who opposed the rule of Kaunda in Zambia, which included the former Barotseland. They were given military training in a secret camp in the Caprivi Strip, under the command of that ubiquitous dirty tricks soldier, Jan Breytenbach.

While both Breytenbach and the commander of the Lozi dissidents, Adamson Mushala, were absent from the camp, a police convoy arrived and ordered the dissident force to get into trucks to be taken to a point where they could cross into Zambia, to start attacks on the Zambian army. The entire force walked into an ambush. There were no survivors. Breytenbach and the military brass were enraged, but rapport was established between Kaunda and Vorster, to the chagrin of the anti-apartheid movements, the South African military and the AB traditionalists.

Kaunda showed his gratitude to Vorster by ensuring that several potentially troublesome South African exiles working in Zambia were moved on. President Felix Houphouët-Boigny of Côte d'Ivoire also hosted Vorster after Eschel Rhoodie had brokered a meeting. President Leopold Senghor of Senegal followed suit. Contacts were also being established with Sudan's dictatorial Muhammad Gaafur al-Nimeiry, and with Egypt, while closer ties with Israel saw the one-time follower of Adolf Hitler visiting the Zionist state as a guest of honour.

At the same time, the security system continued to function both internally and externally. Especially in the Rhodesian bush, South African volunteers were literally being blooded. But there was also involvement with the Portuguese colonial authorities in their wars against independence movements in Angola and Mozambique, the full extent and nature of which are still unknown. Such endeavours cost money, and in 1973 the one essential resource South Africa lacked – oil – soared in price. There was official concern, but it was tinged with optimism.

Because of its golden backbone, the apartheid economy could rise above the crisis. In 1973 the supply of South African gold to a freshly deregulated market was restricted. The price of the metal rose sharply. By December of 1974 it had recorded a more than fivefold increase. This boon helped initially to allay fears that Vorster's grand strategy would come unstuck. Even the outbreak of a wave of strikes (reflecting a sudden surge in the cost of living) in the first three months of 1973 failed to cause deep concern.

All the same, the security police kept a close eye on the labour unrest, for out of it a trade union movement began to emerge which differed from any before it. This came very much from the shopfloor up. Initially at least it tended to eschew permanent leadership: representatives were elected as required and recalled when their workmates so decided. Unlike previous trade union organisations, this one was made up of a series of bodies that functioned collectively; as such, it could not be decapitated. It posed a serious potential threat, especially if it moved outside the field of wages and conditions.

The more aware sections of the business establishment realised that it was better to recognise the unions. As the doyen of South African business, Harry Oppenheimer, noted: 'I was not so foolish to suppose that this would make the life of industrialists like me easier, but I thought it was much better to have this than to sit on the safety valve.' None of the industrialists seemed to realise that, given the nature of apartheid, it was inevitable that the unions would eventually confront the political system. Besides, as the police noted, these embryonic unions tended to rely on radical university students for technical and other assistance. It was just as well that the Security Branch and BOSS project of infiltrating agents onto the campuses was already well under way.

But although Vorster delayed the recognition of trade unions, the traditionalists began to have doubts about the man once seen as the archetypal racial purist. Vorster had shown a remarkable degree of pragmatism. As an internal opposition, coshed into mute submission for years, began again to stir, he employed both the carrot of minor concessions and the usual big stick of repression. Like his predecessor, he felt the need for peace at home and a better image abroad. If this could be bought with a few concessions, then the price must be paid.

For the traditionalists, there was no price worth paying that tarnished the purity of the original apartheid design. This was an article of faith; it brooked no logic and made no concessions to a fast-changing reality. So when Vorster made a minor concession on racially mixed sport, the hard core of the traditionalists split. In 1969, Albert Hertzog and his cronies marched off to form the rapidly marginalised Herstigte Nasionale Party (HNP – reconstituted national party). In the three years since it had helped him to the premiership, Vorster had subtly outmanoeuvred the Hertzog camp in the one area where, in Afrikaner politics, it really mattered: the AB. As 1970 dawned, Vorster was rid of the most outspoken and dogmatic traditionalists. His security chief appeared to have the internal situation under control and his détente policy was starting to pay off. It was the beginning of a few brief years of apparent success.

Despite minor concessions, South Africa remained very much an apartheid state. While domestic war had raged between the 'Broeders', policy stayed on track. Group areas were declared and forced removals followed. Tens and then hundreds of thousands of people – men, women, children, the old, the young and the infirm – were 'endorsed out' of urban areas as surplus to requirements; entire communities were moved as 'black spots' on the map were erased. Those who resisted or showed signs of doing so were beaten, jailed, threatened, blackmailed and banished. The lives of between three and four million people were dislocated and often destroyed in this way.

Banishment, that medieval sanction, became central to maintaining the apartheid state. There were almost biblical overtones in some of the removal strategies as anonymous messengers, paint pots and brushes in hand, moved through humble settlements at night, daubing the doors of homes to be demolished. In the morning, any furniture was carted outside or loaded directly onto waiting government trucks. The bulldozers then crashed into action.

In many cases, these removals amounted to mass banishments. Whole communities, with their belongings, were carted off to remote areas and simply dumped along with timber and corrugated iron sheets with which to build shelter. In others, crude shelter already existed, but there were no toilet facilities, running water or electricity, let alone clinics or hospitals. In several cases, farming communities were moved shortly after they had sown their latest crops or just before harvest time. This was not deliberate. In an echo of a recent and even more horrific European past, officials obeyed their orders because orders were meant to be obeyed. Those who gave the orders and those who made the decisions were not concerned with the detail on the ground. If it was time for a black spot to be erased, then let it be done speedily and, hopefully, profitably as well. So thousands of children suffered permanent damage through the ravages of marasmus and kwashiorkor and thousands more, along with the elderly and infirm, died early, unnecessary and often painful deaths.

Such unthinking brutality, such gross abuse of human rights on so vast a scale, was one of the great realities of apartheid, which should certainly have fallen within the ambit of the TRC. But it was never fully addressed, and could not be, because of constraints of time and the requirements laid out in the legal Act which established the body. Yet these mass removals, the ethnic cleansing of South Africa, were essential for the basic building blocks of apartheid to be put in place. These were the 'homelands'. Verwoerd may have had second thoughts about their viability, but Vorster seemed to have fewer doubts. This was the essential difference between the National Party and sections of the liberal intelligentsia which tended to support the white opposition Progressive Federal Party (PFP).

The PFP itself, having moved from a position of favouring a limited franchise for 'suitably qualified' blacks, supported an undefined 'federation of self-governing states'. Separation or apartheid dressed up as 'federalism' or 'partition' was the dominant aim among the beneficiaries of the system, at least until 1978. The only argument was how best to achieve this. Even well known liberals debated the pros and cons of variable, but essentially racial, division. Most, though, like Leo Marquard, felt that the division should be fairly equitable; none of the federal units should be disproportionately power-ful. Although it tended to be accepted that these units would be racially segregated, there was also an insistence that any wishing to be 'multiracial' should also be permitted.

Vorster had no wish to indulge in these ethnic balancing acts. He stuck to the original design: 13 per cent of the land area, the 'native reserves', would provide the 'homelands' for blacks. But he became acutely aware that Macmillan's wind of change was continuing to blow. The cordon sanitaire provided by Portuguese-ruled Mozambique and Angola and white-ruled Rhodesia still absorbed the worst of these powerful gusts, but they could not stand if the gale grew stronger. Both Vorster and Van den Bergh saw that it would be preferable to win friends in the neighbouring states; to gradually become integrated in the African political scene through the use of bribery, subtle threats and occasional force. This, of course, required some local adaptation, some easing of a few of apartheid's petty rules.

But the wider world refused to accept these gestures as any more than cosmetic. Even at the height of détente, there were problems. Pressure was building and the appellation 'polecat of the Western world', given to the regime and its apartheid system by expelled Anglican (Episcopalian) bishop Ambrose Reeves, had stuck. There were also rumblings from New Zealand in the one secular area which united most of white South Africa with enthusiasm akin to a Christian tent revival meeting: rugby. The exclusion by South Africa of New Zealand Maori rugby players had been glossed over before 1969. When white South African 'Springbok' rugby teams visited New Zealand, they played 'mixed' teams; when the New Zealand 'All Blacks' visited South Africa, Maori players were drafted into a New Zealand Maori side which toured elsewhere. All white All Blacks played in South Africa. Then in 1969, swelling into the 1970s, came the cry from New Zealand: 'No Maoris, no tour.' This quickly developed into 'No normal sport with an abnormal society.'

The task of dealing with these image problems fell primarily to Connie Mulder, minister of the Department of Information established – significantly – by Hendrik Verwoerd. In 1970 Mulder visited Holland, where he met the personable and intellectually capable information attaché, Eschel Rhoodie. Rhoodie, a former journalist whose older brother Nic played a leading role in the segregationist Pirsa, felt there was a need for South Africa's propaganda efforts to be more aggressive. He impressed Mulder both with his enthusiasm and with his apparent grasp of propaganda requirements and how they could be met. He had already made contact with a conservative Dutch publisher, Hubert Jussen of the Elsevier corporation.

Rhoodie encouraged Jussen to launch a conservative news magazine, to counter what both men perceived to be leftwing bias in the media. After visiting South Africa as a guest of the information department and meeting John Vorster, Jussen agreed to launch the magazine *To the Point*. Vorster agreed to help finance it and Rhoodie was seconded to become a deputy editor. So was born what became perhaps the biggest attempt at international media manipulation by a country outside of the major powers.

Two years later Mulder invited Rhoodie to head the department as secretary for information and to launch a massive secret campaign to win friends and influence people, but in 1972 the myriad schemes – ranging from buying political favours in the United States and Britain to setting up an array of front companies and organisations through which passed millions of dollars, pounds, guilder and rands – had yet to get off the ground. Mulder, Van den Bergh and Vorster were enthusiastic and Rhoodie drew in his younger brother Deneys and a friend and former journalist, Les de Villiers. Also among the small group which was to play a role in launching dozens of secret schemes around the world was the young Albie Geldenhuys, son of the police chief Mike Gelden-huys. A fluent French-speaker, he operated in France as a spy for Van den Bergh's BOSS when he first began working for Rhoodie.

Rhoodie's schemes required substantial secret funding, provided at first through BOSS but later, to the extreme annoyance of P.W. Botha, taken from the defence budget, where vast amounts could be hidden from prying parliamentary eyes. Van den Bergh, in the meantime, launched his major long-term infiltration of 'English' university campuses, a scheme aimed primarily at controlling internal dissent. But the demands of the traditionalists grew. They placed even more pressure on Vorster to fulfil the grand design of apartheid. Once the chain of proposed small nation-states, the homelands or 'bantustans', was established and internationally recognised, a number of troublesome questions regarding the permanent residence of 'non-whites' in white South Africa could be dealt with.

Hopefully by then the Rhodesia situation could also be settled. This landlocked country, already heavily dependent on South Africa, might be steered into an arrangement that ensured peace and continued dependence on its southern neighbour. This would require a suitable black leader to take control. Those whites not content with this change would almost certainly move south, which would reinforce the apartheid state in what would amount to a win–win situation. There were precedents for both scenarios. Whites fleeing independence in countries such as Kenya and Tanzania – and classified locally as 'refugees' – had generally joined the apartheid traditionalists.

As for installing a friendly regime, there was always the case of Lesotho, also landlocked, certainly very much smaller, and still a British protectorate, where the South African government had managed to topple the probable winners of the post-independence election. A military coup ensured that Chief Leabua Jonathan and his national party, the BNP, replaced Ntsu Mokhehle and his Basutoland Congress Party (BCP). Perhaps in Rhodesia history could repeat itself on a grander scale. In any event, by 1970 the original paramilitary police presence had been swelled by army and airborne units. Some 4,000 troops were eventually in the field. Among them was a young policeman, Eugene de Kock, later to emerge as South Africa's most proficient assassin.

What was seen as the main anti-colonial force, the Soviet-backed and ANC-aligned Zimbabwe African People's Union (ZAPU), was falling apart through internal bickering. There was also tension in the ANC camps in Zambia following an abortive and poorly organised attempt at infiltration through Rhodesia in 1967. The military threat from the anti-apartheid movement was negligible, although it was trying to pull itself together. In any event, the ANC was penetrated by Van den Bergh's agents to a level where most if not all of its attempts to infiltrate organisers and fighters were known in advance. Zambia's President Kenneth Kaunda was also putting pressure on South African anti-apartheid exiles as a result of the détente policy.

This rosy and quite accurate scenario which Vorster and his ministers had been painting in the early years of the decade was shattered on 25 April 1974 as Portuguese army tanks moved into the streets of Lisbon and General Antonio de Spinola seized control of the country. The full significance of this bloodless coup took time to assess, but one thing was clear: Portugal was lost as South Africa's often sole open ally in arenas such as the United Nations. It also seemed inevitable that Angola and Mozambique were headed for independence. In Angola the CIA had helped to establish and build two guerrilla movements, UNITA and the FNLA, which might prove malleable. But the apparently largest, best-organised and, certainly in the cities, most popular group, despite some internal wrangling, was the MPLA. It was professedly 'Marxist', had the support of the Soviet Union, and was informally allied to the major exiled anti-apartheid movement, the ANC.

Unlike Mozambique, Angola was also potentially wealthy. Oil and diamonds provided a steady flow of foreign exchange, and largely untapped reserves of other minerals were known to exist. It was the last territory that should fall under enemy sway. But although Mozambique was economically crippled, it posed, in many ways, a more dangerous threat. There was only one pro-independence group, Frelimo, which shared the orientation of the MPLA. Several attempts over the years, mainly by the CIA, to establish a rival group, Coremo, had failed. There seemed no alternative to the radical Frelimo movement taking over in Mozambique – and little prospect of creating an opposition movement in the time probably available. Other measures would have to be taken.

On 25 July, in the face of growing political ferment at home, Spinola declared the right of 'overseas provinces' to complete independence. As small European leftwing groups drafted agitators and organisers into Portugal, scenting the potential for a new international revolution, the South African and Rhodesian military began to develop contingency plans. Others with interests in the region, including France, the US, the USSR, and companies such as Elf, Lonrho and De Beers, began to jockey for position. Favours were called in; alliances brokered and broken.

Unlike Indonesia, which was able to march in and annex the Portuguese colony of East Timor in the Pacific, the South Africans could not simply attack and take over, certainly not in Mozambique. Yet the country bordered both Rhodesia and South Africa and was bound to have a hostile government. The solution: destabilise. So the Mozambique National Resistance, the MNR, was born. It comprised South African and Rhodesian special forces together with former members of the notorious Portuguese security police, PIDE, fearful of retribution in an independent country. Together they ensured that one of the most vicious episodes in Mozambique's bloody history got under way.

The experience was to provide South Africa's security planners with an example they felt might be repeated elsewhere: the creation of 'friendly' opposition movements. For, to the surprise of many in the apartheid military, the MNR, better known by its Portuguese acronym Renamo, developed into a major political force after its perhaps 500 members were taken over by the South African army in 1980. It was a lesson quickly absorbed both inside and outside the Broederbond. If it could be done in Mozambique, similar developments could be encouraged within South Africa itself, as well as in Rhodesia and in South West Africa. Apparently ignoring the subtleties presented by there being existing pockets of disgruntlement with Frelimo – and the fact that the Mozambican liberation movement was itself authoritarian and made several serious tactical blunders when dealing with dissent – apartheid's theorists thought they had discovered a formula of general application. All it required was the resources and the right combination of force, fear and philanthropy. The same formula could be applied to the 'homelands' within South Africa.

But in 1974 the prime concern was Angola. With hindsight, the coup in Portugal should have been expected, but it was not. When it came it stunned the South African government. Almost overnight, one of Africa's oldest colonial powers dropped its imperial pretensions and apartheid South Africa's protective cordon vanished. Rhodesia was obviously a lost cause as a white minority-ruled state. But there seemed no viable alternative to continuing to back the government of Ian Smith while trying to broker some sort of deal with the British or within Africa. Doubly worrying was the fact that local young radicals were hailing the victory of professedly Marxist guerrilla movements over colonial Portugal and, by implication, threatening the apartheid state with the same fate.

In those tumultuous months, the fortunes of Vorster's foreign policy ebbed and flowed strongly. The Portuguese coup had triggered a showdown in the great game of the bipolar world. But to the consternation and confusion of many apartheid analysts, it was a game that involved complex and often contradictory alliances. A month after the coup, for example, the FNLA and the majority of the MPLA, which had split into three factions, joined forces against UNITA. Six months later, the FNLA and UNITA joined forces against the main MPLA group. These shifting loyalties were mirrored internationally. Nigeria and Zambia initially backed UNITA, while weapons and cash poured in to the FNLA simultaneously from North Korea, China and the US.

It was a political minefield where the experienced would fear to tread. South Africa's defence minister lacked experience. It is arguable that P.W. Botha was out of his depth. Like several notable US figures, including the supposedly sophisticated Secretary of State Henry Kissinger, he tended to see developments in simple terms. Botha could not conceive of the US 'allowing' what he saw as a 'Marxist' government to take over, especially in Angola. Whether he or Vorster was promised US backing or whether this was merely implied, South African troops began moving into southern Angola in large numbers in September 1975. By then Vorster, in the face of strong protests from the military, had ordered the withdrawal of most South African troops from Rhodesia. This was a sop to President Kenneth Kaunda of Zambia as part of the détente process.

However, Vorster kept up his clandestine military backing for Rhodesia with supplies and helicopters. He also supported the murderous MNR/Renamo destabilisation campaign in Mozambique, while officially seeking friendship with the new Frelimo government. But the prime focus remained Angola. Aware that the main MPLA group under Agostinho Neto was planning to declare itself the government in the capital, Luanda, on the initially jointly agreed independence day of 11 November, the UNITA-FNLA forces and their South African backers determined to pre-empt this seizure of power.

Thousands of UNITA troops in south-western Angola were armed and given additional training; hundreds of FNLA troops under the command of Daniel Chipenda, former head of the MPLA, came south to join them. The bulk of FNLA troops under their leader, Holden Roberto, gathered across the Congo river. A pincer movement of the 'pro-Western' Angolan movements would sweep into the Luanda stronghold of the MPLA and declare an anti-

communist government. Détente would remain in place. A grateful Angolan –
and essentially UNITA – government, backed by the likes of Nigeria, would
ensure the acceptance of South Africa and its 'separate development' alternative. It seems certain that Vorster did not envisage South African troops
becoming involved. According to one of his ministers at the time, he was
taken aback when P.W. Botha, 'like an excited schoolboy', informed him that
South African troops were on the outskirts of Luanda.

South African motorised infantry in French Panhard armoured cars had
headed the 'Zulu' column which attacked northwards sometime between 14
and 23 October 1975. At the same time, FNLA troops crossed the border from
Zaïre, heading toward Luanda from the north. By 6 November the South
African-led invasion force had taken Lobito, but an FNLA force forming the
northern pincer was routed on the outskirts of Luanda and regrouped in the
coastal town of Ambriz. As a consequence, three Angolan republics were
proclaimed on 11 November. The MPLA declared the People's Republic in
Luanda, UNITA the Social Republic in Huambo, which their forces controlled,
and the FNLA the Democratic Republic in Ambriz.

Officially, South African troops were not in Angola, but it quickly became
an open secret. The US administration privately signalled its intentions to
withdraw before the US Senate voted to discontinue support for Angolan
surrogates, and when Nigeria swung its weight behind the Luanda government,
the matter was all but sealed. Facing an Angolan army reinforced by Cuban
troops and Soviet arms, the South Africans were forced to withdraw, their
outward-looking policy in ruins as one country after another rallied to
condemn the military adventurism of the apartheid state.

Botha and his generals were furious. They maintained, with some justification, that they had been betrayed. But Vorster and Van den Bergh were not
prepared to let them commit still more men and materiel to what seemed like
a hopeless case across the border. Better to consolidate at home. Besides, the
scheduled date for the independence of the first 'homeland', Transkei, could
not be delayed. This was the argument that was raging when 16 June 1976
dawned.

On that day the Broederbond's policy of enforcing the teaching of Afrikaans
in township schools triggered a mass uprising in the sprawling Soweto
township complex outside Johannesburg. The unrest spread. The attitude of
the government was summed up in the surviving minutes from a cabinet
meeting in August: just two months after the police had massacred at least 600
school students James – 'Jimmy' – Kruger, the minister of justice, police and
prisons, proposed that 'the police should perhaps act a bit more drastically to
bring about more deaths'.

Vorster appeared to have lost control, and Botha and the generals around him almost certainly saw an opportunity to settle old scores. Extreme concern within the Broederbond was exacerbated by the horrendously bungled torture and murder of Black Consciousness (BC) leader Steve Bantu Biko in September of 1977, which triggered still more international condemnation. Two months later, an arms embargo was agreed by the United Nations. Suddenly Vorster, the tough hardliner, the would-be Führer of the 1930s, appeared to be an ailing old man. In the miasma of Broederbond politics it was a confusing time: none of the ideological anchors appeared to be holding. There seemed to be no clear demarcation between modernisers and traditionalists. But the repression, the removals and the rash of secret wars continued. In the name of a broadly despised ideology well past its sell-by date, the business of governing in a hostile world carried on in an often surprisingly ad hoc manner.

Elements among the political elite who saw the writing on the wall began to make plans for a future in exile. Money flowed abroad into accounts in Portugal, Spain and Switzerland. How much money and who was involved remains the subject of much speculation, but nothing has been proved. The rumours were given added impetus by the gruesome murder of Robert Smit and his wife Jean-Cora in November 1977. Smit, a financial expert and National Party parliamentary candidate, died just eight days before the election, which would certainly have put him into parliament. He had been involved in the transfer abroad of large amounts of money for various supposed propaganda campaigns, including the attempted purchase of the *Washington Star* newspaper in the US. But he had also apparently found large sums of money missing or diverted and had threatened to expose this fact.

The shooting and subsequent stabbing of the Smits and the red-painted graffiti in their house in the town of Springs east of Johannesburg looked superficially like a ritual killing. Perhaps this was the intention. The film *Helter Skelter*, the story of the killing of Sharon Tate by Charles Manson and his group of 'Satanist' followers, had only recently been screened in South Africa. The murders and the murder scene certainly seemed designed to convey a message to some among the living, although the scrawled letters R A U and RAU TEM or TEN seemed meaningless. But to many within and outside the police force, the killings bore the hallmark of Hendrik van den Bergh.

These facts, together with the names of the operatives most frequently linked to the killings and to Van den Bergh – Jack Widowson, Roy Allen and Phil Freeman, as well as Freeman's 'Mr McDougall' pseudonym – were aired at the TRC. The commissioners also noted that attempts by Smit's daughter to investigate her parents' death had met with death threats and possible attempts on her life. There had been no applications for amnesty for the killings and this left no doubt that several of the cancerous growths in the country's body politic remain active. The TRC duly found that members of the security forces killed Robert and Jean-Cora Smit and that 'their deaths constitute a gross violation of human rights'. Years after publication of the finding, there was no sign of serious investigation into the matter, let alone any prosecution.

The earlier murder of journalist Keith Wallace did not come before the TRC, but the Smit killings may have been meant as a warning too. There is certainly circumstantial evidence pointing to this. Yet if it was a warning to plotters around P.W. Botha and within the military who had already begun their attempts to undermine Vorster, it failed. According to one whispered theory, the deaths of Robert Smit and his wife were the last straw, not only for waverers in the military but also for senior police officers such as Johan Coetzee and Mike Geldenhuys. Van den Bergh had finally gone too far in butchering their own. He and Vorster had to go.

The manner of their going should not embarrass their successors – unconstitutional and extra-parliamentary methods could not be risked. And while the vast amounts of taxpayers' money being siphoned off into the many clandestine schemes of the information department provided a wealth of damaging facts which could be carefully tailored and judiciously leaked, it was essential that any exposé should go only as far as Vorster, Van den Bergh and the immediate 'info' department. It should sink the political ambitions of Connie Mulder, but stop short of the extent to which Botha and the military were aware of, and had acquiesced in, the activities at issue. Likewise, those projects launched by the information department which were proving success-ful should not be compromised and should be allowed to continue.

It was a dangerous ploy. Mishandled, it could explode in the faces of the entire Afrikaner political elite as well as damage much of the business establishment. There were other difficulties too. The fractures and factions within the Broederbond made it impossible to use the wholly government-supporting Afrikaans-language media to discredit Vorster and his cronies. It was both safer and more credible if the opposition English-language press exposed financial wrongdoing and some of the extra-parliamentary activities controlled by the 'info' department.

But the opposition newspapers displayed a degree of independence. There was also no way that specific 'friends' or journalist agents working on them could be guaranteed to control the desired investigations, no matter how carefully the plot was handled. The advantage was that the proprietors of the

English-language newspapers would be loath to have the whole political edifice crumble. They and their editors, for all their criticisms, tended to share a perception of the national interest that precluded ever going so far as destroying the credibility of the apartheid parliament. However, they tended to be united in wanting an end to the Vorster Van den Bergh regime.

There was also sure to be substantial counter-propaganda and pressure from the Vorster/Mulder camp. To achieve the desired result against such a background was a tall order, but it was achieved. Information was leaked to selected newspapers such as the *Sunday Express* and the *Rand Daily Mail* and to selected journalists. A degree of control was maintained through journalist agents such as Tony Stirling of the *Rand Daily Mail*'s investigative team, who kept their handlers briefed as to who was saying what to whom. Uncontrolled leaks could be plugged before they caused too much damage.

The tales of high living, especially by the information department's Eschel Rhoodie, and of massive unauthorised expenditure caused a series of sensations. Van den Bergh was clearly outmanoeuvred. Exactly how this was done and by whom makes up more of the unfinished business of South Africa's recent past.

The media exposés of the time not only toppled Vorster and Van den Bergh, and ensured the succession of Botha, they also reinforced the image of South Africa as a parliamentary democracy. Apologists around the world argued that, for all its faults, the country at least allowed a fundamentally free press. It was pointed out that, in the true Westminster tradition, South Africa had a feisty yet loyal parliamentary opposition. Even the apartheid judiciary came in for some international media compliments about its supposed impartiality.

6

Botha, business and foreign friends

P.W. Botha assumed the prime ministership of South Africa with an image untainted by the information scandal which his own ministry had effectively, if often reluctantly, financed. He also took over party and government as an apparent reformer. Although he had been minister of defence for twelve years, he was also untainted by the growing and largely secret brutality and bloodshed visited by the military on targets across the borders. The unlikely image as a potential reformer, standing clear of the financial scandals of 'Muldergate', was desired not only by himself and the Broederbond, but by the business community as well. With such unanimity of purpose, it is perhaps little wonder that the much-hailed exposé of the scandal that put the skids under Vorster stayed within bounds.

But the fall of Vorster and the succession of Botha was not clear-cut. Behind the scenes it was a messy business as the hostile clans at the head of the apartheid state bickered, bartered, bribed and blackmailed to achieve their ends. Favours were demanded and given, all of which had an impact on the process and the way it unfolded. Connie Mulder, Broeder number 4750, fought desperately to keep his chances alive in September 1978 as scandal after scandal enveloped him and his department. Luck also played a part in the bitter battle for succession. The young foreign minister, Roelof 'Pik' Botha, a later arrival on the AB and parliamentary scene, quickly displayed a ruthless streak of personal ambition. He had been put up as the reformist stalking horse for

Broeder 4418, the labour minister Fanie Botha, but then refused to stand down.

The goal for the AB leadership was to hold the Afrikaner establishment together. Mulder, nominated to the AB executive in 1968, still had considerable support. This should be detached to another candidate, but without threatening the unity of party or Broederbond. The bitter struggle between Vorster, Mulder and P.W. Botha had created a dangerous split. A compromise candidate was needed. For many, Fanie Botha was that candidate. He was the epitome of the organisation man, efficient, reliable, uncharismatic: the classic apparatchik whose power and influence lay within, and relied on, the AB and the party.

But the best-laid plans can fail and this one did. P.W. Botha had shrewdly briefed the peculiarly insular and traditionalist 'Free State mafia', the provincial AB and NP leadership, about the financial goings-on within the information department. The Free State leader, Alwyn Schlebusch, was perhaps as swayed by the lure of wielding political influence as he was by the moral indignation he expressed about the financial impropriety of Mulder and his department. He swung his support behind P.W. Botha. Pik Botha also appears to have had private discussions with 'P.W.' on the eve of the elections in the 172-member NP caucus. In the event, the first ballot saw P.W. Botha score 78 votes to 72 for Mulder and 22 for Pik Botha. The second ballot was a formality. By 98 votes to 74, P.W. Botha claimed victory on 27 September 1978.

Inside the white community, it was welcome. After a largely directionless period under Vorster, both the Broederbond modernisers and much of the business elite had come to realise that change was needed, that traditional apartheid was dead. As Anglo American chairman Gavin Relly – also no supporter of majority rule – put it in a 1986 interview, it was an illusion to think 'the old paternalistic process could continue to work'. Botha was seen as the man who would supply the reforms within apartheid that would see off black rebellion and keep up the flow of profits. He also had the toughness to deal with the growing resistance. When Botha outlined his concept of a 'constellation of states' in southern Africa, mining and media baron Harry Oppenheimer, the chief financial backer of the opposition PFP, described it as having both 'imagination and charm'.

But Botha was also subject to other pressures. The core of the traditionalist wing of the Broederbond had stayed on when Connie Mulder was disgraced. Through their influence in parliament, the civil service, the Church and even the military, they advised Botha not to move too fast or too far away from the basics of traditional apartheid. Botha had to accommodate this wing both to ensure his succession and to maintain the tenuous unity of party and AB. As an apparent quid pro quo for the support of Alwyn Schlebusch, he brought several 'Free Staters' into the political inner circle. Among them was Kobie Coetsee, who became deputy defence minister, charged with restructuring the security services, and an unusual academic, Herman Strauss, whose appointment probably allayed the fears of many in the AB about Botha's often casual approach to the Broederbond.

Strauss was a hardline member of the Broederbond executive. As a follower of the twentieth-century Dutch philosopher Herman Dooyeweerd, he held that the will of God devolved on the state. Dooyeweerd's claims that the failure of any state to 'take up the sword' was 'dangerous cowardice' struck a chord with academics trapped in the intellectual laager of Afrikaner nationalism. Strauss was a classic example – as was one of his brightest protégés, Daniel Lukas 'Niel' Barnard, at the age of thirty-one already a full professor at the University of the Orange Free State and a Broederbond member for two years. A political hawk and nuclear weapons advocate, he had studied nuclear strategy in the US, but was almost unknown on the national stage. Then his mentor, Strauss, travelled to Cape Town to join the president's council.

It was almost certainly Strauss and Kobie Coetsee who recommended Barnard to Botha during discussions about restructuring the security apparatus. The upshot was that Barnard was brought in to head the newly revamped intelligence service, which shed its embarrassing acronym, BOSS, to become DONS, the Department of National Security. The appointment was controversial, both because of Barnard's relative youth and for his lack of security experience, but it placated the traditionalists. Besides, Barnard soon proved his mettle. He went on to head the security department for twelve years, playing a key role in the various committees that assessed and approved a multitude of often murderously repressive actions. However, he and Coetsee also managed to bend with the gales of change more flexibly than Botha. Neither man applied for amnesty for any violations of human rights. In fact, Barnard publicly denied that he ever knew about the institutional deployment of murder, torture, poisoning and other gross abuses.

Perhaps the most important appointment made by Botha at that time was of General Jannie Roux, who also showed a remarkable ability to adapt. As the effective head of an enlarged presidential office he was Botha's AB gatekeeper. A prison warder turned clinical psychologist, criminologist and deputy commissioner of prisons, he was an executive member of the segregationist psychological institute Pirsa, and a sometime interrogator. With a reputation for callousness, he had taken a direct interest in Verwoerd's assassin, Dimitri Tsafendas, and drew up, apparently for the perusal of the Broederbond and the cabinet, a major psychological profile of Nelson Mandela that may have had a bearing on Mandela's removal from Robben Island in 1982, along with the core of the old ANC leadership. Roux was also involved in drawing up other, similar, profiles of Mandela and the ANC leadership. In the post-apartheid dispensation, he was appointed South African ambassador to Austria.

But in 1980 Roux still represented the traditionalist wing of the NP, as indeed did Botha. And from the start of his presidency Botha, like Vorster before him, was a reluctant pragmatist in granting concessions that weakened the concept of apartheid. He also soon received some additional external support – and pressure – from the newly elected British prime minister, Margaret Thatcher. She and, in particular, her businessman husband Denis, had close contacts with the apartheid state. Denis's uncle was a businessman in Durban and Denis had numerous investments in the country. The Thatchers' son Mark had been sent out to gain work experience in Johannesburg in 1972. Botha befriended Margaret and Denis Thatcher when they visited South Africa in 1974. He was deeply impressed by Thatcher when he took her and Denis on a tour of the Cape peninsula.

From 1979 Botha felt he had a friend in Downing Street. Although Thatcher did not hold him in very high regard, she also felt Botha was someone with whom she could do business. Her attitude toward South Africa was also heavily influenced by the South African-born mystic and charlatan, Laurens van der Post. His paternalistic brand of racial bigotry, highlighting the noble savagery of the Zulu and the sly communistic traits of the Xhosa, appealed to the prejudices of both Thatchers. It also dovetailed with support for Botha and the apartheid government, especially after Chief Mangosuthu Gatsha Buthelezi and his Zulu-based Inkatha movement broke from the ANC in 1980. This meant that a black political movement potentially acceptable to much of the world might be won over to a managed transition from orthodox apartheid. But there was still no clear idea of where the transition would lead or even if it could, in fact, be halted.

In 1980 Ronald Reagan became president of the United States. This too augured well for the new South African government. Although Reagan knew and cared little about South Africa, his Africa specialist Chester Crocker and Botha became firm friends. It seemed possible that the rising outside pressure would ease just as greater problems were emerging internally and within the region. The idea that South Africa faced a 'total onslaught', with internal instability provoked by communist-inspired agitators across the borders, would be understood in both London and Washington.

The onslaught would have to be dealt with on the ground, so once entrenched within party and government, Botha and his organisationally competent defence minister, General Magnus Malan, set about reviewing the security command structure. It had to be better coordinated, more extensive, and above all, more fully under their control. It was certainly true that the state no longer exercised its former tight hold on security in the country. Concessions on apartheid, often driven by trade union militancy and justified on the grounds of economic expediency, had failed to stem a growing tide of resistance. For all its optimistic rhetoric, the system had its back to the wall. But there was no thought of capitulation, more a hope that a mixture of minor concessions and brute force could ensure survival.

This tactic, essentially one of desperation, received the label of 'total strategy'. At its core was an over-arching plan. Every town, village and hamlet throughout the country must be covered by a fully integrated security net. This would be the National Security Management System (NSMS), and it would bring together as never before the military, the police and the newly established DONS.

At the apex of this pyramid was the State Security Council (SSC) established by Vorster. It was chaired by the president and met every fortnight before the regular cabinet meetings. Botha turned the SSC into a virtual government within a government. The Broederbond, National Party, and the 'Securocrat' inner circle, which comprised the SSC, made the decisions which meant life or death for many considered to be enemies of the state. The rest of the cabinet were usually informed of decisions after they had been made and, in many cases, acted on.

The outlines of this structure were generally known. Through TRC investigations more detail emerged not only of the vast extent and range of the NSMS, but also of how it operated and who served it through the bloody repression of the 1980s. Here was the true heart of the brute maintenance of apartheid.

The tightening up of the security structure was made more urgent by events in Rhodesia. By 1979 it was obvious that preserving a renegade, white-ruled territory was a lost cause. The hoped-for alternative of a relatively friendly, certainly indebted, non-racial government headed by Bishop Abel Muzorewa also crumbled as the more demonised of the two liberation movements, ZANU, swept the board in the first non-racial elections in March 1980. This was largely unexpected, even within the Rhodesian security establishment, which had still kept in place the Renamo training base at Odzi near Umtali (now Mutare) in eastern Zimbabwe. Once the election results became clear, the base was vacated, apparently within seventy-two hours. With the more than 200 fighters trained by a former Rhodesian special forces officer,

Dudley Coventry, went the equipment and staff of the supposedly Mozambique-based Renamo radio station, Voz de Africa Livre. They relocated to a South African base near Phalaborwa, south of Zimbabwe, and close to the border of the Kruger National Park. South Africa's police and military units were withdrawn and the South African military took over the special forces contingent that had operated in Mozambique as the supposed national resistance movement.

This started one of the most enduring, widespread and indiscriminate phases of human rights abuse perpetrated by apartheid. Either through surrogates such as Renamo and UNITA or, most frequently, through its own special forces, thousands of landmines were laid, especially in Angola and Mozambique but also in Zambia and newly independent Zimbabwe. It was standard practice to seed mines throughout an area into which refugees or guerrilla fighters would be driven by a usually pre-dawn attack. Hundreds of thousands of these mines remain today and Angola and Mozambique have perhaps the highest number of amputees in the world. Mechem, the subsidiary of the South African state arms manufacturer Denel, provided the mines and, in the post-apartheid era, successfully tendered for profitable contracts to remove them in Mozambique.

By the time Botha took over as prime minister, the military had already committed what the TRC was to refer to as 'possibly the single most controversial external operation of the commission's mandate period': the massacre at Cassinga. This attack on an Angolan camp of the Namibian liberation movement SWAPO on 4 May 1978 resulted in the deaths of at least 614 and perhaps as many as 2,000 men, women and children, most of them non-combatants. It was the largest of a series of massacres carried out in neighbouring states. Often as a result of erroneous information, people not even associated with the struggle in South Africa died, sometimes at the hands of men from the militarised white community who cut off and dried the ears of their victims to wear as necklace trophies.

Yet Cassinga was described by military chief General Jannie Geldenhuys as 'a jewel of military craftsmanship'. The man in command of the attack, dubbed Operation Reindeer, was General Constand Viljoen. He too hailed it as a major victory. But one of the officers involved, Lieutenant Johan Frederich Verster, told the TRC that Cassinga was 'probably the most bloody exercise we ever launched'. He was sure that most of the dead were civilians and admitted following orders to shoot and kill the wounded.

The finding of the TRC was that gross human rights violations had occurred. The territorial integrity of Angola had been violated and those to be held accountable were Prime Minister B.J. Vorster, P.W. Botha as defence minister, General Magnus Malan as head of the military, together with army chief General Constand Viljoen and air force chief General R.H. 'Bob' Rogers. Since the massacre occurred outside South Africa, there was no need for those held accountable to apply for amnesty. However, with the exception of Vorster, who died in 1983, the other men could face charges, certainly in Angola and probably in Namibia as well.

The same liability applies to the butchery carried out in neighbouring states throughout the 1970s and 1980s, but by the end of 2002 none of those states had taken action to prosecute. Much information never reached the TRC or was never publicly heard. Among this is evidence about the special military death squad based inside South Africa in 1980 at the time of Zimbabwe's independence elections. Guided by members of the Rhodesian Selous Scouts, this squad regularly crossed the border to attack and murder villagers thought likely to vote for one or other of the liberation movements.

There were also numerous attacks aimed at destabilising particularly Mozambique, but also Zambia. Bridges were blown up, roads destroyed and villagers terrorised and killed. As the TRC discovered, by the time of Zimbabwean independence in 1980 the military also had in place a clutch of front companies which dealt in everything from rare timber to ivory, rhino horn and diamonds. The destruction of Namibian and Angolan wildlife and forests and the pillaging of diamonds was done in the name of providing funds for UNITA. From the outset there was widespread corruption, which extended to the upper echelons of the security establishment.

Full details of these operations and who benefited are still unknown, but sufficient evidence emerged at TRC hearings to enable the commissioners to conclude that South Africa's campaigns in Angola between 1977 and 1988 led to 'gross human rights violations on a vast scale'. Held responsible for this campaign, which 'constituted a systematic pattern of abuse', were the South African cabinet, the members of the State Security Council and the security force chiefs, all of whom are known.

When, with the accession of Botha, the military took overall control of security, the plans for an internal 'dirty war' had already been laid. Advice was sought from the Argentinian military, which provided specialist lecturers, including a General D'Almeida and the notorious torturer Lieutenant Alfredo Ignacio Astiz. One of the Argentinian navy's death-squad killers, Jorge Enrique Perren, accused of murders, kidnapping and torture, was based at the Marine War School in the Muizenberg suburb of Cape Town from October 1979 to February 1982. Chile's murderous military also advised and assisted.

The pattern was set in September 1979 at a conference of security chiefs held at the naval base of Simonstown. Known as the 'Simonstad Raad' (Simonstown Council), it was chaired by Botha. Specific tasks were allocated, areas of responsibility defined, and a broad outline given of the tactics to be employed in 'taking off the gloves' in defence of the apartheid state. Here lay the origins not only of the police death squads such as that at Vlakplaas, which was exposed through TRC hearings, but also of the military killer units and their ultimate evolution into the Civil Cooperation Bureau (CCB). It was only during the criminal trial in the year 2000 of chemical and biological warfare expert Wouter Basson that something of the scale of CCB killings was exposed.

Two of the founding members of what started out as 'section pseudo operations' and then became, in quick succession, D40, Project Barnacle and finally CCB were proved responsible for the murder of perhaps hundreds of Namibian prisoners and the disposal of their bodies. Major Neil Kriel, a pilot and former Selous Scout, was the founding commander of the death squad, many of its members recruited from Rhodesian special forces fleeing retribution in a liberated Zimbabwe. Seconded to the unit was Sergeant Trevor Floyd, a founding member of South Africa's 'dirty war' specialists, the Recces.

Kriel and Floyd and other CCB operatives such as Johan Theron were effective executioners and undertakers based at a remote airstrip in Namibia. Working at night, they specialised in disposing of people deemed undesirable who were delivered to them as prisoners. Floyd, who had some medical training, would either poison the prisoners with a spiked drink or inject a lethal drug. On one occasion when Kriel – who was never publicly named – had forgotten to bring the poison, three Zimbabwean prisoners were done to death with hammers. In all cases, the bodies were stripped and loaded into an aircraft with its rear door removed. Kriel, borrowing a technique popular in 1973 with the Chilean military, would fly straight out over the Atlantic, where Floyd would throw the bodies into the sea. They would then return to the airstrip and burn the clothes taken from the prisoners. Similar flights also apparently took place from Lanseria airport, north of Johannesburg, which was a major undercover base.

It was the demands of this operation, as well as for individual assassinations, and the need of the police to overcome and control large crowds, which underlay much of Project Coast, the chemical and biological warfare programme headed by cardiologist Wouter Basson. With money again no object, the most outrageous ideas were taken seriously and experiments conducted. Simonstown was where the earlier experimentation of Verwoerd's secret committees finally matured and mutated. What the Simonstown Council also spawned was a new police killer division in which a newly appointed major, Craig Michael Williamson, was to play a vital role. He was the most prominent of the operatives who emerged from the innocuously named Operation Daisy, run by the security police.

7

Operation Daisy

Operation Daisy began in 1972. It received passing mention at the TRC only because it involved the amnesty applications of Craig Williamson and a group of his cronies for a series of bombings, including the 1982 blast at the London offices of the ANC. Because no direct or gross human rights abuses could be clearly linked to Operation Daisy, it did not warrant a full investigation. Yet this operation, like so much of what was done by the security establishment, contains areas of grave concern. It also left a secret legacy: embedded within the new democratic dispensation are the agents of past treachery and deceit, compromised individuals often in powerful positions who constitute potential toxins in the body politic.

This long-running operation was another for which General Hendrik van den Bergh claimed credit, although it was his intellectually pretentious understudy, Johan Coetzee, who played the major role. It grew out of the first combined operation launched under the aegis of BOSS. Military Intelligence collaborated with the new structure, but was not absorbed by it. In fact, many in the military despised the security police, regarding them as bedroom snoopers and thugs. BOSS in its day certainly merited the label, but it was also very much more, with specialist sections covering everything from bomb-making and electronic surveillance to various areas of infiltration. Van den Bergh, when he established BOSS, hoped it would soon be in a position to take control of military intelligence and become the all-encompassing security umbrella.

Even in those early years, he managed to keep a close eye on many leading lights within the National Party and the Broederbond who therefore both feared and envied him. In 1970, Van den Bergh headed BOSS while Coetzee and his immediate superior, Mike Geldenhuys, chose to remain with the police, Coetzee heading the Special Branch. At that time, the BOSS/SB network had several dozen journalists either in its pay or part of the network, some in positions of considerable influence. This was a long-term tactic, which was to pay handsome dividends. But journalists had their limits. They were not, for example, much good at getting to know the networks of solidarity which extended from abroad and which gave succour to the families of political prisoners or to self-help groups which could provide breeding grounds for resistance to the apartheid system – activities that needed to shun publicity, and in which liberal and radical students from the 'white' university campuses were often involved.

The more radical of these students also seemed to have links with, or at least give support to, an emergent political phenomenon which was causing considerable difficulty for the security services: Black Consciousness (BC). A new approach was needed. For years Security Branch agents had operated on the campuses of the traditionally liberal English-language universities, but such infiltration was aimed primarily at the short-term goals of spotting and quelling any semblance of anti-apartheid or anti-government activity. Agents passed through the universities, were sometimes unmasked and then left prematurely, often to continue with more regular police work.

Military Intelligence too, largely using the military conscription process as a means of reliable recruitment, had some agents in place, apparently as part of a longer-term programme – just as, it was later to emerge, they also had journalists in their pay. But there was little cooperation between the two security organisations. The animosity between Vorster and P.W. Botha made sure of that, despite the establishment of BOSS.

Encouraged by the experience of the Central Intelligence Agency in the United States, with whom he was enjoying increasingly close and friendly relations, Van den Bergh decided specifically to target the universities. The University of the Witwatersrand (Wits) and, to a lesser extent, the University of Cape Town (UCT) had been revealed, through the reports of agents, backed by arrests and subsequent court cases, as areas of radical activity with growing support for BC. One centre of this new development was the Eastern Cape and, in particular, Fort Hare, the oldest black campus in the country and alma mater of many African leaders.

Fort Hare had links to nearby Rhodes University in Grahamstown, so Rhodes, together with Wits and UCT, became a prime focus for infiltration.

But the aim was much grander than to monitor the several staff and students tagged as subversives; it was to place agents on the campuses who would become part of liberal, even radical, university life. They would rise through the ranks of student politics to positions of power and influence both within and outside academia and South Africa. Their role would be to inform on and ultimately to influence and even control organisations seen by Van den Bergh and his cohorts as 'enemy structures'. Given the history of these universities, there appeared little chance, certainly in the short term, of influencing them into wholly conservative, let alone government-supporting, positions, but that too was seen as a long-term option.

No time limit was set on this new operation. It was a long haul in which the prospect of dramatic short-term gains would often be sacrificed in the hope of bigger things to come. In this sense it paralleled the infiltration policy adopted towards the exiled liberation movements, the ANC and PAC, where by 1970 a number of security recruits had already risen to top positions. So the seeds of Operation Daisy were planted. Van den Bergh decided to spend as much time, effort and resources as necessary to infiltrate a new group of agents onto the targeted campuses. Efforts made on the black campuses would consist mainly of repression.

The initial problem was in finding suitable candidates to infiltrate these institutions. They would have to be English-speaking, capable of coping at the academic level, but also reliable and well trained. Ideally, the ranks of the police would provide the men and women needed. Unfortunately, and largely because of the affirmative action policies promoted by the Broederbond and followed by the government, the police force was a predominantly Afrikaner domain. The standard of formal schooling was also fairly low.

Just as in earlier years, Van den Bergh had his scouts trawl through the uniformed branch. One of the policemen selected was a young sergeant, Craig Michael Williamson, a graduate of one of the country's most prestigious private schools. Several other candidates were also identified, trained, and sent off to become students and 'spotters' for further recruitment on the campuses. By 1972 there were agents playing leading roles in student affairs at all the English-language universities. The degree of success surprised the security police establishment, but it said more about the naïveté and inefficiency of the opposition than about the brilliance of the police or their infiltrators.

A classic example is the case of Craig Williamson, who was to become the central figure in a major BOSS project which grew out of Operation Daisy. One of the most lucrative security operations ever mounted, it also brought

Williamson the media sobriquet of 'super-spy', which stuck despite his later grants of amnesty for multiple murders and terrorism. He revelled in this public persona, but it was an amalgam of fact, personal fantasy and the officially generated myth that surrounds the entire Operation Daisy project; it was the offshoot of chaotic times and deft media management. For a government under pressure and desperate to bolster its image and deflect criticism, the creation of a hero figure was convenient. It helped to inject a sense of pride and security into a jaded, frightened and angry constituency. It also tended to intimidate an opposition unable to disentangle fact from carefully designed fiction. Within the security services it bolstered the prestige of the security police in the ongoing turf war with other security divisions.

In the case of Craig Williamson, there was much dramatic fact, which in different circumstances might have reflected rather well on an opposition that was amateurish and often wholly trusting. In many cases, certainly inside South Africa, it was working in humanitarian fields, developing and introducing alternative technologies in rural areas or assisting literacy classes, oppositional only in its disregard for the segregationist and racist mores of the NP government.

Prompted by the security establishment, the 'friends in the media' promoted Craig Williamson as a 'super-spy' who had 'penetrated the Iron Curtain'. The message was hardly subtle: the Western world might disagree with apartheid, but South Africa was still part of the defence of that world against the expansionism of the East. It was a message broadly accepted by the government's constituency in South Africa, but not much more widely. The evidence of 'penetration behind the Iron Curtain', for example, was a holiday snap of Craig Williamson taken in Moscow's Red Square by his wife.

Such local lionisation put considerable pressure on the corpulent spy. When he returned to South Africa to be propelled by myth and ego into a new and murderous role and promoted to major, his peers expected him to perform. Yet if any of his colleagues had looked closely at his background and actual achievements, they might have thought less of his ability. He had also relied heavily on his wife, Ingrid Evita Bacher, who was essential to her husband's success and was an agent in her own right. She had a much better academic record and was as deceitful and cunning as Williamson. Nor did she give herself away, as he did in a fit of panic. Williamson was later to admit that he was 'baffled' by his own survival as a spy. He certainly had no anti-apartheid credentials when he was first sent out by the police Special Branch to infiltrate liberal and leftwing student groups. Quite the opposite, in fact.

Even at school he was known for his rightwing and frankly racist views, which stood out in the very English and at least nominally liberal confines of the Anglican (Episcopalian) St John's College in Johannesburg. He subsequently noted that his first 'political problem' occurred at the school in 1960 at the time of the Sharpeville massacre, when he was eleven years old. There had been no black help to make his bed or sweep his dormitory. This perceived deprivation appears to have had a profound effect on him. He recalled it vividly nearly forty years later when interviewed by Gillian Slovo about his murder of her mother, Ruth First.

As a senior at the school in 1966, an election year, he took part in a major political debate, choosing to represent the rightwing Republican Party. Neither athletic nor academic, he knew how to put his views across and had a small but loyal following at the school. His closest acolyte was classmate Paul Asmussen, who was also destined to become a security policeman and later to play a part in Daisy and other SB and BOSS operations. But for several of his genuinely liberal contemporaries at St John's, Craig Williamson was a 'racist bully'; for others just a bully.

Craig Williamson's apparent rebellion against the liberal spirit of his school was not the reaction of an outsider. He was very much part of that upper-middle-class stratum which formed the student core at schools such as St John's. Ironically, he was born in April 1949 in the Florence Nightingale hospital, overlooking the notorious Fort prison where Nelson Mandela and other ANC leaders were held during their 1964 trial. It was only months after the National Party had swept to power. His Scottish-born father, Herbert Tidby Williamson, and South African-born mother, Ruth, were already moderately prosperous. Ignorant of the conditions in the nearby townships, let alone the far-flung 'native' reserves, they considered themselves intensely patriotic. Racists in the unthinking manner of so many of their contemporaries, they took as their due their relative wealth and the subservient position of their black employees. Herbert had high hopes for his only son, so Craig was enrolled at the prestigious St Stithian's school in the then burgeoning northern suburbs of Johannesburg.

As business continued to prosper, the Williamsons moved to a more salubrious suburb. Craig, at age ten, became a boarder at the decidedly top-drawer St John's preparatory school, apparently in the hope of improving his unimpressive academic performance. Instead he muddled through, distinguished only by his physical size and some verbal facility. To his detractors, the fact that he failed his final examinations was no more surprising than his decision to join the police force in 1968. The police, they pointed out, had a deserved reputation for thuggishness and racism.

His career choice, made in the absence of university qualifications, was apparently accepted by his family, certainly by his parents and younger sister Lisa Jane. Craig and Lisa were almost stereotypical products of their background, and Lisa went on to become a critical figure in Operation Daisy and its offshoots, as well as a lecturer at the police spy school in Pretoria. Only one of the family, sister Pamela, who settled in England in 1972, stayed out of the security establishment.

The web of deceit, treachery, blackmail and murder into which the Williamson family slipped began inauspiciously enough with Craig as uniformed student constable W53076T. He signed up on 6 May 1968 after rewriting some of his final school examinations in March. This time he managed to pass, opening up the possibility of university entry. At the time he expressed the vague hope that the police force would be a stepping stone to a career in the law, perhaps with a law degree. In the meantime, the police force promised excitement, a uniform and power. But for thirteen months Craig Williamson found himself sitting behind the enquiries desk of the Randburg police station, wielding nothing more lethal than a pen. As a student constable, he was not even issued with the standard .38 revolver.

But the die had been cast. In June 1969 he began the six-month course at the police college in Pretoria from which graduates emerged as constables, complete with standard-issue firearms. Almost all the recruits were Afrikaans-speaking and the standard of their schooling generally much lower than that of the boy from St John's. In such a milieu his confidence grew, along with a sense of his own superiority. Then came graduation and a posting to the Parkview police station in suburban Johannesburg. It was something of a letdown. Older and ill-educated policemen failed to appreciate his talents, let alone superiority. They also seemed to resent the fact that his father had bought him a car which none of them could afford. Even black policemen, he once noted, refused to listen to him. When he became a sergeant in 1970 and was transferred to the plain-clothes division, to an anti-housebreaking unit, matters did not really improve.

The school bully was at the bottom of the pecking order again and, worse still, was an English-speaking, private school outsider. Yet it was these very factors which were to catapult him into a world that indulged his fantasies. The summons came out of the blue. Called back to the police station one afternoon in mid-1971, he found a lieutenant, Roy Brand, and a sergeant from the Special Branch waiting. He was given a warm, friendly greeting and invited out by the SB men to join them for a braai (barbecue) and a few beers. Williamson was delighted. These men represented the most feared and powerful wing of the police force: an SB constable could make even a uniformed captain jump. Trying to look nonchalant, he took up their invitation. There was no need for nods or winks. These were SB men. This was how they operated. The abilities and potential of Craig Michael Williamson had finally been recognised.

Later that day, standing around a fire with meat roasting and cans of cold lager in hand, Craig Williamson had his views sought. He was treated as an equal, listened to and joked with. No promise was made, but Brand said he would be back in touch. He had nodded earnestly when told by the burly young sergeant that he was thinking of leaving the police force the following year to go to university. Williamson explained that time served in the force would exempt him from his military conscription obligations.

It was this last fact that struck a chord with then Colonel Johan Coetzee when Roy Brand reported back. Coetzee, who was supervising Van den Bergh's latest trawl through the ranks to find potential spies, knew that there was a small but growing anti-conscription campaign, which was being closely monitored. It was based mainly on the campuses of English-language universities and tended to attract anti-apartheid dissidents who objected to the obligation laid on all young men over the age of eighteen and classified as white to do military service. This meant a full year in one of the armed services and a further twelve years of annual 'camps'. Very few seemed keen to take the option of four years of police service. But it was an option.

Craig Williamson could be said to have taken that option. It would be much more believable than the usual cover story supplied to such recruits. This was a fairly transparent tale developed by Att Spengler with the first group of RS spies a decade earlier. The details varied, but the story was in essence the same: naive young man joins police force; is horrified and disillusioned by the brutality and racism he encounters; leaves, determined to fight an unjust order. Craig Williamson had not only proved ideologically sound by the shallow and fundamentally racist measures applied, but he had provided a viable excuse, a good cover for his time spent as a policeman. To this could be added the standard tale. It would sound much more authentic from someone who could also claim to have entered the police force only to avoid even longer conscription into the army. Coetzee completed the necessary paperwork, obtained the required approval and then instructed Lieutenant Brand to bring Sergeant Williamson in.

Two days after his braai and beer date, Craig Williamson was picked up from work and driven to an office in town. A dapperly dressed, moustachioed Lieutenant Colonel Johan Coetzee welcomed him. After brief pleasantries the two men sat down opposite one another and Coetzee began discussing the South African situation. He talked of the ANC and the Communist Party; of the 'great game' between the democratic West and demonic, communist East. He sought replies and listened intently. Craig Williamson was smitten. Coetzee was obviously an intellectual who recognised ability and intellectual capacity. Sergeant Williamson found that he shared the colonel's conviction that there was a desperate need to cleanse the moral pollutants of liberalism and communism from the campuses of the country. He was keen to play his part, to do whatever was necessary.

By the end of the evening, it had been decided that Craig Michael Williamson would apply for admission to the University of the Witwatersrand in Johannesburg and officially leave the police force at the end of the year. That would give him time to learn how to conduct himself as a police spy and not to get caught out on his cover stories. Coetzee himself would take charge of this elementary training. Although his colleagues at the police station knew that he was about to join the Special Branch, they accepted, with only the occasional nudge and wink, that he was about to become a university student.

It was in this way that the fat, rich 'English' boy in a milieu dominated by poorer working-class Afrikaners became a spy and member of the Special Branch. The only special qualifications he needed were that he was English-speaking and had sufficient schooling to allow him admission to university. Not that he would ever admit to such a mundane progression. In his revealing interview with Gillian Slovo in 1996 he claimed that he had joined the 'glamorous' world of the Special Branch as one of only a handful of men to pass a particular promotion exam.

Whatever the method of his recruitment, his police service, as well as his school background, were poor omens for his career as an anti-apartheid spy. So too was the amateurish way in which the infiltration was initially handled. It was characterised by the same degree of bureaucratic bumbling that plagued several earlier operations. When Sergeant Williamson C.M. number 53076T resigned, he became a paid 'source' of the SO wing of the Security Branch. Only when all the bureaucratic procedures had been followed did he 'rejoin' the police force as W61171R, a member of the secretive Section 4 on full pay. He and other student spies then had to draw their monthly police salaries at a police pay point. As such, they could have been followed and seen to sign in regularly.

Had any professional underground opposition existed, it is doubtful if Daisy would ever have developed. Several of the spies, who were not known as such to one another, met accidentally or at least saw one another during the monthly payout. It was in this way that two Wits students, Derek Brune and Craig Williamson, who were later to serve on the same student representative council with a third spy, Arthur McGiven, saw and recognised one another.

This was at a time when Craig Williamson was still attempting to gain radical credibility as an active member of the National Union of South African Students (NUSAS) to which all 'English' university students belonged. This he managed largely by handling all the essential but boring account keeping and avoiding the intellectual cut and thrust of radical student life. When he spoke, it was forcefully, convincingly, and usually related to the all too often neglected practical side of student affairs. In his early days he was all bounce and bonhomie. A contemporary remembers him as 'a very large, even gross, beer-drinking and jovial student'.

Then one night he over-indulged, was almost involved in a fist-fight with a waiter, and apparently drove the wrong way down a motorway. Whether he was arrested and whether his superiors found out is not known, but he stopped drinking. His attention to workaday detail became still more remarked upon. Reliable, efficient and friendly, steering clear of sectarian squabbles, he was the convincing administrator who argued for the best way to implement agreed policies, managed the books, handled the correspondence and generally made himself useful. In this popular but essentially background role, he became the politically unambitious safe pair of hands in the service of NUSAS and the anti-apartheid cause.

He could not hide his background because there were fellow students who had known him at school and who knew he had joined the police, but he stuck to his cover stories and was believed by most of the students. Even so there were some, such as Cedric de Beer, who were vocal in their suspicions. De Beer had also been at St John's and had regarded Craig Williamson as a 'racist bully'. Another leading student activist, Glenn Moss, also refused to trust him. Both were to be harassed, detained and dragged before the courts, but they did, in those early years, pose a threat to Craig Williamson and the whole security operation.

However, the bureaucratic mentality underlying a Calvinist work ethic ignored such threats and dictated that the student spies should not be left idle during their frequent university vacations. Immersed at university in the ungodliness of liberalism and communism, they had better taste real work during their breaks. It was decreed that the student spies should work during vacations in the offices of the section to which they were assigned. So Williamson reported for holiday duty in the Section 4 offices, situated above a milk powder factory in Johannesburg's down-market Fordsburg area.

The factory was run by former policemen, grateful for the rent received from their secretive colleagues. Almost no one among Williamson's growing circle of radical friends and acquaintances queried in any depth where he went during his holidays or how he was funded. Above all, nobody ever followed the student who was starting to make radical waves in the soon to be banned National Union of South African Students. This was just as well for BOSS and the SB, since Williamson and others like him also carried out 'normal' security police work, which included surveillance operations in black townships such as Soweto.

He also drove an imported Volkswagen Beetle, bought in Bonn several years earlier by Republican Intelligence. It was an official SB pool vehicle, registered to the police, but nobody ever checked with the licensing department. After more than a year, Coetzee corrected this dangerous oversight and bought his protégé a 'civilian' Toyota car from a legitimate dealership. Craig Williamson was obviously going places in student politics, and the investment in tuition fees, salary, incidental expenses and a car might pay off.

The generally sloppy approach to the security of the student spies soon came to an end, but not because of any threat. The ANC and PAC had been driven into exile, their structures on the ground broken, and their internal leaderships mostly jailed and serving long sentences. But Van den Bergh and officers such as Johan Coetzee saw the need for a more professional approach, especially when confronted with renewed stirrings of opposition. These tended to reverberate in the liberal universities and in the various tertiary institutions set up for blacks as part of the 'separate development' policy.

Dubbed 'bush colleges', each of them was administered by a member of the Broederbond, in line with the AB's policy. But despite – perhaps because of – the nature of the administration and the carefully planned curricula, these institutions for blacks seemed to be spawning a new and dangerous radicalism. New figures had emerged to give voice to the voiceless; figures who did not necessarily have any links to the radicals of old. They talked of socialism, but were generally hostile to the Communist Party; they preached liberation, but had few ties to either the ANC or PAC. Black Consciousness (BC) was the political umbrella under which they sheltered.

The administrations at the black campuses had acted swiftly when protests broke out in 1968. They expelled 'troublemakers' and provided their personal details to the police. Hundreds of new files were opened, among them one for Dumisa Buhle Ntsebeza of Cala, a village in the as yet undeclared 'independent homeland' of Transkei and a student at Fort Hare. After he and a group of students had daubed anti-apartheid slogans on the walls of the college, they joined a long line of honourable expulsions from Fort Hare, which included Nelson Mandela. Yet the BC phenomenon had at first been welcomed by some elements within the Broederbond because it demanded separate organisation.

But it soon became obvious that the philosophy of BC embraced not only all the 'black nations' of apartheid but also those people classified by the system as 'coloured' or 'Asian'. Even more worrying was the fact that BC exponents – the most prominent a young Eastern Cape student, Steve Bantu Biko – talked of the goal of a non-racial, unitary South Africa. They became a primary threat.

There were also stirrings on the labour front that needed to be monitored and if need be controlled or suppressed. In all cases, there tended to be an overlap into the 'liberal' universities. It was often through organisations such as NUSAS, at the 'English' universities that anti-apartheid groups got practical assistance or were able to gather support from religious, human rights and radical organisations around the world. These international solidarity links were often the same as those which had given and still continued to give support to jailed ANC and PAC members and their families.

These were organisations such as World University Service (WUS), the International Defence and Aid Fund (IDAF) set up by Canon John Collins of London's St Paul's Cathedral, and the International University Exchange Fund (IUEF) headed by the Swedish social democrat, Lars-Gunnar Eriksson. There was a trail of money, a solidarity trail that could be keyed into, and that led to names, addresses, contacts. The potential of its use for personal gain did not escape some security operatives who appear to have made fortunes in the course of their careers.

The full details of the infiltration of the universities and of the flow of money, primarily through the IUEF, are not known. But fragments of evidence lie buried in the notes and transcripts of TRC meetings and hearings and in the records of a few investigators. Evidence can also be found in the IUEF documents in the National Danish Archives. These fragments have not so far revealed precisely when the security police realised the importance of the flow of aid money to the victims of apartheid, but it was not a hard conclusion to draw.

From around the world, as more of the awful realities of the South African system became known, often through the rumblings of the growing Black Consciousness movement and the formation of trade unions, assistance poured in. Money to pay lawyers defending those charged with political crimes; finance for rural and urban development, or alternative technology schemes; funding for 'leadership training', and to educate those sentenced to prison or banished to remote rural outposts; subsistence allowances for the families of the persecuted, the murdered and the vanished. After the Soweto uprising these trickles and flows of cash turned into a flood. Much of this was organised through bodies such as WUS, IDAF and the IUEF. But there were also contributions made by trade unions, Amnesty International and anti-apartheid groups and individuals that went directly to opposition groups in South Africa.

The London-based IDAF provided funding only for the defence in political trials and for the families of prisoners. This organisation, established in 1956 to support the accused in the marathon treason trial, organised its own methods of direct transfer. The prime conduit for many other inward flows was NUSAS where, from 1974, security police sergeant Craig Williamson was the national finance officer.

Even before he assumed the role of effective treasurer of NUSAS, Craig Williamson and his BOSS and SB handlers had grasped the scale and growing significance of the sums involved. To become part of that flow, both at home and abroad, became an official objective, under the broad heading of Operation Daisy. Williamson's unexpected rise through the NUSAS ranks made him the key person. Fortunately for Coetzee, he also had several other campus spies who were making progress through student ranks. They could provide back-up for Williamson. Chief among these was Karl Zachary Edwards, BOSS agent R1652, of Rhodes University.

British-born Edwards and his younger brother Lloyd both later became members of one of the most notoriously brutal of security police divisions, Port Elizabeth. Neither applied for amnesty. Their rabidly rightwing father, Kurt, was a dedicated writer of letters to the local Press and Karl portrayed his adoption of radical politics as a rebellion against a domineering parent as much as a logical progression for a thinking student. While Williamson moved in circles closer to the ANC and SACP, Karl 'Zac' Edwards sought out contacts among the radical environmentalists and anti-communists. In particular, he made links with the emerging Black Consciousness groups and individuals such as Steve Biko.

Coetzee needed at least two students in prominent positions in order to launch an ambitious project to control funding both to anti-apartheid organisations and to individuals. The government was determined to shut off all external aid. BOSS wanted profits and information. Williamson and Edwards became crucial in this plan. All that was required was that the radical credentials, especially of Williamson, be firmly established.

8

Special Branch larceny

The standard approach to endowing student spies with credibility was to have them arrested alongside genuine dissidents. As a tactic it had become something of a cliché. Craig Williamson was duly arrested at a Witwatersrand University student demonstration in 1973 and charged with riotous assembly – a serious charge which was subsequently dropped. Something more was needed to silence the persistent doubts being voiced about the burly born-again radical. The escape route proved the answer. It was a simple and most successful means of ingratiating Williamson and his cohorts with campus radicals, and in particular with ANC supporters. Faced with conscription into the army, a number of mainly liberal students from the white campuses wanted to leave the country but could not do so legally.

Craig Williamson became known in radical circles as the man to speak to if escape was required. His route to Botswana was said to be the safest available. After the explosion of anger in Soweto on 16 June 1976 and the subsequent brutal police and military crackdown, the trickle of requests to flee turned into a torrent as young black students sought to avoid arrest and detention by leaving the country. Thousands fled, many to Botswana. 'If you wanted to get out safely, go with Craig. That was the word,' former student leader and political detainee Cedric de Beer remembered nearly thirty years later.

But 'going with Craig' merely meant linking into the network he provided. According to verbal evidence and one telegram sent to an escapee in late

1976, 'Paul' ran the route in the early years. The base was the secluded Hertford Farm, near Lanseria airport, north of Johannesburg, owned by English-born Paul Deans, whose stepson Paul Asmussen was a policeman and former school friend of Craig Williamson. After Williamson's own flight, the main campus contact for this apparent freedom train was Zac Edwards. He vetted most of the escapees, demanding their names, addresses and biographies as part of 'security precautions'. The escape route may have begun in 1974 and was certainly running in 1975 when Williamson became the official IUEF contact person in South Africa and began to do underground work for the ANC.

By 1976 it was, in many respects, a family business financed by anti-apartheid donor funds diverted mainly from the IUEF. As such, it was perhaps the most cost-effective operation ever run by the police. The fact that it sent many escapees into exile by different routes did not matter overmuch. Not only were there spies among them as they joined the exile community, but Craig Williamson was also soon travelling to the 'frontline states' to conduct in-depth assessments for his new employer, the IUEF. He was able to check on the efficacy of the escape route.

His sister Lisa Jane was involved, as were other friends from his school days, including Paul Asmussen's brother Mark. Another school friend, Jonty Leontsinis, may also have assisted and was certainly active, with his wife Cindy, in subsequent operations. Paul Asmussen and Lisa Williamson probably joined the security branch at about this time, but the others in Williamson's close circle were classified as 'sources', or part-time operatives paid on a casual basis. The Asmussen/Deans property in Lanseria, which was developed as a hotel, restaurant and pub, became a regular haunt of off-duty Special Branch police. It was here that Karl Edwards maintained a cottage in the grounds from some time in 1978 until January 1980. By 1990 it was the exclusive Hertford restaurant/hotel complex, the venue for the first secret talks in South Africa between ANC and government delegations, effectively arranged by the security establishment.

A decade later it still belonged to Paul Deans, who lived there with Paul Asmussen. Neither had come forward to give any information about the massive acts of larceny or any of the Special Branch activities in and around the property itself. Deans, in July 2000, launched himself as a brash TV chef on South Africa's e-TV channel, promoting his hotel in its idyllic woodland setting. He threatened to sue the local *Mail & Guardian* newspaper, which published an article by me about some of the murky history surrounding the Deans/Asmussen property, but quickly backed down. Instead he wrote a letter in which he denied any knowledge of security police actions. He added: 'Whatever my stepsons' involvement is in the above matters, and who they choose as friends and associates has nothing to do with me. But they are and remain part of my family.'

It was also pointed out to him that not only had I and my researcher/ partner Barbara visited the Hertford Inn on more than one occasion, we had also interviewed an obviously very nervous Paul Asmussen. Only Asmussen insisted his name was Paul Deans, and reluctantly confirmed some of the facts we required before fleeing. There was no direct discussion about the escape route or the theft of anti-apartheid money.

Who played which roles in the escape route and at which times is still not known. All that can be said positively is that the Hertford was the base of the route, that it was established by Craig Williamson and Zac Edwards, was run at one stage by someone using the name 'Paul', and that Edwards controlled it for several years and lived on the Hertford property. How many people used this route is also not known. Nor is it known how many ever reached Botswana, or how many individual journeys may have ended in death rather than exile, directed into ambushes rather than toward the border fence. Those who succeeded in reaching the ANC 'safe houses' in Gaborone included infiltrators trained on the Rietvlei farm outside Pretoria. Some 'special cases' such as Cecilia Masondo, disabled wife of Andrew Masondo, a leading figure in the ANC armed wing, were actually brought over the border and delivered to safe houses. Cecilia Masondo's driver and escort during her escape in 1977 was Lisa Williamson.

Despite the success of the early escape route, the arrest in 1973 of Craig Williamson and others and their subsequent discharge from court on a riotous assembly charge, the doubts persisted. At that time, Williamson was still reporting to Section 4 in Fordsburg. All the same, a year later, when the first information gleaned from the escape route probably started flowing in, Craig Williamson was elected to the NUSAS national executive as finance and administration officer. It was a full-time paid post, based in Cape Town. Married by then to laboratory assistant Ingrid Bacher, an aspirant medical doctor, he was able to explain his rather affluent lifestyle by crediting it to Ingrid's earnings as a medical technologist at Cape Town's Groote Schuur hospital. But still there were doubts, not just among student activists such as Cedric de Beer and Glenn Moss, but also in the South African Council of Churches. They raised an abundance of circumstantial evidence which linked Williamson to the police. But there was no hard evidence, and certainly no confession. There were also powerful political voices that vouched for him – protection not gained only through his obvious ability in establishing the escape route. He had also won the confidence of IUEF head Lars-Gunnar Eriksson – and, much more importantly, of leading members of the exiled ANC.

This protective screen was erected in 1975 when Williamson, as a vice-president-elect of NUSAS, travelled to Europe with its president-elect, Mike Stent. They met with Lars-Gunnar Eriksson and with exiled former NUSAS leaders such as Neville Rubin, then working for the International Labour Organisation in Geneva and a legal consultant to the IUEF. Williamson also met senior members of the exiled ANC, keen to gain first-hand information from back home.

Stent, who had impeccable credentials as a fighter against apartheid, was cautious in his contacts, aware of the possibility of spies and agents provocateurs and wary of the SACP. Williamson obviously had no such qualms. He made himself available. Eriksson was impressed and decided to appoint Williamson as the IUEF contact person in South Africa. He did so despite doubts expressed by Neville Rubin, who felt Stent was the better choice. Although they were later to deny it, senior figures in the ANC, including treasurer-general Thomas Nkobi, were also impressed by the portly student activist and enthusiastic volunteer.

Nkobi was second in command to ANC president Oliver Tambo, and as such wielded considerable influence. He and another senior official, Reg September, met and apparently assessed Williamson. Over tea in a London café an agreement was struck that Williamson would provide information for the ANC. To do so, he would have to meet someone concerned with 'the underground', since both Nkobi and September were 'on the political representation side'. September arranged for the spy to meet 'Ismail Essop', who turned out to be Aziz Pahad, involved at the time in clandestine ANC operations, later deputy foreign minister in the post-apartheid government.

Pahad formally recruited Williamson to provide information on the student movement. His development as a 'political cadre within the country should be built up slowly'. For a start, he was to send 'up-to-date reports on South African affairs' to Nevin Faik at an address in north London. He was also instructed to set up a post office box in Cape Town under a false name.

Through Pahad, the student spy was introduced to other members of the Revolutionary Council (RC) based in London. This group, which included Ronnie Kasrils, who became deputy defence minister and then minister of forestry in the post-apartheid government, and Joe Slovo, head of the SACP and the first post-apartheid housing minister, coordinated various underground activities in South Africa. Despite this apparent acceptance at the top, there were senior ANC members uneasy about Williamson. Prime among the doubters was Satyandranath Ragunanan 'Mac' Maharaj, later to become the transport minister in the first ANC government. To him, Williamson seemed 'too good to be true' and he decided to set a trap for him.

For reasons still best known to themselves, the RC had embarked in South Africa on a programme of 'bucket bombs' – small explosive charges placed in waste bins or buckets which scattered anti-apartheid pamphlets. This was an extremely inefficient way to distribute literature, and because the charges were so small the bombs had drawn scant attention and little or no press coverage. With Williamson volunteering as an activist and with pressure from within the ANC that he be used, Maharaj and Kasrils included him in the bucket-bomb programme.

When Craig Williamson returned to South Africa with his bucket-bomb paraphernalia and pamphlets he and Johan Coetzee fell with some glee into the trap set by Maharaj. They not only ensured that security police agents detonated several bucket bombs, they saw to it that these events received press coverage. For Maharaj this was proof positive that Williamson was a plant. Unfortunately there were others in the ANC who, for the very same reason, felt their trust in Williamson had been vindicated. Prominent among them was Nkobi, but his other supporters included the influential Thabo Mbeki, later to succeed Mandela as post-apartheid president, and Aziz Pahad. However, Williamson would never again come close to involvement in the clandestine 'military' activities of the ANC.

To his supporters he was a doer rather than a talker, a loyal activist rather than a critical thinker and polemicist. It was a reputation he had honed as he rose through the ranks of the student movement. Within much of the ANC he was seen as different from the bulk of the critically polemical and sometimes dilettante 'white Left'. His apparent lack of interest or ability in the field of political theory could even be an asset, given his evident creativity in action. When the authorities withdrew his passport in 1976, this was expected, given his level of overt activity. That he could subsequently meet in Botswana with Lars-Gunnar Eriksson was seen by his influential supporters as further proof of his ingenuity and potential usefulness. To his detractors, it was yet further evidence that he was not all he seemed.

That meeting with Eriksson in 1976 signalled the start of the main financial aspect of Operation Daisy. In Gaborone, Williamson outlined his plans. Because the government was about to clamp down on foreign funding to anti-apartheid groups, as well as on money to assist the victims of the system, he had devised a series of trusts which would be able to circumvent the new rules. They were cunningly disguised in having as a sole trustee a highly reputable university professor who could not in any way be linked to any political organisation. Money supposedly belonging to the professor could be channelled to the trusts, which could then disburse it as local funding. Another channel was through the Danish Confectionery, a bakery and confectionery shop in Johannesburg's Smal Street owned by members of Williamson's network, the Asmussen/Deans family, through whom he had met his wife. Williamson's own sister, Lisa, would act as administrator of the trusts. Eriksson agreed immediately. He thought it imperative that Williamson leave the country and go into exile, which was exactly what Johan Coetzee also wanted.

A few local activists were also informed in broad terms, and in strict confidence, about the plans for anti-apartheid funding. Among them was human rights lawyer Geoff Budlender, who was asked by Williamson to draw up a draft of the trust deeds. Those in the know tended to appreciate the irony of the Danish Confectionery being involved. Much IUEF money originated in Denmark. They were also impressed with the choice of the sole trustee for both the Prisoners Support Trust (PST) and the Education Research Trust (ERT). He was the Anglo-Spanish fine arts professor from the University of the Witwatersrand, Eduardo Joel Fabio Barraclough, a charming, sartorially immaculate, tennis player and raconteur.

Johan Coetzee's friends in the media had created a public profile for Barraclough as a brilliant liberal artist with impeccable credentials, having taught art at Britain's exclusive Rugby School and having served on the executive of the British Royal Society of Sculptors. *The Citizen*, the *Johannesburg Star* and the *Rand Daily Mail* all carried laudatory articles. At a time when universities were desperate to maintain international contacts and recruitment, his failure to produce examples of his work or a promised photographic portfolio of his paintings and sculptures was also overlooked. He had been interviewed in Britain by a tennis-playing vice-chancellor whose academic field was law.

When Barraclough arrived at Wits in 1974 to start a three-year contract, he promptly fell out with colleagues and students in the fine arts department. He was labelled incompetent and a possible fraud. In letters to the university authorities, he claimed that the swell of criticism against him was part of a 'Marxist plot' orchestrated by some members of staff who were inciting the students. The whole affair had the makings of a massive scandal, which might involve the government, so it was kept under wraps, and Barraclough was shunted off into what was effectively a non-existent job as the director of what was to become the Gertrude Posel Art Gallery.

Academics who worked with him now feel that it was at this stage that the Special Branch probably recruited Barraclough, if he was not already a spy. At the time, however, nobody in the department or at the university seems to have thought that he might be any more than a slick-talking mediocre artist who was out of his depth. In the light of subsequent newspaper reports on the prowess and apparent success of Barraclough, even some of his critics began to doubt their assessments. They were not aware how easily the media could be manipulated and that the Barraclough profile was being established under the directions of Johan Coetzee's Section A planners using their media assets.

The image they projected was that of a free-thinking radical artist, the sort of person who could be expected to clash with establishments. Referring in May 1977 to Barraclough's supposed critique of art in South Africa, the *Star's* art critic, John Dewar, noted: 'He found signs of the "averted eyes" approach to the fundamentals of art . . . This resulted in a dehumanised and decorative form of abstraction.' Richard Cheales of the *Citizen*, in an embarrassingly sycophantic art column in October that year devoted to 'this charming man with the volatile mind', quoted Barraclough as finding that 'uninitiated eyes [in South Africa] cannot distinguish between the work of amateurs and professionals'.

This façade was flimsy and would not have withstood examination, but, as Coetzee correctly calculated, nobody would bother to check on the credentials of the man selected to be the trustee of the PST and ERT. The trusts officially came into being in November 1976. Fabio Barraclough's positive public image provided essential protection for Operation Daisy and was so successful that even after he had left Wits (having trashed the university house in which he and his wife and five children had lived) he was widely regarded as a liberal intellectual. When the Wits administration asked him in writing to stop using the title of professor, he claimed in reply that he had it from the University of Madrid – which has no record of this.

Once again, nobody checked. By the time Williamson had to flee Switzerland, and much of the elaborate network established as an offshoot of Operation Daisy had unravelled, Barraclough was already established in his new cover. With the security establishment obsessed with international plots against South Africa, Johan Coetzee devised a scheme to 'infiltrate' the European anti-apartheid movement. It would be done at the highest level, by establishing a national anti-apartheid movement somewhere abroad, which the South African security police would finance and control. The fact that Spain was chosen probably had as much to do with Barraclough's availability as with the fact that no specific anti-apartheid movement existed there.

Spain in general and Madrid in particular was a handy place to have an agent who was in no way connected with the South African embassy and who apparently had anti-apartheid credentials. The country was also a good conduit for money. In Spain, Barraclough led a double life. He was still Professor Barraclough, the apparently retired bilingual academic who listed a telephone number in that name. But he was also Pablo Valls, the evidently affluent anti-apartheid campaigner and funder of the Anti-Apartheid Committee. The committee itself appeared to do little if anything in terms of campaigning, although 'Valls' did address several meetings on South Africa. But he was the most conscientious attender of every anti-apartheid conference anywhere in Europe.

This was a source of great pride in Section A, which lavished substantial funding on the venture. The dapperly dressed and elderly anti-apartheid delegate with an insatiable curiosity was regarded, at best, as 'rather strange' by the mainly younger and very activist AAM core. There was even speculation that he was 'some kind of spy', but it did not matter since the AAM was an open movement without any clandestine cells or secret agendas. So Pablo Valls was tolerated. This enabled him to get close to some visitors from southern Africa and in particular from Namibia. The scraps of information gleaned added to Johan Coetzee's jigsaw of names, places, dates and plans.

During a 1980 summit meeting in Geneva attended by both South African government delegates and representatives of SWAPO, Pablo Valls attended in a supportive role to the SWAPO delegation. He fetched, carried, made himself generally useful, and listened. Every evening he would cross the border into France to the small town of Ferney-Voltaire. In a local hotel he would be debriefed by Craig Williamson, who had returned to Europe only months after he had been exposed as a spy and had fled Switzerland. Williamson would type out reports based on the eavesdropping of Barraclough/Valls, then hand-deliver them to South African summit delegate and SB chief General Johan van der Merwe in a Ferney-Voltaire coffee shop. As a clandestine exercise, it worked. The value of the information gathered seems likely to have been minimal.

If only for reasons of self-promotion and budgetary justification the SB chalked up its intervention at the 1980 Geneva meeting as a major success. Especially since the head of the SB himself was involved, along with Coetzee and Williamson, there would be none who would question where reality ended and myth began. This also served Barraclough well. It secured his position and seems to have kept him in considerable funds. He appears to have flown back to South Africa several times for debriefings or even training sessions. His South African identity document and passport, in the name of Valls, made him three years younger than his actual age. According to these documents he was born on 1 July 1928. Eduardo Barraclough was born on 25

July 1925. Interviewed by telephone in Spain in June 1999, Johan Coetzee's 'Spanish connection' was an obviously frightened man. He admitted to being the trustee of the Prisoners Support Trust and the Education Research Trust and claimed he had been 'under a lot of pressure from the police' in 1976.

SB agent Peter Casselton, a British recruit who was trained at Daisy Farm, the large property north of Pretoria, bought with R40,000 stolen from the trust funds, claimed that the 'professor' who spied in Spain had been made 'an offer he couldn't refuse' by Section A. Whatever the reason, in 1976 Fabio Barraclough became the front for trusts which attracted funding from around the world to finance projects that would promote a non-racial future in South Africa.

Coetzee and Section A had planned well. Because Geoff Budlender had been approached to draft the trust deeds, anti-apartheid activists assumed that the arrangement was above-board. But neither Budlender nor any other anti-apartheid lawyer was involved in registering the trusts. That job was given to one of the leading Afrikaner – and generally regarded as Broederbond – firms in Pretoria, Couzyn, Hertzog and Horak. Problems regarding the trusts would be referred to them. It was an elementary precaution by the security services, yet one that would have rung alarm bells in anti-apartheid circles had it been known. But nobody checked the trust deeds register at the offices of the master of the supreme court in Pretoria until we did in 1999.

Williamson and Edwards now moved to centralise all aid distribution and asked individual agencies to operate only through the PST and ERT. In this way the police were able to seize control of most of the Black Consciousness networks. Security agents also became close confidants of the families of political activists, not just in South Africa but also in Namibia, where the independence struggle was gaining momentum. For years, Lisa Williamson drove to the then South African-controlled South West Africa every month to personally hand over a subsistence allowance to the mother of leading Namibian independence campaigner Toivo ja Toivo, who was jailed on Robben Island. Grateful for this apparently selfless help, the impoverished old woman would present the apparently caring and extremely inquisitive young woman with a chicken for her pains.

For the government as a whole, this project that spanned the decade of the 1970s and ended with another super-spy myth was a small area of success in a decade of setbacks that effectively strangled any hope of sustaining the grand design of apartheid.

9

Washington, Moscow or Stockholm

Global politics had a distinct bearing on the success of Operation Daisy. In a politically bipolar world, the West was in an embarrassed alliance with apartheid South Africa, while the East – in the form of the Soviet Union – backed the ANC through its alliance with the SACP, and claimed the moral high ground. The Scandinavian countries – and in particular Sweden, under Prime Minister Olof Palme – shared the anti-Soviet view of their Western allies, but they were uncomfortable with support or even tolerance for the brutal apartheid regime. Like so many social democrats before and since, they sought an elusive 'third way'. But they did so, certainly at first, on the basis of the same simplistic good-versus-evil, East-versus-West analysis. In the big game, it was the USSR versus the US, and the pieces on South Africa's chessboard were the apartheid government and the ANC-led alliance.

So the kitchen cabinet around Olof Palme welcomed the emergence of anti-apartheid forces hostile to the Soviet system and to the SACP. Close friends Bernt Carlsson, general secretary of the Socialist International, Lars-Gunnar Eriksson, head of the IUEF, and Palme formed the core of this group. They met and corresponded frequently: South Africa was an intense focus. As the decade of the 1970s unrolled, it seemed to them that the apartheid state provided a perfect laboratory for the development of a third way. Black Consciousness as the leading force on the ground there had its limitations, but was an understandable development, given the racist realities. But there were also the self-proclaimed social democrats and even Marxists at several of the English-language universities who tended to dominate the national student movement, NUSAS. This was the 'white Left' that had emerged in the years after the first mass bannings and detentions had driven the ANC and its allies, together with the PAC, into exile.

The new forces coming into their own in the 1970s were infused with socialist ideas, but these were ideas which derided as grotesque the ideological distortions of Josef Stalin. They stressed liberty – even libertarianism – and condemned the tyranny and barbarism of the gulag. Inspired as much by the Parisian student revolts of May 1968, as by the American Black Panthers and the writings of everyone from Jean-Paul Sartre and Amilcar Cabral to Herbert Marcuse, this was a loose, largely university-based movement, clear only in what it opposed. Imperialism, whether Portugal's increasingly tenuous hold on its colonies or US intervention in Vietnam, was universally condemned. So too was apartheid. To be considered part of this new revolutionary current it was generally enough simply to oppose both capitalism and what passed for socialism in Eastern Europe or China. The socialist future was seldom defined other than in vague terms of human liberty and the extension of democracy – goals with which social democrats, socialists of any other stripe, and liberals could all concur.

This white Left, while feeling uncomfortable with the exclusivity of Black Consciousness, tended to accept that its role should be one of support to a political movement led by BC. Particularly for Lars-Gunnar Eriksson, here were the makings of a beacon of hope that could combine the best of all known worlds in providing a 'third way' alternative both to the brute authoritarianism of the USSR and the conscienceless capitalism of the US. The mixture of clarity and confusion, of strategies, resentments, ideals, hopes and fantasies, which was BC, was the major visible anti-apartheid force within South Africa. It had emerged while the exiled ANC created a highly successful international presence and the PAC fell into bickering disarray. The Swedish kitchen cabinet resolved to provide as much support as possible to encourage the growth of this perceived new force while remaining on non-sectarian terms with the ANC.

Later this position changed quite fast when the third way advocates got to know the ANC's exiled president, Oliver Tambo, better. They were also impressed by his apparent protégé, Thabo Mbeki, who seemed decidedly undogmatic, despite his senior position within the SACP. These realisations coincided with the havoc sown by Operation Daisy and with the ANC becoming the only major piece on the political chessboard both at home and abroad. But that would wait for the following decade. Throughout much of the 1970s, the attempt to build a distinctive third way was a priority. This meant operating in an often clandestine manner; it created a milieu in which spies could function.

It was this desire to create a third way which helped propel Craig Williamson into the position of IUEF liaison in South Africa through his position in NUSAS. He and his handlers were only too happy to play up the prospect of a social democratic movement developing in South Africa. It formed one of the bases for the briefing of Williamson before his trip to meet Eriksson in Gaborone on 30 July 1976. Williamson gave the impression that SSD – Students for Social Democracy – groups were being established on all campuses. Eriksson was impressed, and said as much in an information note he penned. 'The basic intention is that they [SSD groups] should keep issues alive and provide a platform for people working for a different society,' he noted. 'They will concentrate on meetings, publications, etc but will not get involved with action which will have to be handled in a different way in order not to compromise these bodies.'

There were obvious delusions of grandeur; of sitting in the cockpit of a major revolution in the making. The note made mention of a putative 'national organisation' which would involve 'hand-picked people' and would be numbered 'in the hundreds rather than thousands'. It also made casual use of the names of various activists, including Glenn Moss, the student leader who was one of a minority who still maintained that Williamson was suspicious. Among the others was Fink Haysom, who was later to become legal adviser to President Nelson Mandela.

The importance of the BC groups is clear in a statement that 'Craig would set up the necessary mechanism for the information service, the value of which has been emphasised by the black groups'. This would be a two-way arrangement, with the IUEF as the hub. Payments would flow one way and information the other. The note also states that 'it has in principle been agreed that [Craig Williamson] will be employed by the IUEF to handle our publications production, particularly in regard to Southern Africa, the utilisation of Southern African material etc as well as being involved with our Southern African programme in general'. Apparently sent to members of the Socialist International group with a copy to Neville Rubin, the file note also mentioned that Craig Williamson's 'intention is to leave illegally at the end of the year via Botswana'. Arrangements were made to 'get him cleared' and there was mention of finding out 'about medical studies in Geneva for his wife'.

Williamson wrote a report of this for the police, and he later sent on the

Eriksson file note, stolen from Eriksson's filing cabinet in Geneva, which confirmed his version. He and his handlers also composed the report sent to Eriksson some weeks later. Although dated 3 September, it was only received in Geneva on the 22nd, apparently delivered by a courier. It gives a good illustration of how the security forces operated in terms of protecting themselves and their spies by means of confusion. The report states that Neville Rubin, the IUEF legal adviser, had prepared the deed to establish the Prisoners Support Trust. Rubin did indeed draw up a trust deed for the PST, just as Johannesburg-based anti-apartheid lawyer Geoff Budlender had done. The fact that cursory checks would reveal that such deeds had come from such sources provided an aura of legitimacy to the exercise. With Rubin and/or Budlender involved, there was no need to delve any further.

The SB report included the nomination of Williamson's undercover IUEF successor, BOSS agent Karl Edwards, a proposal eagerly accepted by Eriksson. At last it appeared that things were starting to move in South Africa. The townships were still in uproar in the wake of the school students' uprising in Soweto, and talk of revolution was in the air. Eriksson was excited. His undercover man in South Africa seemed well connected and the IUEF, the Swedish kitchen cabinet and the Socialist International seemed to have the inside track on what was happening. Craig Williamson's warning that it would be premature to launch a national Movement for Social Democracy was seen as a sign of his political maturity rather than an indication that very little if anything of the sort existed on the ground. For the police, and for Williamson in his discussions with Eriksson, it was a simple matter to imply that the numerous groups and agencies striving for a better society were mere fronts for the grand social democratic project. Edwards, for example, was the leading member of the university-based Environmental Action Project (Envirac). He was already, by that stage, the conduit for funds from sources such as the World University Service.

The September report from Williamson mentioned that Envirac 'is presently in the process of being formed into an independent national organisation'. This was the Environmental Development Agency, which was to have Edwards as its first director. 'This is then the most perfect cover for a chap such as Karl to carry out a co-ordinating and initiating role,' Williamson's report enthuses. It also notes that Edwards had arranged for a financial grant from WUS, which had agreed to provide R7,000 in 1977 and R15,000 a year thereafter. The PST was to start out with a R50,000 grant from the IUEF and with Lisa Williamson as secretary. Of this amount, R5,000 was earmarked for administration and R25,000 for 'support of dependents and ex-prisoners'. The fate of that sum will probably never be known.

The legitimate Cape Town-based prisoners education trust (SAPET) was supposed to be paid the remaining R20,000 of this initial donation. Its secretary, Laura Schultz, recalled no donation of that size. For security reasons, individual donations were not listed, but SAPET was funded from a wide variety of sources. In the year to April 1977, total income was R33,747. In 1977 the IUEF supposedly made donations of R35,000 to SAPET, but from May 1977 to April 1978 total donations recorded were R15,000. So SAPET, which deliberately avoided Craig Williamson's appeals to channel all funding through the PST, had a total income for 1976 and 1977 of R48,747. Yet the IUEF alone was suppose to have donated R55,000. Craig Williamson explained such discrepancies twenty years later, when he privately admitted before several witnesses that large sums of money were diverted. But he claimed that neither he nor any of the individual spies or security officials had profited from this. Their subsequent affluence could be attributed to their business acumen. It was, however, true that much of the stolen money did go toward security operations and purchases, including paying spies in Europe.

Among the purchases was Daisy Farm, near Pretoria, bought by Coetzee under the name John Davis with R40,000 of stolen anti-apartheid donations. Even before Williamson left for 'exile' he had access to large sums of money, much of which went to 'secret projects' on behalf of the supposed social democratic cause or the IUEF. Edwards was in a similar position. Even before the formal IUEF leg of Operation Daisy got under way with Williamson crossing to Botswana as a refugee from apartheid, the entire project was paying off in terms of names, addresses and other information, as well as financially.

Like a gang of delinquents admiring and serving their gang boss, Johan Coetzee's thieving troupe lied, stole, blackmailed, threatened and eventually bombed and murdered. Some of these actions were simply gratuitous, such as stealing a painting of a Boer general on a horse from a London art gallery as a present for Coetzee. It hung in pride of place in his home.

While much of the apartheid state might be slipping out of control, here was an operation that brought results. Whatever happened, it should be protected. Since Edwards, Williamson and his sister Lisa were fairly frequent visitors to Botswana, there was always the danger that some unreliable journalist might decide to investigate how and why these apparent radicals were able to cross borders with such impunity.

To the security establishment, it seemed best to restrict access to journalists. Where the South African media was concerned, this really meant only one newspaper, the *Rand Daily Mail*. It had sometimes overstepped what the government and the security establishment considered reasonable opposition, giving critical coverage to deaths in detention, and at one stage exposing horrific prison conditions. This was one of the reasons that the police Special Branch and Military Intelligence had established 'reliable contacts' on the newspaper, some of them paid agents.

As a result of information passed on to one of these contacts, three *Rand Daily Mail* staffers, Mervyn Rees, Geoff Dalglish and Ingrid Norton, travelled to the airstrip at Selebi Pikwe in Botswana in July 1977. It was from here that a chartered Viscount aircraft was each week ferrying hundreds of refugees – mainly from Zimbabwe, but increasingly from South Africa – to Lusaka. Botswana could not cope with the influx and the liberation movements in the region were all headquartered in Lusaka. Over two days – on 7 and 8 July – the supposedly liberal and anti-apartheid *Rand Daily Mail* published front-page and major 'Inside Mail' features on a 'terror pipeline'. The first report also used United Nations figures illustrating the increase in refugees from South Africa. It also added to the image of Craig Williamson, who had by then left South Africa via Botswana.

In the same issue of the paper, the 'Inside Mail' feature was headlined 'The terror charter'. It noted: 'For several hours at a dusty airstrip in northern Botswana last week, three *Rand Daily Mail* reporters secretly watched as a group of black refugees embarked on a flight that will take many of them to secret guerrilla camps for military training.' Although most of the references were to 'Rhodesians' the flight was also referred to as an 'ANC charter'.

Next day there was a front-page headline 'Terror airlift: bomb threats' above a report about anonymous bomb threats to the South African-based aircraft charter company. It quoted Charles Tibone, the administrative secretary in the Botswana presidential office, who was infuriated by the approach of the newspaper and its description of the refugees. 'They come to us as refugees and leave as refugees. It is absurd to refer to them as guerrillas or terrorists because they are refugees,' he was quoted as saying.

The 'Inside Mail' feature on that day, by the same reporting team, professed to be 'the story of a refugee living in self-imposed exile'. The interview with 'Joseph' publicised the police-run escape route from South Africa to Botswana. 'Joseph' was also quoted as stating that refugees, when they arrived in Botswana, could 'opt for asylum, further education or guerrilla training'. Such offers were contrary to Botswana policy, and there is no record, apart from the *Mail* report, of this ever having occurred. But the impression was created that the subsequent murderous attacks on Gaborone by apartheid hit squads had some justification.

The Botswana government reacted by barring *Rand Daily Mail* journalists from the country. One of those who suffered from this ban was staff reporter Paul Bell, who tried several times, months later, to enter Botswana. It was exactly what the security establishment had hoped for.

The police-run escape route continued to function throughout this period. Craig Williamson himself used it. Before he left, however, Coetzee sent him for six weeks' training at Rietvlei Farm, then run by National Intelligence. This agency, together with the police, would oversee the operation. Tai Minnaar and Att Nel of Military Intelligence were the trainers, and Williamson once proudly listed the aspects of this training: memory; report writing; surveillance and counter-surveillance techniques; secret writing; photography (general); report photography; personal meetings; dead drops – choosing, using etc; emergency procedures. He did not have to concern himself with the internal funding network and escape route; they continued to function, and the escape route had become part of the underground links to the country for the ANC.

With his training complete, it was decided that Williamson would leave for Botswana in early January 1977. He would take with him the liberal student radical Eric Abraham, who Coetzee knew was known and trusted by Lars-Gunnar Eriksson. Abraham, who was later to become a leading film and television producer in Britain, had been severely harassed and was ready to leave. So far as the security establishment was concerned, he was better gone. He was, in BOSS parlance, a 'troublesome child' – the term applied to a student who refused to spy.

Abraham had done much more than that. Working as a freelance journalist, he twice exposed BOSS agents. In the first case, while on a working visit to England he spotted a known student spy taking photographs of protesters at an anti-apartheid rally. Abraham, who had his own camera with him, immediately sneaked a shot of the Cape Town student poet and spy, Michael Morris. London's *Guardian* newspaper bought the picture and the story, bringing to an instant end the attempt to relaunch Morris's spying career in Britain. He returned to South Africa, where he worked in various security research and front organisations before finally migrating to the United States.

Abraham's effort cut no ice with some of the anti-apartheid establishment. When even the liberation movements had not been able to do such a thing, here was a young student unmasking a BOSS agent. It was rumoured, with the probable encouragement of BOSS, that Eric Abraham's exposé had been a carefully staged event to gain him credibility in anti-apartheid circles. This, it was said, was necessary because his father was a senior officer in the South African Navy. In a British anti-apartheid milieu dominated by the SACP,

Abraham was certainly considered suspect. He was isolated from the main-stream of anti-apartheid activity. It was a situation tailor-made for BOSS.

When Eric Abraham returned to Cape Town, he received a friendly telephone call from a Captain Basson. The two of them should meet. Perhaps they had more in common than might be supposed. Abraham recognised the approach for what it was: security recruitment. He also recognised its potential as a newspaper story. He agreed to meet Basson, but only in a public place of his choosing. Basson agreed, and the following afternoon a confident Captain Nic Basson strolled along a pathway in the historic gardens behind Cape Town's St George's cathedral. There, on a park bench in a quiet corner, sat Eric Abraham. Unknown to Basson, a photographer was also in position, hidden in the shrubbery, his telephoto lens focused on the bench.

It was an excellent story and the *Sunday Tribune* made great play of it. The personal tale, with picture, of how the security police tried to recruit students to spy on the local university campus outraged BOSS. It was bad enough that Abraham had rejected the advances, but that he had twice gone public with the fact was an acute embarrassment. He would be punished. He was. Banned, excluded from university, harassed and driven to the brink of suicide, Eric Abraham simply wanted to get out. This suited Coetzee's purposes. He knew that Abraham, who had worked with Amnesty International in London and had been a key person in the IUEF-sponsored student news agency, SANA, was highly regarded by Eriksson. He could be used to provide extra credibility for the next big step in Operation Daisy: Williamson was instructed to 'escape' with Eric Abraham.

The plan Williamson proposed was simple. Eric Abraham was to wait for a telegram. It would come from 'Paul', and if it wished him 'Merry Xmas and happy New Year' he was to fly to Johannesburg on 5 January on the evening flight and be met at the airport. The telegram arrived. Abraham took the flight, was met at the airport and driven to what was then the secluded Hertford Farm, north of Johannesburg. He waited nervously for several hours, until Williamson turned up and the great escape and the next phase of Operation Daisy got under way. Abraham had served his purpose.

Although Williamson was later to preen himself on his successful exit, he did not know that he only narrowly avoided destroying Operation Daisy only days after crossing the Botswana border. Before going into 'exile', he had made a point of maintaining contact with NUSAS anti-apartheid activist Jeannette Curtis. She had married political prisoner Marius Schoon shortly after he emerged from a twelve-year jail term as the victim of a police agent provocateur. The Schoons fled to Botswana, using the escape route established by the police. When, only months later, Williamson staged his own escape, he sought out and stayed with the couple. Ten years later he was to send a parcel bomb to the Schoons, who were then teaching in Angola. The bomb killed Jeannette and her six-year-old daughter, Katryn.

When he arrived in Botswana Williamson played the role of the angry activist, eager to strike back at the system which had victimised him and gunned down so many hundreds of innocent schoolchildren in Soweto and elsewhere. He would, of course, need introductions, especially since he would be travelling to Lusaka to be debriefed by the ANC. At his request, Jeannette agreed to write a letter to Ray Alexander-Simons, veteran trade unionist, communist and confidante of many of the leading figures in the liberation movement, asking her to introduce the new exile to 'the leadership in Lusaka'.

As a young activist new to the exiled underground, Jeannette was not to know that this sort of request was simply not acceptable. Not only did it flout the hierarchical etiquette of the liberation movement, it also contravened security. Although the exiled ANC was often grossly amateurish and naïve in its actions, its senior members did try to adhere to the 'need to know' principle. Williamson's push for a letter of introduction was therefore a blunder, but a relatively minor one. Ray Alexander was merely annoyed when she read the letter handed to her in the garden of the Lusaka home which she and her husband Jack Simons sometimes shared with as many as twenty comrades who were passing through. She thought it presumptuous and silly. But she calmly looked up at the large, beaming man standing in front of her and told him that she did not know any leaders.

Craig Williamson, who was scheduled to leave for London next day, then tried a desperate gambit to ingratiate himself. In an obvious effort to enhance his credibility, he mentioned that Mary – Ray and Jack Simons's eldest daughter, who had recently been banned in Cape Town – had also suggested that he call. This was a major blunder. Mary and her mother did, at various times, send emissaries to one another, and had developed a very strict rule for the identification of trusted comrades. Unwittingly, Williamson broke it. He left empty-handed, and Ray Alexander told her husband and other senior ANC members that Craig Williamson 'cannot be trusted and is probably a police spy'.

Among those who received this information was Thomas Nkobi. He would not accept it. Craig Williamson, he said, was a reliable person who was of great help to the liberation movement. Even husband Jack, who was to receive press clippings and other information from inside South Africa, arranged for by Williamson, felt that Ray's suspicions were groundless. As he had done in

NUSAS, Craig Williamson provided the goods; he did the work while so many others merely talked about it. Besides, it was said, he only worked in a support capacity for the movement; as an aid agency worker, however senior, he posed little danger.

This naïve and trusting attitude allowed Craig Williamson to move freely in exile circles from his base in a comfortable apartment at 29 Rue St Victor in Geneva. He had access to funds and fed them to various projects, especially where new exiles needed assistance. For these purposes he was usually supplied with their names. He was also behind the appointment of Zanele Mbeki, wife of the ANC foreign affairs chief and future South African president, as IUEF representative in Lusaka. She did not know about the trust funds, set up in South Africa by Williamson, which were being used to channel at least some of the available anti-apartheid money to legitimate sources within the country.

Because the IUEF gave funding to exiles, Williamson demanded and got lists of all ANC houses and their occupants. He was even provided with lists of young people trapped in landlocked Lesotho and who required air fares to move them further afield. In Williamson's own words, he was a 'vacuum cleaner' siphoning up, collecting and passing on every piece of paper, scrap of information or whisper which came the way of himself or his wife, Ingrid Bacher. As such, he pinpointed many targets who were subsequently kidnapped, tortured and murdered. He and his wife, who went on to become a lecturer at Williamson's alma mater, the University of Witwatersrand, and a psychiatrist in private practice in Johannesburg in 1999, would sometimes spend nights locked in the IUEF office in Geneva. They photocopied memoranda, receipts, orders and private correspondence, rifling through filing cabinets and drawers. These late-night sessions earned Williamson a reputation within the IUEF as a hard worker.

But the doubts about his bona fides persisted, especially from the South African Council of Churches. That so august a body should have doubts worried Lars-Gunnar Eriksson. Quite chaotic in his organisation, and a heavy drinker with a cavalier approach to financial accountability, he relied on Craig Williamson and trusted him. Yet he still checked. Senior members of the South African student movement, students such as Karel Tip, dismissed the allegations as false. But Eriksson also checked with the ANC, which he thought was the only one of the liberation movements with a counter-intelligence capability. Craig Williamson was cleared 'at the highest levels'. ANC treasurer-general Thomas Nkobi trusted him, as did Thabo Mbeki and his virtual 'shadow' Aziz Pahad.

At some stage over the next three years, some doubt does seem to have surfaced within the ANC even among those who had once completely trusted Williamson. By and large, they failed to see any real problem. 'We get more from him than he gets from us,' Mac Maharaj confided to a fellow doubter. This was probably a reflection of the fact that, since the advent of Williamson, the IUEF had provided substantial funding to ANC projects, as well as apparently steering other funding toward them. Even if Williamson was a spy, it was reasoned, he could not do much damage within the IUEF.

This analysis completely misunderstood the function of the international body and the range of information that came through it, almost all of it passed on to the security analysts in South Africa. In some cases, Ingrid Williamson carried bundles of material back with her when she flew to 'visit her family' in South Africa. The fact that she still possessed a South African passport and was free to come and go rang no alarm bells.

Ingrid, who was found a job with the World Health Organisation by Neville Rubin, was also active in her own right. Although there was little WHO information which was in any sense confidential, she stole or copied anything that might be of use to her spy bosses. She also regularly visited the offices of the International Labour Organisation (ILO), ostensibly to see Rubin. He later noted that some material, including maps, went missing. It amounted to a vast pile of dross, interspersed with nuggets of information, especially names and addresses.

All the while, one of the greatest acts of larceny the security services are so far known to have committed was under way. The prime focus abroad was the IUEF; at home, the various trusts established by Craig Williamson and by Karl Edwards. Williamson also directed other anti-apartheid groups to support either the PST or the ERT. Such an instruction went, for example, to Group 227 of the Amnesty International West German section on 17 April 1977. But this Amnesty group was particularly security-conscious. Its secretary, Georg Sehl, contacted the PST directly through its listed PO Box in Johannesburg. He also tried to check the bona fides of the PST with groups such as the Anti-Apartheid Movement and Amnesty International's secretariat.

Not surprisingly, the newly launched trust was not known, but Georg Sehl noted that the trust sent 'many informations' and appeared to have 'a lot of money'. He wrote back to the IUEF in July, pointing out that his group was 'rather suspicious about this trust'. Where, he wondered, had the IUEF got the address of the PST in the first place?

Williamson's reply was short and to the point. He noted that 'due to the confidential nature of this work, we are not prepared to endanger these programmes by further explaining them'. He added: 'Your suspicions about the Prisoners Support Trust are unfounded and I request that you treat the information already given you about organisations channelling funds to political prisoners as confidential. I am disturbed that you have been making public enquiries all over Europe about this group and I hope that it does not result in the police in South Africa acting against the Trust.' He had informed the trust of the Amnesty group's attitude, 'and they would be glad if you did not contact them again'. So far as is known, it was only the Amnesty group in Neuwied, West Germany, which ever seriously questioned the arrangements made by Williamson. Some of these were blatant give-aways. One note simply listed the recipients for R50,000 of donations as '1. Mr M.P. Asmussen 2. Mrs J.E. Asmussen.' Their address was 66a Smal Street, Johannesburg, the premises of the Danish Confectionery firm run by the Asmussen/Deans family.

How much of the IUEF funding was passed on to Lisa Williamson at the PST/ERT offices in this way is not known. Nor is it possible to know exactly how much disappeared before reaching its supposed destination. Certainly money to pay for cases handled by the anti-apartheid lawyer Griffiths Mxenge failed to arrive on several occasions. This was probably part of a policy of harassment aimed at Mxenge, who was later hacked to death by killers from Vlakplaas. But it was obviously quite profitable as well for those who were siphoning off the Mxenge payments.

Craig Williamson, who dispatched the bulk IUEF payments from Geneva, also profited by sending the donations in South African currency, bought at a discounted rate from banks in Switzerland. He could make as much as 20 or 30 per cent on a single bulk transaction. At least some of this profit was apparently deposited in a slush fund used to pay the spy network that operated in Europe after Williamson's exposure as a spy. It was a widespread operation, which produced a great deal of information of dubious value. Pride of place in security branch mythology was given to the anti-apartheid group established in Spain by Fabio Barraclough/Valls.

As with other agents, the former Wits professor seems to have been regularly debriefed about matters not known to him at first hand. Many of these reports, written by Brussels-based Security Branch husband-and-wife team John and Patricia Adam, were practically worthless and could easily have been culled from newspaper clippings. But there was another level of activity and there were other reports about which less has emerged. John Adam, for example, was involved in the bombing of the ANC London office in 1982, for which he was granted amnesty together with operatives including Johan Coetzee, Craig Williamson and the man who exposed the operation, Eugene de Kock. Over the years in various parts of Europe there were burglaries, assassination attempts, killings, vandalism and attempted blackmail, all of which pointed to the South African security apparatus.

During the bloodiest period of repression in South Africa and terror abroad, John and Patricia Adam were central to South Africa's covert operation in Europe. Adam, a captain in the notorious Koevoet force in Namibia, had been recruited there by Williamson, along with Eugene de Kock, to join the security police group that bombed the ANC London office. After that mission, De Kock returned to northern Namibia while Adam was brought into the new network being set up in Europe by Coetzee. It was in June 1984 that he and Patricia were posted to Europe under cover of running an import-export business in Brussels. They reported to a desk officer in the Security Branch headquarters in Pretoria. They, in their turn, handled 'sources' and agents including Barraclough and the chief representative in the London ANC office, Solly Smith (Samuel Setotane Khunyeli). They also handled Williamson's senior policeman friend in the Netherlands, Colonel Bart de Beaufort, and the Swedish medical academic who reported on the ANC office in Stockholm.

John and Patricia Adam were English-speakers and key to the empire Williamson started to construct after his return to South Africa from Switzerland. This included taking charge of the ongoing Operation Daisy, which he later claimed to have extended to every campus in the land. Ingrid Bacher continued to be active, first at Pretoria University and later as a lecturer at the University of the Witwatersrand. But while the Adams were in Brussels, their sponsor changed tack. Williamson left the police and joined military intelligence in 1985. In 1987, John and Patricia Adam returned to South Africa expecting high praise and promotion. Neither was forthcoming. John Adam kicked his heels in a desk job at security police headquarters before resigning to join the Anglo American Corporation as a security officer in the gold division.

Much of the information collected by the European network was low-grade or useless, but there is no denying that some of it led to a string of official murders and mayhem. Furthermore, resistance had to be fluid: addresses changed and individuals moved. So a number of the bloody cross-border raids approved by the State Security Council killed men, women and children who had little or nothing to do with the anti-apartheid opposition, let alone the ANC or SACP. 'We shot anything that moved,' a special forces officer admitted.

From the security police viewpoint, one highlight of Williamson's career in the IUEF was his knowledge of the movements of Black Consciousness leader Steve Bantu Biko and the intentions of the BC leadership. The police had hit hard at BC, and shattered its organisation – a plan apparently coordinated by Johan Coetzee, making BC increasingly reliant on aid from the IUEF. Through Craig Williamson in his eventual role as deputy director of the funding body and Karl Edwards, who liaised with the PST and ERT, funding was provided for conferences and for fares and transport, subject to proper accounting. And so the security establishment learned that Steve Biko was attempting to unite the various anti-apartheid organisations; that he also intended speaking to the ANC in exile.

Only weeks before his detention in 1977, Biko was arranging through Eriksson and the IUEF London representative, Chris Beer, to meet with Oliver Tambo. This was part of the drive by Eriksson to bring together what he saw as the non-communist resistance. Biko had requested information about possible military training for BC volunteers, and Eriksson scheduled a meeting in Lisbon with Algerian ambassador Mohammed Sahuoun to explore the prospects of such training. Minutes relating to these plans were intercepted by Williamson, and copies sent at once to Coetzee in South Africa. Those minutes amounted to a death warrant for Steve Biko.

Craig Williamson has maintained consistently that he does not specifically remember passing on the information about Biko. He passed on all such information. What came next was none of his business. In another of those glaring lapses that left essential issues unresolved, Coetzee was never asked. Neither was Edwards, although he was the IUEF and Security Branch contact with Biko. Edwards was also linked to the notorious Port Elizabeth Security Branch, several of whose members were responsible for the brutal murder of the BC leader.

The information on Biko was among the more important material culled by Williamson. The IUEF provided no access to the families of apartheid victims and prisoners who were aligned with the ANC and SACP. Most of the support to these families came through the London-based International Defence and Aid Fund (IDAF). Despite continued efforts by Eriksson, encouraged by Williamson when he reached Geneva, to persuade IDAF to amalgamate, or at least to share information, with the IUEF, the organisations remained separate. On one important level this was a result of the Cold War; the tussles between IDAF and the IUEF represented a sideshow in the big bipolar international game.

The accused in the 1956 treason trial in South Africa comprised members and supporters of the ANC, many of whom belonged to the underground SACP. Canon John Collins, dedicated anti-apartheid campaigner and dean of St Paul's cathedral in London, set up a defence and aid fund to pay for the legal defence of the accused and to provide financial assistance to families suffering as a result of political persecution. From this grew IDAF, with its various fund-raising national bodies in a number of other countries. But the national DAFs only raised money, which was sent to IDAF for disbursement. From its earliest days, IDAF employed exiled South Africans in its three departments: Legal Aid (Clause 1), Assistance to Dependents (Clause 2) and Information (Clause 3). Publications research and archive functions also developed. In all cases, perhaps unsurprisingly, given the origins of the organisation, the departments were eventually headed by members of the SACP. Other employees also tended to be SACP members or, in a few cases, members of the British Communist Party.

Eriksson was worried about this CP dominance. In a 'Strictly Personal and Confidential' report to Bernt Carlsson which found its way into the South African security files, he noted: 'apart from Canon Collins himself and his personal assistant, Freda Champion, [IDAF is] fundamentally controlled by the South African Communist Party in co-operation with the British Communist Party . . .' This he saw as dangerous, not because of any knee-jerk reaction to communism, but because of the tendency of the Soviet Union to use affiliated communist parties as instruments of Soviet foreign policy. The SACP and the British CP, he complained to Carlsson, 'belong to the group of completely Moscow-controlled Communist parties'.

What also concerned Eriksson and the small circle of Swedish social democrats around him was the role played by individual SACP members in apparent support of Soviet foreign policy. Some of this social democratic group had influence with the leadership of the Namibian independence movement, SWAPO, and were working for UN action on Namibia. At the urging of the social democrats, SWAPO drew up a compromise resolution to present to the Security Council. It steered clear of direct confrontation with South Africa, which would make it acceptable to the West, but provided for enough direct action to make it acceptable to the Afro-Asian bloc and impossible for the Soviet Union to reject. It would be the third way in operation. But the resolution never made it to the floor.

'At the crucial point, Abdul Minty appeared on the scene,' raged Eriksson about the South African exile he considered part of the SACP 'brains trust', together with SACP chief Joe Slovo and his wife Ruth First. Minty arrived 'behaving as if he was speaking on behalf of all third world countries and liberation movements, but without consulting SWAPO, and presented an uncompromising demand for a total arms boycott of South Africa,' Eriksson added. This made it politically impossible for SWAPO to be seen to be backing away from militancy by putting forward the compromise resolution, with the result that the Soviet Union and the Afro-Asian bloc supported Minty's resolution, which was promptly blocked by a triple veto. Eriksson protested some months later: 'He [Minty] is actively working as a political agent and is single-handedly responsible for having created the US/UK/French veto in the Security Council on the Namibian question.'

Behind this manoeuvring, Eriksson maintained, was the desire of the USSR to block any resolution on the continued illegal control of Namibia by South Africa, which enabled Soviet fishing vessels, along with trawlers from several other countries, to pillage the rich fish resources off the coast. Eriksson did not know or did not care that there were also reportedly agreements in place between the US and USSR. These restricted any military aid provided to the ANC to conventional warfare training, involving artillery and tanks – not much use in the conditions of the time. But for Eriksson the 'extremely intelligent and competent' Abdul Minty was a particularly dangerous agent of the international 'enemy'. That Minty was subsequently employed by Canon Collins as the IDAF liaison with foreign governments was also annoying – doubly so when it emerged that his salary was being paid by the Swedish government.

That IDAF 'under communist control' used its substantial assets to support 'various South African committees, information services and so on' also meant greater influence for the SACP. IDAF itself provided full-time jobs in a key area of the anti-apartheid struggle to SACP members, and this meant greater influence for the USSR and its allies. It was this perception, as much as the current conditions, that drove Eriksson to further diversify funding. Except that almost all the IUEF funding came with strings attached: it was supposed to be used only for clearly stated objectives. So Eriksson, with the help of Neville Rubin, established a company, Southern Futures Anstalt, through which funds were passed and hidden and overdrafts could be used to cover shortfalls. As Williamson was known to boast, 'this was real struggle account-ing', where the books gave the barest hint of the true position.

It was this fact, combined with some shallow analysis of his political orientation, which was to convince Coetzee and Williamson that they could hire Lars-Gunnar Eriksson to work for South African security. The roots of this analysis lay in the IDAF report that Williamson sent to South Africa, but the attempted recruitment came only after he had panicked and blown his cover as a spy.

The IDAF report revealed some background that made the South African security establishment even more determined to infiltrate the organisation. Some two years before the report was written, Eriksson and the Canon had discussed their mutual concern about the degree of SACP influence in IDAF. One result was the appointment of journalist and former ARM political prisoner Hugh Lewin to head IDAF's information department. Eriksson and Canon Collins then met again to outline plans for IDAF that would minimise the influence of the SACP. Hugh Lewin would eventually become the director of IDAF, while Eriksson would take over as president from the ailing Canon Collins. Eriksson made detailed notes of the meeting and mailed a copy to Hugh Lewin at the IDAF offices, but Phyllis Altman, IDAF secretary general and in charge of legal work, opened all mail which arrived there. Eriksson was exaggerating when he later wrote of Hugh Lewin that 'everybody in the secretariat stopped talking to him, in an absolute and literal sense'. Nevertheless, with their plotting Eriksson and Collins had made Lewin's position untenable. He resigned after only three months at IDAF.

Another non-SACP member, Horst Kleinschmidt, also an exile and former political prisoner, eventually succeeded as director of IDAF. He maintained the distance between the IUEF and IDAF, if only to avoid unnecessary problems now that their relations had soured. He saw no reason not simply to get on with the job, much of which entailed sending monthly subsistence grants to victims of apartheid and their families. It was this financial pipeline which the police had longed to tap and constantly failed. But then even the SACP members at IDAF were unaware in any detail of how the system worked. It had grown up through Christian church contacts established by Canon Collins, and while names and addresses were collected, collated and approved at the IDAF offices, it was individual church members and their families who passed on the monthly stipends.

Unlike the IUEF, which on Williamson's initiative had installed a system of trusts designed by the security establishment, the IDAF system relied on hundreds of individuals and families, each dealing with one or two recipient individuals or families. The whole exercise was coordinated by a parish priest from north London who met once a week with the director to pass on correspondence from individuals from as far away as Australia or Canada who were the contacts of one or two victims in South Africa. The priest shipped the money and arranged for new contacts to take on new names when necessary. The various contacts, who were reached through their churches, bought postal orders once a month and sent them to 'their' family or individual in South Africa. When many of these postal orders began to be stolen the matter was dealt with by means of individual governments, at the insistence of church support groups, putting pressure on the International Postal Union and threatening to have South Africa expelled. 'Membership of the IPU meant more to them than the money, so the thefts stopped,' Horst Kleinschmidt remembered in 1999.

The most important difference in the approaches of the IUEF and IDAF was that the IDAF method required no personal contact. There was no Lisa Williamson, Karl Edwards or any other false friend able to use the monthly stipend to exploit the trust of activists and their families.

To Eriksson, who understood that control of resources meant influence, the IDAF system of disbursing aid would almost certainly have made sense had he known about it. He might even have wanted to adopt it. After all, the IUEF pursued the same method for financing the defence in political trials – which was not surprising, since both had basically been set up by Neville Rubin and his father, Leslie, who was also a lawyer in exile. Eriksson's arguments had to do with who got support and, more important, how other funds were spent. The fact that a number of ANC/SACP exiles in London received financial support from IDAF he saw, with some justification, as a way of strengthening the influence and resources of the SACP.

In the global battle, he was against the USSR and its supporters. Just as he was opposed to apartheid and its supporters. He did not see the one as a greater and the other as a lesser evil. Quirks of history might have put apartheid South Africa within the general Western orbit, but just as there were criminals in any society, so too could there be criminal states. South Africa was a classic case. This seems to sum up Lars-Gunnar Eriksson's view of the Cold War and apartheid. It was a view that the South African security establishment found impossible to understand. Likewise, many members of the SACP could not see Eriksson and the Swedish group as any more than 'agents for Washington'.

Craig and Ingrid Williamson fairly quickly exhausted the backlog of information accessible through the IUEF. Thousands of documents had flowed south, where the threat was increasingly perceived as coming once again from the ANC-led alliance, especially with the collapse of the cordon sanitaire provided by Angola and Mozambique. The dream had faded of controlling every aspect of the ANC and its armed struggle and demolishing the organisation from within. Most of the thousands of youthful BC-influenced activists who had fled into exile had found that there was only one organisation able to absorb and deploy such an influx: the ANC had military camps in Tanzania and Angola, farms in Zambia and Mozambique, and access to scholarships.

Its political fortunes soared as the rebellion in South Africa spread; the ANC became the only game in town, one in which Williamson was sidelined. From within the IUEF he could sometimes confirm how many new exiles had stayed where, but what the security chiefs now craved was information from deep inside the ANC. It was time, they thought, for Williamson to use his fraudulent reputation for activism on behalf of the Revolutionary Council to move into real activism, as a member of the ANC armed wing, MK, and hopefully as a senior member of the SACP.

Although Williamson was to write lengthy reports for his bosses after his return to South Africa in January 1980, his views and analysis counted for little if anything: the analyses had already been done and often acted on. Even the snippets of information suitable for future blackmail had been carefully filed. It had been noted, for example, that in 1978 Dame Judith Hart, as Britain's overseas development minister, made a grant to the IUEF of £238,000 for 'Christian care' in Zimbabwe/Rhodesia. This was quite a coup for Lars-Gunnar Eriksson, and witnessed to the obligations felt by members of the Socialist International. The IDAF was also seeking British government aid at the time. In the following year, before the Conservative Party swept to power, Judith Hart authorised a further grant to the IUEF of £450,000. But what interested the South African police was the quid pro quo when Judith Hart found herself on the backbenches. She approached the IUEF on 13 September 1979 for financial help 'to enable me to continue my international work on third world development'. She wanted to maintain the office at her home and her research assistant. In 'strict confidence', and illegally, a £3,000 grant toward Judith Hart's £12,000 budget was paid to the former minister.

The funds earmarked for 'Christian care' in Zimbabwe seem eventually to have reached there, although some of the British money appears to have been lodged for some time in a high-interest account. Like so much other funding, it made its way through the shambles that passed for IUEF accounting, which was bound to be exposed before long, and possibly sink the IUEF. By then, Johan Coetzee hoped that his man at the IUEF would be well away, preferably ensconced with a grateful ANC and SACP. Williamson would not be held responsible, although he had played his part. Lars-Gunnar Eriksson was no bookkeeper and his organisational ability, perhaps hampered by his heavy drinking, was poor.

Williamson was a bookkeeper, and capable enough to compound the chaos to his own advantage and that of the various hands which diverted funds. He, like Karl Edwards in South Africa, often carried large wads of cash. Eriksson too often dealt in cash for purposes such as air fares or accommodation for figures in the exile movements, as well as for unauthorised loans to several friends. He had created the opportunity to divert funds and would be held responsible. Here there was the potential for blackmail that Johan Coetzee would later try – and fail – to exploit.

Under instructions from Pretoria Craig Williamson was preparing to distance himself from the IUEF in 1979 when in an apparent fit of pique a BOSS agent, Arthur McGiven, 'defected' to Britain with a stack of files and began telling his story to the *Observer* newspaper. But McGiven did not mention Williamson. In fact he maintained, even after Williamson's flight back to South Africa, that he did not know that the man who had served on the Wits SRC with him was a spy. Years later, Williamson admitted while under brief arrest in Angola that McGiven had lied. He had stolen a number of important files and fled into exile when he was about to be dismissed from BOSS as a suspected homosexual. Apparently to protect himself after he had fled, he had agreed with a BOSS contact in London that he would not expose Williamson as part of his revelations.

Whatever the truth of the matter, it provided Williamson with a perhaps convenient exit from a spying exercise that could earn him a bullet through the head. He confessed his identity to Eriksson and arranged a meeting in Zurich at which he introduced him to Johan Coetzee, who had flown in on a false passport and brought another for Williamson's use in the name of Jacobus Hendrik Smidt. Coetzee put pressure on Eriksson to collaborate. He argued that 'we are on the same side'. There were threats that the IUEF would collapse, with damaging exposure of Eriksson's financial mismanagement. Coetzee also made it quite clear that Eriksson's wife and family might not survive refusal of the offer. What followed often veered between tragedy and farce and involved Swiss police, British journalists, an alleged MI6 agent and various IUEF employees. It resulted in Eriksson's family going into hiding, guarded by Swedish security, and Eriksson going public to announce that Williamson was a spy.

By then, Williamson was back in Britain as Mr Smidt. He was told to spend a couple of days lying low in Southampton before going directly to Heathrow to fly to Johannesburg. His wife, whom he had left at a health farm on the outskirts of London, would be taken to Brussels. At the airport a nervous Craig Williamson waited until the final boarding call before checking in. Only inside the aircraft did he discover that Ingrid was also on board. She comforted and reassured him. It was one of those shrewd touches for which Coetzee was renowned: it strengthened the bonds of loyalty he demanded from his operatives.

Coetzee had returned to South Africa to oversee the propaganda circus. Since he alone knew where the Williamsons were and when they would be returning, he could not be pre-empted by any other agency. It also gave him time to brief the Williamson and Bacher families and to orchestrate interviews and coverage in the media. It amounted to a major coup for the Special Branch. The opportunity to promote another super-spy myth was also a godsend for the new regime of P.W. Botha. As well as deflecting public interest from too close an examination of the toppling of John Vorster and Hendrik van den Bergh, it promoted an image of security force brilliance under Johan Coetzee in the post-Van den Bergh era.

Once again the reliable journalists, sucking in one or two dupes, did their job. Williamson became a 'super-spy' managed by a 'brilliant' Coetzee, described as 'the Clark Gable' of the security police. On the day Williamson returned and reports appeared in Europe about his spying activities, the security agent and then chief reporter on the *Rand Daily Mail*, Tony Stirling, interviewed former Wits University vice-chancellor Guerino Bozzoli about 'the IUEF claim' that Williamson was a spy. The report, headlined 'Student spy is no surprise – Bozzoli', included the observation that 'Security Police penetration' of campus and student bodies seemed to be 'more widespread than widely believed'. This added to the atmosphere of suspicion and fear on campuses.

Three days later, in a report that lauded Johan Coetzee, Mervyn Rees wrote in the *Rand Daily Mail* that the revelations surrounding Williamson's operation promised to prove it 'spectacular in its achievement'. Coetzee was said to be a 'brilliant and tough-as-nails policeman' who was, at one and the same time, 'an academic with an obsession for knowledge'. Most important, he possessed 'a limitless depth of knowledge about his pet subject and enemy – communist doctrine and dogma'. Williamson was almost certain to be revealed as 'yet another product of the Coetzee school of secret agents'. Over the following week, the myth of Williamson, and the 'QO18 spy' Gerhard Ludi before him, having 'travelled behind the Iron Curtain on dangerous missions' was also promoted. The *Sunday Express, Sunday Tribune, Cape Argus, Johannesburg Star* and other major 'opposition' newspapers all uncritically published the 'super-spy' tale.

White South Africa was presented with two new hero figures as part of a new beginning under the supposedly incorruptible and reformist regime of P.W. Botha. But this was no new beginning; it quickly emerged as prolonging the ad hoc defence of the indefensible that had so paralysed Vorster's administration during its final years. Just like Vorster before him, Botha had to face up to the particular problems set by what had once been promoted as the apartheid dream in action: the Transkei homeland in the eastern Cape Province. Significantly, in 1980, when the military recruited Selous Scouts for its new dirty war detachment, the founder of that notorious Rhodesian force,

Colonel Ron Reid-Daly, took up the post as commander of the Transkei army.

At that time there were fears among the security establishment that a new Soweto was in the making as student unrest erupted in the eastern and western Cape. There were strong familial ties between the eastern Cape with its Transkei homeland and the black townships of the western Cape. Once again, the cornerstone of grand apartheid, Transkei, had emerged as a millstone around the neck of a government still theoretically committed to what had clearly become an unworkable racial master plan.

FILE TWO

End of the apartheid road

History, despite its wrenching pain, cannot be unlived. But if faced with courage, need not be lived again.

– Maya Angelou

1

The model bantustan

The core of apartheid was the concept of homelands or 'bantustans', territories into which the linguistically defined African 'nations' of South Africa were to be corralled. The groundwork for this grandiose and inequitable scheme had been laid by the Land Acts of 1913 and 1936, which provided for reserves or reservations to which the bulk of the black population could be confined, labour reservoirs that would hopefully keep much of it securely out of sight and out of mind.

Apartheid demanded more: not only should each of the designated 'black nations' be housed in these areas, but the areas themselves should become independent nation-states, part of a grand 'constellation' of states on the subcontinent. This was the moral justification for apartheid, the idea behind 'separate development'. Once the mythology of incompatible 'nations' and their definitions was accepted, the concept of separate nation-states became not only logical but also desirable.

The racial moralists among the apartheid traditionalists argued for equipping the proposed 'Bantu states' with the wherewithal to become viable national entities. Total segregation should be the object. Most, however, also considered that the neighbouring and former British protectorates of Bechuanaland, Swaziland and Basotholand should be part of this grand scheme: it was only the perfidy of Britain in acceding to demands for the independence of

Botswana, Swaziland and Lesotho which had prevented their incorporation into larger, more viable bantustans.

In this debate, and contrary to popular belief, Hendrik Verwoerd was a moderniser. He accepted that there could not be total separation; that the economy of South Africa could not survive, let alone thrive, without black labour. A balance should be struck which made the bantustans economically viable enough to house most of the black population, but not so independent that they ceased to need the remittances of migrant labour.

So Verwoerd turned down most of the costly proposals for development contained in the sixteen-volume report of a commission set up shortly after the Nationalist Party power in 1948. The Commission for the Socio-Economic Development of the Bantu Areas within the Union of South Africa tabled its report in 1956. Known as the Tomlinson Commission, after its civil servant chairman, its developmental terminology was adopted. This helped to boost the image abroad of the scheme that centred on a single 'reserve' area: Transkei.

It was inevitable that Transkei, undulating from the high Maluti mountains of Lesotho to South Africa's south-eastern seaboard, should become the focus of the apartheid experiment. Poor, ruggedly beautiful and mainly rural, this 'native reserve' was the only such designated area large enough to be promoted as a national entity. More than twice as large as Wales and slightly larger than the combined area of the US states of Maryland, Connecticut and Rhode Island, Transkei also contained a relatively homogeneous population. If apartheid could not work there it would work nowhere, especially since the other nine proposed 'homelands' comprised more than eighty fragments of land scattered around often remote corners of the country.

For Verwoerd, and for Vorster after him, Transkei was to be the model bantustan, the first 'independent' state within South Africa, and one that would blaze the trail for others, not only within the country but also in what was then South West Africa (Namibia). Such developments would point the way forward to an ultimately grateful world. They would pioneer a system of territorial partition designed to solve the problems of racism and nationalism once and for all, a commonwealth of independent states under what Verwoerd saw as the benign leadership of an ethnically European, Christian National and Afrikaner-led state.

Land area alone however, does not a nation-state make. For all its size and the linguistic and cultural affinities of its population, Transkei contained within its boundaries far more contradictions than the Afrikaner ideologues could iron out. It was already poor, overcrowded and overgrazed before the ravages of Verwoerdian apartheid exacerbated the situation. Formal apartheid merely followed a long history of depredations by settlers and successive governments that had forced the growth of migrant labour.

The custom and practice of big business, driven by greed and oiled by hypocrisy, further embittered the conditions of migrant labour under apartheid. There was no legal stipulation, for example, that ill or aged workers should be sent 'home' with little or no financial compensation to die, or that men should be housed by the thousand in giant, single-sex hostels on concrete shelves. The motive here was profit; questions of human rights, dignity or humanity did not compute. The men housed in brutish conditions in the compounds of urban South Africa came from throughout the country, as did many women who lived in the backyard rooms of white suburbia. Decades of such development had blurred and often obliterated the distinction between peasant and worker.

But many, traditionally, came from the Eastern Cape, from the isiXhosa-speaking areas of the country, which were among the first to receive the mixed blessing of missionary education. This promoted literacy and modern numeracy within the framework of a still largely traditional society. The result was a strong traditional rural base, reliant on migrant wage labour. It also mustered enough reasonably educated individuals to staff the infrastructure of apartheid's first satellite state.

Transkei was where the apartheid experiment began, where it first faltered and where it finally failed. Although mainly rural, with no major mineral deposits or any industrial centres that could not be hived off into 'white' South Africa, Transkei was one of the most politically developed regions in the country. The migrant labour system had widened the vision, experience and expectations of what had been a traditional peasantry in a broader region which also housed the oldest 'black' university, Fort Hare. But the timetable for change was not dictated only by events at home and assessed levels of development. Transkei's accession to self-governing status in 1963 and to nominal independence in 1976 came about under a combination of internal and external political pressure.

As part of a progression towards what it intended to be the eventual separation of black from white within the boundaries of South Africa, the Broederbond planners and their successive governments resolved to strengthen 'tribal' authority in the bantustans. By this they meant that traditional, hereditary, governance, under the indirect control of the NP government should be maintained, reinforced and even, if need be recreated. The system of councils which contained both elected and nominated members, which had been instituted in Transkei in the nineteenth century and had spread around the country, should be ended. This system had failed in its goal of focusing the attention of local residents on their own parochial problems. Instead, the councils had tended to provide a platform from which regular calls were made for wider, non-racial representation in the central parliament.

Some of this agitation also came from traditional leaders who still held office, so greater control of the process of choosing chiefs was deemed necessary. A combination of financial inducements and manipulation of the form of tradition was encapsulated in the Bantu Authorities Act of 1951, which converted traditional chiefs into formal employees of the government, often wholly reliant on state payments. Install these chiefs at the head of communities and they would be obeyed, just as they would obey their paymaster. Unfortunately for the Broederbond and government, only half of this thesis held good: bought chiefs did tend to obey. Their nominal subjects, most of them caught up in the migrant labour system, showed a marked reluctance that often grew to fierce resistance.

It also took time to implement the new system, especially since there were problem chieftainships which had first to be dealt with. However, persuasion worked in a number of cases, as it did in Transkei. There several chiefs and prominent members of the council system had grown vocally impatient about ever achieving representation for themselves and their people in the national parliament, and felt bitterly disappointed with the frankly inferior new system of Bantu Education. They provided a ready audience for the nationalistic case made by the government. If they had full control over their territories, they could introduce whatever schooling system they wished. The new dispensation would also restore the power and status of royal houses and the institution of chieftainship. As a first step toward this goal, all they had to do was disband the council system – the Bunga – in Transkei and accept the new Bantu Authorities system. (This was administered by a department that soon became known by its appropriate English-language acronym, BAD.)

In 1955 the Transkei council dissolved itself and accepted the new system that promised so much. There was a great deal of confusion, but there was one young chief whom government officials had correctly assessed as having the ambition and ability to make him invaluable in the bantustan cause. Kaiser Daliwonga Matanzima was a chief of the abaThembu royal house and the nephew – although his senior – of another local aristocrat, Nelson Rolihlahla Mandela.

KD, as he was widely known, had been a mentor to Mandela at college, but was soon to reveal himself as a master among the stream of often cunning compromisers produced and used by the apartheid system. He recognised behind its professedly noble ideals the unscrupulous drive of prejudice and self-interest, yet he saw how by steering into the vortex of patronage, cruelty and corruption he might further his own ends. This he argued with his young kinsman Mandela, who tried hard to persuade KD not to support Bantu Authorities. Mandela's pleas fell on deaf ears, and he and his one-time mentor went different ways. Nelson Mandela went on to serve twenty-seven years in prison and to become the first president of a non-racial South Africa. KD Matanzima became the first chief minister of the Transkei bantustan and waded deep into the mire of bloody collaboration before emerging into comfortable retirement. He died in June 2003.

But in 1960, with the government showing clear signs of fright after Sharpeville and the protests in Cape Town, and with the ANC and PAC banned, Matanzima was consolidating his grip on what he saw as the apex of political power to which a black man could aspire. Other chiefs too were attempting to assert an often new level of authoritarianism. None more so than Botha Sigcau, the elderly and disputed paramount chief of East Pondo-land. He had been appointed by the government in 1939, ahead of a brother seen by most Pondos as the rightful heir to the chiefdom. Acutely aware that his authority was at best grudgingly accepted, Botha Sigcau sought ways to ensure and extend his power. Bantu Authorities appeared to provide the answer, with the promise of much greater authority for tribal leaders. The problem was that his nominal subjects refused to agree.

Of all the isiXhosa-speaking peoples of Transkei, amaMpondo had tradition-ally been the most quiescent. As a result, their tribal structures had been left more intact than most others. Colonial, union and apartheid authorities tended to focus their attention on those groups which had a history of confrontation, so the tradition of the imbizo, the communal meeting to debate all matters of common interest, with a chief in the role of chairman and arbiter, had been maintained. Wesleyan missionaries in the area were also less encumbered by distant authority. They certainly preached obedience, but they also tended to give their students a sense of self-worth. In any event, until the apartheid government took office in 1948 there was always the vague notion that somehow, at some time, improvement and even democratic change might come.

During the 1950s, as the state refined its bureaucratic infrastructure, such thoughts evaporated. The once quiescent Pondo peasant/migrant worker families began to show signs of unease. The advent of the Bantu Authorities system placed relatively democratic and quite efficient community and judicial structures under the autocratic control of Botha Sigcau, backed by the apartheid regime. Corruption spread fast. Tribal councillors no longer owed their places to the will of their constituents, but to the patronage of Sigcau, who endeavoured to spread the system. Anger erupted when some chiefs turned their backs on tribal consultation. Increasingly, it was the police with their batons and bullets and the apartheid magistrates with their fines and jailings who enforced the will of the new authorities.

By 1960, the majority of amaMpondo had had enough. The government added fuel to the fires of discontent when student activists were expelled from Fort Hare. Firebrands of the ANC Youth League such as Anderson Khumani Ganyile were forced to return home to towns already in ferment. When one of Sigcau's senior councillors refused to attend a meeting called by the community, amaMpondo struck back. The councillor's house near the town of Bizana was burned down.

The government responded with two battalions of troops dispatched in armoured personnel carriers. It was the time of the shootings at Sharpeville and of the emergence in the Western Cape, mostly among migrant workers from Transkei, of the militant Poqo movement. News of these events spread rapidly through the scattered groups of huts on the hills and in the valleys of Pondoland as well as through the rest of Transkei. The presence of the troops increased the anger: barefoot youths and blanket-draped horsemen on sturdy mountain ponies carried news and responses from homestead to homestead, and a vast movement took shape.

Mass meetings were held on ridges and on hill or mountaintop sites where none could come close without being seen. This was the birth of the Intaba movement, a number of whose leaders, such as Ganyile, were also members of the recently banned ANC. Others were associated with the leftwing Unity Movement, but most were not aligned to any specific political grouping. Members of Intaba also sometimes called themselves iKongo, explained by some participants as a reference to the independence struggle then under way in the Congo, by others as derived from the Congress or ANC. Both meanings were probably in use at the time, for it is certain that among the horsemen of the mountains there was a sometimes acute awareness of the world beyond Transkei and South Africa. As the Intaba meetings grew and spread, news of them relayed by police spies and the spies of the chiefs spread alarm through the security establishment.

The presence of ANC members was one factor, the sheer size of the movement a bigger one. The most terrifying aspect for the authorities, however, was the form of the rebellion. Its intensely democratic substance challenged not only the racial mores of the established order but also the basis of tribal and, by extension, all imposed authority. There were also rumblings of rebellion in the districts of Xhalanga and in Thembuland. It was something the government wanted eradicated as quickly as possible and as ruthlessly as necessary. The instructions to wipe out Intaba also provided a good opportunity for the police in particular to practise crowd control and counter-insurgency measures. According to more than 200 statements received by the TRC, detentions, torture, killings and disappearances were key features of the official response.

The police and the emerging special forces elements in the army were able to operate with little danger of political fallout. The remote locale and the reporting restrictions under emergency regulations distanced the world from what transpired in Pondoland in the early 1960s. Even more than thirty years later, at TRC hearings, only general observations surfaced. The smaller-scale jailings, harassment and beatings in Xhalanga and Thembuland did not get even a mention.

Evidence presented at the TRC, however, indicated that the police and military took full advantage of the amaMpondo rebellion as a training exercise. According to Clement Gxabu, who attended a mass meeting on Ngquza Hill near the rural centre of Lusikisiki on 6 June 1960, it was broken up by the use of airdropped teargas and troops. As the police had neither aircraft nor paratroops, the attack must have involved both air force and army, but the army maintains that there were no operations in Transkei at the time. Police records of the event no longer exist, but the police were as sure as memory would allow that Ngquza Hill had been a joint police/military operation.

Nor was Ngquza Hill one of the many secret or unauthorised meetings called by the Intaba opposition. It had been widely publicised and the organisers had invited government representatives to hear the complaints of the community. The crowd gathered, unconcerned, as they waited for official-dom to arrive. They never did. Instead came clouds of choking teargas and submachine-gun fire. At least eleven died. An unknown number of wounded were carried off to be treated secretly. Contemporary reports noted that several of the dead had taken a single bullet to the back of the head. Not one of those who commanded, planned or authorised this massacre has been exposed, let alone brought to book.

Yet Ngquza Hill was only one of many similar incidents, though perhaps the most perfidious and lethal. That year and later the police were constantly active, frequently backed by the military. For some six weeks between March and May 1960, under the heading Operation Duiker, nearly 200 officers and men, using six British-made Saracen armoured personnel carriers, were deployed in Transkei. The defence force admitted that this was followed by Operation Otter, which was headquartered in Durban. On 7 December 1960 Operation Swivel appears to have been a military exercise aimed at supporting the police in rounding up suspected rebels. Thousands of men, women and children were detained and more than 2,000 eventually charged in court. Twenty were sentenced to death and hanged.

Most of those detained were tortured, some of them horribly so. They complained at the time and some complained again during TRC investigations nearly forty years later. Victims told how much of the torture was carried out at a tent camp set up by the police at Mkambati. It was here that sadistic thugs such as Theunis Jacobus 'Rooi Rus' Swanepoel and others practised the cruder elements of their trade, beating and kicking shackled detainees.

On the few occasions when their victims dared to go to court, the cases were dismissed. It was always the word of one former detainee against that of someone like Swanepoel and at least two or three of his cohorts. So far as loyal magistrates were concerned, it was the aim of communists and their liberal fellow travellers to besmirch the name of brave policemen and the force in general. They followed apartheid's rule: believe the police, ignore all other evidence. None, including the judges who sentenced the twenty amaMpondo and the hundreds of other resisters to death on the gallows, have been called to account. Most, like Swanepoel, went on to more senior positions or new careers and to eventual, comfortable, retirement.

The fragments of information gleaned from this brief period in Pondoland alone show how much unfinished business still festers beneath the veneer of reconciliation. On the basis of the evidence it heard and uncovered, the TRC deduced that the Pondoland experience enabled the police to rehearse and develop techniques of interrogation and assassination. Which techniques, and who was killed by whom, where and when, and under whose orders, will probably never be fully known. But a trail of evidence leads to some who were responsible not only for torture and murder, but also for poisoning. In fact, Pondoland may have been one of the first areas in which the military experimented with techniques of chemical and biological warfare, though it is doubtful that the relevant records remain.

Once the Pondoland rebellion had been crushed, the pressure was on Verwoerd to move more quickly with his bantustan plan. Under mounting international criticism, he was only too aware that without a solution the 'native problem' would flare up again with potentially serious consequences for the economy. His vision of grand-scale social engineering rested on the assumption that it would be shared by those who would inhabit the homelands and welcomed by those who would govern them. But right from the start there were deep contradictions. The apartheid rationale of the Afrikaner nationalists was never fully accepted by even the most craven individuals among the elites whom they promoted to govern the homeland territories.

K.D. Matanzima was no exception, but he used government largesse and authority to undermine his own paramount chief, Sabata Dalinyebo, and to consolidate his personal power.

Matanzima accepted the idea of bantustans as the only means to preserve the authority of hereditary leaders like himself. This he equated with the best interests of the amaXhosa, the isiXhosa-speaking people of South Africa. On one issue, investment, he and Verwoerd were in full accord: 'white' capital should be kept out of Transkei. This ignored the recommendations of the Tomlinson Commission, which saw an inflow of capital – largely a 'white' preserve – as essential to 'homeland' development.

The ban on outside investment also ignored the wishes of the main modernising tendency in the Broederbond, whose most prominent representative was academic turned international entrepreneur Anton Rupert. He and other industrialists wanted to expand their markets and to tap into competing labour pools. Verwoerd's refusal to budge was hailed by Matanzima and other bantustan recruits as a sign of good faith. For, as the prime minister's supporters hastened to point out: 'Dr Verwoerd was exceedingly wary of and sensitive to any reproach of neo-colonialism or economic imperialism.' Verwoerd, on one reported occasion, put it more obnoxiously. His embargo, he said, would 'keep the Jews out'.

In any event, Verwoerd had a plan to bridge these countervailing pressures: border industries. His government would provide financial incentives to national and international business to set up industries on the borders of the homelands. These would utilise homeland labour, whose wages flowing back into the bantustan would stimulate smaller industries such as butchers, bakers and other retailers to service the new wage-earners. Like so much apartheid planning, it was superficial. It ignored basic elements such as transport and availability of skills and markets as well as grossly underestimating the cost. In practice, the border industry scheme was a disaster – but not only in terms of attracting industries. The projected two-way flow of labour and wages also failed, with labour clustering close to the industries.

Yet the die was cast. The commitment to independent homelands was complete, and after John Vorster succeeded Verwoerd it appeared to gain greater credibility. Vorster continued to talk up traditional apartheid, especially among the leaders of other African states, but in the wake of the 1974 coup in Portugal and the independence of Guinea-Bissau, Angola and Mozambique those leaders who had shown interest began rapidly to back away. The need to translate the apartheid idea into practice became a matter of dire political necessity. The existing order everywhere in the region was collapsing; Harold Macmillan's wind of change was rattling the doors of South Africa. Before doubt could supplant support for the segregationist proposition among all sections of the white electorate and dilute the strong indications of sympathy from Europe and the United States, a bold move needed to be made: independence must be granted to an internal African 'nation'.

Such independence – allowing for the pursuit of integrationist or segregationist policies – could even damage the professedly liberal parliamentary opposition. It was, after all, the leading Cape Town liberal Leo Marquard who had advanced the notion in 1971 of a federation of eleven 'states' in South Africa. The Progressive Party opposition in parliament, which had once advocated an essentially racist extension of the franchise to qualified 'non-white' people, stood solidly behind the federal proposition. In its ideal scheme of things, segregation of schools, public amenities and residential areas would be permitted. 'Integration will not be forced on communities: but no legislation will be valid that prohibits voluntary integration,' wrote the PP's sole member of parliament, Helen Suzman, in 1974.

Having to pander to a racist white electorate meant that parliamentary criticisms of apartheid tended to focus on practicalities, not principle. It was the substance, not the fact, of apartheid that gave rise to much of this opposition. If, in whatever form, a 'homeland' could be shown to be both viable and truly independent, then the problems of the NP government should vanish. This was the credo of the ideologues, and of a government which had expended massive secret funding to promote the apartheid ideal at home and abroad.

So in order to sway an increasingly hostile world, and once Matanzima's demands had been satisfied, it was decided that Transkei could become at least nominally independent. Scores of invitations were sent to governments around the world to attend the independence celebrations in the 'homeland' capital, Umtata, on 25 October 1976. In the event, only South Africa was represented. On the same day, in New York, the United Nations General Assembly adopted resolution 31/6A, which rejected Transkeian independence and banned all formal dealings with the territory. The rigours and brutality meted out during its gestation ensured this near-unanimous decision: only the United States abstained.

Transkei was stillborn. It was a measure of the government's desperation that prisons minister James – 'Jimmy' – Kruger effectively offered Nelson Mandela his freedom if he would only recognise the independence of the Transkei and agree to move there. Mandela refused. Any hope for an apartheid future vanished. But legacies endured, as they always do. The corpse of the grand ideal continued to be promoted only because there seemed no alternative. It would be some time before the Broederbond modernisers gained the upper hand and managed to stage an exit from this ideological morgue. In the meantime, forces of uncontrolled change had to be kept at bay.

This was a time of merely holding on to power whatever the costs. The state came increasingly under the influence of the military as South Africa entered a decade and more of systematic terror for the oppressed majority. Any who dared to stand up to the decaying monster or were thought to pose a threat suffered often grievous harm. Much of the region was devastated.

All too many tales of this period remain untold, but some emerged from the hearings of the TRC and most of them epitomise the time. Transkei seemed marginal to the dramatic events that unfolded around the country in the years from 1976, but an umbilical cord of migrant labour bound it to almost all the major upheavals. Its founding and failure as a nation-state heralded the dawn after apartheid's long dark night. For Transkei contained all the often conflicting elements that marked the birth and death of the crime of apartheid. It was also sons and daughters of Transkei, of amaMpondo, abaThembu, amaGcaleka, amaMpodomise, amaBaca, amaBomvana, amaMfengu and abeSotho who, as South Africans, played leading roles in the anti-apartheid resistance. Six of the seven members of the underground leadership of the ANC and its military wing, Umkhonto we Sizwe (MK), who were classified 'black' and were sentenced to life terms in 1964, had their roots in Transkei. Five, including Nelson Rolihlahla Mandela, were nominally citizens of that supposedly self-governing homeland. The seventh man, Elias Motsoaledi, came from another centre of rebellion, Sekhukuneland.

For K.D. Matanzima, the sentencing of his uncle Mandela and his radical commoner comrades Govan Mbeki, Walter Sisulu and Raymond Mhlaba, together with the Johannesburg-born Andrew Mokete Mlangeni, was the ultimate vindication of his own policy. The only way forward was collaboration. But it was still a difficult road to walk even for someone as astute and ultimately as ruthless as Matanzima. On a different level he faced many of the same problems as the central government: to balance the demands of traditionalists and modernisers while desperately striving to win majority support.

His brother, collaborator and prime minister, George Matanzima, delivered the official line in 1972 to a group of 'expatriate' soon-to-be Transkeians in Cape Town. He maintained that he and his brother shared the goals and ideals of Mandela and others incarcerated on Robben Island. Where they differed was that, rather than go to jail, they chose to take the longer view and were patiently forging 'the keys to the doors' leading to eventual liberation. Theirs was the pragmatic and ultimately sensible view.

In his sometimes desperate attempts to give some credibility to this perspective and to refute accusations that he was a mere puppet, K.D. Matanzima found it necessary, within the narrow limits allowed him, to provide some evidence of independence. So Transkei dumped the loathed Bantu Education system. It also adopted its own Publications Act and Control Board. Publications long banned in South Africa became readily available in the land of Matanzima, though only because of administrative incompetence and the fact that Reverend Majija was the dominant member of the publications control board. He took to heart the authority delegated to him and, since he was opposed to censorship, especially of any 'educational texts', ensured that no books were banned.

The fact that publications were not banned did not stop the police from raiding homes and bookshops to confiscate material banned in South Africa. They did so regularly. But Majija's stand meant that the confiscations could be taken to court, and the police ordered to return books they had taken and to pay for any they destroyed, lost or damaged. This concession helped to encourage many of the new wave of opponents to Matanzima's rule and to the entire apartheid structure. Neither Matanzima nor his paymasters in Pretoria foresaw this, and the flow of published ideas remained as a chink in the fearsome armour that developed in response to growing resistance. As resistance and repression spiralled, Matanzima, his prime minister brother and the ruling establishment were sucked deeper into the bloody maintenance of the apartheid order. All the same, the personal material benefits were substantial.

K.D. Matanzima had become adept over the years at seizing advantages. When, in 1975, the apartheid state felt itself under intense pressure to demonstrate its seriousness about 'separate development', Matanzima backed off. He would not agree until he had gained more land. So it was that in a give and take of parcels of property, Glen Grey was acquired. So too was Herschel, a mountainous territory bordering on the south-west corner of Lesotho. An unforeseen consequence of this was that it opened a door to escape into, and infiltrate from, Lesotho. For Matanzima it was merely a case of territorial aggrandisement, for Herschel was a classic example of the ravages of colonialism and apartheid.

Well into the later nineteenth century it was a prosperous community of small farmers. In less than a hundred years, it was reduced to destitution. It had become a dumping ground for the old and the sick, a place where women tilled the depleted soil and children suffered the diseases of malnutrition. Younger, fitter, men worked in the factories and mines of white South Africa. After October 1976 it was part of the at least nominally independent Transkei, the empire of K.D. Matanzima. As such, it could provide sanctuary for someone wanted in South Africa.

Rick de Satge, a young environmentalist and anti-apartheid campaigner, was one of those on the run. He lived and worked in Herschel for four years, staying with the Siyatsha family, whose main breadwinner, Mthethonzima, a fit, youthful-looking man in his forties, had left to work as a migrant labourer for a company in Cape Town.

Mthethonzima, whose name in isiXhosa means 'tough law', returned home unexpectedly on the evening of 12 June 1979. De Satge, owner of the only car in the district, was called to the bus stop at the nearby Gugulethu Store to fetch him. There was a heavy dusting of snow on the surrounding mountains and a bitter chill in the air. De Satge noted in the diary he regularly kept:

12 June: Mthethonzima 'returned' today – having become an old man whom I did not recognise at the bus halt, carried to the car, an invalid home with TB, empty wicker basket, two blankets, no laces in his shoes. The silence of the sick man, his children backed against the stone wall of the hut unspeaking, shocked at the break in routine, at the shuffling father supported in the arms of other men; lowered down to the mattress by the open hearth fire hastily kindled by neighbours. His wife is away at a funeral . . .

13 June: The night of the 12th June has been the coldest night of the year. The temperature fell way below zero. The light burned all night in the small hut next to mine. The next morning at dawn many people gathered. The approach of death seems to have a magnetism. People crammed into the hut to hear the last words. I was supposed to take Mthethonzima to hospital but just before we were to leave he changed his mind and called for an old woman to pray for him. By 9:30 he had died.

Such was the lot of many under the laws of the apartheid state. In countless distant areas of South Africa, fresh mounds of earth were continual reminders of the regular interment of the very young and the prematurely aged.

But there were also anomalies. One such was the district of Xhalanga, and in particular the town of Cala at its political and social centre.

2

The Cala connection

Ringed by distant mountains to the north and west, the town of Cala straggles up a hillside some 140 km west of Umtata. Perhaps its only distinguishing physical feature is an extraordinarily wide main road with an incongruous avenue of Australian bluegum trees down the centre. Goats, chased lethargically by spindly-legged herdboys, roam amid the thorn scrub. Everywhere in the surrounding bush, snared on the bone-white spikes of thorns, are shreds of plastic, known wryly in urban areas as 'township flowers', the unsightly gifts of the supermarket age to the rural poor. Everywhere there is dust: in winter and summer, autumn and, especially, spring. Powdery, red-brown dust that vanishes from walls and roofs, trees and bushes only when a heavy downpour of rain sluices in copious rivulets down the unmade roads, making deeper the gouge marks of years and collecting in still brown puddles in the potholes.

But the mud, the puddles and the moist freshness never last long under the scorching sun of an African summer. Soon the dust, scuffed from the flaking cracking mud by hoofs, feet and vehicle wheels, settles again on the town, on to the large, brick-built bungalows on the lower slopes and the homemade mud huts on the rockier ground above. The tender shoots of grass and leaves barely have time to gather their coating of dust after the rain before being eaten by goats, or the sinewy cattle that snuffle along the hillside and are shooed from the small vegetable plots alongside the huts. It is much the same in winter when frost or, occasionally, a light dusting of snow covers the hillside, holding the dust in an icy grip in the brief moments of dawn. Then the sun, a paler but still metallic orb, burns away the blanket of cold.

Here is a place of evident poverty and no obvious wealth; a town barely distinguishable from the many remote and run-down rural hamlets that dot the former homeland areas of South Africa. Yet this is a town proud of its reputation as a centre of intellectual ferment and rebellion. It, and the surrounding Xhalanga district, has produced a disproportionate number of business leaders, lawyers, academics and prominent trade unionists, most of them steeped in the anti-apartheid struggle.

Here, as in so much of South Africa, God and history are readily invoked. But it is the God of paternalistic missionaries and the history of resistance to authority, traditional or imposed. Unlike almost any other area of the country, in memory and oral tradition stretching back into the last century, Cala was never ruled by an hereditary chief. In the whole district there were only two minor chiefs whose authority extended no further than the boundaries of their own farms.

The town and its inhabitants, as well as those who lived outside the two chiefly farms, fiercely resisted the intrusion of 'tribal authorities' when remote colonial and South African governments tried to impose them. These were property owners, farmers and peasants who deferred to no chief. Without such authority they seemed to manage perfectly well. How the people of Cala and most of the Xhalanga district came to this basically democratic dispensation is still unclear. It is part of a long-term study by Cala-born academic Lungisile Ntsebeza, the brother of lawyer and truth commissioner Dumisa.

But the fact is that Cala had a democratic tradition and a broad commitment to education. This was encouraged at an elementary level by the Anglican (Episcopalian) and Roman Catholic churches and, ironically, by the Dutch Reformed church which provided the theological apologia for apartheid. On the southern side of the rutted twin lanes that flank the avenue of bluegum trees is the convent and Roman Catholic mission. On the outskirts of town are the Arthur Tsengiwe school, initially a Dutch Reformed Church secondary school and today a teacher training college, and the Matanzima secondary school set up by the Methodist Church in apparent opposition to the Dutch Reformed institution. In 1998 it was renamed the Bathandwa Ndondo Senior Secondary School.

The founding principal of the Arthur Tsengiwe school was DRC lay preacher Whyte Bafana Ntsebeza, father of Dumisa and Lungisile and their sister Matuse. He became a somewhat reluctant local hero when he walked out of the school while Dumisa was still an infant after the church decreed that a black man could no longer be head. Offered a demotion to deputy under an imported head teacher of the approved pigmentation, he refused even to discuss the matter.

A quiet and quite conservative man, he found himself allied with the many more radical teachers who quit as the syllabus of state-decreed 'Bantu education' slowly entered schoolrooms. Unlike them, he did not desert the system. Schools and schooling mattered too much, however corrupt and distorted the bureaucracy that controlled them.

This attitude – a puzzle to his sons – was the very essence of the man who, at sixty-five, was awarded a BA degree through correspondence. He had taken his junior secondary certificate examinations as a private student and, without benefit of teachers or school, had taught himself enough to attain a senior secondary matriculation. Armed with this qualification, he trekked north to what was then Rhodesia.

Whyte Bafana Ntsebeza went north to gain experience and make the money to marry and settle down. He taught in a school on a mission station run by Garfield Todd, later prime minister of Rhodesia, and whose principal was one of the founders of Zimbabwean nationalism, Ndabaningi Sithole. Another of the young teachers was Robert Mugabe, first president of independent Zimbabwe. Why Ntsebeza left in an apparent hurry is not known, or why he returned with nothing but the clothes he stood up in. It was said he had been robbed on the way home. But another tale was whispered down the years: Ntsebeza had been involved in a strike at the school against the corporal punishment of women and had fled when the authorities clamped down.

The latter tale makes sense; it was the sort of experience that could have inculcated what became a rooted dislike of political action in the elder Ntsebeza. He had fought too hard for what he had to sacrifice it on the altar of some futile fight against a powerful bureaucracy. So he went on to work, together with his teacher wife, Nozipo, at a number of schools throughout Transkei. It was this spirit, as much as that of the more radical teacher-rebels, that enabled Cala and the Xhalanga district to preserve much of its intellectual vibrancy.

The hamlet and the surrounding district were remote enough from the central bureaucracy and had a strong enough intellectual tradition to deflect or block directives from white authority. Parents raised in this tradition brought to bear a culture of respect for learning and critical thought that was boosted in 1963 by the advent of 'self governing status' for the territory. With Umtata instead of Pretoria in control after October 1976, when Transkei agreed to nominal independence, the focus of resistance in Cala shifted to somewhere closer. Even so, there was greater leeway to study and learn. English was the medium of instruction and only one book – *Render unto Kaiser*, a critical study of Transkei president K.D. Matanzima by student activist and journalist Barry Streek – and a published speech by ANC acting president Oliver Tambo were ever banned by the government.

This was the environment in which Dumisa Ntsebeza and his siblings were raised. It also nurtured the academic turned major business figure Wiseman Nkuhlu, who in 2000 became an economic adviser to President Thabo Mbeki, and the eminent trade unionist political prisoner Moses Mayekiso. Here too the student activist Bathandwa Ndondo, a cousin of the Ntsebeza children, was murdered in broad daylight by a death squad partly drawn from the notorious Vlakplaas. The Cala tradition also often spread through individuals who grew up amid the hills and valleys of Xhalanga and moved further afield. The more politically active of them gravitated towards and attracted like-minded individuals. Matthew Goniwe, a teacher from Cradock who met up with the Ntsebeza brothers in Umtata, became a leading figure in the anti-apartheid struggle before being butchered with three of his friends by a government death squad.

Cala's status as a rural stronghold tended to encourage pride and resourcefulness, despite the decrees from distant authority that often washed over it. In other areas the daily humiliations of racist rule and pressures to seize land tended to cripple communities and often to breed sycophancy and self-loathing. In an environment such as Cala the greater self-confidence that thrived among the young propelled the more fortunate and academically inclined to university, and often into outright conflict with the apartheid authorities.

Dumisa Ntsebeza was a classic example. With a brilliant school record behind him, he arrived at the University College of Fort Hare in 1967, by his own account politically naive and academically ambitious. He and his sister had spent most of their early school years in Cala with two young cousins, in the care of an elderly aunt. They looked after themselves and never missed a day at school – a fact their father would check when he, their mother and younger brother returned for each vacation from the latest school with which Whyte Ntsebeza was associated. It was expected that Dumisa, Matuse and Lungisile would attain academic heights. All did. Dumisa became a lawyer, Matuse a school principal and Lungisile a sociologist. But the road was long.

During his first year at Fort Hare, Dumisa Ntsebeza worked hard and listened well. This was a place of intellectual ferment where ideas of liberty were being discussed and news sought and relayed about anti-imperialist struggles; in Vietnam, Angola, and in particular Guinea-Bissau. The students also read the writings of Amilcar Cabral and, of course, Frantz Fanon.

Fanon was an inspiration to a growing legion of young black students struggling to understand their situation and to find a way out of it. He epitomised the fight for national liberation, for black pride and for a greater and more democratic future. The descendant of slaves who became in turn an anti-fascist war hero and major figure in the Algerian war of independence, Fanon was admired and his writings, particularly *The Wretched of the Earth*, were avidly read and discussed by Dumisa Ntsebeza and his colleagues.

Then came May 1968. There was no television in South Africa, but there was radio, and newspaper reports could be read and analysed. The doings of Daniel Cohn-Bendit – Danni the Red – caught the imagination of the students of Fort Hare, who felt bitter about the imposition of another Broederbond principal. J.J. de Wet came from the proclaimed 'Christian National' university at Potchefstroom, one of the intellectual heartlands of segregation. His brief was to turn Fort Hare, alma mater to resistance leaders in many parts of southern Africa, into 'an exclusively Xhosa institution'. The students disagreed and staged a strike and a series of demonstrations on campus.

They were also kept up with events by the numerous anonymous posters, satirical verse and political commentary known as Ndikubhekile, a wall newspaper that flourished on noticeboards around the campus. Sometimes these emerged under the English headings of 'Morally Bound' or 'Morally Disgusted'. By July of 1968 De Wet warned that seventeen 'student leaders' he named would be expelled if there was any more trouble. Among the seventeen was Barney Pityana, later to become a priest, head of the Human Rights Commission in post-apartheid South Africa and head of the University of South Africa. Later the list expanded to twenty-one. The students were outraged, both at the threat of expulsions and at having De Wet dictate who their leaders were supposed to be. They marched on the administration and, reflecting events in Europe, staged a sit-in. The police were called and the expulsions went ahead. The student body was dispirited. They did not know that a similar, much smaller protest was held 'in solidarity' by a handful of white students at the nearby Rhodes University. It probably served to feed police paranoia about conspiracies.

'Some of us felt we had to do something to show that resistance was still alive,' Dumisa Ntsebeza remembered thirty years later. The use of Ndikubhekile on a big scale seemed appropriate. Operation Catwalk was born. A meeting of seven trusted friends was called and all turned up. So did one extra person, the friend of one of the seven. When they met in the biology lab, Zonke and her boyfriend were already there, seated at the table, as the others arrived. 'What is this woman doing here?' Mzamo Tena hissed to Dumisa Ntsebeza as they entered. Ntsebeza shrugged and neither of them thought any more about it. After all, she was the friend of a friend. She was also very helpful, making notes and helping to keep the meeting on track during the debate that followed. When agreement was reached, Zonke put away her notebook and Operation Catwalk began.

Paint and brushes were liberated from nearby Lovedale College. It was a simple graffiti protest, carried out at 2 am on a Monday in late October, but it electrified the campus. It also incensed the authorities to walk past slogans that not only mentioned the Broederbond but also included such blunt instructions as 'GO HOME POTCHEFSTROOM SCUM'. The university had no immediate means of removing the slogans, and for nearly three weeks the seven proudly watched the crowds admiring their handiwork. There was local publicity, and on the streets of the Rhodes campus slogans mimicking those at Fort Hare appeared. They were signed by the 'Provos', leading local newspapers to fear an international conspiracy. The police apparently shared this fear.

It was at this stage that the note-taker left Fort Hare campus for the nearby city of East London. After several days she returned, and within twenty-four hours the campus was abuzz with rumour. Four students had been arrested, all of them members of the Catwalk group. Two days later, after a Saturday night movie at the theological college near the campus and some talk in another friend's room, Dumisa Ntsebeza and Mzamo Tena, two of the three remaining, returned to their adjoining rooms. They had barely closed their doors when the security police burst in with handguns drawn. Donald Card, later to become the mayor of East London and a prominent member of the Democratic Party, together with another SB man called Scheepers, had come for the nineteen-year-old Dumisa Ntsebeza. They hustled him out of his room and he saw Mzamo Tena being dragged from his. Suddenly there were more police. He counted seven. Three cars stood in the road outside the student residence.

Dumisa Ntsebeza felt frightened as he was shoved toward the open back door of a car. 'Here is one who might need some persuasion,' said Card, slamming the door behind the terrified student. Card took the wheel, Ntsebeza sat bolt upright in the middle of the back seat, and Scheepers got in beside Card. Soon they reached the police station in the small town of Alice, across a shallow river gorge from the university.

The car pulled up behind the station. Card switched off the engine and turned slowly round, his left arm leaning casually on the back of the seat. Suddenly, without warning, Ntsebeza was struck by a savage blow to his head, then hands closed around his throat in a strangling grip. Shaken and dazed, he was dragged from the car and into a grimy little room behind the police station. A single electric bulb revealed stains and splatters on the walls.

'Stand against the wall,' Card ordered. Ntsebeza obeyed. He felt the plaster cold against his back. While Scheepers watched, Card moved in purposefully and grabbed the lapels of Ntsebeza's jacket. His face was contorted in rage, but he made no sound as he pulled the young student's face towards his own before slamming him violently back. Again and again his body was slammed against the wall, his neck jolting back and his skull making an almost hollow sound as it struck. If he screamed in pain and fear, he does not remember.

Ntsebeza came to lying on the floor against the wall and was aware of screams and thuds from the adjoining room. Card was bending over him, his hands around his neck, strangling and pulling him up. Ntsebeza, choking, struggled to his feet, only to be tripped. He fell heavily and was kicked in the ribs. 'I am going to kill you,' Card hissed at him. 'I've done it before.' Then he turned on his heel and left the room.

Scheepers, who had not said a word until then, looked resigned as he addressed Ntsebeza in fluent isiXhosa: 'Inyanisile landoda, iyakukubulala' (It is true what the man says, he will kill you). The matter-of-fact statement took on a chilling note when Ntsebeza realised that the screams coming from next door were those of fellow student Mzamo Tena. After Card, Scheepers seemed eminently reasonable. Still speaking isiXhosa, the Special Branch man named all the activists who had attended the Catwalk meeting. Only the note-taker was left out. He knew who had suggested which slogans and who had painted them. It was as if he had memorised Zonke's notes. There was nothing to add. 'You should tell us everything,' he said, 'because we already know all about you.'

Almost without thinking, Ntsebeza responded: 'If you know everything, why are you asking me?' It was a simple statement of bemusement and of fact, but made at the wrong time and place. Scheepers was enraged. He bounded across the room and smashed his hand into the side of the student's face. The calm voice and the Xhosa were gone. He shrieked: 'Just because you are in university you think you are big stuff.' Then, switching to Afrikaans: 'Maar julle bly mos altyd kaffirs' (But all of you will always remain kaffirs). With that, he spat repeatedly in Ntsebeza's face and stormed from the room.

Then there were other policemen. All seemed convinced that the prisoners were part of some wider conspiracy. All of the arrested students were later to report that the police wanted to know about associates. What was their organisation? The only organisation Dumisa Ntsebeza belonged to was the University Christian Movement. Although it had links with emerging student radicals such as Steve Biko and Barney Pityana, it was no subversive or clandestine body.

For four or five hours the beatings and tirades continued. One white security policeman named Davis was not much older than Ntsebeza. He was chattily informal and spoke fluent isiXhosa. 'I don't touch people,' he told the student. 'I don't believe in hurting people.' Like all the others, however, he tried to persuade Ntsebeza to reveal the greater conspiracy. It was frightening and confusing. But Ntsebeza's responses were seen as insolence. 'You are the youngest of the group and the cheekiest, you Cala scum,' noted Card shortly before Dumisa Ntsebeza and Mzamo Tena were pushed outside again and into the back seat of a waiting car. 'It's 180 days for us,' Tena whispered before being ordered by Scheepers to sit on one side of the car and Ntsebeza on the other for the drive to the city of East London.

Dumisa Ntsebeza spent nearly two weeks alone in a cell at the Cambridge police station in East London before being suddenly removed and driven to the nearby Fleet Street police station. There he was left all day in an office. The policemen who delivered him had gone. Nobody spoke to him. He sat on a chair and waited. It seemed as if he had been forgotten. Perhaps no one knew what to do with him. Perhaps he was about to be released. He didn't know, but didn't dare to ask. Then in the late afternoon two more plainclothes policemen, evidently SB (Special Branch), strode in and marched him out to a waiting car. They drove him out of the city and into the police station in the black township of Duncan Village.

Formalities were completed at the front desk, and Dumisa Ntsebeza noticed with a sinking feeling that the dossier with his name on it contained in the section listing charges a single word: sabotage. Then he was ushered into the back of the police station, across a concrete courtyard to a steel door with scuffed paintwork. The key turned and the door swung open to reveal another, barred, gate. It opened, and Ntsebeza was pushed in.

As his eyes adjusted to the gloom he made out perhaps thirty or forty men of various ages standing, squatting or sitting in what amounted to a large concrete box. Two small barred windows high up in one wall were covered by heavy steel mesh that blocked out most sunlight. The only open area was in one corner where a hole in the floor and a chain hanging down off a lever in the wall identified the toilet.

As the door slammed shut the young student found himself the object of silent stares before an older man, obviously the boss, flanked by several lieutenants, ambled up to him. 'Name?' he demanded. Dumisa Ntsebeza stammered out his name and a greeting. The boss appeared not to hear. 'What are you here for?' he snapped. 'Sabotage,' said the student. The atmosphere changed instantly. Other prisoners introduced themselves. Dumisa Ntsebeza suddenly found himself surrounded by an aura of respect that had nothing to do with his education, erudition or grammatically correct speech. He was gallows bait, the top of the penal hierarchy. In addition, he was political. He faced the big drop for resisting authority. 'Hei! Iza kudontsa lendoda' (Hey! This man is going for a long time) noted the boss with a note of admiration.

As a result, Dumisa Ntsebeza did not have to eat the stinking and inadequate police station rations. Other prisoners awaiting trial who received food parcels from their families insisted on sharing their rations with him. Soon he was able to reciprocate. For some inexplicable reason his own rations suddenly improved. He remembered decades later that he had been given the unheard-of luxury of sausages, which he was able to share with cell mates in that fetid purgatory of overcrowding and lack of privacy.

After nearly three weeks in the Duncan Village holding cell, Dumisa Ntsebeza was again called out and put into a car by silent policemen. Two hours later he was back at the Alice police station. The other six members of the Catwalk group were already there. They had been held in police cells in different parts of the eastern Cape. The reunion was shortlived. Donald Card was in charge and he summed up the position.

The seven, he said, could appear in court, where they would be charged with malicious damage to property. There was no mention of sabotage or any other serious offence. Should the students plead guilty, they would be fined and released. It was obvious that he wanted the issue dealt with fast. He even adopted a fatherly tone, and referred to the 'evils of apartheid'. But apartheid, however bad, did not justify crime. With that homily ringing in their ears, the seven were left to make their decision.

The police had made a mistake in assuming that the students were part of a wider conspiracy. That fact had obviously dawned on them and their superiors, so the aim was to tidy it all away. With this in mind Mzamo Tena and Dumisa Ntsebeza argued for a not guilty plea. They wanted to retain a lawyer. Enraged at their treatment and furious at their betrayal, they wanted to make a political statement through the case. The note-taker, Zonke, would also be publicly exposed as a spy. The other five were unconvinced. They felt powerless. Discretion would be the better part of valour. Their votes carried the day.

Late that afternoon, the seven were rushed to a side entrance of the Alice court. The whole business was over in five minutes. The students were ushered before a magistrate, the charge was read, each of them entered a guilty plea and was sentenced on the spot to a R60 fine or 60 days in prison. The official court day was all but over and there was no one present but themselves, the court officials and the police. The seven went back to the cells. Unknown to them, a lawyer from Grahamstown, retained by supporters who had heard of their case, arrived only minutes after the sentencing.

Chief among those supporters was a young Anglican priest and lecturer at a nearby seminary, Desmond Tutu, who was later to become archbishop of Cape Town and chair of the TRC. When he heard about the malicious damage charges he started a fund to pay the fines. None of the students had the money and they faced more time in prison. But they paid what they had – in Ntsebeza's case, R35. Within a day, the Reverend Tutu had raised the R420 and the seven were free, but not to return to Fort Hare.

They were all barred not only from Fort Hare but from any other campus. Tutu had thought it likely that whether the students were jailed or released, they would require help to continue their studies, probably by correspondence. He arranged scholarships from the University Christian Movement for the seven. It was with this knowledge that Dumisa Ntsebeza returned home to face his father. Whyte Ntsebeza was not impressed with what had happened, but he was happy to give advice on how to study privately. Gaining an education was a priority.

Yet the young man who returned from Fort Hare was not the eager young Christian scholar who had embarked not long before on the second year of a Transkei government scholarship. He was, if anything, more intense and determined to find out more about the world around him and the system he was starting to know. He stayed at home studying and earned pocket money working in his uncle's shop some 40 kilometres from Cala. He also devoured books such as Ndabaningi Sithole's *Rise of African Nationalism* and discovered to his surprise that he could discuss it with his younger brother Lungisile.

Just fourteen and at school in Umtata, Lungisile agreed that Sithole was worth reading. 'But there are other books,' he said. Which books he did not detail at the time, but his influence seemed to be the Cala-born lawyer Sobantu Mlonzi, the uncle of a close personal friend, Godfrey Meluxolo Silinga. Sobantu had recently been released from a term as a political prisoner and was held in high respect by several of the growing band of young firebrands in the area. Based in Johannesburg, he returned to visit Cala each June. It was the time of the school holidays and much of it was spent in political debates and discussions with his nephew and friends. Although none of them knew it at the time, this was the start of the People's United Front for the Liberation of South Africa (Puflsa), a grandly named discussion group and embryonic revolutionary political party that provided the basic political education for many anti-apartheid activists.

But in those first years after his expulsion from Fort Hare, Dumisa was not one of the socialist grouping around Sobantu Mlonzi. His precise orientation was unclear: he knew what he opposed, but not exactly what he supported.

Nor was he sure how he should resist a system he knew to be wrong. Like most young people of his generation, he was strongly influenced by the currents of Black Consciousness which eddied through the communities, propelled by news of heroic battles against all the apparent odds by oppressed black and brown people – the Panthers in the United States, the guerrilla fighters of Guinea-Bissau, Angola and Mozambique – above all by the battering of the American giant in the jungles of Vietnam.

Dumisa Ntsebeza completed a BA degree in history and African languages by correspondence and in 1971 followed his father's footsteps into teaching, first at Tsomo and then, together with his father, at a school in Tsolo which was easier to reach from Cala. Father and son travelled home every weekend. The move to Tsolo was significant because of the existence just three kilometres away of the Jongilizwe College for the sons of chiefs and headmen. It was a special project of apartheid, an institution designed with the blessing of the Broederbond as an intellectual incubator to hatch and train a compliant tribal leadership. Its principal, Jan Taljaard, was an AB member and he and the college provided an excellent example of how the best-laid plans of the AB could quite unintentionally be frustrated.

Taljaard, an affable man, was far keener on maintaining a relaxed lifestyle than on supervising details of curriculum. His role, as he saw it, was merely to keep the college running smoothly. Well known throughout the region, as a former principal of the Arthur Tsengiwe school he had earned his reputation for laziness. Nozipo Ntsebeza had taught there at the time, and Lungisile Ntsebeza had been a student there for a year, with Taljaard as his Afrikaans teacher. The Cala connection went even deeper. Almost everywhere Taljaard went, he was accompanied by his driver and personal factotum, a well-built, very dark-complexioned Cala man who was known to everyone by an Afrikaans nickname, Spierewit. This was a play on the Afrikaans words for muscles and lily white. Spierewit was totally loyal to his Afrikaner master, but knew and respected the Ntsebeza family.

Such contacts were to stand Dumisa Ntsebeza in good stead when he later applied for a teaching post at Jongilizwe. It paid no more than any other teaching job, but the much smaller classes would mean less pressure, preparation and marking time, hence more time to read and study. These thoughts were foremost in his mind when he returned from the mid-year vacation of 1973. While he was away he discovered a new direction, a set of potential answers to his questions about the nature of society and how it might be transformed to the benefit of all. He needed time to clarify this new direction that he had happened upon almost by accident.

As a graduate and student of the University of South Africa, the distance learning institution, he was invited to its centenary celebrations in Pretoria in the June and July of 1973. He travelled to the country's administrative capital to discover that students 'of colour' were effectively segregated from the campus. Although they paid the same fees, took the same courses, often came out first in examinations, they had to stay in the township of Atteridgeville outside the city. This situation had been accepted over the years, but now there were complaints. It was a reflection of the time. The black townships were rife with talk of the newly emergent trade unions and of the twelve miners shot dead for daring to strike at an Anglo American mine near Carltonville, west of Johannesburg. Links were being made between capital and state, apartheid and big business, the urbane Anglo head, Harry Oppenheimer, and the former wartime fascist, John Vorster, and his thuggish police.

It was against this background that Dumisa Ntsebeza left Atteridgeville to visit his younger brother and his friends in the dusty, treeless sprawl that was and is Soweto. Lungisile, Godfrey Silinga and another young friend had travelled up from Cala to stay with Godfrey's uncle Sobantu Mlonzi in his two-room 'matchbox' house in the Mofolo East section of the township. They came to listen, to debate and to learn. Dumisa joined this intellectual coterie, reading, arguing, eating and sleeping in the one small concrete-floored room that served as kitchen, living room, debating chamber and guest quarters. This was his introduction to the ideas of socialism, the writings of Marx and Engels, the concept of the widest possible social and economic democracy. Although the texts were banned, Mlonzi had some available. When he didn't, his phenomenal memory could source ideas to authors from Rosa Luxemburg to Leon Trotsky. It was a turning point.

Dumisa was impressed with Mlonzi and began to consider a legal career; it seemed a useful way of fighting the system. He had also begun to believe that Black Consciousness, which had earlier proved so appealing, had over-emphasised race and colour. It was class that seemed to matter. BC also seemed to lack a clear strategy. It offered slogans when what was needed was education – not the predigested, narrowly focused schooling delivered from above, but encouragement to critical thought that could lead to meaningful action. When Dumisa Ntsebeza left Johannesburg to return to Tsolo it was with a commitment to find work that allowed more time to study, and to build an organisation to spread the ideas of liberating humanity. Puflsa had started to take shape.

Jongilizwe offered the opportunity for study and reflection, so Ntsebeza applied to teach English and history to the putative traditional rulers of Transkei. He was accepted, but also offered the post of assistant boarding master. It meant free board and lodging in exchange for spending one weekend a month at the school. 'If you are half as good a teacher as your mother, I'll be happy,' Taljaard announced as he, with a broadly grinning Spierewit in the background, welcomed Dumisa Ntsebeza as the newest staff member at the Jongilizwe College for the sons of chiefs and headmen.

He was delighted when the keen young teacher jumped at the additional responsibility of handling the daily current affairs lesson and volunteered to take charge of the library. For Taljaard, 'Mr Ntsebeza' was a find, even if his sartorial style was unorthodox. He affected a dress code that seemed informal, even flamboyant, but he was very popular with the students. His denim dungarees and dark glasses caused the students to dub him Cat – 'the coolest cat we'd ever seen'. With classes as small as five students and none larger than twenty-four, Ntsebeza was in his element, even if the students were the offspring of the local, and now compromised, aristocracy.

To Taljaard's delight, he also took over the ordering of publications for the library, many of which were devoured to provide background for the suddenly popular current affairs sessions. These took place every morning and entailed listening to the radio news and the subsequent commentary by a promoter of the apartheid order before discussing the broadcast. Ironically, one major source for reliable information was the magazine *To the Point*, sponsored secretly by the South African Department of Information. To make it seem halfway legitimate, 'Info' had to allow *To the Point* to carry a range of material seldom found in local publications reluctant to transgress the host of security laws. Dumisa Ntsebeza and his students noted the subtle propaganda: they could read between the lines. The discussions were lively, the students obviously bright and interested. Jan Taljaard was pleased.

Outside the college, much of the next year and more was spent in shabby rooms, student residences and community halls, debating and arguing. There was interest in ideas of a revolutionary transformation of society, but it was among young men and women scattered around Transkei and beyond. Transport was a major problem. Lungisile had bought a car in 1975, but they needed another vehicle. Working at Jongilizwe, Dumisa did not earn enough to buy a vehicle and none of the others had prospects of earning much money, so he resigned from the college and took up a job at twice the salary at the Standard Bank in Umtata.

A year later, he had enough money to buy a small secondhand pick-up truck, one of the ubiquitous 'bakkies' of South Africa's rural roads. Time now became the priority, so he resigned from the bank and reapplied to join Jongilizwe College. Jan Taljaard was only too pleased to welcome the bright young teacher back. So too were the students. Dumisa Ntsebeza shared their enthusiasm, but not for the college's sake. His interest was in the long school holidays.

Dumisa Ntsebeza's battered brown bakkie was to provide transport to innumerable small gatherings of interested, mainly young, people. It made its dusty way along mostly unpaved roads from one end of Transkei to the other. Puflsa was established and was starting to grow. It promoted the idea of a society that would liberate humanity, one that would allow the maximum possible democracy, the maximum possible choice. There seemed to be no current models. The dreams of the European Enlightenment and the optimism of the early socialists seemed to have run aground on the rocks of self-interest and nationalism. Yet such dreams and such optimism still seemed valid and attainable, despite the confusion created by the so-called 'socialist' states.

The problem was charting the path. This meant critically analysing the ideas and practice of the past in order better to understand the present and so to plot a course to the future. In the meantime a barrier loomed: apartheid. The group dismissed bombs and insurrection, not for any moral reasons but because the tactic would not work. The way forward was education: to develop the skills of critical analysis, and waken that dormant will to question which they felt resided in the mass of oppressed and exploited humanity.

They would help to light the spark of self and class awareness, so that a democratic mass movement could usher in a new world, discarding the relic of apartheid on the way. The only prerequisite was that it had to be a home-grown, home-based movement, so exile was out of the question. This was their mission, and they took to it with a dedication remembered nearly thirty years later by Dumisa Ntsebeza's students. One of them was Bantubonke Holomisa, destined to become an army general, military ruler of the Transkei, a deputy minister in the first ANC government and the co-founder of the opposition United Democratic Movement. Although he had graduated from the college in 1975, he and other former and later students could describe as vividly as the class of '76 the day when Louis le Grange came to visit Jongilizwe. The story has assumed almost legendary proportions.

Louis le Grange, Broederbonder and deputy minister of information and the interior, arrived unannounced at Jongilizwe College in April 1976. An impressed Jan Taljaard ushered him in to the history class. The teacher was Dumisa Ntsebeza, the subject the rise and fall of the Portuguese empire. Dumisa Ntsebeza was decidedly not impressed, but he was worried when the principal introduced the deputy minister.

Angola was the topic at the time, among both students and staff. The government position, reiterated constantly on the official radio, was that there were no South African troops in the former Portuguese territory. But the students at Jongilizwe had access to uncensored foreign news magazines and to the government's subtle propaganda magazine *To the Point*. Even *To the Point* had implied that there were South African troops in Angola and that they had been forced to beat a retreat. Ntsebeza's silent hope that the principal and the minister would simply leave quickly faded. Taljaard was desperate to impress. Le Grange, all magnanimity, was introduced to the class.

Then came the moment the young teacher knew, with a sense of both pride and foreboding, was probably inevitable. Questions to the minister were invited. Hands shot up. The first question saw Le Grange's demeanour change. How was it that Cuban troops had apparently 'made mincemeat' out of the South African army? The minister visibly blanched and then retorted angrily: 'Let me tell you, South Africa's involvement was limited. If we had gone into Angola in full strength we would have been in Luanda in a week.'

There was an almost unanimous exclamation from the class. So the minister admitted it? There were South African troops in Angola.

Taljaard beamed as he escorted the minister and Dumisa Ntsebeza from the class. Were these not truly bright students? Leaders in the making? 'They seem very well informed,' Le Grange answered curtly as the party made its way to the library. Dumisa Ntsebeza began to feel decidedly nervous, a feeling reinforced when they entered the library. Nearly thirty years later he could still recall the look on Le Grange's face as he scanned the array of publications in the library. 'The students read all of these,' Taljaard announced proudly, 'and it's all thanks to Mr Ntsebeza here.' Le Grange looked over at the young teacher, who smiled wanly and shrugged. A thin smile flickered on Le Grange's lips. 'All of these?' he noted almost absently. Turning to Dumisa Ntsebeza, he almost hissed: 'Small wonder those questions.' Then he nodded, turned and left the room, followed by Taljaard, still enthusiastically singing the praises of Jongilizwe, the students and Mr Ntsebeza.

Two months later, Dumisa Ntsebeza was in jail, detained without trial. So too was his brother, along with Godfrey Silinga and the young teacher and community activist from Cradock, Matthew Goniwe. It was just days before the massive student explosion of 16 June 1976. Michael Mgobozi and most of the Puflsa activists, together with many others, were also taken into detention in the days and weeks that followed.

3

The trial of the 'Puflsa Five'

The 'Puflsa Five' were arrested as the world of South African prime minister Balthazar John Vorster began to tilt out of control. Images of school students armed with sticks, stones and dustbin lids facing the armoured cars and paramilitary might of the South African police galvanised world opinion. Although the five men detained knew nothing of the eruption in Soweto, they knew that the wounds the South African state was nursing went much deeper than just another slide for its international image.

Most of white South Africa was only vaguely aware in the 1970s of the wars of independence raging in the Portuguese colonies to the north. Few knew or cared where Guinea-Bissau and the Cape Verde islands were. As for Angola and Mozambique, the Portuguese had always been able to handle their natives. A few troublemakers, armed and incited by an undefined demonic entity known as 'the communists', would be eradicated sooner or later.

In marked contrast, in schools, colleges and universities attended by black students these African countries and the struggles within them often formed the focus of discussion. Student orators such as Abraham Tiro, murdered by a parcel bomb in Botswana in 1974, and Steve Biko, who suffered a prolonged and horrific death in police custody in 1977, spread the word about these struggles in candle-lit huts, mass student meetings and every venue in between. They spoke of noble fights for freedom against Portuguese imperialism in Africa and US imperialism in South-East Asia.

Above all, they promoted what they termed Black Consciousness. This concept surfaced among black students on university campuses and gave rise to the South African Students' Organisation (SASO). It was a breakaway group formed by the victims of apartheid from the National Union of South African Students (NUSAS), a mainly English-speaking organisation dominated by the more liberal wing of the beneficiaries. By 1970 SASO, and its most prominent member Steve Biko, were part of a rapidly evolving political current.

At first the Broederbond and the security establishment were not sure how they should deal with this phenomenon. According to the simplistic theory adhered to by most government agencies, for black university students to have split from their white counterparts and set up an all-black organisation was a welcome development. It was hailed as such by the Afrikaner Studentebond (ASB), the segregationist student organisation of Afrikaans-speaking whites.

At a conference at the University of Cape Town in January 1971, the ASB saw in SASO a parallel movement. Johan Fick of the ASB pointed out that 'Afrikaner' students had decided to separate themselves from the 'English' in 1933. The existence of SASO, he said, made the claim of NUSAS to be nationally representative even more tenuous. 'I hope that SASO will grow to the benefit of the students it represents,' he added. Here, organically, apartheid seemed to be growing just as Verwoerd and other believers had always assumed it should. Such naïve hopes soon evaporated as the reality of the SASO position finally dawned on the ASB, for SASO's politics were the antithesis of the dogma of separate ethnicity.

At the 1971 conference, which brought together representatives from NUSAS, SASO and the ASB, Steve Biko clarified the SASO and Black Consciousness perspective. Black Consciousness 'made the blacks sit up and think again', he said:

It heralded a new era in which blacks are beginning to take care of their own business and to see with greater clarity the immensity of their responsibility. The call for Black Consciousness is the most positive call to come from any group in the black world for a long time. It is more than just a reactionary rejection of whites by blacks.

The quintessence of it is the realisation by the blacks that, in order to feature well in this game of power politics, they have to use the concept of group power and to build a strong foundation for this . . . The philosophy of Black Consciousness, therefore, expresses group pride and the determination of blacks to rise and attain the envisaged self. At the heart of this kind of thinking is the realisation by blacks that the most potent weapon in the hands of the oppressor is the mind of the oppressed. Once the latter has been so effectively manipulated and controlled by the oppressor as to make the oppressed believe that he is a liability to the white man, then there will be nothing the oppressed can do to scare the powerful masters.

Hence thinking along lines of Black Consciousness makes the black man see himself as a being, entire in himself, and not an extension of a broom or additional leverage to some machine. At the end of it all, he cannot tolerate attempts by anybody to dwarf the significance of his manhood. Once this happens, we shall know that the real man in the black person is beginning to shine through.

Biko, SASO and BC were certainly not in the business of creating or accepting ghettos in which to proudly seal themselves off. They were out to scare their powerful masters and to seize what was rightfully theirs. Close examination of the utterances of Biko in particular revealed that the strong stress on pigmentation was largely a reflection of passing South African political reality – a tactical step. Hence Biko, the BC philosophy and its various offshoots quickly joined the list of enemies of the state.

Although formal organisations existed, BC also seemed capable of spreading in a manner impossible to monitor. Some of the security establishment likened this proliferation of social resistance to the way the mutant viruses cultured in the secret laboratories of the apartheid state multiplied, spread and mutated. The state hit out, but blindly, its efforts often futile. A realisation of potential collective power was growing in all strata of the oppressed. In every protest, strike, riot, uprising or militant demand over the next decade and more, BC was present and often dominant.

The collapse of the Portuguese empire, brought to its knees by African guerrilla movements, fed all of these sprigs of opposition. The white community had lived for years on a myth of European superiority, ignoring the facts on the ground. Now that the myth had been punctured, among the politically aware minority, mainly among the black population, there were ecstatic feelings often almost religious in their intensity, the sense of a new world in the making.

The retreat of the South African army from Angola lifted hopes and spirits even more. The 'Boer' army, once endowed with an aura of invincibility by supporters and victims alike, could be beaten by black brothers and sisters. Even in the dustiest and most derelict of townships there was a scent, however faint, that victory in the battle against apartheid was actually possible.

There was also the discovery of recent history, talk again of the ANC and the PAC, of the Freedom Charter and the South African Communist Party's programme. But these were, in the early 1970s, still eddies amid the winds of Black Consciousness. There were whispers, too, of revolutionary socialism and these seemed to be growing, fanned by the emerging trade union movement.

Outside the mainstream of BC and the slowly strengthening links with the exiled movements, there were a number of small groupings emerging, among them Puflsa. These looked beyond the struggle against national oppression and talked of the South African system not as apartheid but as apartheid-capitalism. Groups such as Puflsa also talked of international socialism, but looked neither to Moscow nor Beijing. Internally based, Puflsa was aware and supportive of the emergent trade unions, but had no contact with them. Nor was it linked to any of the exiled groups, and was therefore seen both by the state and the exiled groups as a 'loose cannon'.

To the security forces, certainly at the operational level, any political group which seemed – or placed itself – to the left of the 'terrorist' ANC, let alone the SACP, looked plainly bent on violence at its worst. While it seems certain that the more senior analysts within the apartheid system understood the power of ideas, those lower down the scale equated Left and Right with a fanatical willingness to use violence. Violence from the Left was identified with chaos; violence from the Right with keeping order. So the security forces sought for weapons and for details of plots to murder and maim, to poison and cripple: the mirror of the state's own behaviour and policies.

Known activists waited for the midnight knock on the door or the sound of it being kicked open. Or else they fled. Those who stayed hoped only that they would not disappear without some witness present; people who would note where they had gone and who had taken them. It was the best – the only – insurance against possibly disappearing for good. So when three security police barged into the Jongilizwe College for the sons of chiefs and headmen in the afternoon of 11 June 1976, Dumisa Ntsebeza was almost relieved. He had been expecting trouble ever since Louis le Grange's visit.

In any event, there had been police surveillance when he attended some meetings, and Puflsa's nerve was further tested when one of its members at Fort Hare confessed to being a security police spy. As a result, the group had discussed the possibilities of arrest, detention or exile. They had decided that even a fifteen-year prison term would be preferable to leaving the country. Besides, for a discussion group, prison did not seem likely. All the same, Ntsebeza felt it was only a matter of time before he was picked up, if only for questioning.

On 11 June, the time was up. Although the police assured him, as they did as a matter of coached routine to all those to be detained, that he would be 'back again soon', he knew it might be weeks or even months before he re-emerged. He was certainly going to miss his sister's wedding, due next week.

As the shocked teaching staff looked on, Dumisa Ntsebeza was escorted out to a waiting car. 'Look after my stuff, it's going to be a long time,' he called out. They were the last words he would speak as a free man for the next five and a half years.

A new Section 6 'terrorism' detainee, he was taken first to the security police offices on the fourth floor of a commercial bank building in Umtata, where a Colonel Dreyer demanded in Afrikaans: 'Where are the weapons?' The worst part of the time spent with Dreyer and his cohort was when he saw his sister Matuse brought in. She had little interest and no involvement in her brothers' political theories and activities, but she had been observed welcoming them into her house one Sunday after a Puflsa meeting. They had stayed for lunch – a gesture that cost Matuse hours of solitary confinement interspersed with interrogation.

But these details Dumisa only discovered after he emerged from Libode prison, some 20 km outside Umtata. This squat old building had served as the local lock-up for many years and bore the grime of decades. A single tiny cell in the isolation section was to hold him for the next three weeks. He was escorted by sneering guards down echoing corridors over polished concrete floors, the clang and rattle of steel doors and grilles signalling his progress. Then he was inside.

The door slammed shut, the key turned, and there was a quick double scratching sound as the cover over the judas peephole in the door was lifted and fell back into place. Then there was the sound of retreating footsteps. Although it was a bright sunny day outside, the cell was chilly, the gloom made more oppressive by the dark walls. There was no light; no sign of any electricity. In the corner stood a bucket, the toilet arrangements; on the floor a tin mug containing water. Also on the floor was a single rectangle of felt, about 25 mm thick, with two dark grey blankets folded neatly at one end. There was a musty, dank smell about the place.

On that first day Dumisa Ntsebeza did not eat. He could not. The food smelled foul and the metal plate looked dirty. Only when hunger finally numbed his other faculties did he start to eat. But he had to sleep and the nights were cold, so the felt mat and the blankets could not be avoided. The mat did not seem to lessen the hardness of the floor, but at least it reduced the bone-chilling cold rising through the concrete. There were marks on it too, of what he did not know. It was the same with the blankets. Two standard-issue prison blankets, grey. They were stiff and scratchy and smelled of vomit and urine, relics of who knew how many incarcerated souls. But he was not alone. Others were held in similar solitary cells.

Welcome whispers floated down the empty corridors after the guards had gone. A number of PAC people had been arrested. Somebody was also sure that Dumisa's brother Lungisile had been picked up. But everything outside this squalid, claustrophobic little world seemed light years away. Brief respite came when an exercise period was announced. There was supposed to be one of an hour every day, from Monday to Friday, which would allow the prisoners to take a cold shower and to walk in an anti-clockwise circle around a small enclosed yard. But the warders often forgot or ignored the requirement.

After three weeks Dumisa Ntsebeza was ordered out of his cell, back through the gates and grilles, and bundled into a car. He was driven back toward Umtata, to the still incomplete and brand-new Umtata Central prison, an independence gift to Transkei from the South African government. At least it was clean. And there was light, although the single neon tube hummed incessantly, and after a month the cold silence of Libode sometimes seemed preferable. But the isolation cells were larger and Lungisile was there. Soon to join them were ex-Robben Island prisoners Fikile Bam and Clarence Makwetu (later the leader of the PAC). There was also much more time to exercise. The Ntsebeza brothers revelled in this, reasoning that they would at least emerge extremely fit. But they were not released.

On 18 October 1976, Dumisa Ntsebeza as accused number 1 stood with four co-accused – Lungisile Ntsebeza, Godfrey Silinga, Matthew Goniwe and Michael Mgobozi – in the dock of the Umtata supreme court, Chief Justice George Glaeser Anderson Munnik presiding. They were charged with 'furthering the aims and objectives of communism', which implied support for an armed struggle. The case was immediately adjourned to give the accused time to find pro deo counsel, since the charge was a capital offence. It was only then, faced with the prospect of death, that the young men came to take the charges seriously. Thirty years later Dumisa Ntsebeza remembered that he and his co-accused had not even conceived of the possibility of facing the gallows. Until then, their tangle with the law had seemed something of a laughing matter: the state exerting draconian powers against non-criminal actions. To think – to promote critical thought and concepts of extended democracy – might not be liked, but it was not illegal. The prospect of being among the first to take a final walk through the brown-painted door that led to the brand-new gallows at Umtata came as a sobering shock. But soon there were other matters to distract them from morbid speculation.

The accused were remanded to Libode prison, to the packed holding cells with sentenced criminal prisoners. Here assaults were routine. Warders armed with short sjambok whips, or sticks or canes, provided a gauntlet through which prisoners had to pass on the way to and from the stinking ablution block or the exercise yard. Whipping, interspersed with kicks, seemed to be an almost bored, reflexive action on the part of many warders; others enjoyed the experience.

Brutality was also encouraged among the prisoners, with control in the vastly overcrowded prison maintained largely by bullying and in-fighting among themselves. It was this aspect Matthew Goniwe tackled first. He spoke with care and patience to the convicts. The 'politicals' – who were also, in their own words, 'super fit' as a result of their rigorous training schedules while in detention – carried more than moral authority. They were listened to and Goniwe's advice was largely heeded. The young Cradock schoolteacher also demanded to see the administration to highlight the fundamental message that prison was punishment and did not exist for punishment to be meted out. Conditions improved.

Then there were the consultations with the lawyers. The state case was to be based on the piles of literature seized by the police. Prime document among these was *The Organisational Tasks,* by Sobantu Mlonzi, which spoke of the need to educate and agitate among the poor and dispossessed and build a strong revolutionary organisation within South Africa. All copies were confiscated and destroyed. There were also books by leading German/American leftwing academic Herbert Marcuse, Lenin's essays 'What Is to Be Done?' and 'State and Revolution', a book entitled *The Essential Left* and even Alexander Solzhenitzyn's *The Gulag Archipelago.* This radical study group, which was reading classic Marxist texts as well as critiques of 'communist' practice, was to be portrayed as a revolutionary organisation hellbent on the violent overthrow of the state.

This in itself raised an interesting technical point: the five had been arrested and the charges formulated in South Africa, under South African law. Yet they were now being tried in a supposedly independent Transkei. Munnik, transformed into the 'Chief Justice of Transkei' – he was later to become Judge President of the Cape Provincial Division in South Africa – was indifferent to such quibbles. The charges stood, along with the possible penalties. The state would bring an expert witness in the theory and practice of Marxism and communism to testify that its charges were valid. He was Professor Stoffel van der Merwe of the Rand Afrikaans University in Johannesburg, who subsequently became a minister in P.W. Botha's cabinet.

His grasp of the topic was expected to be slender and confused. Expert refutation was necessary. But who could provide it? The first choice was the Durban academic Rick Turner, who fell victim to a death squad outside his home less than two years later. But Turner was under house arrest. Special permission was refused.

Rick Turner suggested André du Toit, from the country's leading Afrikaans university, Stellenbosch. Dumisa Ntsebeza in particular was horrified at the suggestion. An Afrikaner academic and one from Stellenbosch was bound to be a disaster, biased and racist, with a closed mind. Certainly not a real academic in the grand Socratic tradition. But André du Toit turned out to be precisely what all the accused agreed was a 'real' academic. His dispassionate dissection of political texts and refutation of Van der Merwe's shallow propaganda and the equally inane and bullying interjections of the judge created a lasting effect on the accused. It certainly saved them from the possibility of a death sentence.

The experience changed the lives of the Ntsebeza brothers. Du Toit's testimony inspired Lungisile to reject accountancy and switch his interests to political science and philosophy. Dumisa was persuaded finally to pursue the law as a career. He had become acutely aware that the system that oppressed him and the vast majority of South Africans adhered to the form of parliamentary democracy. Even the most apparently arbitrary actions had to be justified, somehow, by the law. He decided to play the game; to become a lawyer and fight an unjust society on the basis of the rule of law it purported to uphold. This, he felt, would give at least some of apartheid's victims more of a chance. It would be a future to strive for, if indeed he had any future beyond a few months.

With the prospect of death hovering on the legal margins, such planning for the future in the early days of the trial acted as a talisman to ward off morbid fears. As the legal duel progressed, however, the prosecution case became increasingly exposed as a flimsy farce. Long-term plans began to look achievable. Du Toit had clearly shown that remarks such as 'the days of peaceful pleading are over' did not constitute a call for armed rebellion; that what the group was involved in was an often intense dissection of society. Its object was to find some clear way out of the social and economic morass in which most of humanity was stranded.

On Wednesday, 31 August 1977, the trial was over. Judgement would be handed down on the following day. When it came, it was a mild shock: guilty. Then came the sentence: four years' penal servitude for the Ntsebeza brothers, Godfrey Silinga and Matthew Goniwe, a suspended sentence for Michael Mgobozi. As political convicts, the four men jailed would receive no remission. In terms of the evidence offered and its conduct, the trial was such a patent farce that an appeal would be sure to succeed. But the right to apply for leave to appeal relied, in the first place, on receiving the written reasons for the guilty decision from the judge. In the meantime, the four convicted men were sent to jail. Not to Robben Island, where all other South African and Namibian prisoners of officially darker pigmentation were sent, but to Umtata.

There was national pride at stake for Kaiser Matanzima. 'These are ours,' he announced. So three of the four new political convicts were housed in the single cells for female condemned prisoners, on one wing of death row. A corridor separated it from the male section. Matthew Goniwe, who had been diagnosed with tuberculosis of the spine, went to the prison hospital, where he was to remain for twenty-three months.

Munnik's written judgement was expected by November. When it failed to appear before the long Christmas break, there was little prospect of starting the appeal procedure before the new year. The application for leave to appeal was eventually lodged on 12 February 1978 – again with Judge Munnik. He reserved his decision in order, he said, to consider the issue more fully. If he rejected the right to appeal, the matter could be taken to higher levels. If he granted it, the case would go to the appeal court, where there was a good chance that it would be thrown out, if only to preserve the academic reputation of the appeal judges. Everything relied on Judge Munnik, and Judge Munnik was in no hurry.

The weeks of waiting dragged on into months. The regime on death row, where the lights stayed on for twenty-four hours a day, was also maintained, although there were no condemned female prisoners. But there were men in the other wing, waiting their turn with the hangman. He made regular visits over the next four years, and all through that time there was at least one of the politicals present in the female section. For nearly three years the Ntsebeza brothers and Godfrey Silinga kept their silent vigils on those days. It was always the same, although the first hanging remained the clearest memory.

Awareness that something out of the ordinary was about to happen came at 5 am on a Tuesday, shortly after the four-year sentence had started. From the male wing, the hymns and doleful counterpoints began. Two warders who used the kitchen at the end of the row of cells that housed the three 'politicals' chatted loudly as they prepared the final meal for the condemned. 'Well, we'll be getting rid of . . .' the name became blurred in memory. The warders left as the singing floated on the chill morning air, all but drowning out the sounds of opening gates and the slam of a single door. Then there was silence, an eerie silence that seemed to suspend the whole prison in time and space until it was broken obscenely by the chatter of warders' voices, the clatter of keys in locks and the slam of that same door again.

For the politicals, breakfast was always delayed on such days. They were kept in their cells until the ritual was complete before being let out to walk to the linking corridor between the two sections and pick up their food at the gates looking on to the gallows door. Barred windows in the corridor looked on to similar windows in the hospital section where Matthew Goniwe was held. In the more relaxed environment of the hospital, dealing with warders who were friendlier, he had been able, every so often, to get hold of a newspaper. In a series of whispered words and hand signals, he conveyed a means of passing them over.

A piece of string tied to a cake of soap could be thrown between the bars of a hospital window towards the pair of arms reaching out from the corridor window opposite. Goniwe had a strong throwing arm and one throw was usually enough. As soon as the soap was captured, he would tie the newspaper to his end of the string and his three comrades on death row would eagerly reel in their reading matter. Goniwe, whose powerful voice had not been diminished by his illness, loved to sing, and a song would signal whenever a newspaper was available. For some reason he chose a Nat King Cole version of 'Mona Lisa'. There was no real danger from the warders. Their access to the courtyard was via a conventional steel-clad prison door. It gave a warning of any intention to patrol outside by the clang of a key in the lock and the drawing of bolts.

In this way the Ntsebeza brothers and Godfrey Silinga gained fitful information about the world beyond their concrete and steel cocoon with its obscene adjunct. This was how they heard of the death of Steve Biko and the controversy it had stirred. Every day they would wander down the corridor, longing to hear Goniwe's baritone croon, 'Mo-na Li-sa, Mo-na Li-sa . . .'

More taxing than waiting for newspapers was the protracted wait for news of the appeal. Despite continual pleas to have their applications heard, nothing happened. The same inaction greeted their requests to the prison authorities for exercise, leave to study, and for the lights to be switched off. Protest was obviously necessary and the only means seemed to be a hunger strike. Matthew Goniwe, still ill and in hospital, was eager to take part, but, through messages passed via long-term prisoners, the others managed to persuade him that he would not be selling out by not joining the strike.

For twenty-one days the three prisoners drank sugared water and took vitamins, but refused all food and rapidly lost weight. When word leaked out about their protest the authorities were infuriated, especially when the hunger strikers demanded to see the commissioner of prisons. However, at least some of the more annoying aspects of the warders' behaviour stopped. Improvements began, the hunger strike stopped, and bureaucracy relapsed into its rut: the prisoners were charged with bringing the prisons into disrepute. They were duly found guilty – and sentenced to several days of 'spare' (reduced) diet.

All the while they knew that Matanzima was signing detention orders. Word came through the grapevine of individuals or whole groups of men and women being brought in to various prisons to be housed in solitary cells. News came too of torture and of banishments. The information was sporadic and often incomplete, but it indicated that Transkei's government was operating in much the same way as its patron in Pretoria, and probably in direct collaboration.

Still the façade of legality was being preserved, so they waited in hope for Munnik to respond. In the meantime, they continued to study. In one of those ironies that litter the political landscape of South Africa, the Puflsa prisoners were started on their further academic careers with funding that came partially from the Geneva-based International University Exchange Fund. But no word came from Mr Justice Munnik, who sustained his reputation as one of the government's more reliable retainers. In fact, it was not till 25 February 1980 that Judge Munnik finally communicated. After nearly four years, he released a statement of just two sentences: 'Application for leave to appeal refused. Reasons will follow in due course.'

Without the reasons, of course, there could also be no further action. By then, Dumisa Ntsebeza had been moved to another prison in Mt Fletcher, 250 km to the north of Umtata. Lungisile went to Mt Frere, 100 km away. Godfrey Silinga was moved to another section of Umtata prison. But Matthew Goniwe simply refused to move.

There were many further instances of the nastiness, the petty viciousness, they endured. When Nozipo Ntsebeza died, for example, Dumisa was not told. He heard a month later through a letter from his sister. Lungisile was informed, and at the same time told that he would not be allowed to attend his mother's funeral. As the months dragged on, it became apparent that Munnik might wait until weeks or even days before the end of the sentences before giving his reasons. In the event, the reasons never came. On 31 August 1981, the sentences expired.

Munnik never explained himself. Nor was he officially asked to. He remained a senior member of the judiciary, adapting himself after 1994, without apparent difficulty, to the new democratic dispensation. He became the chief justice of the Western Cape before going into retirement.

4

The killing of Bathandwa Ndondo

When the Ntsebeza brothers, Godfrey Silinga and Matthew Goniwe emerged in 1981 from their fundamentally illegal incarceration, it was into a Transkei and a South Africa that superficially had changed little. There was a new head of state in Pretoria in the unappealing shape of the former defence minister, the finger-wagging P.W. Botha, but for the state machine it seemed to be business as usual. There had, however, been a major subterranean change. The foundations of certainty in the success of apartheid as a system had dissolved with the failure of détente, the Angolan misadventure, and the worldwide rejection of Transkei as a nation-state. South Africa was the 'polecat' of the world, and with no apparent hope of improving that status.

The exiled ANC, bolstered by an influx of militant young men and women fleeing police and military repression, was again becoming a serious security threat, for all the infiltration of its ranks. Apartheid had effectively collapsed as an option, yet there seemed no way to provide for its demolition. The structure had to be kept at least nominally intact while some way was found to transform it, yet still to maintain control of whatever succeeded it. All pretence by the planners of serving a nobler cause had vanished. The era of secret slaughter had begun. It was not so much a case of letting loose the dogs of secret war, but of unleashing all the pent-up vileness, racism and corruption which the system had fomented over generations.

But while the substance had grown more insanely brutal, the form was still adhered to. Torture was even more widespread, but still denied and nominally illegal. More opposition activists disappeared or died in suspicious circumstances, but others were still charged and brought to court. And opponents were still banished and banned. On the day of their release in Umtata, the Ntsebeza brothers and Godfrey Silinga were banished to Cala, where Whyte Ntsebeza had opened a small bookshop. Matthew Goniwe was 'deported' to his home in Cradock.

Within a year, following moves by Umtata lawyer Temba Sangoni, the banishment orders were lifted. Dumisa Ntsebeza packed his bags and joined the Sangoni Partnership as a candidate attorney. Lungisile stayed behind and became more involved in the bookshop, importing and selling books, most of them 'political' in the broad sense of the word, and most of them banned in South Africa. The brothers had continued on courses that would lead to frequent conflict with the authorities. But it was Dumisa's willingness to take on and use the legal system that made him a special target.

Even before he had fully qualified, Dumisa took on political cases. Unlike many of his peers, he did not allow the social norms of apartheid society to follow him into the courtroom. Having recognised that the form of parliamentary democracy meant that a defence lawyer had to be treated as an equal in court, even in the apartheid state, he strode into courtrooms with relish. His rhetorical flourishes and displays of erudition often left poorly educated prosecutors, police and magistrates floundering and barely able to contain their fury. He was the epitome of all they most feared and hated: a confident, educated and articulate black man; the ultimate 'cheeky kaffir'. Often he was able to win cases by delving behind the bare evidence and beneath the façade of the rule of law.

His first case provided a classic example. Pan Africanist Congress activist Lawrence Vumankosi Ntikinca did not stand any real chance of acquittal for his political activities, but he had been terribly tortured. Dumisa Ntsebeza not only defended him; he sued the state and the security police for the injuries inflicted on his client. Vumankosi Ntikinca served four years in Umtata prison, but he won compensation from the Transkei state for the injuries inflicted by torture. However, with rebellion erupting, there were demands for legal assistance in South Africa too, especially in anti-apartheid hotspots such as Queenstown, across the border from Transkei. It was there that the Sangoni Partnership opened a branch office as more and more appeals were made for legal assistance.

The lawyer who took on many of these cases was the young firebrand Dumisa Ntsebeza. It earned him a deserved reputation among political activists as a tough fighter for justice, but it also earned the hostility of the South

African security establishment and the Transkei authorities. Transkei security police regularly raided the homes of the Ntsebeza brothers and continued to harass Godfrey Silinga. The bookshop in Cala was a target for squads of security police. What followed became almost a ritual: the police would carry off boxes of books; Dumisa Ntsebeza would issue a letter of demand, and the books would be returned, together with any replacement costs. It was a tense and often frightening game of intimidation and resistance, using the fragile legal independence of Transkei.

Outside Transkei there was less protection. The security police often made clear what lay in store for those who dared to continue to oppose them, in however non-violent a form. In late 1983, Lungisile Ntsebeza and Matthew Goniwe arranged by telephone to meet in Queenstown, which lies midway between Cala and Goniwe's home in Cradock. The telephone was tapped. No sooner had the two men shaken hands than they were surrounded by police, arrested and dragged before the head of local security, a Captain Venter.

Venter gave them a chilling warning that Lungisile never forgot. After saying that the likes of Ntsebeza and Goniwe were not welcome in his town, Venter looked at them coldly. 'It is no use arresting communists like you,' he said. 'You just come out and do the same things. There is only one solution,' he added, slowly drawing his finger across his throat. After four hours, the two men were released.

There was no doubt about the message. Less than two years later, in 1985, as the country was convulsed by another series of uprisings and protests, especially in the Eastern Cape, P.W. Botha, his defence minister Magnus Malan and law and order minister Adriaan Vlok visited the region. As senior members of the State Security Council (SSC), the centre of the vast security web, they were concerned. The Eastern Cape, which housed both the Transkei and Ciskei 'homelands', had become largely unmanageable. Stability must be restored at any cost. Instructions duly flowed down the chain of command, from the SSC, via assessment in the coordinating committee, to the counter-revolutionary assessment and targeting centre and so on to the security units and death squads on the ground.

Terror was the chosen tactic. In May, only weeks after the SSC trio's visit to the Eastern Cape, Sipho Hashe, Champion Galela and Qaqawuli Godolozi of Port Elizabeth's Black Civic Organisation disappeared. They had in fact been abducted and butchered, their bodies burned on makeshift pyres while their killers roasted meat on a smaller fire and swilled cold beer. The ashes of both fires were thrown into the nearby Fish River. Two months later the mutilated and partially burnt bodies of Matthew Goniwe and his companions Fort Calata, Sparrow Mkhonto and Sicelo Mhlawuli were found dumped on open ground outside the city. It was a stark warning to activists. For broader consumption, the state propaganda machine, through its friends in the media, pumped out claims that factional feuding had been responsible. This suited the perceptions of the government's white constituency and was tailored to the prejudices of sections of the foreign media.

But the message to activists on the ground was always clear. At the mass funeral of Matthew Goniwe and his comrades, Victoria Mxenge rose to speak. Far from being cowed, this widow of activist Griffiths Mxenge, who had been hacked to death in 1981, openly scorned the unknown killers. 'We are prepared to die for Africa,' she said. Twelve days later, Victoria Mxenge was dead, shot and stabbed in front of her own children. The death squads were becoming even more brazen, and one of the most brazen acts of all came on 24 September 1985. It took place in Cala and it was aimed again at the Ntsebeza family.

Lungisile Ntsebeza still remembers that clear spring morning. He had left his home to drive to the regional centre of Elliot. Just outside Cala a white minibus – a 'kombi' – approached. It was almost identical to a vehicle he owned and it carried an XS registration number, denoting Cala. Automatically, Lungisile waved as the vehicle passed. For an instant he thought it strange that he had never seen it before, since all local vehicles tended to be known by everybody in the district. But he could not see whether his wave was answered, since both the windscreen and windows of the bus were heavily tinted; they glinted like patches of patent leather. He thought no more of it, apart from noting the coincidence of the registration number: XS 1889. His own kombi bore the number XS 1885.

As Lungisile Ntsebeza's car wound down the pass towards Elliot, the kombi with the tinted windows pulled up outside the house in Cala that Lungisile shared with his student cousin Bathandwa Ndondo and a friend, Victor Ngaleka. Bathandwa Ndondo was working as the local coordinator of the Cape Town-based Health Care Trust after being refused readmission earlier in the year to the University of the Transkei in Umtata. A former member of the Catholic Student Association, he had played a leading role in the university's first democratically elected student representative council. This SRC had incurred the wrath of the authorities by organising a commemoration of the Sharpeville massacre. His suspension was on the grounds that he was 'inciting the students to be involved in political activities'. Victor Ngaleka worked in the bookshop run by Lungisile Ntsebeza.

On the previous day, Bathandwa's friend and fellow student activist Thobile

Bam had arrived unannounced from Mt Frere, some 200 km to the north-east, having decided to spend a few days with his friend in Cala. He and Bathandwa had seen Victor off to the bookshop and were relaxing in the house when there was a knock at the door. Thobile went to answer it. Standing on the doorstep was a slightly built, unsmiling man who introduced himself as Dandala. He asked to see Bathandwa. Thobile nodded. He did not know the man and did not introduce himself, an oversight that probably saved his life. As he was later to discover, Detective Constable Gcininkosi Lamont Dandala had started the day early, in Mt Frere, looking for Thobile Bam. So Thobile left the man standing on the doorstep and went to call Bathandwa. He watched as Bathandwa walked to the door and then accompanied Dandala out towards a white kombi with dark windows. The two men were in apparently earnest conversation.

After several minutes, Bathandwa came back into the house. He pulled Thobile aside. There were three men, including Dandala, and a woman in the vehicle parked outside, he said. They wanted information and wanted him to accompany them, but he was worried. They seemed to be police. Bathandwa had also noticed that all the windows of the kombi were heavily tinted and that there did not appear to be an inside handle on the passenger door. But on a sunny September morning there seemed little prospect of anything untoward happening. Still, it was best to take no chances. Like most of the community, he knew what had happened to Matthew Goniwe and his three friends. But such horrors happened under the cloak of night, so Bathandwa Ndondo decided to join the group in the kombi, but only after ensuring that Thobile Bam was ready to follow at a safe distance. If he was being taken to prison or detained, then Thobile should notify Lungisile and his lawyer brother, Dumisa.

But Thobile lost the kombi. When he saw it again, after speeding around in a frantic search, it was leaving the police station and driving towards the hospital. Something strange was going on. Where had the kombi gone before turning up at the police station and why had it headed to the hospital? Thobile raced to the bookshop, where he picked up Victor and, briefing him in the car, sped up to the hospital. The kombi was parked in the street outside the building. Thobile parked a short distance behind it and Victor got out and walked up to the driver's door. The window was wound down and the driver was sitting behind the wheel.

Victor greeted him and received a muffled reply. 'I'm looking for Bathandwa Ndondo,' he blurted. The driver turned to him and demanded to know who he was and what business he had with Bathandwa. Victor was taken aback by the aggressiveness of the response. But then a chill ran through him as he realised that there were spots of blood on the driver's shirt. There also seemed to be blood spattered on the dashboard of the kombi, in which a woman and two other men were sitting. He stammered out his name and the fact that he shared a house with Bathandwa. The driver seemed hardly to listen. He cut Victor short, waving him away. 'We are police,' he said. Bathandwa was in their hands. Victor nodded and backed away to join Thobile. Uncertain of what to do, they stood by the roadside and watched as the white minibus drove off. On their way back to the bookshop, they spotted Lungisile Ntsebeza's car and flagged it over. Victor leapt out of their vehicle and raced up to Lungisile, blurting out what had happened. 'Those people are wicked,' he gasped.

Was Bathandwa dead or alive? Given the brazenness of the police action, did it mean that all of them were soon to be arrested or killed? Lungisile was determined to find out about Bathandwa and try to ensure some protection for those who might be threatened. The only access to a telephone was at the bookshop and it was through a manual exchange. Calls had to be booked. The three young men made their way there. They would telephone Dumisa and the press. Although Cala was remote, it should not be forgotten.

Once in the bookshop, but before the calls could be made a local taxi-driver, Nceba Mbulawa, ran in. He had a grim tale to tell. Bathandwa was dead, shot again and again as he lay on the ground by people who matched the descriptions given by Victor and Thobile. Told that they were police, Mbulawa refused to believe it. Local bus inspector 'Mzalwana' Bulwana arrived at the bookshop minutes later and backed up this version of the shooting. He was sure that there was no chance that Bathandwa had survived.

With the scent of death in his nostrils, Lungisile Ntsebeza contacted his friend and former prison mate, Godfrey Silinga. Not trusting the telephone and not wishing to draw attention to Silinga, he went to see him at the local secondary school where he was teaching. 'I thought that whatever information I had should be known by some people who would use it in the event of me being killed as well,' Lungisile remembered years later at a memorial meeting for Bathandwa Ndondo. Having briefed Godfrey Silinga, Lungisile left for the hospital, where he was told that Bathandwa could not be seen. He was a 'police case' and police permission was necessary. But this was Cala, so it was only minutes before Lungisile found someone else who ushered him into the morgue. Bathandwa was dead, his upper body torn by several obvious bullet wounds. Later, an independent pathologist would report that the student leader had been shot eight times, once while he was standing and seven times while lying on his back.

A shaken Lungisile made his way back to the bookshop. He knew what he had to do. He must report the killing to the local police. Not because he had any faith in them, but so as to offer no procedural excuse for any failure to investigate the killing. Transkei – and South Africa for that matter – still claimed adherence to the rule of law. But precautions needed to be taken. Once he set foot inside the police station, Lungisile knew that he could disappear. The sight of Bathandwa's body and the recent murder of Matthew Goniwe and his friends made him nervous. For the umpteenth time he shut out thoughts of fleeing, of running for the border and disappearing into the Maluti mountains of Lesotho. He went again to Godfrey Silinga, his frail insurance policy, to tell him where he was going, why and when. Silinga would tell others, who would watch out to ensure that he emerged safely from the police station.

Filled equally with fear and resolution, Lungisile Ntsebeza strode into the police charge office. He wanted to lay a charge of murder for the death of Bathandwa Ndondo. Very well, said the policeman behind the desk, but had Lungisile seen the killing? If not, he could not lay a charge. Only eyewitnesses could do so. Was Lungisile aware of any eyewitnesses? Lungisile was not in the business of providing names. He wanted only to register the fact of a murder having been committed. So he sought for another police officer. Again he was unsuccessful. A message sent to the station commander, Lieutenant Jilili, brought the reply that Jilili was too busy to see anyone.

There was an obvious nervousness among the police, and Lungisile Ntsebeza realised that since he was being left unharmed inside the police station, the rule of law must still be outwardly in place. He should gather what evidence he could as fast as possible. There might still be time before the police stepped in to cover their trail. As casually as he could, he strolled from the police station to his house, where he collected his camera and made his way to where he had been told his friend had died.

It was in a side street near the centre of town, outside the home of Nontobeko Thunzi and her elderly mother. Both women gave graphic accounts of what had happened and Lungisile took pictures of the scene. The women told how a young man appeared to hurl himself out of the window of a kombi driving past their house. As he scrambled to his feet, shouting for help, the vehicle slid to a halt and the doors burst open. Three men and a woman, all carrying guns, sprinted after him. The young man ran around the house and, as he headed towards the front door, shots rang out. He seemed to trip and fall on the doorstep. His pursuers caught up. There were more shots.

Old mother Thunzi was horrified. 'Whose child is it you are shooting like a dog?' she demanded, with all the authority of her advanced years. 'He is a terrorist,' came the reply. Bathandwa's body was twitching, his mouth trying to form words. The old woman leaned down. In a croaking whisper she heard the words: 'I am from the Ntsebeza family.' Then the woman in the death squad snapped: 'This dog must not pretend to be dead before he has given us the information we want.'

After conferring among themselves, the killers dragged the still body roughly back to the vehicle. The dying or already dead student was thrown in and the killer squad sped off.

Armed with this evidence and his photographs, Lungisile returned to the police station. As he got to the front door, he paused. Standing with his back to him was Lieutenant Jilili, his voice raised, speaking on the telephone. He seemed to be speaking to a major in Umtata. He described the shooting of Bathandwa and mentioned two names as involved. Lungisile, nervously straining to catch every word, recalled only one name. It was Mose or Moss. Later it was to emerge that this was Sergeant Silulami Gladstone Mose, an askari drafted in from Vlakplaas whose deadly work earned him promotion to captain before he died of a heart attack in 1990.

That was as much as Lungisile heard. Just as Jilili finished speaking another policeman spotted the young man hovering in the doorway. Jilili spun around. He was clearly taken aback and almost apologetically invited 'Mr Ntsebeza' to join him in his office. Trying hard to conceal his nervousness, Lungisile followed. Jilili sat down behind his desk. In a matter-of-fact tone he admitted that he knew of the death of Bathandwa.

The killers had reported to him that they had shot someone, he said. He knew who they were and he had opened a murder docket. As Lungisile questioned him, his posture tensed and his tongue slid nervously over his lips. No, he had not detained the killers and was not at liberty to divulge their names. Jilili was becoming increasingly agitated and Lungisile started to feel decidedly vulnerable. 'Come back this afternoon,' Jilili said. 'At four o'clock.' Then more information would be available. Lungisile thanked him, promised to return, and left the police station, walking slowly, half expecting a shout telling him to stop or the thud of a bullet in the back. Only when out of sight of the police station did he relax, having already decided he would be as far away as possible by four o'clock that afternoon.

As news of the killing spread, an atmosphere of fear seemed to seep into every corner. Suddenly Cala felt terribly isolated. Friends and family agreed that Lungisile should leave town to get help. He should drive to Queenstown, where his lawyer brother Dumisa was based, and together they should let the world know what had happened. As Lungisile drove out on one road, he was unaware that vanloads of heavily armed police were pouring into Cala on another. Shortly before four o'clock, they drew up outside the Ntsebeza home. The building was searched, books and papers rifled through, and several cassette tapes of music bearing the name of Bathandwa Ndondo were removed.

The local family doctor, Khaya Mfenyana, observed the scene from a distance. He had heard what had happened and was horrified. Although he was in no sense a political activist, he decided he could not stand by and see Lungisile Ntsebeza arrested or worse. As a doctor, and given his apolitical reputation, he would not be stopped if he left town. So he shut up his practice, got into his car and drove to Queenstown to warn Lungisile not to return; that a police trap awaited. Hours later in Cala, with Lungisile nowhere to be found, the squads of police left town while others, local police, kept watch.

It was extreme intimidation, but it showed that the country had not changed; that wholesale slaughter was not on the cards. Form would be preserved. While the search was going on in Cala, Lungisile was briefing his brother. Warned by Khaya Mfenyana, he stayed on in Queénstown. With the cooperation of the Sangoni legal partnership, he and Dumisa spent the rest of the afternoon and all that night ensuring that as many people as possible, including the local and international media, were made aware of what had happened. Using the networks of family, clan, school, university and political connections that abounded in the region, they also gathered more information.

Within a week they had established who the killers were. It had not been very difficult: the death squad had felt so safe from official censure and prosecution that they had eaten lunch at an Umtata restaurant only hours after the murder. The four had sat around their table, still wearing blood-spattered clothes, laughing and talking.

The publicity surrounding the incident and the fact that the rural grapevine spread and often embellished every detail probably saved the lives of the Ntsebeza brothers and their friends. But it infuriated the authorities. Less than a week after the death of Bathandwa, police again raided the Ntsebeza home in Cala. They dragged out Victor Ngaleka, who disappeared into detention. Dumisa and Lungisile Ntsebeza soon followed. As did Godfrey Silinga, the late Monde Mvimbi, and Zingisa Mkhabile, who was later to go on to become the Eastern Cape PAC leader. They were held incommunicado, but were neither interrogated nor charged. Nor were they allowed out for the funeral of Bathandwa, where mourners were harassed by police.

The detentions triggered more adverse publicity and more criticism. It had become impossible for the Transkei and its police to deny involvement in the killing. There was also strong evidence pointing to the role of elements from South Africa. The issue could not be hushed up – the Ntsebeza brothers and their friends had ensured that. Somewhere within the security hierarchy it was decided that damage limitation could only extend to confusing the issue so far as possible and to making any links with South Africa impossible to prove.

Dandala was a local Umtata security policeman and so did not pose a problem. But the other three killers were from Vlakplaas, former ANC fighters 'turned' to become askaris. While their masters plotted options, Dandala and the others made intimidatory forays into Cala to ask openly where Lungisile Ntsebeza or other witnesses to the murder of Bathandwa could be found. Then suddenly such intimidation stopped. Two of the askaris, Mose and the former ANC women's unit commissar turned apartheid killer, Xolelwa Sosha, disappeared.

What no one, outside a small group of security planners, knew was that this formed part of the damage limitation exercise. While Mose and Sosha were posted to other areas of South Africa to ply their deadly trade, Mbuso Enoch Shabalala stayed on in Umtata. Only he ceased, officially, to exist. On the instructions of Brigadier Willem Schoon, the Vlakplaas boss, Eugene de Kock, destroyed all reference to Shabalala: it was as if he had never been. In his place there was Johannes Mavuso, complete with a new, authentic identity number 530518 5734 08 6. This made it possible for Mbuso Enoch Shabalala to be charged, along with Gcininkosi Lamont Dandala, with the murder of Bathandwa Ndondo and for the case to collapse when Shabalala disappeared and was found never to have existed in the first place.

The 'sweeper' elements in the security establishment specialised in this sort of confusion. These were the people who covered up the murders and mayhem, often using methods that, with hindsight, outdo the inventions of fiction. They were able to do so because of the complicity of an entire bureaucratic community held in thrall by the gains of apartheid – and, at the upper levels, by the solid discipline of the Broederbond.

Time was also a factor. Delaying legal action for nearly a year meant that media and general public interest waned. It was also helpful that a good friend of the security establishment, Francois van Zyl, was attorney general of Transkei. It was he who decided, contrary to eyewitness evidence, that only two people were involved in the killing of Bathandwa Ndondo and that the former student leader had been shot while trying to escape from legitimate arrest. It was also he who decided, against vociferous protests, that Dandala and Shabalala should be released on their own recognisance after being charged. Finally, it was Francois van Zyl, later to represent police accused before the TRC of human rights abuses, who decided that the case against Dandala should be withdrawn 'pending the arrest' of the missing Shabalala. Since Shabalala did not officially exist, the case was effectively dropped.

It was a farce; a complete sham. And Dumisa Ntsebeza immediately categorised it as such. To do so implied a conspiracy that would have to involve not just senior police, but also the Transkei attorney general, the home affairs department and, therefore, senior government officials, perhaps even to ministerial level. This was something white South Africa would not, could not, accept.

By the time of Bathandwa Ndondo's death, Kaiser Matanzima's collaboration with apartheid had, inevitably, already sucked him deep into a murky vortex of corruption and deceit. Matanzima decided that attack was the best means of defence – a tactic that was to backfire badly. Addressing a meeting in the southern Transkei hamlet of Idutywa in early October 1985, Matanzima lied brazenly:

'I want the whole world to know that here in Transkei we know the people who are causing trouble. Recently a young man called Ndondo was killed in Cala. Many people are asking why Ndondo was killed. He is the one who came from Lesotho with others and exploded a bomb in Umtata. The petrol depot that exploded and should have killed the whole of the Umtata population was destroyed by this young fellow, Ndondo.

'You will see the communists will be asking what has Ndondo done. Must you all be killed because of these people? Your president, your prime minister, will not allow such atrocities to take place in Transkei.'

It was obvious why this attempt to deflect popular anger failed. Not only was there widespread sympathy for anyone who might have bombed anything associated with President K.D. Matanzima and his prime minister brother, George, but the Ntsebeza brothers refused to take the crude bait. They announced that the issue was not what Ndondo had or had not done, but whether Matanzima was condoning state-sponsored murder without trial. K.D. Matanzima promptly authorised a second period of banishment for the brothers.

5

The forgotten people

There remain in South Africa many wild and distant areas where habitation is sparse and the environment hostile. These were the places most often selected for banishment, an extra-judicial punishment resurrected by the National Party government and adopted by its homeland progeny. It had echoes of the avaricious and brutal Dutch East India Company and its removal to the Cape, three centuries earlier, of troublesome individuals from Java and other islands of the Pacific archipelago that became Indonesia and Malaysia. But its immediate roots were in the 1927 Native Administration Act. This allowed the governor-general, as head of state, and representative of Britain's king or queen, to order 'any tribe or native to proceed forthwith to any designated place' and not to leave again without permission.

It was a most efficient piece of legislation, for it did away with the time-consuming chores of judicial procedure and allowed the state to choose each destination. There were pointers to this thinking in the 1963 General Laws Amendment Act that introduced ninety-day detention without trial, although this law was much more specific in its purpose. It allowed any police officer to detain 'in any place he deems fit' any individual who he had cause to believe had information about any act, or the intention to commit any act, detrimental to the good order of the state.

Detention therefore existed primarily as a means of extracting information. And where the sensory deprivation of solitary confinement failed, the torturers waited: those men – and a few women – who could inflict pain and humiliation or instil fear to such effect that many, if not most, of their victims would cooperate. Ninety days soon gave way to 180, and finally to indefinite detention without trial. The rationale was the same. And detention could lead to trials and to long prison sentences for those who had transgressed the laws of the land.

Then there were those who broke no laws, concealed no information, but whose very presence presented a problem. Often these were community leaders or elected chiefs in the rural areas who did not toe the line, leaders perceived as insubordinate – 'cheeky' – by some authority. Or there were those who tailored the language of resistance and carried out their practice of opposition in ways which were effective, but which remained within the law. In the last decade of apartheid rule, such people were often singled out for assassination.

But more usually these were the people selected for banishment. They were the forgotten, the living dead of an authoritarian system, wrenched away from family and friends, to await in penury either death or an official change of mind. As with so much of South Africa's recent brutal history, we shall probably never know exactly how many people were banished and what happened to them all. But thanks largely to one brave campaigner and her two companions, we have documentary evidence, dating from 1962, of the lives, the circumstances and in some cases the fates, of thirty-six individuals who were consigned to this legal limbo. These stories were not investigated by the TRC and there were no amnesty applications from those responsible.

The issue of banishment was however raised at the TRC and some evidence was heard. Two brothers, Marelane and Dalagubha Joyi, who had been banished for five years by K.D. Matanzima, told a TRC hearing in Umtata what had happened to them. The Commission considered the issue of banishment as well as the practice of restricting individuals by means of banning orders and found these to be gross violations of human rights. Although the TRC also held the 'former government and, in particular, the ministers of justice and law and order' accountable, no further action was taken.

The evidence from 1962 was collected and publicised by Helen Joseph, the 'other Helen' from Johannesburg whose many trials and sufferings tended often to be associated with Helen Suzman, the Progressive Party parliamentarian and darling of the liberal media. Both were from Johannesburg's northern suburbs. Suzman represented the parliamentary constituency of Houghton, which allowed the journalistic penchant for alliteration full rein: she became

'Helen of Houghton', a Trojan echo that portrayed her as a lone opponent of apartheid.

Helen Suzman could be freely quoted and was the most outspoken opponent functioning within the bounds of the apartheid system. It was she who demanded in parliament to know who and how many people were banished. She also visited and spoke out about some of the later banished. But it was Helen Joseph, of the rather less salubrious suburb of Orange Grove, who took to the roads and tracks of rural South Africa to find those banished people. It was Helen Joseph who brought back their stories of horror and frightful loneliness and who suffered the wrath of the state for doing so.

Helen Joseph left on her journey to uncover some of the hidden business of apartheid only hours after her first banning order lapsed at midnight on 30 April 1962. It had restricted her to Johannesburg and banned the publication of any word she might utter or write. Nevertheless, Helen had still been active in establishing the Human Rights Welfare Committee which the then already outlawed ANC had wanted set up to find and help those who had been banished. Through occasional newspaper reports and other contacts, the committee gradually located some of the victims. It was also able to establish that, rather than the eighty people whom the government claimed to have banished, there had been at least 116 held between 1950 and 1962. In that year, the government said that forty people remained in banishment, and it was these that Helen Joseph and two friends set off to find on that crisp autumn morning in May 1962. For most of this journey, which took two months and covered some 15,000 km, she was accompanied by Joe Morolong and Amina Cachalia. They traced and interviewed thirty-six of the 'forgotten people'.

For her pains, Helen – who had already been imprisoned, tried and acquitted of treason, and then banned – was banned again. Because she had written and sent abroad the stories of the banished, published in Britain as *Tomorrow's Sun*, she was prohibited from writing or preparing anything for publication. She also became the first person to suffer house arrest, restricted to her home for twelve hours a day during weekdays and day and night during weekends and holidays. Even the twelve hours of relative freedom were hedged with restrictions and with the demand that she report – again on pain of prison – to the central police station in Johannesburg between noon and 2 pm on each weekday.

The mainstream media largely ignored Helen Joseph's findings. Likewise, after a spike of publicity, her twilight existence (and that of all the others who were later also served with house arrest orders, some of them for twenty-four hours a day) was soon forgotten. But at least the 'house arrestees' lived in their own homes, albeit on some strange, legally created margin of society. There was even occasional interaction: usually clandestine, sometimes dangerous and frequently nerve-racking. But even this, Helen Joseph often reminded herself, was more than the other banished could hope for.

She and her companions discovered that many of the banished had died. Others had disappeared, perhaps across a border. Still others continued to survive on 'wild and uncultivated stretches of arid land, far from any town or even any African village'. The tragic stories of those days continued in the decades ahead. Among those that surfaced at the TRC hearings was the case of the Siliza family. Mzwandile Siliza, a torture victim and Robben Island prisoner, and his wife were banished after his release from Robben Island. In the desperate conditions in which they were forced to live, their child died, aged three months. With no money for a coffin, they buried the child in a cardboard box.

Jojo Titus was another Robben Island prisoner. He served six years there before being released in 1972. Returned to Transkei, he was served with a banishment order. The next ten years he spent in a hermit's existence in a remote rural area of western Transkei, hearing only fragments of news from the world beyond. But by 1982 he had heard enough to convince him that the battle he had fought all those years was still going on. He decided to escape. He walked to the Lesotho border, crossed at night, and kept walking across the mountains until he reached the Lesotho capital of Maseru on 8 December 1982. There he was given directions to an ANC house. For the first time in sixteen years he was free and among friends. Little more than twenty-four hours later, Jojo Titus and his new-found friends were dead, mowed down in a cross-border raid by apartheid special forces. That night in 1982, forty-two men, women and children died in Maseru.

The highest-profile case of banishment recorded was that of Winnie Madiki-zela-Mandela. The militant wife of Nelson Rolihlahla Mandela was banished in 1977 to the dusty township of Phatakahle outside the tiny Free State town of Brandfort. There was an irony in the name, for Phatakahle means 'handle with care'. She was no normal target for banishment, and the place she was sent to no normal locale for such punishment. The object was to remove her from Soweto, where she had become an icon for the rising tide of student rebellion, to a more rural, conservative area where the main languages were seSotho and Afrikaans as opposed to Mandela's isiXhosa and English. Brandfort was also close enough to the provincial centre of Bloemfontein to allow the security police to provide round-the-clock monitoring without too much difficulty.

Winnie Mandela spent eight years in Phatakahle and Brandfort, turning the town into a Mecca for visiting politicians seeking anti-apartheid credibility and for foreign journalists keen to interview this figurehead of a burgeoning popular resistance movement. But in the process she also influenced local lawyer and Broederbonder Piet de Waal. Small-town lawyer and hardline segregationist though he was, De Waal was aware of the wider problems facing his government; of the sometimes confusing interplay between modernisers and traditionalists as the system and 'the volk' sought a way out of the morass they floundered in. As the only lawyer in town, he also handled the affairs of Winnie Mandela. He had not wanted to, and had tried at first to avoid the responsibility but the rules of the legal façade that cloaked apartheid obliged him to deal with her. He got to know her well, and it was in his office overlooking Brandfort's main street or at his home that Mandela met and talked with her numerous guests.

Kobie Coetsee, who became minister of Justice, Police and Prisons in 1980, was a close personal friend of De Waal. By then, De Waal was convinced that Winnie Mandela and, obviously, her imprisoned husband, were not the demonic terrorists of legend. He mentioned his view to Coetsee, though it merely reinforced the assessment made of Mandela by the Broederbond prisons chief and clinical psychologist, General Jannie Roux. That De Waal underwent this almost Damascene conversion is the only recorded case of a banished person and the place and circumstances of her banishment playing such a role.

In 1985 Winnie Mandela's small house in Phatakahle was fire-bombed. She simply packed her bags and moved, without permission, back to Soweto. She was not an assassination target: to kill her would create another martyr and would almost certainly trigger a huge national and international backlash. Something similar could happen if she were to be arrested yet again or 'removed' back to Brandfort. The official decision was instead to surround her with security agents and, as one of them commented years later, 'give her enough rope to hopefully hang herself and the ANC'.

But Winnie Mandela was not the only banished person who managed effectively to turn the tables on her persecutors. Mamphela Ramphele was a young woman doctor, close associate and lover of Steve Biko. Pregnant with Biko's son Hlumelo, she was banished to a remote rural area in the north only weeks before Biko's brutal murder on 12 September 1977. She had only just begun to settle in to a village of poverty and illiteracy where she did not speak the language when the news of Biko's death reached her. She was shattered, and said later that she 'nearly disintegrated'.

Instead she resolved to carry on and to fight back with the ideas of self-help that Steve Biko had promoted. In the process she transformed the dusty backward village of Lenyenye and the entire district. Her Ithuseng clinic, financed by donations from business and church groups, became a major medical facility and sprouted branch clinics in other villages. Literacy projects and gardening clubs that taught the rudiments of modern agriculture followed.

When her five-year term of banishment was not renewed in 1983, she stayed on in Lenyenye for another year to ensure that the projects she had helped to create were on a sound footing. Only then did she leave to start an academic career that was to make her vice-chancellor of the University of Cape Town and then one of the four managing directors of the World Bank.

Shortly before sunrise on 8 October 1985 in a quiet back street of Umtata, a squad of security police pulled up outside the home of Dumisa Ntsebeza. The lawyer was half expecting the loud knocking on the door. When it came, it was almost a relief. For weeks he had heard rumours of his impending arrest and detention. They confirmed the information given by a security policeman who had sought him out secretly at a funeral and warned him to be careful. This self-declared 'mole' stayed in touch throughout the bloody years that followed, passing on scraps of information that aided and ultimately reassured Dumisa. It was the mole who first warned that the police would use banishment.

Five days before Dumisa's arrest, his brother Lungisile had been detained, apparently in relation to the funeral arrangements for Bathandwa Ndondo. Both brothers had been outspoken about his death, openly blaming the Transkei Security Branch. They and Victor Ngaleka, Godfrey Silinga and two other friends, Zingisa Mkabile and Monde Mvimbi, were central to planning the funeral. All were arrested without charge. Nothing they had done was illegal. In the case of Dumisa Ntsebeza this was in accordance with a pledge made to himself when he decided to take to the law as a career and as a means of fighting the apartheid system.

He still expected to be picked up and locked up, if only because annoyance and frustration might goad the authorities to stage a show of power. Such detention, he felt sure, would not be for long, but he took precautions. The Sangoni Partners law firm of which he had become a partner in January that year was instructed to institute legal action for his and his brother's release should they be detained. This action would be a precedent for any other detainees.

With Dumisa's arrest, the application to release Lungisile became one for the release of the Ntsebeza brothers. It was set down to be heard on 1 November in the Transkei Supreme Court.

The Transkei police then clamped down hard on the funeral for Bathandwa Ndondo. They harassed and terrorised anyone even vaguely associated with the arrangements. The Roman Catholic Church, which the family had counted on to provide a priest to officiate, refused. Ministers of other denominations were also reluctant to involve themselves. Some churches feared their priests would face deportation, others gave no reasons. A minority said they would be prepared to officiate, but only if there was no alternative. So it was that an Anglican, the Reverend Edgar Ruddock, conducted a service where the mourners were supervised by heavily armed police and armoured personnel carriers. White mourners were barred and police and troops turned back all the buses and cars that headed to the funeral from outside Cala. Young mourners wearing specially printed T-shirts which bore the slogan 'Rest in Peace Bathandwa Ndondo', were also arrested. By the end of October, fifty-one people had been detained in the name of the security of Kaiser Matanzima's state.

In their solitary cells, the Ntsebeza brothers and their four close friends knew that – barring some radical turn for the worse – it was only a matter of time before the issue of their incarceration would come before the courts and they would be released. Tensions rose, for there was no hint of what might happen, but on 30 October, two days before the application came to court, Lungisile was released from prison. Next day Dumisa and the others walked free.

There was no time to celebrate. The six friends were at once handed orders, signed by Kaiser Daliwonga Matanzima as the head of the Transkei 'state', banishing them to various remote rural areas. The Ntsebeza brothers were ordered to be banished to the 'Mhlahlane administrative area in the Tsomo district'. The mole had been right. Their presence 'in Umtata or any other place in the district of Umtata' was not considered 'in the general public interest'. However, they were given a choice of dates by which they should 'withdraw from the said district of Umtata'. The latest was 26 November, which meant that they could still be in Umtata for the Supreme Court action on 1 November regarding their detention. The upshot of that hearing was that the minister of police agreed to pay the costs of the action. It was another minor victory, and cause for still greater annoyance within the security establishment.

With that out of the way, the Ntsebeza brothers immediately instituted legal proceedings against their banishment. Then, armed with a camera, they travelled out to the rural area beyond Tsomo, some 100km south of Umtata, to see and record at first hand the conditions to which they had been banished. Although they had expected rural squalor, the reality came as a shock. In the first place, it was impossible to reach the two dilapidated mud huts by vehicle. They lay more than 2 km beyond the end of a rutted, boulder-strewn track which itself led off 5 km of gravel road. It brought home, for the first time, a realisation of what banishment must have meant for all those who had suffered it in the past. Here, at least, they still spoke the language, and their families knew where they had been sent. The bleakness that confronted them, they realised, amounted to better conditions than those most other victims had endured.

There was, they decided, no way this order should be obeyed. In a notice of motion to the Supreme Court, Dumisa Ntsebeza contended that the banishment order was malicious and invalid since it sought to punish and humiliate him. The effect of the banishment would be to reduce him 'to the status of a subsistence peasant in the rural areas with no means of earning any livelihood'. He included photographs of the huts that he and Lungisile had been allocated as 'residences'. Noting that 'both places have neither running water nor toilet facilities. They have large gaps in the roofing; in the walls and have gaps in the doorways. Both places are extremely damp and the door joints are rotting.' He added, almost as an afterthought, that neither had electricity nor lightning conductors. The urgent notice was brought after lengthy representations by his law firm to the commissioner of police had met with a two-sentence response:

1. Contents in your above quoted letters are hereby acknowledged.
2. This office is only concerned with the issue of a written permit when your clients have to leave the Districts to which they have been referred by the order.

Using the law in this way, the Ntsebeza brothers managed to gain 'interim relief' from banishment for themselves, and by extension for their four banished friends. They were also able to extract from the authorities various admissions, justifications and statements which gave some insight into the bureaucracy of the period and how deeply the attitudes of the masters were imprinted on their trusted servants. It fell to Transkei's President Matanzima to justify the conditions chosen for the brothers in their banishment. Without ever having seen the area, he informed the court that the two huts and the area itself were highly suitable.

'The Mhlahlane area is, in a Transkeian context, the home of the Ntsebeza clan,' said Matanzima's affidavit to the court, 'even if they themselves had not grown up in that area.' Irrespective of their or their family's connection with Mhlahlane, it was an 'appropriate area' to contain the brothers 'without undue harm to the general public interest'. The complaints about the huts and their insanitary conditions were dismissed as being from 'a white or a European point of view and not in the Black or African context'. The president admitted that he had not seen the huts in question, but even if they were inadequate this would not invalidate the banishment, although it might entitle the brothers to refuse to live inside the huts. Earlier in the statement, he had informed the court that any Transkei citizen should be able, if need be, to build a hut. He did not add that this was something many of the banished in the past had been forced to do.

Demands by the brothers for reasons for their banishment were met by Matanzima and his Security Branch police chief, General Leonard Kawe, with the bald statement that they both posed 'a threat to the security of the state': the 'general public interest' would 'best be served' by their banishment. Denials by the brothers that they were involved in any illegal or subversive activities, said Kawe, were 'neither strange nor unexpected'. This was the stock reply of 'people who conspire against the state'. He assured the court that the security police had information that the brothers presented 'a real risk to the security and peace of the republic of the Transkei'. He could not disclose his sources, nor could he describe them generally, since disclosure 'could cause some diminution of their effectiveness'.

What General Kawe could say was that the information that justified the arrest of the Ntsebeza brothers had been 'similar to that which led to the arrest of Mr Ndondo'. That Ndondo had died, and Dumisa Ntsebeza in particular had publicly blamed the police, had nothing to do with action taken against the brothers. Kawe showed how badly their prisoner had rattled the authorities when without any prompting he angrily announced that it was simply untrue that Dumisa Ntsebeza was being badly treated by the police because he was a 'champion of human rights'. The truth was that Ntsebeza had 'an abrasive personality and was frequently ill mannered'. This, he explained more calmly, would sometimes 'elicit from police a similar discourtesy'.

As this argument unfolded, publicity mounted. Questions were asked in the South African parliament. On 26 November, Mr Justice van Reenen postponed the case pending a final determination. It was likely that the orders could be set aside, thus acutely embarrassing the Transkei authorities. Alternatively, political pressure might turn the judgement the other way. The Ntsebeza brothers wanted an end to uncertainty. They also knew that the outcome of their case would affect the four others.

For many in the security police establishment – and, in particular, the triumvirate who controlled the Transkei division – the public furore about the case was the last straw. Generals Kawe and Gladile and Captain Joe Ntwasa resolved that Dumisa Ntsebeza should be 'eliminated'. Now the mole surfaced again. Dumisa should flee, he suggested, or else he would be dead in a matter of weeks. Dumisa told his wife Nontobeko. What should they do? Should they, as a family, go into exile? Should he go alone? Was there any other action they could take? A thought struck Nontobeko. 'Hamlet Manci is a close friend of Kawe, Gladile and Ntwasa,' she said. 'I'll speak to him.'

In any place other than the close-knit community of a region like Transkei, its population pushed closer together by the pressures of apartheid, this might have seemed a crazy thing to do. But Hamlet Manci was both a long-time family friend of Nontobeko's and a boyhood friend of Ntwasa, and maybe the fresh air of publicity would blow away some of the festering conspiracies. Dumisa agreed and Nontobeko challenged Hamlet Manci. How could he associate with men who wanted to make her a widow and her children orphans? Hamlet Manci, in his turn, confronted Joe Ntwasa, who denied any knowledge of a murder plot. A day later a puzzled mole reported that the murder plot had suddenly been shelved.

That bit of good news was followed by an approach from the state for negotiations on the banishment issue. The Ntsebeza brothers accepted. In the horse trading that followed, it was obvious that the authorities wanted some face-saving quid pro quo. It eventually came down to money. The Transkei government would withdraw the banishment orders in exchange for all six of the banished agreeing to pay R10,000 toward the state's costs. The agreement was struck on 15 October 1986 and duly announced, although no money changed hands.

Dumisa Ntsebeza was convinced by then that elements of the apartheid state apparatus were directly involved in episodes such as Bathandwa Ndondo's murder. That apparatus, through management committees and the State Security Council, probably extended all the way to the South African president, his trusted ministers and generals. Transkei, however, contained a barrier, a slight rupture in the chain of command, because even the most devout homeland supporter would not overtly endorse apartheid. Family, clan and pigmentation might provide an element of protection. It certainly gave more confidence to the activists.

In January 1987, for example, Dumisa's mole approached him once more to warn him that he, his brother and the others were about to be served again with banishment orders. Although Kaiser Matanzima had already retired as president, he was still pulling the strings. The banishment issue had come up at a meeting of the whole Transkei cabinet called at KD's home in Cofimvaba. The Ntsebeza brothers and the other four were to be served with orders within the week. Because there were so many people present at the meeting, the source of the information would be safe.

On this basis, Dumisa Ntsebeza wrote to the Transkei government. He noted: 'We are reliably informed that you are about to banish us again,' and mentioned the limit of a week. The letter worked: the orders were withdrawn. But celebrations were shortlived. On 3 March 1987 a security police major barged into the offices of the Sangoni legal partnership in Umtata and thrust another banishment order into Dumisa Ntsebeza's hands. Dated 26 February, and signed by Kaiser Matanzima's successor Tutor Ndamase and by George Matanzima as prime minister, again it ordered the lawyer 'in the general public interest' to relocate to the Mhlahlane district of Tsomo.

Dumisa Ntsebeza shook his head in disbelief, but the major was serious. He produced a warrant for the arrest of Ntsebeza should he fail to comply. The order must apply without delay. There would be no time for telephone calls. He grabbed the lawyer and hustled him into the street to a waiting police car that drove at speed through town to the Ntsebeza home. They gave him a matter of minutes to throw a few belongings into a suitcase before being shoved outside again.

There he made a stand, a token of resistance to affirm that he was no mere piece of political flotsam. He would go to Tsomo, but only in his own car. The police at first refused, but finally a compromise was agreed: a policeman would drive Ntsebeza in his own car and the police car would follow. So it was that a two-car convoy turned up at the magistrate's office in the hamlet of Tsomo. But the magistrate was not there. He had learned only that day of Ntsebeza's arrival and was arranging for a 'residence'. By the time the magistrate returned, Ntsebeza's legal partners were also in the office and the police left. They had no wish, they said, to inspect Ntsebeza's new home.

But Temba Sangoni had questions. Was there a bed? What about cooking utensils? The magistrate looked uncomfortable. 'There is nothing,' he replied, and directed his assistant to escort the lawyers to the new, and legally defined, residence of Dumisa Buhle Ntsebeza. Although it was possible to get closer by car than to the quarters previously deemed fit for the Ntsebeza brothers, this hut was in worse condition. It was part of abandoned school premises and had never been lived in. Ntsebeza stated in a notice of motion filed before the supreme court of 2 April that:

> There is no furniture of whatsoever nature, no cooking utensils, no firewood or lighting paraphernalia; no electricity, no running water . . . the place is, with respect, a wilderness.
>
> To add to my miseries, the one window had broken windowpanes. The other window would not lock from the inside, so that anyone could simply push it open and gain access into the hut. Near the door and taking about a third of the floor area, there is a place which appeared to be damp and smudgy.

Information from a local official that the hut had been built over a perpetual spring that kept it permanently damp allowed Ntsebeza to inform the court drily that 'the spring in my mud hut would appear to be the closest approximation to running water that there is'. There was clearly the intention, once again, to humiliate and to punish. But this was to be his 'residence'.

While his partners hurried off to file the necessary legal motions, Ntsebeza consulted a dictionary. 'Residence', it informed him, was a place where a person normally resides. Normally, but not always. And since conditions at his official residence were far from normal, he got into his car and drove to a nearby hotel where he registered as a guest – temporarily, he said, away from his normal residence.

The Sangoni Partnership and Dumisa's wife Nontobeko made applications to the courts to have the banishment order overturned. While the judicial wheels ground on, they also applied for permission for Dumisa to handle the various cases he was already involved with and others that demanded his attention. All this made a mockery of the banishment order, but the police persisted. Even when his young son was ill and in hospital, permission had to be sought to visit. It came in the usual, curt manner:

1. Application to visit his child in hospital by Mr Ntsebeza on 17/3/87 is approved.
2. Application to remain in Umtata overnight is not approved. He must leave Umtata not later than 19h00 on 17/3/87.

Finally, on 18 June 1987, the matter came to court and was set aside. Dumisa Ntsebeza was able to return to his Umtata home and his wife and two young children. He was perhaps the last prospective victim of a gross human rights abuse that had been part of the state apparatus of repression for nearly forty years.

Although the banishment experience of the Ntsebeza brothers and the battles surrounding the orders took place relatively recently, they illustrate the nature of banishment and the mentality of those who ordered and inflicted it. By the 1980s, in most of South Africa – and following the experience of Winnie Mandela and Mamphela Ramphele – banishment gave way to more chilling and final solutions. This was one factor that stepped up the tensions within Transkei, in particular between the totally compromised security police and the imported former Rhodesian Selous Scouts under Colonel Ron Reid-Daly on the one side and a group of Transkei military officers on the other. Among the Transkei officers were several who supported the ideals of the ANC and

PAC. Chief among these was one of Dumisa Ntsebeza's former students, General Bantubonke Holomisa. Another former student, General Temba Matanzima, was a nephew of both K.D. and George Matanzima. He had been one of the leading questioners of minister Louis le Grange at Jongilizwe College in 1976 and went on to become a major-general of the post-apartheid defence force.

In January 1987 Holomisa had himself been detained by security, although it was one of Reid-Daly's men who interrogated him. After two months he was told he would be released to face charges in court and would be allowed to apply for bail. Holomisa refused to appear in court without his lawyer: Dumisa Ntsebeza. The stalemate was resolved when fellow officers in the Transkei army gave an ultimatum to George Matanzima, KD's brother and righthand man. Holomisa was unconditionally released. Reid-Daly and the Selous Scouts who had joined him in Transkei were briefly detained before being expelled from the territory. The tide was turning, but slowly. General Kawe still held sway with his spies, thugs and killers and continued to cooperate with his 'amaBhulu' (Boer) counterparts.

6

Hit squad horrors

In the 1980s Transkei operated a perpetual state of emergency, a reflection of the rest of South Africa. In this environment, Dumisa Ntsebeza remained a prime target of the security establishment, not only because of his legal defence in political trials as far afield as East London and Wepener in the Free State province, but for his role with Prisoners' Welfare Programmes. This organis-ation, known by the acronym Priwelpro, documented human rights violations in Transkei and campaigned on behalf of political detainees. It was the local equivalent of the Detainees' Parents' Support Committee (DPSC) set up in South Africa in the wake of the wave of detentions that followed the 1976 student uprisings.

Dumisa Ntsebeza was the legal adviser and board chairman of Priwelpro, which was established by Lawrence Vumankosi Ntikinca when he was released from prison, and by a former ANC prisoner, Mzwandile Mbete. Ntikinca was the field officer and Mbete the administrative officer. The security police had never forgiven these two for the embarrassing damages claim they had brought and won. Shortly after the formation of Priwelpro, they sent a questionnaire demanding details such as its sources of funding, and the names and personal particulars of directors. In his capacity as legal adviser, Ntsebeza formally refused to comply. The police were enraged, but were hampered by the shifting political realities in the homeland. Their tactics toward the lawyer consisted mainly of indirect intimidation, overt surveillance and cold hard stares. Others were not so fortunate: kidnaps and killings continued, among them five of Dumisa Ntsebeza's clients. The message had been underlined again in blood.

While the Transkei police were apparently wary of direct conflict with Ntsebeza, their South African counterparts cared nothing for the political tensions in Transkei. Unlike their Transkei counterparts, most of them were white, with all the insecure arrogance this fact implied in the apartheid state. Dumisa Ntsebeza clashed again with the Eastern Cape security police soon after emerging from the banishment deal with the Transkei government in October 1986. He was retained to defend Nomatamsanqa Mbilini, a woman from Queenstown who was charged with furthering the aims of the ANC, which, by South African police definition, was a communist organisation. She had been badly tortured, but the only evidence against her comprised some notes in her own handwriting, which were alleged to be copies of ANC and SACP material.

In preparation for the case, the lawyer needed to have a copy of the handwritten document, so he drove to the regional court in Queenstown and made his way to the office of the prosecutor. The door was open. Inside he found Captain Venter, the head of the local Special Branch who had threatened Lungisile and Matthew Goniwe, sitting with another, older, man in plain clothes and the woman prosecutor behind her desk. As he walked in, Venter rose angrily from his chair, shouting in Afrikaans: 'Wat maak jy hier?' (What are you doing here?) 'I don't want to see you anywhere I am . . . have you no manners . . . why don't you knock?'

Dumisa Ntsebeza was taken aback and, he remembered decades later, positively frightened. Then cold anger overwhelmed his fear. He stared back at the red-faced captain and, struggling to keep his voice as calm as possible, asked why Venter found it necessary to quarrel every time they met. Venter was nonplussed and Ntsebeza should have left matters there. But, gaining confidence from Venter's silence, he ventured to add: 'After all, I am not here to see you – and this is not your office.' With that he turned to the prosecutor and informed her in measured tones that he intended reporting the incident to the magistrate. It was, as Lungisile Ntsebeza used to note in exasperation, 'just the right thing to say at probably just the wrong time'.

The incident had also given Dumisa Ntsebeza ammunition for his argument about the ill-treatment sustained by his client. Venter's colleague Tollie le Roux had also engaged in the torture. When he came up for cross-examination, Dumisa put it to him that Venter's evidently uncontrollable rage was an indication that he was capable of the sort of vicious beatings that Nomatamsanqa Mbilini had suffered. The allegations caused a major stir. Venter was furious.

So too was Brigadier Griebnauw, who turned out to have been the other man in the prosecutor's office when Venter had flown off the handle. Griebnauw had reasons of his own to dislike the lawyer from Cala. On the following day he too had had a run-in with Ntsebeza, who appeared to have no respect for social protocol. He had told Ntsebeza that he, a security branch brigadier, was an expert on the ANC, SACP and communism. He would be testifying in the case and had prepared a document containing what he said were quotations from banned ANC and SACP literature. These would clearly show that Mbilini's handwritten document was orientated toward the ANC and SACP.

It was meant to be a pre-emptive strike before the final confrontation in court, only Dumisa Ntsebeza refused to accept it. He demanded the original documents from which Griebnauw had taken his quotations. Only with these, he pointed out, could he ensure that Griebnauw was not quoting out of context. The brigadier was flummoxed. These were banned materials. Subversive literature. It would be inappropriate, not to say illegal, to show them to anyone. In any event, said Griebnauw, he did not want to commit an offence. In terms of the Act, to show Dumisa Ntsebeza the original material would constitute 'training' in communism.

It was a classic example of the insane logic of the system. Ntsebeza could not stop himself. 'What if I am already trained?' he asked in a conspiratorial tone. Griebnauw, who was linked to one of the notorious Eastern Cape death squads, failed to see the joke. He became even angrier when he was informed that if he did not provide the original documents, Ntsebeza would object to his 'communist quotation' document being admitted before the court. The objection was lodged and the court adjourned when Griebnauw reluctantly agreed that Dumisa Ntsebeza could view the original documents in East London.

Ntsebeza congratulated himself on another minor victory and thought no more about the incident, pleased only that he could return to Umtata. There, with a free weekend ahead, the family decided to go shopping in East London on the Saturday. They left Umtata early in the morning, which, as it turned out, was a fortunate decision. Dumisa Ntsebeza's absence from Umtata probably saved his life, since a death squad spent much of the day cruising the Transkei capital looking for him.

That evening, at dusk, Dumisa and Nontobeko and their children, Samora and Castro, returned from their day out. Coming into Umtata, they stopped at a set of traffic lights. Another grey-green sedan, the virtual duplicate of the Ntsebeza car, drew up alongside. It was Joseph Miso, also a lawyer and, coincidentally, also from Cala. He hooted and waved. The Ntsebezas responded but, having promised the children a video, they turned off the normal route home to go to the shop. Miso drove on, with a white car behind him. What happened next was first relayed to Dumisa Ntsebeza in a garbled telephone call at three o'clock in the morning. The caller was Joseph Miso. He was in the Butterworth hospital, 120 km south of Umtata, where he had been admitted with multiple injuries after being severely beaten.

Next day the story was pieced together and passed on to local and foreign journalists. The anti-apartheid *Weekly Mail* made great play of it, and this was again a form of insurance policy, for Ntsebeza realised with horror how narrowly he and perhaps his family had avoided almost certain death. After waving goodbye at the traffic lights, Joseph Miso had driven on for about five minutes before he was forced off the road. The door was wrenched open and three white men bundled him out. With kicks and slaps, they forced him onto the floor in the back of the other car. One of the men had taken his keys. The two cars sped off along the road toward East London.

Crouched on the floor, Joseph Miso was punched and stamped on by the man who had got in with him. Where was all the communist literature, the man wanted to know. Miso, crying in pain and terror, protested that he knew nothing. He admitted that he was from Cala and, yes, he was a lawyer. The beating resumed immediately. 'So you are Ntsebeza,' his assailant said triumphantly. He seemed incapable of understanding that there could be two black lawyers from Cala. The more Miso denied that he was Dumisa Ntsebeza, the more the blows and kicks rained down. His life, he knew, was in the balance. He had to prove he was not Dumisa Ntsebeza. Then, through the pain and fear, he remembered: his passport was in the glove box of his car.

He remembered later that he had screamed this information. The beating stopped as he lapsed into semi-consciousness. He was only vaguely aware of the car stopping, doors opening and more angry voices, before hands pulled him roughly from the car. He was at Kei Bridge, the border post between Transkei and South Africa. One of his assailants was demanding of a Transkei policeman, Stofile, that the bloodied and battered Miso be locked up in the police station cell at the border. Stofile refused. 'I am not having anyone dying in my cell,' he insisted. He would not budge and, after hasty consultations, Joseph Miso was again thrust into the back of the car. It sped off back towards Butterworth, while one attacker kept a foot on his neck.

Joseph Miso passed out. He came to, aware that he could taste gravel. He was lying, face down, on the roadside. His car keys were beside his head and his car was parked a short distance away. After some time, he was able to get to his feet, stagger to his car, get in and drive to Butterworth. Both he and Dumisa Ntsebeza decided that the best defence was publicity. There was nothing else to do, since Miso did not know his attackers, and anyway the target had clearly been Ntsebeza.

There were no further attacks on Dumisa, but the open intimidation continued. Then there were the clients who died. Sithembele Zokwe, a political activist represented by Ntsebeza, was arrested in January 1988 and taken to his home by two Transkei security policemen, Gumengu and Tyani. There, using automatic rifles, they shot him at point-blank range, almost ripping his upper body apart with sixty bullets. In a crude attempt to cover their tracks and to claim that Zokwe was a grenade-throwing terrorist, they set off a handgrenade in the room as they left.

This was the third attempt on Zokwe's life. In September 1985 a group of men in a white minibus with tinted windows had drawn up alongside him in the town of Butterworth. In broad daylight, they attempted to bundle him into the van. He resisted and called out. Passersby responded and the men leapt back into the kombi and sped off, but not before Zokwe had a good look at one of them. He gave a description, which matched that of the askari Mose. It was only days before Bathandwa Ndondo was invited into what was perhaps the same vehicle. Once again Mose, one of the most prolific killers in the security police, was present.

Before the month was out, Sithembele Zokwe was again waylaid, this time on the outskirts of Umtata. He was shot several times and left for dead on the banks of the Umtata river. Suffering from multiple gunshot wounds and loss of blood, he was found and rushed to hospital. This time he recognised among his assailants a Cala-born man known only as Shologu, who had left the district of Xhalanga when he joined the police. Shologu simply disappeared and the Transkei police denied all knowledge of him. On the third occasion, the killers took no chance that Zokwe would live, but this was 1988 and the balance of power was in flux within Transkei. A military council, under the chairmanship of Bantubonke Holomisa, had taken over.

To Dumisa Ntsebeza's surprise, the two security policemen were arrested. He wrote at once to the attorney general, expressing the view that the policemen responsible for the killing would be allowed bail. Then, like the murderers of Bathandwa Ndondo, they would simply disappear. The letter brought in a threat of libel from the attorney general, but the killers were refused bail.

While these arguments were still raging, three more of Ntsebeza's clients were murdered, shot dead in broad daylight in their car as they drove through suburban Umtata. A fourth passenger was seriously wounded, but survived. It was Friday, 5 February 1988, and Zolile Sangoni, cousin of the lawyer Temba Sangoni, and his friends Zonwabele Mayaphi and Thozamile Nkune had attended a political trial in the Umtata court defended by Dumisa Ntsebeza. In the public gallery the three young men met up with 'MK' Gift, a young man reputed to be an ANC guerrilla. When the court adjourned early for lunch, the four decided to drive out to the well-known Nqadu butcher's in Ncambendlana township. It was a sunny day and they decided on a 'braai' (barbecue).

As they pulled away from the butcher's, they noticed a car following. It was a Husky, a small station wagon. It came very close, and when the driver flicked his lights Sangoni pulled further over to the side of the road. As he did so, someone leaned out of the following vehicle and opened fire, shattering the rear window. The car lurched onto the sidewalk and stalled. The Husky drew level and paused for the few seconds it took for three automatic weapons to empty their magazines into the car and its occupants, before speeding off.

Several of the bystanders who had seen the shooting noted the registration number of the Husky. They and others confirmed that the death squad comprised four people, one of them a white man and one a black woman. Once again, the close-knit nature of the region displayed itself. When Dumisa Ntsebeza got to the scene to collect statements, he was given more than a simple description of the death squad and the vehicle they used. At the inquest, one of the killers was identified as Mpumelelo Mandliwa, an East London-based askari. Another was a Transkei security policeman known as Wana.

Dumisa Ntsebeza and Vumankosi Ntikinca made their way to the hospital where the shattered bodies and the seriously wounded Thozamile Nkune lay. The scene was to haunt him for years. The death squad had used expanding dumdum bullets. It was almost a miracle that Nkune had survived. Well into that evening Ntsebeza and Ntikinca shuttled between the hospital, the police station and the scene of the murders. They took statements, asked questions and demanded action.

As Saturday dawned, Lungisile 'Bra Lu' Stofile, a car-mad member of the Sangoni legal firm, turned up in his highly tuned little 16-valve VW GTI. There was always the chance that the death squad was still in town; their vehicle might still be in Umtata. Bra Lu volunteered to cruise the highways and byways of the Transkei capital to see if he could sight the Husky or any of its occupants. Vumankosi Ntikinca went with him. Maybe the killers' car had been dumped somewhere. They certainly did not expect to see it being driven. Yet at midday, as they turned a corner in the Mbuqe Park township, they saw ahead of them a car that matched exactly the description given by eyewitnesses. The clincher was the registration number.

This was a situation they had not planned for. It would be foolhardy to try to stop the car, which seemed to contain a driver and two passengers, a man and a woman. After a hurried consultation, Ntikinca and Stofile decided that the best bet was to follow at a safe distance and to be as inconspicuous as possible. Since there were only two cars on the road, this was a forlorn hope. Outside of what they had seen in the movies, neither Vumankosi Ntikinca nor Bra Lu Stofile had any experience of 'tailing' anyone. When the quarry speeded up, so did they, and when it slowed down, they followed suit.

Obviously aware that he was being followed, the driver of the car in front abruptly turned a corner and accelerated. Bra Lu, whose 'hell driver' reputation was not unwarranted, followed. It was a frightening experience, racing through the streets of Umtata, jumping stop signs and traffic lights and screeching around corners. The Husky could not lose the chasing VW, piloted by a determined Stofile. Had it stopped, neither of the pursuers had any idea what they might do. It did not stop, presumably because the pursued trio did not know who was behind them. Almost without realising it, Bra Lu was speeding down one of the main streets toward the central police station. It was here that the car in front braked and skidded into the driveway leading behind the station. The two pursuers were elated. Here was further confirmation of what Priwelpro had long maintained: the death squads were official or, at the very least, were linked to the police. While Stofile kept watch, Vumankosi Ntikinca ran to the legal firm's town centre office.

It was only minutes before Dumisa Ntsebeza, together with a breathless Ntikinca, arrived in Ntsebeza's car. They barely had time to confirm from Bra Lu that nobody had left the police station when the road was sealed off. Cars screeched in at either end, doors slammed and suddenly the street was filled with what could only be police reinforcements. The death squad must have radioed for help. It was, Dumisa Ntsebeza remarked later, as if there was some Security Branch convention going on. The atmosphere was decidedly hostile, especially the glares from a number of white, and apparently South African, operatives. But there was no backing down. In the most authoritative tone he could muster, Ntsebeza demanded the arrest, on suspicion of murder, of the trio who had sought refuge behind the police station. He was still declaiming when several policemen approached and announced that Ntikinca was under arrest. He was bundled off. How could this be happening? Surely not under the new military council, with Holomisa at its head? Then Ntsebeza and Stofile were escorted into an office in the police station. They were to be held for questioning. The interrogator was Colonel Booi, who had tortured and mutilated Ntikinca five years earlier.

Only minutes into the interrogation, it was obvious that Booi was stalling. His questions ranged from banal to downright silly. The reason why became clear when the two men were released two hours later. The corridors and offices were almost deserted – no sign of any of the white or black security police. In two hours the South Africans could already be safe across the 'border'. Hunched, his fists clenched in frustration and anger, Dumisa Ntsebeza marched out of the police station and drove to the home of his former student, the general and then head of the military council, Bantubonke Holomisa, stopping only to pick up the father of the murdered Zonwabele Mayaphi. Holomisa was pleased to see 'Cat', but not at all pleased with what he learned. He would do what he could, he said, but things were not so straightforward.

Holomisa was walking his own tightrope, trying to consolidate his control, keep closer contact with the exiled ANC and PAC, and at the same time ensure that he did not trigger too harsh a reaction from the apartheid state. In part this meant dispensing reassurance to the ever watchful security contingents, especially in Port Elizabeth, Queenstown and East London. While he was mostly sure about the army, he knew that the police were badly compromised. Evidence of this emerged shortly before the scheduled trial of the killers of Sithembele Zokwe. They had been kept in a rural jail and they managed to escape. According to the police, they forced the door of a van transporting them to a doctor in the village of Nqamakwe and vanished without trace.

It was frustrating for Ntsebeza, Priwelpro and its supporters, but at least it had been clearly established that the killers belonged to the police. A similar blend of frustration and success surrounded the drive-by killing of Zolile Sangoni and his friends. At the inquest, the police admitted killing in self-defence: 'MK' Gift had been about to throw a handgrenade at them. They had spotted it lying on his lap and had opened fire before he could pull the pin. This was a stock excuse used by police when murdering alleged guerrilla targets. This time, given the circumstances, the claim was especially outlandish. Magistrate D. Ncapayi rejected it. The police, he found, were culpable.

To nobody's surprise, the prosecuting authorities ruled that there was insufficient evidence to proceed. But the Sangoni Partnership instituted a civil action against the Transkei state and won substantial cash settlements for the families of the victims. Years later it seemed that more light might be thrown on the matter when one of the killers, Wana, applied to the TRC for amnesty for his crime. Shortly before he was due to appear, he withdrew his application and the matter was not pursued. It was just like the old days in Transkei, days when Holomisa felt he had to make concessions as long as his own position within the military council remained insecure.

After the furore following the Zokwe and Sangoni, Gift and Mayaphi killings, the military government banned Priwelpro and demanded the forfeiture of its assets. Vumankosi Ntikinca had had enough of pressure, of dealing

with the ever-present prospect of, at best, a bad beating or a quick death in a
hail of bullets. He fled into exile, using one of the demanded assets, Priwelpro's
van. Dumisa Ntsebeza stayed behind, aiming to use the law to fight the
banning and resist the seizure of any other assets. What little money there
was, was hidden, along with all the records. Even the office furniture
disappeared into friendly hands. A few items of stationery, some books and a
few other odds and ends were all that remained for the state to seize. But by
1989 the military government, with Holomisa clearly in command and more
and more openly allied with the ANC, lifted the ban on Priwelpro and thirty-
two other organisations. Ntsebeza duly applied for and had returned what the
police had taken.

It was a time when the tide was turning rapidly; in South Africa as well.
Holomisa openly associated himself with the ANC and called for round-table
discussions on the future of South Africa between the apartheid government,
the liberation movements and the homelands. He also provided sanctuary to
PAC leaders who were still on the run. Most importantly from the angle of his
own survival, Holomisa also ensured that a number of trained ANC soldiers,
members of the organisation's armed wing, MK, were placed in the Transkei
army. It was they who played a significant role in 1992 when the apartheid
government, then under F.W. de Klerk, decided to get rid of Holomisa.

De Klerk and his ministers and generals knew that Transkei would be
assured of a seat in any negotiations about the future dispensation for South
Africa. As long as Holomisa represented the homeland, this vital element
would be allied to the ANC. If the leadership of Transkei changed, the ANC
could hardly object to the presence of a Transkei delegation, even if the new
leader decided not to support the liberation movement. This was the thinking
behind the two coup plots that were launched. The first was aborted, but the
second, supported by both the military and police, with weapons supplied by
Eugene de Kock from the huge Vlakplaas arsenal, went ahead – and failed.
Colonel Craig Duli, who had pledged to replace Holomisa with the utterly
discredited K.D. Matanzima, died in the attempt. Holomisa continued to lead
a Transkei delegation to the Convention for a Democratic South Africa
(Codesa) talks. He did so as part of a 'patriotic front' led by the ANC. Another
of the government's carefully laid plans had misfired.

The move toward a negotiated settlement, obviously largely engineered by
the apartheid government, introduced other political tensions. The PAC
initially refused to be part of the talks. So too did the Black Consciousness-
orientated Azanian People's Organisation (Azapo). The Black Lawyers' Associ-

ation (BLA) – president: Dumisa Ntsebeza – neither supported nor rejected Codesa. This was in accordance with a professed non-sectarian stand. Dumisa Ntsebeza had, in fact, joined the BLA and resigned from the National Association of Democratic Lawyers (Nadel) in 1988 when it came out in support of the Freedom Charter of the ANC. This, he correctly saw, was a party political stance. In his view, organisations of lawyers or workers in trade unions should be inclusive, worker or professional unity being the protection behind which various political currents could contend. At the time, he explained: 'I insisted on taking a neutral stand in the politics of our country, electing to support the entire liberation movement.' Besides, he pointed out, this did not stop the BLA – it did not have a racially exclusive constitution – and Nadel working together on such issues as the demand that exiles be allowed to return to South Africa without preconditions.

Real and imagined differences over Codesa gave the security establishment an opportunity to try to isolate certain groups and individuals from the broader liberation front. The securocrats also continued to target Holomisa by alleging that he was supporting armed attacks carried out in South Africa but planned in Transkei. (Some attacks were still taking place, mainly staged by elements of the PAC armed wing Apla, which was, in any event, quite heavily infiltrated by the security police.) It had already become obvious to black security operatives that the times might be changing. They were not privy to the planning and overall strategy of the white security establishment, but at senior levels they had access to the documents derived from such planning, and a lot of them reached Holomisa. One was secret information note 59/238 dated 28 April 1992, and addressed to the commissioner and deputy commissioner of the South African Police. It purported to be an assessment of Apla military activities in Transkei.

It also contained a list of what were said to be Apla training bases in Transkei. Among them was 'The house of Dumisa Ndebeza [sic], Cala' and the Ntsebeza family bookshop. The homes of several of the lawyer's clients were also listed. Holomisa passed the secret note on to Dumisa Ntsebeza, who publicly announced that he had been placed on a hit list by the security forces; that he had seen the list, and it named a large number of innocent people. The link between them was that they had been anti-apartheid activists and were not members of the ANC or its allied organisations. Publicity, yet again, seemed the only protection.

Although he did not announce the fact, Ntsebeza knew that Major-General J. Kuen had signed the information note as 'Chief: crime intelligence'. The compilers, listed on the document, were Captain J. Meyer of 'Unit C20' and Captain J.J.C. Shulz, described as 'Unit A50 co-ordinator'. The report was 'perused and concurred with' by Brigadier J.C.S. Oberholzer. Even without the 'friends in the media' and other means of propaganda, a report authorised by such high-ranking policemen would surely cast doubt on Ntsebeza's innocence and that of others listed in a similar way. In an unpublished analysis, he wrote:

> '[The police] have calculated that if they link me with the PAC, people in the ANC will not sympathise with me . . . I believe the police want this to be the case so that a hit at this time will not raise any widespread protest. The police know that I am not in the PAC and have never been. They know I am not in the ANC and have never been. They also know that I support the liberation movement with my legal skills . . . after all, to them it does not matter whether I am in the ANC or PAC or in none of them. In my work I disturb them. In the BLA I disturb them. In Priwelpro I disturb them. In other non-governmental organisations in Cala, I disturb them.
>
> However, they are also aware that my neutralist stand on Codesa etc has lost me a lot of those who are unequivocally supportive of Codesa. If they can show that, far from being neutral I am in fact taking sides with the PAC which is trying to wreck the peace process by armed attacks, they will successfully create an atmosphere in which, when the hit takes place, there will be confusion as to whether in fact it was THEY who did it, or over-enthusiastic supporters of those in Codesa.

It was, Ntsebeza added, similar to the tactic employed with a number of other murders carried out by the South African security forces. Even in the case of the brutal slaying of Matthew Goniwe and his comrades, the police and military had initially tried to blame Azapo. It was clear that the list's information was grossly inaccurate. Yet it was an official report. As such, it provided the bureaucratic pretext for the murder of opponents.

Having exposed the existence and inaccuracy of the information note, Dumisa Ntsebeza felt he had scuppered this excuse for slaughter. He was wrong. Little more than a year later, as F.W. de Klerk tried to hold together his increasingly critical right wing, he launched one of the last and bloodiest of raids into Transkei. It was the night of 8 October 1993 in the Umtata suburb of North Crest.

7

The North Crest massacre

Nothing stirred in the sleeping houses. Suddenly volleys of gunfire ripped through the night. The weapons were silenced; the men in balaclavas who wielded them did their work fast and efficiently. The only outward disturbance was the quick series of flashes, that shone through the curtains of the darkened room as one of the men took pictures of their handiwork. Then the group slipped out, led by the informant who had brought them, as silently as they had come.

In the small front room of number 47, A.C. Jordan Street, only the television set was still intact. Five bodies lay crumpled in front of it, riddled with bullets, laced with blood. Dark puddles of blood oozed onto the mattresses laid on the floor and there were scarlet splashes on the walls, pockmarked with ricochets. There were bullet holes, too, in the cupboards and ceiling.

The front door was slightly ajar, green insulation tape wrapped around the handle. Number 47 was still and silent as nearby curtains and doors opened and the smoke and smells of breakfast greeted the rising sun. The attackers of the night were already many miles away, in the coastal city of Port Elizabeth. They had been congratulated on another job well done, had filed their reports and forwarded the Polaroid pictures to the higher levels which had requested them.

The date was seared into the memory of Sigqibo Mpendulo, branded on his mind. A local North Crest butcher and PAC activist, Mpendulo owned the house at 47 A.C. Jordan Street. He had been away for the evening, but had left it in the care of his twin school student sons and three of their young friends. The boys were staying with him for a few days as part of the arrangement with his divorced wife. They had intended watching television until the midnight close, and he fully expected to find that they had fallen asleep in the front room as they had done so often in the past.

As he pushed open the door, Mpendulo sensed something wrong. It was ajar yet there was no sign of life. When he glanced into the room, he saw not just the bodies, but the blood. He still does not remember what he did in those first moments.

Then questions tumbled through his mind. Who had done this? How and why? He had been part of the anti-apartheid resistance: as a result, he had spent five years in the grey stone prison and working in the lime quarry of Robben Island. He knew of the killings and bombings visited on neighbouring states over the years. But this was 1993. South Africa was under the international spotlight. This was the time of talks about setting a date for non-racial democratic elections, a time when peace and reconciliation were the dominant themes promoted from on high.

There were, of course, the various fragments of the self-professed White Right, pouring out their racist bile and threatening a southern African apocalypse. Apla, known to be heavily infiltrated by the security services, was also still officially at war. Elements within it had launched several attacks apparently aimed at sowing terror throughout the white community, which it saw as being complicit in the crime of apartheid. These attacks, one on a golf club, another on a church, and yet another on a restaurant, were calculated to bring home to the white community the reality of sudden blind brutality with which black South Africans had lived for years. Whatever the rationale and however tragic the consequences, these seemed to be little more than the final throes of a doomed armed struggle. In just twenty days, a meeting was scheduled between the government and the PAC about a formal cessation of hostilities.

Yet, in North Crest in 1993, here was yet one more example of the terror inflicted over the years on the homes of activists in Lesotho, Mozambique and Botswana. Could it be that a maverick 'Third Force' really did exist? Had the khaki-clad, swastika-wearing elements of the Afrikaner Weerstandsbeweging extended their influence into the special forces and police death squads? After all, De Klerk had maintained, contrary to all the evidence, that death squads did not exist; that he and his government would not tolerate them. There had even been official commissions of inquiry that delivered the same verdict, although questions were already being asked about the way they were set up and how they had reached their findings.

Such questions were logical at the time. Umtata was the capital of Transkei, which was still a nominally independent state. And although De Klerk and his ministers were being labelled sellouts by many in their former constituency, they seemed unlikely to indulge again in bouts of official terror. Or did the National Party leadership feel the need to prove themselves still capable of wielding the brutal power – the kragdadigheid – so often demanded of Afrikaner leaders?

Sigqibo Mpendulo roused neighbours, called the police, and broke the terrible news to the parents of the three boys whose bodies lay crumpled beside those of his twin sons. Then he telephoned Dumisa Ntsebeza, whose law practice and home were nearby. Perhaps in justice lay the chance at least to blunt the pain of loss.

Within hours, rumour and speculation were rife throughout the region. The common assumption was that the sixteen-year-old twins Samora and Sadat, seventeen-year-old Thando Mthembu and their young friends Mzwandile Mfeya and Sandiso Yose, both just twelve years old, had been killed by 'the Boers'. Perhaps as a message to all political activists that 'they' could still get you wherever you were, and then walk away. Who else would sneak in and butcher five school students with such savagery? An independent post-mortem later established that 16 bullets had been fired into the body of Sadat Mpendulo, and 11 bullets into Samora. Between them, Sandiso Yose and Mzwandile Mfeya, both 12 years old, had been shot 37 times. Six bullets had ended the life of Thando Mtembu.

This must be the work of trained killers, of one of the specialist death squads. Dumisa Ntsebeza, when he examined the scene, recognised the signature of the apartheid state, but he foresaw a lengthy and possibly futile task ahead to identify and prove responsibility. Unlike the killings of Bathandwa Ndondo, Sangoni and his friends, or of Sithembele Zokwe, there were no witnesses. It had happened in the dead of night. No trace remained of the killers. Somewhere behind it stood the system, but to pinpoint the planners and the source of the ultimate orders was surely a hopeless task.

But the North Crest atrocity proved different, maybe unique. For the first and only time in South Africa and perhaps anywhere, the head of a state accused of systematic and gross human rights abuses stepped forward and claimed the credit. While the gunmen and their immediate superiors lay low, President F.W. de Klerk announced that he had ordered the destruction of 'an Apla facility' in the Transkei. Acting on sound information from his intelligence sources, he could confirm that the house in North Crest was a base used by Apla to launch attacks on South Africa. Stern-faced and forceful, he said he had been 'fully informed' of every aspect of the raid. To underline the lethal success of the venture, there were even colour photographs of the bodies.

The police also issued a statement. It described the raid on the house as a '27-minute operation' and claimed that the 'five terrorists' killed had 'offered resistance'. The defence force also stepped in to back De Klerk, announcing categorically that 'the house was a confirmed Apla facility'.

Nelson Mandela, speaking from Glasgow during a visit to Scotland, described the attack as 'an act of thuggery'. His statement summed up the feelings of Dumisa Ntsebeza and the bereaved families. Yet their outraged protests attracted little media attention and Mandela's comment was merely noted; most of the mainstream newspapers and certainly radio and television were content with the president's version. But the independent anti-apartheid *New Nation* newspaper, which was financed by the Catholic Bishops' Conference, checked the facts on the ground and produced a banner front-page headline: SLAUGHTER OF THE INNOCENTS.

Within twenty-four hours, the question of who had been killed became an issue. The ages of the boys, and the fact that they had apparently been shot while asleep, was briefly a topic for public debate. De Klerk and the security apparatus vehemently denied that the victims had been young school students. The boys, they asserted, were much older than claimed and had been trained Apla operatives. Defence minister Kobie Coetsee, the leading Broederbond moderniser who had played a major role in steering the system toward negotiations, joined hardline securocrats such as SA Defence Force (SADF) chief of staff General Kat Liebenberg, police chief General Johan van der Merwe and Liebenberg's designated successor General Georg Meiring, in supporting De Klerk. A barrage of misinformation spread confusion about ages, weapons, and even who had been shot by whom and why.

Exactly a week to the day after the massacre came an announcement that heaped insult on to the injury felt not only by the families of the victims but by growing numbers of local supporters: Mandela and De Klerk had jointly been awarded the Nobel Peace Prize. 'I felt physically ill when I heard that,' Ntsebeza remembered years later. Holomisa promptly called for foreign governments to 'suspend prizes to De Klerk'. But this was a call from the margins of mainstream society by 'a known supporter of the ANC and PAC'. It barely warranted public mention. Nor did the finding announced on the following day by pathologists who had examined the bodies of the victims and who confirmed that the dead were in fact as young as their families had claimed.

A massive funeral in Umtata, attended by an estimated 30,000 people, had some repercussions, not least within the negotiating forums at Kempton Park. But there was virtually no attention paid outside Transkei. Kobie Coetsee also assured the Codesa forum, where Mandela and other anti-apartheid delegates continued to complain about North Crest, that he would produce fresh evidence to justify the raid. 'Although regrettable,' he claimed their deaths were unavoidable.

On a television talk show two weeks after the raid, Mandela spelled out exactly how he felt. 'For a president to authorise the killing of children is a blatant act of terrorism,' he said. It was a forthright statement which was noted by embassies and analysts – and largely ignored by the popular media. De Klerk, Mandela added, 'did not have the decency to apologise. That confirms our accusations that, when it comes to blacks, he is absolutely insensitive.'

In terms of general public awareness, there the matter lay. But Ntsebeza continued to press for information, probing and building up a case. By early December he was ready to launch a civil action demanding compensation for murder from De Klerk, his foreign minister Roelof 'Pik' Botha, law and order minister Hernus Kriel, and defence minister Kobie Coetsee. The indictment was filed with the Transkei supreme court only days before De Klerk and Nelson Mandela were due to leave for Oslo for the Nobel prize giving. Ntsebeza's action infuriated De Klerk and the security establishment. They need not have worried: no major newspaper, radio or television station took up the issue, which tended to be seen as a shabby attempt at political mud slinging. Mandela, however, had by then grown weary of what he perceived to be the duplicity of De Klerk. He accused the National Party leader of being a murderer, a man with 'blood on his hands'.

A year later, De Klerk was to complain bitterly to American author and journalist Patti Waldmeir about the accusation. He was horrified to be labelled in this manner. It was unfair. Mandela had failed to understand 'the complexity of the situation'. But De Klerk talked in general terms. There was no mention of North Crest. The world at large knew nothing of the tension between the two men as they made their separate ways to Norway.

De Klerk flew in the presidential jet, NAN, via an audience with the British queen and a lengthy and 'extremely helpful' talk with British prime minister John Major and his foreign secretary, Douglas Hurd. Neither raised the issue of North Crest, nor of De Klerk's involvement in human rights abuses. Then it was on to Oslo, where De Klerk later noted with obvious chagrin that his reception had been 'reserved', as opposed to the 'effusive and unrestrained' welcome accorded

Mandela. He lodged similar complaints about the Nobel ceremony, where he again felt that he had enjoyed too little prominence.

By that stage he seems to have become convinced that he was the star in a morality play of his own scripting and deserved international adulation. En route, he had received the attention he felt was his due, but not here. Yet had he not been the first South African president invited to Moscow? And had not the Russian leader, Boris Yeltsin, just a year earlier, told him that Mandela would also be welcomed to Moscow, but not as the president of the ANC, merely as 'an international figure, a campaigner for human rights?' De Klerk had, indeed, received the sort of plaudits that helped inflate a burgeoning ego.

Such praise continued. Russian journalist Boris Pilyatskin wrote about the Nobel award in *Isvestiya* in December 1993: 'One could understand if the Peace Prize were awarded to De Klerk three years ago when he single-handedly changed the course of the ship of state away from apartheid. But what did Nelson Mandela have to do with it? It was De Klerk who released him from prison and provided the opportunity to legalise the ANC.' Such commentaries reinforced De Klerk's own impression of himself and his role. They also offered some balm for the rebuffs he suffered. Outside the Nobel ceremony, for example, there were protesters who hailed Mandela and shouted: 'De Klerk – go home!'

De Klerk was mortified. Yet, had the protesters known about the five dead boys, his reception might have been far more hostile. Mandela's disdainful observation that De Klerk had blood on his hands could have been magnified a thousandfold, to echo around the world and eventually bury De Klerk in calumny. The world did not know, and the award was generally perceived as a dual triumph. Yet North Crest would not go away.

While Mandela and De Klerk were in Oslo, Ntsebeza and the families sought to prove the ages of the children. In their gamble that the victims' births had not been registered, the intelligence services had forgotten, or never knew, about another fact of Transkeian society: it is generally religious. Births might not often have been registered with a remote and often despised state authority, but children were and are baptised in their first year. Where birth certificates were not available, Ntsebeza discovered baptismal documents. The case made public by De Klerk was starting to fall apart.

So then the police, in order to rig cover for the primarily military unit which had orchestrated the raid, maintained that the boys killed in North Crest had been armed. They also claimed that an arms cache had been discovered at the house; the squad had 'fired in self-defence'. It was a panic reaction to the

charge of mass murder levelled at a time when a democratic transition was
under way and the risk of retribution existed. Besides, at that stage North Crest
provided the only clear example that deliberate murder behaviour was not the
aberrant act of 'rogue elements' but part and parcel of the security structure of
the state.

But there was a problem with this police revelation: none of the photographs taken by the killers revealed any weapons. This lack was corrected in a
manner familiar over the years: the police produced photographs of a weapons
cache they claimed had been seized in the raid. This was another blunder. For
one thing, the notion that a gun is a gun might satisfy lay observers, but
specific weapons were favoured by different armed groups. The weapons
displayed in the police photographs were not those associated with Apla.
Examination might reveal where they had come from.

So Ntsebeza demanded sight of the weapons and arranged for a leading US
firearms expert from the Chicago police force to examine them. It was
common knowledge in the broader anti-apartheid movement that the police
and army kept stocks of weapons for use in framing suspects or for planting at
the scenes of assassinations. (This was a fact which evidence to the Truth and
Reconciliation Commission was later to confirm. It was admitted for example
by Kobus 'Chappies' Klopper, who was granted amnesty for planting hand
grenades in the home of 'people's poet' Mzwake Mbuli.) Not one of the 'North
Crest weapons' ever appeared. Repeated requests – including court orders –
for these vital pieces of material evidence to be produced finally elicited the
response that they had been lost.

By then, the constitutional negotiations at Kempton Park were nearing the
compromise that was to pave the way for South Africa's first non-racial
democratic election. 'Homelands' such as Transkei were being reincorporated
into South Africa and the concept of reconciliation was being heavily promoted. In all the political deal-fixing, the North Crest case fell from public
notice. Mandela and De Klerk, their relationship still strained, agreed that the
matter could be settled out of court with 'ample' payments from the government to the bereaved families. But the fact that the head of state had admitted
authorising the raid could not be erased. Five years later, in a self-serving
autobiography, De Klerk expressed regret about the raid. He claimed he had
acted in good faith and that he had instructed the attackers to 'use minimum
force'.

He added: 'If there had previously been any weapons in the house, they
had already been removed, because none were found.' The smear, the
implication of wrongdoing, remained in a book in which De Klerk admitted
always to supporting the police and armed forces. By then, too, the investi-

gations unit of the TRC had been wound up and the lengthy process of hearing the applications of those seeking amnesty had begun.

Frederik Willem de Klerk did not seek amnesty. Nor did his predecessor, P.W. Botha, or most of the high ranking military and political figures of the recent past. Only Adriaan Vlok, a former police minister, and a tiny handful of police and army generals – out of all apartheid's top promoters and enforcers – actually sought amnesty. Vlok had been implicated directly by police bombers as having authorised the August 1988 bombing of the Khotso House building in which the South African Council of Churches had its offices. In his amnesty application, he noted that Botha had not only personally ordered the bombing, he had also congratulated Vlok on the success of the attack at a meeting of the state security council of which De Klerk was a long-standing member.

Botha simply refused to attend hearings of the TRC, and denied ever having ordered Vlok to plant bombs. De Klerk, who did attend, refused to accept that 'something is true because it is in an amnesty application'. It was Vlok's word against Botha's and De Klerk's, and it was only Vlok who had conveyed the instructions to police general Johan van der Merwe. Vlok had also been the only politician to attend the celebration party after Khotso House in central Johannesburg was all but demolished by some 80 kg of high explosive. The party was staged at the Vlakplaas Farm base of South Africa's leading death squad. And the last commander of Vlakplaas, Colonel Eugene de Kock, the apartheid state's most proficient assassin, also became perhaps the only 'foot soldier' to tell all. Vlok could not deny his involvement.

Nor could De Klerk disown his self-admitted role in at least one case of gross abuse of human rights. But Vlok's involvement was made public because it was investigated and the evidence heard through the TRC. As such, it featured in the massive, five-volume TRC report that was launched in 1999 with a series of high-profile international media events. The effect of this media blitz in Africa, Europe and the United States was to draw a flimsy and temporary curtain over decades of hurt, anger, deceit and duplicity resulting from a mountain of unfinished business. The final report also contained one blanked-out page, demanded by De Klerk and enforced by a legal injunction that threatened to sabotage the timing of the carefully orchestrated media launch. That blanked-out page read:

> F.W. de Klerk presided as head of the former government in the capacity of State President during the period 1989 to 1994. On 14 May 1997, he testified before the Commission in his capacity as head of the former government and as leader of the National Party. In his submissions, Mr De Klerk stated that neither he nor his colleagues in cabinet and the State Security Council authorised or instructed the commission of unlawful acts.

Given the centrality of former State President De Klerk to the transformation of South African politics and his role in the 1990–94 period, the Commission has made the following finding:

The Commission finds that, when Mr De Klerk testified before the Commission on 21 August 1996 and 14 May 1997, he knew and had been informed by his Minister of Law and Order and the Commissioner of Police that they had been authorised by former State President P.W. Botha to bomb Khotso House.

The Commission finds that the bombing of Khotso House constitutes a gross violation of human rights.

The Commission finds that former State President De Klerk displayed a lack of candour in that he omitted to take the Commission into his confidence and/ or to inform the Commission of what he knew, despite being under a duty to do so.

The Commission finds that Mr De Klerk failed to make full disclosure of gross violations of human rights committed by senior members of government and senior members of the SAP, despite being given the opportunity to do so.

The Commission finds that his failure to do so constitutes material non-disclosure, rendering him an accessory to the commission of gross violations of human rights.

The Commission finds Mr De Klerk morally accountable for concealing this from the country when, as the executive head of government, he was under obligation to disclose the truth known to him.

This omission from the final TRC report highlighted the fact that there were many more questions than answers raised by the report and by the whole TRC process. The TRC then began a lengthy exercise to strike a compromise – rejected by De Klerk – to produce a watered-down version of this section.

But the TRC did uncover some of the tragic and frequently blood-stained episodes of the past. It also touched on the tangled history of the homelands and on Kaiser Matanzima's key role at a time when apartheid was still seriously touted as a practical solution for South Africa and even further afield. From 1960, for a decade and a half, the Broederbond ideologues laid down their foundations for the system of grand apartheid. This web of prejudice and self-interest posing as progress ensnared a selection of greedy, craven and unscrupulous individuals and a few fools among the oppressed. It provided a handy rationale for collaborating with the system. So it was that George Matanzima could make his statement about sharing the vision of Mandela.

By 1980 there could no longer be any pretence. The keys to the various evolutionary doors offered as lures by the apartheid system had to be bought at the cost of increasing bloodshed and compromise. As each was opened, it led nowhere. Finally, only the central system itself remained; by then, George and Kaiser Matanzima and their cohorts found themselves tied by blood and betrayal, openly on the side of their oppressors.

The manipulators and manipulated, the masters and their manikins, found that they had common cause only in trying to defend the indefensible; to maintain the status quo when all reason for its existence had dissolved. Stuck fast in a trap of their own making, the more desperately they struggled to get out, the more they were forced to turn loose their heavily indoctrinated hounds of war. In order to buy time they hit out ever more viciously and indiscriminately. Thus was launched the most brutal – and probably most corrupt – decade of apartheid rule. This period that began under P.W. Botha and ended under F.W. de Klerk was drenched in death and blood. It ended with the ruthless massacre of innocents at North Crest, but it also left a bloody legacy, especially in KwaZulu-Natal. This was the decade that the TRC examined most closely, but the fact remains that too much of the deadliest business of a brutal time remains concealed.

FILE THREE

From cul-de-sac to compromise

To shroud the horrors of the past in a collective amnesia would leave posterity with a legacy of festering guilt and unrelieved pain.

– Mac Maharaj

1

Planning the bloodiest decade

It was difficult for minds numbed by apartheid ideology, and made paranoid by Cold War propaganda, to accept that rising popular anger could have roots within the local black population. The emergence of militant trade unionism, the Soweto uprisings in 1976, the roar of international condemnation – all these were seen as examples of a 'total onslaught' by the malevolent forces of international communism. Such was the simplistic view that dictated planning and policy in the South Africa of the 1980s. Even in its crudest form, it counted as considered analysis throughout the lower ranks of the apartheid apparatus.

These were years of increasingly brutal and futile attempts by P.W. Botha and the military to dam the tide of democratic change. The 'total strategy' they developed, justified by the perceived existence of a 'total onslaught', acknowledged the need to relax traditional apartheid with a view to winning the active support of crucial sections of the black community. It also called for the most brutal 'iron fist' response to continued resistance. Constitutional affairs minister and Broederbond moderniser Chris Heunis noted in parliament in 1983: 'Though committed to the process of constitutional development and change the government is not prepared . . . to jeopardise order and stability in this country.' At its most hypocritically benign, this was paternalism, which believed in never sparing the rod or the rope.

The voice of the military throughout this period was P.W. Botha. His finger-wagging belligerence made him an unlikely reformer. Yet reform was being called for and supported, if only within the context of total control. Botha remarked when he introduced his Defence White Paper to parliament in 1977: 'The resolution of a conflict in the times in which we now live demands interdependent and coordinated action in all fields: military, psychological, economic, political, sociological, technological, diplomatic, ideological, cultural, etcetera.' This action should be 'coordinated with all the means available to the state'. By 1979, now firmly in charge as prime minister, Botha was able to put his ideas fully into practice. The launch pad was the September 1979 'Simonstad Raad' (Simonstown Council). It laid the formal groundwork for postwar South Africa's bloodiest decade. Yet this critical initiative was not the subject of any amnesty applications or investigations by the TRC.

This was a gathering of the top planners and officers of the various armed forces of the apartheid state. At this Simonstown meeting they articulated the rationale and tactics necessary to preserve and reform a system deemed by most of the world to be a crime against humanity. Here, ultimately, lay the responsibility for the state's conscious decision to carry out human rights abuses on an even more massive scale.

To the military brass the previous regime had seemed incapable of absorbing the lessons of Soweto, Angola and Mozambique. They, with their greater experience and generally better education, saw themselves much better placed to guide and protect South Africa. For the most part, the training and experience of senior military officers did tend to be much broader than that of almost any police officer. As a result, the higher levels of the military found themselves more and more in tune with the 'liberals' of big business who had realised that traditional apartheid was a dead end. Just as business had found that more and more skilled black labour was required, so too had the military found that it could no longer cope in a racially exclusive way. Extending conscription had effectively put almost every young man classified white into military service. The step had proved inadequate. Even opening the services to women – there were 6,000 women in uniform by 1977 – had not begun to fill what was becoming a yawning gap.

One of the men acutely aware of the problems of strict racial exclusivity was the military chief, General Magnus Malan. He was the officer most closely aligned with P.W. Botha, who had appointed him defence minister. Malan not only had the recent experiences of Angola to draw on; he had also learned valuable lessons when attached to French forces fighting in Algeria in the 1960s. Together with a period spent at the General Staff College of the US Army Command, these experiences gave him a subtler theoretical approach than was usual among police generals and lower-ranking officers of all services. It modified his iron-fist instinct by adding a perceived need to develop a velvet glove, woven of socio-political tactics and softened by judicious compromise. Malan knew that he needed numbers to create the biggest, toughest iron fist, but the only way to gain such support was to win the hearts and minds of the majority of the population in any target area. He spelled out this approach to a military/business conference as early as December 1977. Referring to the problems facing the apartheid state, he noted:

> This war involves so many different fronts, unknown to South African experience, that it has gained the telling, but horrifying name of total war. This different, all-encompassing war has brought with it new methods and new techniques which, in turn, have to be met by total counter-measures.

The conference, at the Rand Afrikaans University in Johannesburg, had brought together senior military strategists and senior representatives from all the major South African companies. Entitled 'Manpower and Defence – Crucial Issues', it was jointly chaired by Standard Bank chairman Ian McKenzie and General Neil Webster, the head of military logistics. Much of it was held behind closed doors and all the participants signed the Official Secrets Act. It further consolidated the close links between the military and business. It was, as the preamble to the conference proceedings stated, 'an attempt to find solutions for the critical problems encountered by both sides in the field of manpower planning. The vital link is obvious – the continuing close communication on all crucial issues between management and the military.'

This 'vital link' has never been closely investigated. Like so many links in the chain of apartheid repression, it received only superficial attention from the TRC. Yet 'close communication' between big business, the military and the political establishment was essential to maintaining the system. It may even have played as great a part as the journalist agents and other 'friends in the media' in ensuring that the newspaper exposés that toppled Van den Bergh and Vorster did not go any further. At the time it was speculated that the initial leaks in what became known as 'Muldergate' or the 'Info scandal' had come from the military. The defence minister was known to have been fully aware that the money allegedly misused had come from his own budget. Not only was it obvious that Botha knew about the secret projects that were financed in this way, but it was openly admitted that many survived the fall of Van den Bergh and Vorster and were continued into the next decade.

The absence of further revelations meant that the system remained intact. This suited both the political and business elite. For all the bitter infighting at a political level, the transition was smooth: Van den Bergh was shunted aside and the military and their police supporters such as Johan Coetzee and Mike Geldenhuys took over. Inter-service rivalry persisted, but it lessened. Cooperation became the order of the day. The media had helped lay the groundwork in the years leading up to the coup, so the changes at the top caused relatively little disruption even within Broederbond ranks.

The military, certainly from 1977 onwards, had become more publicly involved in political debates. These increasingly avoided the traditional apartheid themes of race and racial segregation. Partly as a reaction to growing international sanctions pressure, the public stress tended to be on defending the system of 'free enterprise'. In this regard the military and big business spoke with one voice, and it was one that government began slowly to adopt after the departure from the National Party in 1982 of Connie Mulder and a small but influential core of traditionalists.

Business and much of the business establishment had come to trust the military, and Botha was the military's man, so his assumption of parliamentary power was broadly welcomed. The doyen of big business, Harry Oppenheimer, publicly greeted Botha's initial proposals for a 'constellation of states' as having 'imagination and charm'.

The degree to which the state had become militarised played an important role. It provided lucrative contracts as the government strove to become self-sufficient in armaments production. The military also seemed more flexible and efficient in a managerial sense, and this impressed the business leaders in organisations such as the largely Anglo American-backed Urban Foundation. Businessmen from major corporations acted in advisory roles to the military, especially on manpower issues, and several held high rank in the armed forces reserves or part-time 'commando' units. Roy Anderson, the Stock Exchange chief, for example, was a brigadier. At a local level, business people were brought into 'joint liaison forums'.

Even the schools of the business – and largely 'English' – elite were drawn firmly into the armed forces' web. There had for many years been military cadet detachments at schools. These undertook weekly military parades and occasional camps. Until 1976, only a few were formally attached to the military, often through regimental connections such as that of the Witwatersrand Rifles with Germiston Boys' High. All that changed in the wake of the Soweto uprising. From then on, all cadet detachments became adjuncts of the military. Wealthy private schools excelled in this new militarised environment. The Anglican Diocesan College in Cape Town established its own air wing, naval division and 'battle school'. It possessed two aircraft of its own and training was linked to the air force base at Langebaan. Naval cadets attended annual camps at an SADF base.

This enlistment of support and winning the hearts and minds of even those nominally opposed to National Party rule went on throughout the latter years of Vorster's rule. It seemed to prove to the military the lessons some had learned from their US and European trainers. It had become starkly clear that the entire white community, however militarised, was numerically too small to contain a mass uprising; that any victory scored would be pyrrhic. Yet the turmoil of 1976, the increasingly militant trade unions, and the growing tensions in Namibia, seemed to point towards just such a rising. The trade unions in particular seemed to be developing a radical and independent political perspective.

Out of these realisations came the germ of an idea, which was to develop into an elaborate attempt to co-opt the 'coloured' community and those South Africans of Indian descent. In its full-blown form it produced the tricameral parliament, which gave the vote to adults classified 'coloured' and 'Indian', in separate chambers of parliament. At the same time, attempts went on to be made to alternately control, co-opt and repress the often fractious but gradually uniting trade unions.

Major propaganda exercises were also launched throughout the bloody 1980s, especially in the rural areas, involving what the army called the Civic Action Programme. This entailed using university graduate or undergraduate conscripts as volunteer teachers, engineers, medical assistants and in other roles in support of local communities. In most cases, such conscripts were given a six-week crash course in the vernacular language of the area to which they were assigned.

Many of these conscripts tended to be the 'soft underbelly' of the military machine. Some were opposed to the NP government and, in a general sense, to apartheid. Some were liberals. Others merely wished to avoid getting involved in any shooting war on the borders. Whatever their motivation, the CAP recruits could usually be relied on to work hard to improve the lot of the communities to which they were assigned. At all times, however, they had to wear their uniforms and carry their rifles. The more astute saw how they were being used, but short of desertion, felt there was nothing they could do. A few brave individuals deserted, most stayed put.

At the same time there was a concerted attempt by the military to recruit black soldiers in addition to 'coloureds' and 'Indians'. This was a far cry from the confident statement made by Botha in parliament in 1970. 'If the Bantu wants to build up a defence force, he should do it in his own eventually independent homeland,' he noted at the time. That was before the collapse of Portugal's African empire, the military debacle in Angola, the Soweto uprising, and the crippling failure of Transkei. It was also before the wave of strikes in the Durban area in 1973 announced a new and independent trade unionism. Botha was forced to change his mind. In 1982 he introduced his Defence

White Paper by stating categorically that 'all population groups' should be represented in the SADF; it should become 'a defence force of the people for the people'.

Aping their foreign mentors, the military invested heavily in 'winning hearts and minds', a project based on the strategies outlined by J.J. McCuen of the US and the French Indo-China and Algerian strategist André Beaufre. But, as the US and France had discovered in Vietnam, a 'total strategy' involving bribery, terror and blackmail had very limited success. People who were oppressed and exploited refused to cooperate. Collaboration had to be seen to be in their interests. That is what the original apartheid scheme had aimed at. It had failed.

Although traditional absolutist separation was unworkable, not to say immoral, the alternative of a non-racial parliamentary democracy was still anathema to the overwhelming majority of the white establishment. The more 'progressive' and 'liberal' elements of this establishment did, however, contemplate the possibility of a non-racial system, but only under their firm guidance and patronage. The central question for most of the elite, including P.W. Botha, was how to relax apartheid without totally betraying the segregationist ideal. This was summed up in the twelve-point plan outlined in August 1979 and which combined the requirements of reform within the limits of traditional apartheid.

The minority view, which grew stronger throughout the 1980s, was to consider possibilities beyond segregation. It was held by some of the Broeder-bond modernisers and extended into the upper ranks of the military and the party political machine. One moderniser was Maritz Spaarwater, a product of the vicious crucible of military intelligence. Another was Kobie Coetsee, who became minister of justice in 1980. They belonged to a group of powerful individuals who gained ground throughout the bloody decade.

Coetsee in particular was influenced by the political and psychological assessments of Nelson Mandela produced by the prison warder turned psychologist, Jannie Roux. As the decade of the 1980s dawned, he noted about Roux's observations: 'This kind of thing must be immediately brought to my attention.' In February 1981, he duly received a summary about Mandela's background and approach to prison life. He asked for more, and received an expanded assessment a month later.

It was obvious from this that Mandela was no communist and that the ANC orientation was towards non-racialism. Mandela remained unbroken by the years in prison, he was very much the leader, and he accepted that there was a place for Afrikaners in a future democracy. Most significantly, given subsequent events, Roux reported to Coetsee, and presumably to other fellow Broederbonders, that Mandela foresaw a five-year transition period to majority rule. This, the ANC leader felt, would enable the white minority to accustom itself to the change. Such a display of pragmatism – of magnanimity – surprised Broeders brought up to see Mandela as the devil incarnate. Roux considered that the ANC leader, if not the exiled ANC, would probably have to be part of any future settlement. This would mean dismantling the homelands and introducing some form of largely integrated society.

For the modernisers as much as for the traditionalists, this raised the issue of minority group rights and how to protect and guarantee them – how to preserve the benefits of a racially exclusive economic cocoon while at the same time weakening, if not demolishing, that cocoon. The moderniser vanguard, most of whom, like their counterparts in business, claimed anti-apartheid credentials when the democratic transition took place, had no clear way forward. They tended to agree, however, that the direction and pace of any change should be under strict control. Peace and stability were the keys to any managed change. The already draconian powers of the state must not only be maintained, but strengthened and made more efficient.

This was what the military argued for as internal and international pressures continued to build. Simonstown opened the door, and there was a great deal of optimism that some new way forward would be forged. There were also solid indications that international support might be forthcoming.

2

Foreign influence and hidden repression

The optimism stemming from the effective council of war in Simonstown was bolstered politically by elements within the United States security establishment who were busy planning armed resistance to the new Soviet-leaning governments in Nicaragua and Afghanistan. The coming to power of such governments in 1979, while South Africa faced the prospect of Rhodesia going the way of Angola and Mozambique, fed into the paranoia of the time. South Africa, it seemed, was back in the front line of the fight to preserve the 'free world'. The evil empire had gained some advantage, which the CIA and the Pentagon were trying to claw back, having been betrayed by their politicians.

Botha and his generals saw themselves as heroes in this struggle. South Africa would play its part in fighting the Red menace and so earn the thanks of the world. The enemy could be resisted and overcome by sponsoring opposition from within the very communities that might at first have backed the new governments. An iron fist could be created, wielded by converted hearts and minds. Besides, as Botha was especially pleased to note, in Britain the woman he regarded as a friend, Margaret Thatcher, had swept to power. There was also the prospect of a Republican victory in the US presidential race, which would install the rightwing Ronald Reagan. The CIA and the Pentagon would come into their own. In Germany the conservative Helmut Kohl seemed on the way to eventual victory. Robert Muldoon, regarded as a friend of the apartheid state, was back in charge in New Zealand.

On the home front, detailed intelligence confirmed the schism between the ANC and Chief Mangosuthu Gatsha Buthelezi's Inkatha movement. In this the security planners saw the prospect of an alternative, acceptable, anti-racist movement to the ANC. They knew that Buthelezi had been a member of the ANC and had, with its approval, given up his legal training to take up a chieftainship in KwaZulu. His cultural movement, Inkatha Yenkululeko ye Sizwe (Freedom of the Nation), had been established as a stalking horse for the ANC. But that was in 1975, when the fortunes of the exiled movement were at a low ebb.

One of Buthelezi's chief advisers was the banned lawyer Rowley Arenstein, a former member of the SACP, who had adopted a fiercely anti-Soviet approach following the ideological dispute between China and Russia, the so-called Sino-Soviet split. He categorised himself as a Maoist and argued that the potential for revolutionary change had to come from within South Africa and from the 'peasants and workers'. Buthelezi and Inkatha, he felt, provided the basis for such a change. He also claimed that the exiled ANC was manipulated by the SACP, which was 'a mere tool of Moscow'.

Buthelezi's own hostility to and suspicion of the SACP was reinforced by Arenstein. When a group of leading ANC members led by Tennyson Makiwane broke from the ANC in 1975, complaining about the influence of the SACP, Buthelezi saw himself and Inkatha more and more as embodying the true spirit of the nationalist movement. Then, suddenly and unexpectedly, the fortunes of the ANC changed as thousands of young militants fled in the wake of the Soweto uprising. All thoughts of working within the homelands system were ditched. Many of the exiled leadership had, in any event, become concerned at the 'dual power' situation that was developing. Buthelezi had to be pulled into line. The final attempt to do this came in 1979 at a meeting in London. Buthelezi made it clear that he would not toe the line of the exiled movement, especially with regard to economic sanctions.

The ultimate wedge was driven in when Buthelezi was informed that, at a subsequent meeting in Lusaka of the ANC political-military council, a proposal had been made to assassinate him. According to the version that reached Buthelezi, the proposal was put by the SACP's Joe Slovo and vetoed by Oliver Tambo. In accordance with the simplistic Maoist doctrine that 'the enemy of my enemy is my friend,' Buthelezi was prepared to seek help from anyone who could help him fight what he saw as perhaps an even greater evil than apartheid: Soviet communism. For the South African security apparatus, this was manna from heaven. In 1980 they prepared to exploit the opportunity. Besides, internal resistance had faded. As Caryle Murphy, the *Washington Post* correspondent at the time, told media researcher James Sanders: 'It was almost as if black resistance had received a lobotomy.'

Inkatha could provide a surrogate force that deflected criticism from the apartheid state. Where violence erupted, it could be 'black on black' and portrayed as part of the greater struggle of Christian good against communist evil. The more traditionally minded apartheid ideologues also saw in this the prospect of continued white patronage if not overt dominance, with the segregationist regime enshrined as the only guarantor of peace and stability. The emergence of a black 'anti-communist' force would send a signal that things were changing; that black and white 'nations' were united in their opposition to 'communism'. Such a message had become essential now that even friendly foreign politicians demanded some dismantling of apartheid, some change that would ease the pressures they too were feeling. At the same time they should not be deterred from overt state-sponsored brutality. 'Non-standard' procedures should be secret and, where possible, their origins deflected. That and the need to centralise control, was at the core of the Simonstown talks.

Along with laying the foundation for professional death squads, the Simons-town conference provided the infrastructure for running guns to Inkatha and training its 'soldiers'. More information, more spies, more agents, more operatives – this was the booming security market that enabled Craig William-son, lionised as a returning 'super-spy', to extend the range of Operation Daisy. He did so through the 'G' section of the security branch. In an unpublished confidential note, he later boasted:

> I also developed a recruitment, training and placing process which meant that we covered all campuses in different faculties and aimed at going on after university into different areas . . . to have people who would flow through to newspapers, trade unions, church organisations etc etc.

Only a few of the operatives put into the field in the 1980s through Operation Daisy were exposed. The best-known was Olivia Forsyth, a graduate of Rhodes University in Grahamstown. She was one of a trio of agents who came from the same university, and probably the least successful. She lived with one of the ANC underground couriers in Harare, Zimbabwe, before being caught out and jailed in Angola by the ANC. She managed to escape and to seek refuge in the British embassy in Luanda. On New Year's Day 2001, she migrated to Britain.

Much more successful was Joy Harnden. When she left university she became a journalist in Johannesburg, where she was active in anti-apartheid organisations such as the End Conscription Campaign, the Black Sash and the Johannesburg Democratic Action Committee (Jodac). Through these she met, and moved into a house with, Sheila Weinberg, the banned daughter of long-time exile SACP members Eli and Violet Weinberg. This put her at the centre of established ANC circles and enabled her to monitor the activities and contacts of the various known and banned activists.

Like Craig Williamson before her, Harnden developed a reputation for efficiency and reliability. But she was also soon suspected when two meetings that only she could have exposed were raided by the security police. She was expelled from Jodac. Although the ANC in Lusaka was informed of this, and of the suspicions that Harnden was a spy, the information was never circulated, and anyway Sheila Weinberg refused to believe it. She readily accepted Harnden's offer to accompany her when she visited Maputo to see her widowed mother Violet in July 1986, having been granted permission on compassionate grounds.

This was a tremendous opportunity for agent WWR 805 Harnden to widen her contacts. It would also provide an opportunity to check on the truth of the information coming from the two agents in the ANC office in Maputo. Officially, by that stage, following the 1984 Nkomati agreement between South Africa and Mozambique, the ANC was allowed to keep only eight members in Maputo. The retention in the city of this already infiltrated contingent obviously suited the South African security establishment, as the Mozambican capital remained the hub of ANC underground activities. Operatives moved from Maputo into Swaziland and then on to the vital Witwatersrand region.

Harnden's handlers Brigadier André Oosthuizen and Colonel Chris Deetleefs apparently hoped that the agent could further endear herself to the exiled movement; that she might even be given tasks that could lead her to other underground contacts. In her guise as a known anti-apartheid activist, living in the home of a banned person who was the daughter of leading communist exiles, she could not hope for more. But when she volunteered in Maputo to 'do work for the movement' she was recruited into the MK underground.

One of the people she was introduced to at the time, under the name of 'William', was the East Rand-based MK commander Ignatius 'Iggy' Mathebula. She was assigned to his unit and was apparently trained by him in making bucket bombs for distributing pamphlets. Like Craig Williamson before her, she carried out her first bucket-bomb exercise successfully and with attendant publicity. However, by then there was word of a leak within the security branch and Olivia Forsyth was arrested. On his way to a meeting that ANC sources say was with Joy Harnden, Iggy Mathebula disappeared. No trace of him has ever been found. Joy Harnden also vanished.

The Mathebula family and the ANC appealed to the TRC to investigate, but nothing was done, although the woman known as Joy Harnden could have been subpoenaed. The police told ANC officials that by 1996 Harnden was working as a journalist under her 'real name'. She was 'in receipt of a police pension' and her name was given as Ronel Botha. However, the newspaper she was said to be working on had no record of anyone of that name, nor had any newspaper in the group.

The police did not tell the ANC – nor did the TRC discover – that Lieutenant Joy Harnden in fact became Sandra Joan Patterson when she gave up her previous identity. In a touch of apparent vanity, Harnden, born in 1961, reduced her age as Patterson by more than two years. Sandra Patterson was said to have been born on 1 April 1964. Her new identity number 640401 0682 00 1 made this clear. What she did and where she went under this name is still unknown, but as Patterson she held a South African passport – P00080528 – issued in April 1988.

The police also failed to inform the ANC that Joy Harnden had married a South African diplomat. As Joy Crane, she had lived for a time in Glasgow, Scotland. As Joy Crane she also worked for a timber industry trade publication in Johannesburg in 1998. In the following year she told an acquaintance that her husband had left the foreign service and that she would be relocating to the Western Cape.

The most successful of the trio was Gordon Brookbanks, who was also a lieutenant in the mid-1980s when he was posted to London, apparently because he held a British passport. There he took over the running of the European spy network established by Craig Williamson and Johan Coetzee. It was he who ran one of the most important spies of the time, the ANC chief representative in London, Solly Smith. He is also credited with having recruited as an agent the ANC executive member and historian Francis Meli.

After the unbanning of the ANC, Brookbanks was withdrawn from London and posted to the Western Cape, still as a member of the security police. In 1995 he held the rank of Senior Superintendent and took over as the provincial commander of intelligence coordination. He was also a member of the provincial intelligence coordinating committee before moving, as a senior officer, to the renamed National Intelligence Agency, a division of which he commanded in 2002.

Operation Daisy was one of the major vehicles used to compromise vulnerable young men and women. Some began informing under the impression that they were assisting the anti-apartheid cause. But these 'false flag' operations applied only in a minority of cases. In others the simple inducement of cash was enough to ensnare the desperate, the greedy and the simply unwary.

Today there are hundreds of severely compromised individuals who have never come forward. Several of their number remain ideologically committed to the cause of racial supremacy, but most may wish merely to hide. All are vulnerable to blackmail and manipulation so long as they stay in the shadows.

The highly secretive security backbone, reinforced at Simonstown, catered for this widespread corruption. The broad outlines of the system were made public, but a hidden network underlay it, and only part of this has been exposed.

The all-encompassing security plan to combat the proclaimed 'total onslaught' meant that every town, village and hamlet throughout the country was covered by a tightly integrated security net. This was the National Security Management System (NSMS). It was designed to bring together, as never before, the military, police and national intelligence. The military would hold overall command, while the security police did most of the internal information gathering. By 1979 the NSMS was fully functional. Simonstown confirmed and refined it, and it remained in place for more than a decade, through two name changes and some restructuring.

As the TRC investigations got under way, more detail began to emerge not only of the vast extent and range of the NSMS, but also of how it operated and who carried out the various tasks throughout the bloody repression of the 1980s. Some of this information came into the public domain, much did not. Yet here was the true heart of the brute maintenance of apartheid, a vast structure whose planners and minions carried out most of the violent acts which became the focus of the TRC. A clear hierarchy was exposed. It linked the state president, members of the cabinet and the security chiefs serving on the SSC, all the way down to the hired killers and the agents in neighbouring states.

3

The nature of the beast

Throughout its existence, the State Security Council of South Africa comprised the ministers of Defence, Law and Order, Justice and Foreign Affairs, together with other senior cabinet members. Other permanent members were the chiefs of the military, the police and intelligence, as well as the two senior civil servants – the directors general – in the foreign affairs and justice departments. Other members were co-opted from time to time, while a permanent secretary played a vital role in an administrative 'working committee' made up of the directors general of the various ministries represented on the SSC. Most, like the security chiefs and ministers, were members of the Broederbond. None were called to account.

This working committee was also charged with liaising with the large secretariat (SSCS), which comprised between 80 and 100 full-time officials seconded mainly from the military, police, national intelligence and prisons services and was divided into four sections: administration, intelligence inter- pretation, communications and strategy. It was this SSCS that interpreted the directives issued by the SSC and whose members assessed information from the spy agencies to pass on to the SSC. They translated directives into specific instructions as part of a 'coordinated counter-revolutionary strategy' and passed them on to the relevant departments. To assist the secretariat, there were twelve to thirteen inter-departmental committees which developed counter- revolutionary concepts and ensured their implementation. One of these committees, charged with dealing with security, later evolved into the National Joint Management Centre which met each day to assess perceived threats to the state.

These national structures were replicated at regional level, where at any one time between eleven and fifteen Joint Management Committees functioned. These usually comprised sixty members drawn from the various security forces and chaired by either a senior military or police officer. Like the SSCS, JMCs contained four divisions, commonly known by the Afrikaans acronyms: Veikom (security), Komkom (communications), Semkom (social, economic) and GIS (joint intelligence). The JMC chair, and the chairs of the four subcommittees, appear to have operated as an executive. Directly answerable to the regional JMCs were some sixty sub-JMCs responsible for various districts which, in their turn, were linked to about 350 mini-JMCs covering specific cities, towns and townships. When needed, temporary local management centres (LMCs) were established, sometimes down to neighbourhood level. Such actions were invariably coordinated with local business operations; in particular with those enterprises designated as 'key industries'. The JMCs also established 'joint liaison forums' on which local business served.

Facts, gossip and hearsay, spiced by vindictive rumour, were absorbed into this massive web and passed for analysis up the chain of command to give rise to new orders which flowed back down. These covered everything from instituting social welfare programmes to staging cross-border raids. Throughout, everything was premised on the paternalistic assumption that only a small minority of the 'non-white' population – usually put at no more than 10 per cent – were either 'agitators' or active dupes of an international communist conspiracy. Most of the population was deemed either to be satisfied with the existing situation or apathetic. However, this generally silent majority was widely believed to be prone, by its nature, to emotional outbursts. It could be exploited and manipulated where real or perceived grievances existed. This attitude is summed up by a passage from a police college criminology textbook that noted:

> The Bantu are less civilized. The more primitive a people is, the less they are able to control their emotions. At the slightest provocation they resort to violence. They cannot distinguish between serious and less serious matters. They are less self-controlled and more impulsive.

Given this perception, naked state terror always went hand in hand with any social and economic advancement. At the same time as this new, integrated, security network was being established, its agents moved swiftly into Southern Rhodesia, soon to become Zimbabwe. Brigadier J.J. 'Tolletjie'

Botha, who was to play a key role in the shadowy Directorate of Covert Collection (DCC), was in charge of establishing a network of agents and saboteurs. He briefed Major Neil Kriel, a former Selous Scout, to sign up as many of the 'hard men' he could find to serve the apartheid state. Botha's name was mentioned in amnesty applications as the head of the DCC, but he was never interviewed. Kriel's name never even appeared.

Kriel, who was a founder of what became known as the CCB, recruited mainly from the Rhodesian special forces and Selous Scouts. Most of his recruits came south and were absorbed into the Recce groups of the army or into the Civil Co-operation Bureau (CCB). The apartheid state's 6 Reconnaisance battalion, for example, was made up of former Rhodesian special forces troops who fled south before Zimbabwean independence on 18 April 1980. With them came the 200 'MNR' or Renamo fighters who were to form the core of 'internal' armed resistance to the Mozambique government.

Such developments added to the confidence felt by Botha and his generals. After a precarious period, things did seem to be changing for the better. The economy had begun to pick up, supported by a surging gold price. As the yellow metal reached $800 an ounce there were many who felt that God was at last smiling on them. Even the sports boycott, which had had a profound psychological effect on the beneficiaries of the system, appeared to be cracking. Robert Muldoon, in New Zealand, indicated that, despite Commonwealth sanctions, he would welcome a Springbok rugby team to his rugby-mad nation. With the reformist mantle of P.W. Botha, apartheid South Africa seemed to be creeping back into acceptability.

But then the school students of Soweto started protesting again at exactly the same time that a fresh wave of industrial strikes began. This time in Soweto it was a backlash against one of the military's key 'hearts and minds' tactics: the use of armed and uniformed national servicemen in classrooms. On 2 February 1980 school students in Soweto boycotted classes and demanded the removal of the soldiers. Within weeks the protest spread across the country. Schools and universities became involved as all the old grievances were aired. It was the start of nearly eight months during which little schooling took place outside of the affluent white ghettos.

While there were similarities with 1976 in clashes with the security forces, in marches and rallies, the slogans of 1980 were markedly different. Black consciousness had given way to condemnations of 'apartheid-capitalism', an echo of the slogans emanating from the trade unions. A new and possibly more dangerous militancy was emerging. But it was still embryonic. The government responded in June by calling for a report on the education system. The up-and-coming Broederbond moderniser, Pieter de Lange, rector of the

Rand Afrikaans University, was appointed to head a commission that would report in the following year.

The announcement of the De Lange commission did nothing to calm the protests among students from all the oppressed communities. They also tended to refer to themselves as 'black', irrespective of which community they came from. In the midst of this furore, which remained restricted to the townships and largely out of sight and mind of white society, a petition to free Nelson Mandela began to gain momentum. Launched early in the year in the *Sunday Post* newspaper by campaigning editor Percy Qoboza, it had received a controversial and unexpected endorsement from Hendrik van den Bergh. The disgraced former security chief noted of the ANC leader: 'I know the man's history well and I challenge anyone to produce one shred of evidence to prove that Mandela was a member of the Communist Party.' Yet this was the reason advanced for keeping Mandela behind bars. Louis le Grange, the man who, as deputy minister of information, had reacted so strongly toward Dumisa Ntsebeza at Jongilizwe College, was the minister of police in 1980. He announced that Mandela was 'a staunch communist'. He should remain in jail.

This exchange, in April 1980, was apparently an attempt by a bitter Van den Bergh to fuel the ongoing and bitter battle within a Broederbond that he felt had turned against him. The battle was real enough. There were already a few modernisers, such as De Lange, who were contemplating eventually having to do a deal with the ANC – and that meant Mandela.

Having demonised both the man and the movement, such thoughts could not be openly expressed at that time, certainly by those in authority. Besides, certain security requirements needed to be satisfied first. Although the ANC provided little military threat, the exiled movement was starting to tap into the initially BC-fuelled unrest. For example, the major school student organis-ation, COSAS (Congress of South African Students) had adopted the ANC's Freedom Charter in 1979. The 'Charterists' were starting to emerge as a challenge to the potentially more troublesome 'Workerists' who did not regard the Freedom Charter as radical enough and who called for 'worker control' of society.

But while the apartheid modernisers conceded that talks would eventually have to be held with the ANC, they preferred a weaker movement. In propaganda terms, the ANC was starting to have greater impact because, since the independence of Mozambique and Zimbabwe, it was able to use states on South Africa's borders. Mozambique in particular had become a base, and there were signs that guerrilla operations were becoming more sophisticated.

Agents could not penetrate all of the routes and cells, so on 30 January 1981 the Matola raid – 'Operation Beanbag' – was launched. It was the first major joint Security Branch/military operation under the newly centralised security structure, and involved a column of heavily armed vehicles disguised in Mozambican military colours and carrying a group of 'Recces' including the newly recruited 'Rhodesians' of 6 Recce. They invaded a foreign country, committed murder and mayhem, and abducted several 'suspects'. Yet not one single participant appeared before the TRC.

Among those kidnapped was Vuyani Mavuso, who simply refused to cooperate with his captors. Evidence emerged at the TRC that he repeated a constant refrain: 'Charge me or shoot me.' Brigadier Willem Schoon of the Special Branch reportedly told the then Vlakplaas commander, Dirk Coetzee: 'Get rid of him, we can't let him go free.' Handed over to the death squad, Vuyani Mavuso, one of the bravest of the many unsung heroes of anti-apartheid resistance, was first fed with experimental poisons from police general Lothar Neethling's laboratory. When these failed to render him unconscious, he was made to kneel on two bricks and to recite the Lord's prayer while his face was reduced to a bloody pulp by kicks every time he faltered. Not once did he plead or ask for mercy. Eventually he was shot and his body burned to ashes.

This kind of brutality and inhumanity was commonplace in the 1980s, but was always publicly denied. Raids such as that on Matola, could not be denied, however. They resulted in some international condemnation. But Margaret Thatcher stuck up for the Botha government and Robert Muldoon repeated his assurances that a rugby tour would be welcome. However, the Australian government confirmed its support for sports sanctions. Another of the rugby-playing 'white' Commonwealth countries, it lay across the main air route to New Zealand. No landing or overflying rights would be allowed to any aircraft bearing an apartheid sports team. It was a heavy psychological blow to the sports-starved and rugby-mad white community in South Africa and another fillip for the anti-apartheid activists. But there was much worse to come.

Sport, and especially rugby, provided a popular outlet for the xenophobia promoted by the form of narrow racial nationalism that was the political face of apartheid. The game had been played in South Africa since the late nineteenth century in the Cape Province, and on a largely non-racial basis. As a result, the South African Rugby Union (SARU) had a non-racial constitution, obliging the racial purists to establish a Rugby Board that catered for 'whites only'.

It was this board that was recognised by the British rugby unions and by two other colonial rugby playing nations, Australia and New Zealand. Apartheid was adopted by New Zealand rugby at the insistence of a regime that refused to allow Maori players into South Africa. This was the origin of the

New Zealand Maori team. When all-white All Blacks toured South Africa, the best Polynesian players were given a Maori tour somewhere else. It was the most blatant example of the export of apartheid practices. Internally the non-racial SARU and its players and officials were forced to the margins, deprived of playing fields and other facilities.

This fate was shared by other sporting codes. The police and municipal authorities, often with the active connivance and encouragement of the apartheid sports authorities, ensured that non-racial sport was punished. Even after the slight relaxations under international pressure, thousands of sports men and women had their potential stunted. World champion weightlifter Precious McKenzie, for example, lost years of international competition before migrating first to England then to New Zealand. Despite his age, he repre-sented both adopted countries at Olympic and Commonwealth Games.

More famous was the cricketer Basil D'Oliveira, who also represented England. They were among the fortunate few who managed to break out of the shackles of apartheid, elsewhere kept locked by a system that enjoyed the active collaboration of a white sports establishment that has still not been called to account. But in July 1981 that establishment received its biggest shock. It came from New Zealand, which was, ironically, to become a destination for a large number of apartheid's beneficiaries who fled South Africa after the 1994 transition.

Robert Muldoon's announcement in 1980 that New Zealand's National Party government would welcome a tour by an apartheid South African rugby team was a slap in the face for the Commonwealth, whose secretary-general Shridath Ramphal noted diplomatically that Muldoon had 'let the side down'. However, the news also caused massive consternation within New Zealand itself.

This small island nation boasted proportionately the biggest anti-apartheid movement in the world. It was a product not only of the history of sporting contact between the two countries, and local battles against racism, but also of the way the movement was organised. Unlike most anti-apartheid groups in the rest of the world, which tended to play a supportive role to the ANC's diplomatic efforts, the New Zealand movement was a grassroots anti-racist front. It organised numbers rather than names; sought support from workers and students rather than from the professional elites, and fought apartheid on the same basis that it challenged local racism and the importation of racist practices to local sport.

The New Zealand movement had also kept in touch with anti-apartheid groups in South Africa and invited the non-racial South African Rugby Union to tour. SARU never made it because the apartheid government banned the tour and confiscated the passport of SARU's president Abdul Abbass. It was actions like these that swung the support of leading rugby players such as Chris Laidlaw and Bob Burgess behind the anti-apartheid movement. They were among its early supporters along with almost every major church, trade union and student group.

Being non-sectarian – the unofficial ANC and PAC representatives shared platforms in the country – and clearly not anti-sport, let alone anti-rugby, what started as a small but active movement had grown into a mass organisation by 1980. A new generation of activists had flooded in after seeing coverage of the 1976 student uprisings in South Africa. They tended to feel a particular responsibility since, on the day the uprising began, 16 June, an all-white All Black team played the Springboks in Pretoria. This was also the year when African countries boycotted the Montreal Olympic Games in protest against apartheid.

But petitions and mass demonstrations failed to sway Muldoon any more than surveys that revealed a majority of New Zealanders were opposed to a Springbok tour. Protests about the cross-border raid into Mozambique and the killing of thirteen people in January 1980 left him unmoved. For South Africa's white electorate, starved of international sporting contact, Muldoon's attitude was a blessing. As they saw it, the traditional links would be restored and the misguided rabble put in their place.

The news reports and television coverage that followed shocked South Africa's white electorate. For many New Zealanders caught up in the events, it was a deeply traumatic experience. The male preserve of rugby found itself challenged as never before. Often to the forefront were the mothers, sisters and daughters of the rugby fraternity.

Exiled anti-apartheid campaigners Donald Woods, Andrew Molotsane and the priest and bomb victim John Osmers toured the country appealing for a halt to the tour. They followed in the footsteps of Frene Ginwala, later to become the Speaker in the South African parliament. It is perhaps a measure of the importance that Botha and Muldoon attached to it that the tour still went ahead.

The Springbok team was forced to fly a circuitous route to avoid African countries and Australia. In mid-air they received a small taste of what was to come when Mary Baker, a member of the anti-tour coalition in Christchurch who was on the flight, loudly abused them. The anticipated official welcome in Auckland turned into a nightmare. Thousands of jeering protesters and a 'service of repentance and solidarity with the black people of South Africa' staged by theological students, clergy and a clutch of bishops ensured that the apartheid team had to skulk away onto a flight to the provincial city of Gisborne.

The tour went ahead amid scenes of unprecedented protest. The second game was cancelled when Pat McQuarrie, a former World War Two fighter pilot, flew toward the provincial capital of Hamilton to support the thousands of protesters who had managed to pull down the fences surrounding the local rugby ground. The police took fright when they heard McQuarrie was in the air. He had had his licence revoked several years earlier after a low-level flour-bomb attack on a visiting apartheid softball team. As the elite police 'Red Squad' booted and battered protesters trying to make it onto the playing field, the game was cancelled.

On the Wednesday after the debacle at Hamilton, a march comprising a high proportion of women and older, middle-class New Zealanders set off in Wellington to protest outside the South African consulate general. They never made it. In what was to be a turning point for many who had sat on the political sidelines, the police attacked the march. A then middle-aged mother who had joined the demonstration with her teenage daughter remembered years later 'the most frightening time of my life'. Blood flowed and bones were broken. For many of the younger protesters this was the last straw, as Muldoon used the police to ensure that the tour went ahead.

That nobody died during those weeks of protest is remarkable. From Christchurch, where the police estimated that between 10,000 and 12,000 protesters gathered, to Nelson and Napier there were increasingly violent clashes as the police force tried to stamp out resistance. Protests erupted around the country every Wednesday and Saturday to coincide with scheduled games. Police resources were strained to breaking point, and eventually the army had to be called in.

In response to police tactics, the protesters too began to adopt body armour, made for the most part of cardboard tubing, to wear crash helmets and to carry hardboard shields designed at earlier 'protest training camps'. A lack of security resources meant that the scheduled game in Timaru was called off, and every game was accompanied by pitch invasions by core groups, some of whom took terrible beatings. Motorways and airport runways were blockaded; sit-ins staged and broadcasts disrupted. As Tom Newnham, the teacher, author and doyen of New Zealand anti-racism campaigners, commented later: 'Many of the elements of civil war had arrived in New Zealand, courtesy of apartheid. It would only have taken some martyrs to be made and the mad cycle of revenge and retaliation would have begun.'

John Minto and other coordinators of the protest had achieved their aim: to illustrate that apartheid should only exist within a repressive environment and a virtual state of emergency. The final test in Auckland was no exception, although the planned aerial invasion of 120 kites and a radio-controlled zeppelin trailing more than 30 km of nylon line never got off the ground. Instead another pilot, Marx Jones, and his passenger, Grant Cole, buzzed the playing field fifty-eight times, dropping more than 60 flour bombs. To the cheers of thousands of protesters around the ground, they reduced the test to a farce. There never was another tour, and twenty years later many of those who braved the batons and barbed wire were part of the New Zealand Labour/ Alliance government.

White South Africa was still reeling from its rugby tour experience when Britain's former Conservative Party prime minister Edward Heath arrived in Johannesburg in August and delivered an unexpectedly harsh warning to the apartheid state. The West, he said, would not stand in an alliance with South Africa so long as the country pursued a 'system profoundly insulting to the rights of the overwhelming majority of its population'.

But Heath was perceived as a has-been. Margaret Thatcher ruled in London and Ronald Reagan was in the White House. Reagan had also apparently shown his colours in what Botha assessed correctly to be three important appointments for his regime. Jeane Kirkpatrick was United Nations ambassador, the journalist and editor Herman Nickel became ambassador to South Africa, and Chester Crocker took the all-important post of secretary of state for Africa. Crocker, the architect of 'constructive engagement', saw apartheid South Africa as an important 'strategic partner' of the US and South Africa's military chiefs as 'modernising patriots'. He and Botha became firm friends.

More importantly, sentiment in the money markets also appeared to be turning in favour of Pretoria. After a period of stress with several of the major banking houses, loans were again available, even if the interest rates demanded carried a premium. A threat to some of the senior informants inside the exiled ANC and its military wing had also been removed with the murder in the Zimbabwean capital, Harare, on 1 August 1981 of Joe Gqabi, a journalist and ANC representative. He had been working to establish a separate intelligence organisation within the exiled movement to counter the high level of infiltration, and had already gathered evidence that pointed to at least one informant at the very highest levels. His death was listed by the TRC as a human rights violation, but the background to it was not explored.

The South African military blamed the killing on internal feuding. This, as the TRC was later to establish, was a tactic employed by the security forces, especially in the late 1980s and into the period of transition. KwaZulu-Natal, where tons of arms and ammunition were supplied, was a particular target. But the tactic extended eventually to having 'blacked up' operatives on speeding trains shooting, stabbing and throwing commuters onto the tracks. This was calculated to encourage the impression of mindless 'black on black' violence, to cow the general populace by its random nature, and to simulate a form of instability that only the security forces could control.

This hideous spiral began when Botha's minor reforms resulted in increased resistance, which in turn triggered greater repression. Once again, it was rumblings from within the burgeoning trade union movement that most concerned the apartheid establishment. It also worried the exiled ANC. It exemplified the classic observation from French philosopher Alexis de Tocqueville's book *Democracy in America* that: 'the most perilous moment for a bad government is when it seeks to mend its ways. Only consummate statecraft can enable a king to save his throne when, after a long spell of oppressive rule, he sets to improving the lot of his subjects.' Botha lacked the statecraft and was unready to pursue any course but the one he and his generals had embarked upon.

4

Reform, revolution and repression

The great surge of unionisation that began in 1973 bypassed the mining sector. In 1980 South Africa may still have had a golden economic backbone, but it was not unionised. The migrant labour system so thoroughly exploited by the mining companies also continued. All that had changed after 1974 was that recruitment switched away from the neighbouring states, to the homelands. This labour system allowed for gross abuses of human rights over decades and was largely overlooked by the TRC.

By 1984 nearly 60 per cent of miners were reckoned to come from the 'homelands'. After the independence of Mozambique in particular, the mining companies began to fear that radical politics might be imported with immigrant miners. Ever since the strike by black miners in 1946, which was brutally crushed, the workforce had been largely docile. The companies wanted to keep it that way, and the strictly policed compound system, with miners segregated by language and geographic group, made union organising extremely difficult.

But the mine compounds could not remain immune from the turmoil in the surrounding environment. In 1982 there was a series of wildcat strikes in various mines, and evidence of growing union organisation. The largest of the gold-mining houses, Anglo American, had by then already expanded into other enterprises. As the premier representative of South African private capital, it was one of the first major companies to recognise that the traditional system of racial exploitation had started to become unprofitable. Anglo American therefore recognised trade unions and called for a more flexible approach to apartheid. Other mining companies were not convinced. Some even judged that the clock could perhaps be turned back.

The 1982 strikes did, however, see several mine owners grudgingly accept that it would be better to permit unions than to suffer industrial anarchy. This opened the door to the Congress of Unions of South Africa (CUSA), a trade union federation with a radical although unclear commitment to a form of black consciousness and socialism.

The CUSA-affiliated National Union of Mineworkers (NUM) was established in August 1982 and won its first recognition agreement in June 1983. It was not easy going. Two mining houses in particular, Gold Fields and Gencor, resisted worker demands and responded in the traditional way to industrial unrest, with batons, bullets and mass sackings. Despite the occasional outbreaks of resistance and the growth of the unions in the early 1980s, the companies and the state were obviously in control.

The government was also gaining greater respectability in the financial arena. National and international banks were rallying. Locally, Barclays Bank and Standard Bank made record profits in 1983 and the locally-based Nedbank opened a New York office as its first step to international prominence. More important for the government was the fact that foreign loans were again available at quite reasonable rates. These were, almost without exception, short-term loans. It was a recipe for disaster, which few seemed to notice at the time.

The fact that white South Africa and external bankers and other businesses regarded South Africa with a degree of optimism was due in part to media coverage. The local media tended almost exclusively to see things through the eyes of the beneficiaries of the system. The foreign media, which relied largely on reports from local stringers or whose correspondents lived and moved among apartheid's chosen people, tended to mimic the viewpoints of their hosts. Many who persistently did not were simply banned from entering the country.

The media output was also skewed by journalist agents and the government's various 'friends in the media'. So it was that Botha's tricameral reform initiative, and even the reluctant acceptance of independent trade unions were greeted as major breakthroughs by most of the white establishment. The tricameral proposal in particular was hailed as a significant reform. It proposed that the existing 178-seat white parliament be joined by two smaller chambers, for 'coloureds' and for 'Indians'. These would act in an advisory capacity on national policy.

The Progressive Federal Party and the hardline apartheid traditionalists both campaigned for a 'No' vote in the referendum: the PFP protesting that the new constitutional dispensation did not include blacks, the 'white Right' that it gave too much. The continued exclusion of the majority of the population was seen as a problem by many of the PFP's former financial backers, including Anglo American's Harry Oppenheimer, but on balance organised business supported Botha's proposals as 'a step in the right direction'. Gavin Relly, successor to Oppenheimer as chairman of Anglo American, openly campaigned for a 'Yes' vote.

Saatchi & Saatchi, the British Conservative Party's advertising agency, masterminded the government's campaign. In the event, on 2 November 1983 there was a 76 per cent voter turnout and 66 per cent of that number gave the thumbs up to Botha's reform package. They also effectively approved the new legal dispensation that differentiated further between black people living in rural and urban areas. This gave councils in the segregated black townships the right to manage their ghettos.

The fact that overwhelming majorities of local residents boycotted elections to the resulting township councils seemed not to concern the government. The state and the security forces regarded the low poll turnouts as examples of apathy and minority intimidation rather than deep-seated anger. They also failed to take heed or any action when the councillors, openly referred to as impimpis ('sellouts' or quislings) by their communities, proceeded to enrich themselves at the expense of their communities. Instead, there were numerous laudatory articles and statements about South Africa moving away from apartheid.

International banks and businesses were obviously impressed, but they remained cautious about the longer term. 'Many people felt that the republic had entered into a new and more hopeful era,' wrote J.D.F. Jones, the editor of the British *Financial Times*. In a survey in February 1984 he also pointed out: 'It is difficult to avoid the impression that the frustrations of [the] black majority are intensifying even while the whites are increasingly unsure about the answer to their country's unique problems . . .'

Jones and other more astute observers had noted the formation in June 1983 of the National Forum of radical and Black Consciousness groups and the launch in August of that year of the larger and much more broadly based United Democratic Front (UDF). Nor were they taken in by the blinkered approach adopted by both the government and the reformist parliamentary opposition whose policies Botha was apparently embracing as his own. They pointed to the potential volatility of a system that excluded most inhabitants from their country's constitution. But Jones and others like him were minority, though influential, voices.

In the wake of his referendum victory, Botha embarked on a nine-nation European tour. It began in Britain; the first visit to that country by a South African head of state since Hendrik Verwoerd had stormed out of the Commonwealth twenty years earlier.

The tour was preceded by a major diplomatic victory, the Nkomati Accord. Signed between South Africa and Mozambique, it prohibited guerrilla incursions by either country. What this meant, in effect, was that the ANC and its armed wing were excluded from Mozambique – a major setback – while South Africa continued to support the Renamo rebels who maintained their rear base in South Africa. The Accord was presented as a major step toward peace in the region. Roland 'Tiny' Rowland, the head of the Lonrho industrial conglomerate, claimed to have played a leading role in brokering it, but it was Botha who was generally given the credit.

Although unpublicised, the South African government had also concluded an even more far-reaching agreement with the government of Swaziland. This allowed South African death squads to operate within Swaziland and endorsed collaboration by the Swazi police with South African security units. It opened the way for a series of murders and kidnappings in the following years, many of which were publicised through later TRC hearings, but the complicity of Swazi government officials and police was never investigated.

What has also never been fully investigated was another source of Botha's confidence: the mutiny in the ANC camps in Angola that began in January 1984. At the time, MK fighters were increasingly being used to support Angolan government troops against the rebel UNITA movement. As with the mutiny in Tanzania in 1964, the major reason behind the revolt was poor conditions combined with the hunger to return to South Africa to fight. Survivors of both the 1964 and 1984 mutinies confirmed in interviews that their view had been 'rather die fighting at home than rot in exile'. Especially among fighters with a Black Consciousness background, the fact that they were fighting black people seemed absurd. They also had specific complaints about the brutality and high living of MK chief Joe Modise and national commissar Andrew Masondo.

A contributory factor was the abuse of authority by members of the ANC security unit in which several apartheid agents were active. Following the arrest of several agents in 1981 and after the murder of Joe Gqabi later in that year, attempts to restructure the security organ had been halted. The atmosphere of paranoia that prevailed within the various ANC communities led to numerous false allegations and further abuses by security units. Even senior ANC member Pallo Jordan, later a minister in the first post-apartheid government, was caught up in the swirl of innuendo. He was detained in appalling conditions largely on the basis of allegations made by an ANC security officer, Francis Malaya.

Malaya was one of the agents who succeeded in exploiting the very real grievances that gave rise to the mutiny. However, these agents provocateurs almost all took a background role and the leaders of the revolt appear to have been genuine anti-apartheid fighters. Malaya later transferred to the ANC's department of information and acted as a courier between Mozambique and Swaziland for the apartheid security police. He was arrested in Lusaka in 1987 on suspicion of being a spy, but escaped through a toilet window and sought refuge in the US embassy. He later re-emerged in South Africa as a member of the security police.

In the first post-apartheid dispensation, Modise became the minister of defence. He died in 2002 amid allegations that he collaborated with apartheid Military Intelligence. Masondo became a general in the army. Both men had played leading roles in suppressing the mutiny. It was brutally done and resulted in numerous deaths, including at least seven mutineers shot by firing squad. But in 1984, outside the senior ranks in the ANC and Angola's MPLA government, few except the intelligence services in South Africa had more than an inkling of what had occurred. While they could not claim full credit for having caused it, the state security planners and their agents had obviously seized their chance. The mutiny weakened the ANC and encouraged levels of distrust throughout the organisation. Even the charismatic MK leader Chris Hani was once sought in Lusaka by a security 'posse' intent on rounding up suspects. Hani maintained that Modise had set it on him.

All this was good news for Botha, but he had still more reason to feel confident. The astute manoeuvring of the new Broederbond chief, Pieter de Lange, had contained the schism within Afrikaner ranks. As had been done only twice before in the organisation's history, all members of the AB were called upon to reregister. This enabled the moderniser wing, which had taken control, to weed out the core of traditionalists. From then on, the thrust of the Broederbond would be towards finding ways out of what was perceived as the impasse of apartheid. Although Botha remained a member, he tended to see himself as free to make his own decisions. However, AB members surrounded him, and the security establishment continued to be dominated by the Broederbond.

On his return from Europe, Botha looked forward to another milestone along his carefully crafted path of paternalistic reform and tight security: the tricameral elections, scheduled for August. A growing movement called for a boycott. The government responded by detaining most of the UDF executive and sending more and heavily armed patrols into black, Indian and coloured ghettos. If anything, this encouraged support for the boycott call. The elections were a farce, with an average turnout of 11 per cent. One new parliamentarian received just 154 votes. It was a repeat of the council elections in many black townships a year earlier.

The result was a major boost to the confidence of anti-apartheid groups and a severe embarrassment for the government. The government blamed a minority of 'agitators' who had 'intimidated' the majority. It was pointed out that on the last day of tricameral voting, Tuesday, 28 August 1984, there were clashes in the Indian area of Lenasia, west of Johannesburg. A further crackdown was ordered. On the following Sunday night, a trigger-happy policeman in the Bophalong township south of Johannesburg shot dead local sporting hero Reuben Twala. The bottled-up anger of the township burst out in protest. It was the start of the most sustained uprising South Africa had seen.

Just two weeks later the first legal strike by the NUM began. It spread rapidly to other, non-unionised, mines. The mining companies responded by calling in the police to back up mine security. Striking miners were forced underground at gunpoint and at least ten were killed. There were reports that one of the larger mining houses, Gold Fields, had even patented its own rubber bullet. But this was a watershed for the mining companies. Not only did the strike compel them to concede the demand for unions, they also decided to explore the possibility of a negotiated settlement with the ANC.

The response of Botha and the State Security Council was to unleash the reorganised agents of repression. Massive intimidation, murder, torture and detention savaged the rebellious communities. But for all their ferocious response the police were losing control. Now the army was drafted in. By late September there were more than 32,000 troops in ninety-six townships around the country. Lumbering armoured personnel carriers – 'Hippos' – protected the patrols, but even they could not travel through certain townships such as Alexandra, north of Johannesburg, at night. Several that did so got stuck in hastily constructed 'tank-trap' trenches dug across the rutted gravel roads. Troops filled them in during the day only to have them dug again as soon as darkness fell.

Many townships were clearly becoming ungovernable. The rent and rates increases announced in August were met with a simple boycott of all payments. Massive 'stayaways' shook industry. Consumer boycotts began to bankrupt white businesses that relied on township trade. It was this that, for example, drove the large Hepworths departmental store out of Queenstown in the Eastern Cape. Even more worrying for business and government was the fact that many of the militant elements, especially within the burgeoning trade union movement, were hostile not only to apartheid but to capitalism. To the consternation of the ANC, they also tended to be dismissive of the exiled movement, some of them referring to the Freedom Charter as a 'bourgeois' document. The scent of revolution was in the air, and it seemed to bode no good for either business, government, or the movement that proclaimed itself the legitimate representative of the South African majority.

These developments did not at first move Botha and the generals toward thoughts of a deal with the ANC. If ever such talks took place they wanted to dictate conditions, and this required a position of overwhelming strength. The government had lost ground and was determined to regain it before any conciliatory moves were made. So the 21st of July 1985 brought the first of a series of states of emergency that were to cover almost all of South Africa almost continuously until 1990.

This was the period that provided much of the grist for the TRC mill. Disappearances such as the Pebco Three, later found to have been beaten with lead pipes for hours before being strangled, and the slaughter of the Cradock Four were among the higher-profile tales of horror that emerged during TRC hearings. The parade of victims and the tales of poisoning, torture and sadistic slaughter that the TRC revealed were only part of a particularly brutal aspect of enforcing a system that had uprooted and educationally and emotionally crippled millions of citizens.

But the 'total strategy' in its brute sense extended beyond the borders of South Africa. Throughout the decade the apartheid military, assisted by the police and national intelligence, rampaged through the region. The financial cost to countries attacked and undermined as part of the destabilisation campaign has been estimated at more than $50 billion in 2000 values. The human cost of uprooting millions of people, causing the deaths of hundreds of thousands of children, ruining agriculture and wrecking infrastructure nation-wide can never be quantified. The outline of who planned, ordered and carried out so many acts of institutional terror is known. But this too was never investigated: it lay outside the scope of the TRC.

Many of the known individual cases within South Africa classed by the TRC as human rights abuses also remained unexplained. During the security crackdown of the 1980s, suspected opponents were detained in their thousands and most of them were tortured. Of 600 released political detainees examined by a panel of doctors from the National Medical and Dental Association in 1985, 93 per cent complained of torture and other physical abuse and 83 per cent bore medical evidence of abuse, sometimes weeks after the abuse had occurred. More than 350 of those examined were classified by the doctors as 'severely injured'. This pattern was to continue for years. Many of the victims never knew the names of their torturers, although many could probably identify them by sight. Others, who were blindfolded or otherwise unable to see their tormentors, knew the locations where they had been tortured.

When the investigations unit of the TRC was established it was this fact that caused a young investigator in Johannesburg, Piers Pigou, to collect the names of all officers who served in the security police during that era. He pointed out that it would be a relatively easy, if time-consuming, exercise to discover which officers were serving in which areas at any given moment. These could be matched with the hundreds of cases of human rights abuse where the date and place were known. National investigations unit director Glenn Goosen turned the suggestion down flat. The TRC, Pigou was told, did not 'have time for that sort of thing'.

For some of the TRC staff, to veto such an obvious investigation smacked of stupidity or worse. However, it probably had much more to do with time constraints and with a fundamentally religious attitude toward reconciliation. It was summed up in the phrase 'we will have no witch hunts'. What this meant was accepting that the process concerned individual perpetrators and victims, and giving the perpetrators the opportunity of confession to clear their consciences. None appear to have done so.

Confessions, in the form of amnesty applications, tended to come only after perpetrators were positively identified and could not deny their guilt. This was admitted bluntly by mass murderer and security policeman Paul van Vuuren. He applied for amnesty for the murder of eighteen people, while his colleague Jacques Hechter admitted to killing twenty-six. All of these were murders in which another police killer, Joe Mamasela, had implicated him. Van Vuuren admitted to author Jacques Pauw that there were several more incidents that he would not talk about. 'Sometime Jacques Hechter and I went on operations. We are not going to split on each other and it will remain our secret. Nobody will ever know.'

Van Vuuren, Hechter and their commanding officer Brigadier Jan Hatting Cronje were part of a security police death squad that operated in the then northern Transvaal province. They boasted of being 'better' than Vlakplaas in terms of their records as killers and terrorists. But they were only one of numerous units around the country that kidnapped, fire-bombed homes, murdered and tortured with impunity.

*

Despite the most ruthless efforts, by 1986 the level of repressive violence had failed to quell resistance. As banks, business and even the friendliest of foreign governments began to show decided concern, Botha once again restructured the security command and stepped up the military's terror capabilities.

Greater use of information technology was seen as one way to enhance the performance of the system. Three separate streams of data, along with recommendations and advice, some of it contradictory – from the police Security Branch, from Military Intelligence and from the National Intelligence Service – poured in to the State Security Council and its secretariat. Decisions derived from this material had failed to stop the political and social fabric fraying at the edges. Botha and his generals resolved to crack down even harder.

Despite pressure for sanctions, access to more centralised and efficient information processing was not a problem. The whole racial classification system, from 'influx control' for blacks to the 'books of life' – detailed identity documents – for other categories, had been maintained since the 1950s by electronic hardware and software provided by companies such as ICL in Britain and IBM and the Burroughs Corporation in the United States. The shortage of military personnel in the 1970s had been partially overcome by the use of computers supplied by 'Big Blue', the IBM corporation. By the 1980s, South Africa had become the biggest spender on computers in terms of percentage of national wealth (GDP) after the US and Britain.

These close collaborative ties with international business and the links through South African corporations were little explored by any local media and not at all by the TRC. It was left to individuals, such as a group of Stanford University students in the US, to uncover the details and often the horrible consequences of such connections. But technology could not make up for deficits in popular support. For all the assistance received – at a price – from business interests at home and abroad, the state machine could still not cope.

So Botha and his generals decided to retain the SSC and its working committee, along with the joint management structures. But in 1986 they established a new, high-powered, coordinating body known as KIK (Kordinerende Intelligensie Komitee – Coordinating Intelligence Committee). Members included the heads of the police Security Branch, Military Intelligence and the National Intelligence Service. NIS director Niel Barnard chaired it for much of its existence. KIK was, in fact, another working committee of the SSC to which it reported. Barnard, in his role as head of the NIS, also reported directly to the state president. He was later to maintain consistently that he knew nothing of the human rights abuses that occurred and had not been involved.

The actual work of collating and analysing material fell to another new body, a subcommittee of KIK, known as Trewits (Teenrewolusionre Inligtings-taakspan – Counter-Revolutionary Information Task Team). This Pretoria-based unit became a major known hub of intelligence gathering and assessment, a lodestone for the fragments of information that poured into the spy agencies in South Africa's nine regional military command divisions and from the various agents in countries far and near. The role of Trewits was to assess such information and to build up 'target dossiers' on the individuals and organisations named. An elite body, which never numbered more than twenty members, seconded mainly from the police Security Branch but also from the NIS and Military Intelligence, it was also tasked with drafting detailed plans to eliminate opponents.

The instructions for compiling target dossiers were specific. They comprised all individuals and organisations that:

1. Already contravened security regulations or that are expected to do so in the future. Here it is the duty of the regions to identify the most important individuals and supply such information to Trewits to enable them [sic] to perform the necessary research in conjunction with the desk at Security Branch Head Office, Military Intelligence and NIS.
2. Are acting in such a manner that it endangers safety and good order.
3. Render assistance to individuals or organisations already mentioned.

KIK also instructed Trewits to 'identify the operational, strategic and tactical aims' of opposition organisations. Specifically mentioned were the ANC, the PAC, the communist party (SACP) and the Black Consciousness Movement (BCM). The order also mentioned several rightwing organisations, but stated that this information should be dealt with only by the chairman of Trewits on a 'need to know' basis. In any event, Trewits appears to have concentrated almost solely on the ANC (which included the SACP) and on the PAC. Most of the dossier building focussed on individuals and structures associated with the ANC.

Organised administratively as a 'C' unit within the Security Branch of the police, Trewits was always chaired by a senior security police officer. When it started, it shared an office with the rest of the Special Branch 'C' unit, including the Vlakplaas death squad, in the Security Branch headquarters in Pretoria. It later moved to offices in nearby Bosman Street, and finally, to the Southern Life building in the city in November 1990.

From 1986 until 1992, Trewits gathered and assessed information, drew up target dossiers with recommendations for action, and passed them on to KIK and so to the SSC, which usually approved the recommendations and returned

them to Trewits. Trewits then relayed the instructions to the appropriate
operational units. To liquidate individuals or groups, this often meant C1,
Vlakplaas or one of the other police death squads. However, both MI and the
NIS continued to maintain their own assessment structures and operational
units and all seem to have been able to use the services of Botha's newly
launched Civil Cooperation Bureau (CCB).

A secret defence force report dated 28 April 1987 spells out the attitude of the
military toward the CCB. Arguing against a formal structure, it classed the
CCB as a 'longer term project'. The report notes that 'methods which are
being proposed' should not be regarded as murder, but rather as 'an attack on
an individual (enemy) target with non-standard-issue weapons in an unconven-
tional way so as not to harm innocent people'.

So it was that University of the Witwatersrand sociologist and anti-apartheid
campaigner David Webster died in a blast of shotgun pellets fired from a car
driving down a suburban Johannesburg street in broad daylight. The CCB
operative who wielded that non-standard-issue weapon, gangster and convicted
murderer Ferdi Barnard, was identified, tried and sentenced to life imprisonment for the murder. It was only when Barnard, together with seven other
former CCB members, applied in September 2000 for amnesty for a series of
apartheid 'dirty tricks' that some of the facts emerged. The amnesty applications related to the attempted murders of ANC transport minister Dullah
Omar and journalist Gavin Evans, and to the bombing of the anti-apartheid
Early Learning Centre in Cape Town's Athlone in 1989. None of the men had
applied for amnesty for the murder of David Webster. As leading anti-apartheid
lawyer George Bizos noted, 'Their attitude is: killing is our business. Don't ask
any questions about it.'

But at the hearing Barnard, already serving two life sentences, finally broke
ranks. He confessed to having murdered David Webster. The order, he said,
had come from Colonel Joe Verster. Verster had refused, at TRC hearings, to
discuss the inner workings of the CCB. He had been appointed head of the
military death and dirty tricks squad as 'managing director' with the salary
scale of a general, while retaining the rank of colonel. With a background in
what the military refer to as 'pseudo ops', he had served in 1976 with the
Selous Scouts in Zimbabwe as part of a 'practical experience' exercise. A
former parachute instructor and 'Recce' member who also served in Namibia
and Angola, Verster was handpicked for special training at the warfare school
in Taiwan. Perhaps most significantly, he was sent for 'special training' in Israel
before taking up his 'pseudo' civilian post at the head of the CCB.

He and fellow amnesty applicants Carl 'Calla' Botha, Abram 'Slang' (Snake) van Zyl, Eddie Webb, Daniel 'Staal' (Steel) Burger, Leon 'Chappies' Maree and Wouter Basson, nephew of the chemical and biological warfare chief of the same name, listened impassively as Barnard confessed and named names. 'Calla' Botha, he said, had been the driver for the drive-by shooting of David Webster. The academic had been 'taken out' because of information he had gleaned about military activities and which, it was feared, he would pass on at the United Nations.

Verster and Botha, both of whom could now be charged with the murder of David Webster, have refused to speak on the issue except to brand Barnard a liar. No charges were laid against them. The same applies to the other members of what was effectively a state-run Murder and Terror Incorporated. From what is known of the way the system worked, a target dossier on David Webster would certainly have existed, drafted by Trewits, or by one of the MI units or the NIS. In any case, it would almost certainly have been processed through KIK with approval given by the SSC. Unfortunately, the inner workings of Trewits, KIK and the SSC, let alone MI or the NIS, were never examined by the TRC. In fact, the TRC rejected an urgent application made by its own investigators in mid-1998 to have seventeen leading military officers subpoenaed for questioning. The official reason: 'not enough time'. The priority, the commission ordered, should be to produce the report that would cover the activities of the TRC to that date.

But while the TRC mandate to uncover the truth of the apartheid past was frequently curtailed by time constraints, lack of capacity and an absence of political will to delve too deeply or to expose responsibility at too high a level, some clarity was achieved. From evidence at amnesty hearings, from scraps of documents, interviews and TRC hearings, the chain of command, which existed to control every aspect of state terror, was laid bare. It was made clear who held ultimate responsibility for the hundreds of deaths, detentions and tortures that are known about. But the facts of the deaths, detentions and tortures had been known about publicly for years before the TRC came into being.

On 6 November 1986, for example, opposition MP David Dalling read into the parliamentary record the affidavits of several eastern Cape torture victims. He stated pointedly: '. . . when the Nuremberg trials are held in this country – and it will happen – I do not want any members of this House to say: I did not know.' What Dalling himself did not know at the time was that some members of the House, including Wynand Malan, who was later to become a truth commissioner, had already been briefed by Dirk Coetzee about the murderous activities of Vlakplaas. He also did not know then about how far the talks and talks about talks had already gone.

5

The talking begins

In the midst of the bloodletting and the widespread mounting chaos as Botha tried with increasing desperation to put out the fires of revolt, a self-effacing Afrikaner academic arrived in Lusaka. It was September 1984 when Hendrik Willem van der Merwe travelled north for talks with Olivier Tambo, Thabo Mbeki and Zambia's President Kenneth Kaunda. Known as 'Har-vee' after the Afrikaans pronunciation of his initials, Van der Merwe was the head of the Centre for Conflict Resolution at the University of Cape Town and a committed member of the Society of Friends. He had joined the Society – the 'Quakers' – in the late 1950s. He then turned his back on his segregationist past and became a friend of the Mandela family. He knew that, throughout its history, the ANC had stood for a negotiated transition to majority rule; that it had been pushed reluctantly into armed resistance.

His barely noted visit to Lusaka was to provide the opening both for the Broederbond and NP modernisers and for those senior members of the ANC who saw in the general turmoil the opportunity to strike a deal with the apartheid state. As a pacifist and head of a centre dedicated to the peaceful resolution of disputes, Van der Merwe was grieved by the widening spiral of violence. He carried assessments and comments between the Lusaka ANC leadership and Mandela. His own analysis of events would have been part of this, although he was never known to press a personal viewpoint; his strength and reputation lay in the fact that he was ever the facilitator. He also kept open contacts to every sector of South African society and, as an Afrikaner, was well aware of the realities of Afrikaner power politics.

Shortly after his return to Cape Town he contacted Sampie Terreblanche, with whom he had been at university, a Stellenbosch political economist known to be one of the leading modernisers within the Broederbond. Van der Merwe suggested that Terreblanche and three other known AB modernisers, Stellenbosch philosopher Willie Esterhuyse, leading Dutch Reformed Church theologian Johan Heyns and journalist Wimpie de Klerk, should meet with the ANC. Terreblanche was interested, as were the others. They agreed to discuss the proposal.

Van der Merwe also had messages for Mandela from Lusaka. He relayed these to Winnie Mandela, and it was she who invited him to visit the imprisoned ANC leader on 11 October. Mandela was then held in Pollsmoor prison, where he, Walter Sisulu, Raymond Mhlaba, Andrew Mlangeni and Ahmed Kathrada had been moved in 1982 after Kobie Coetsee had become aware of the psychological profiles drawn up by General Jannie Roux. The unofficial rector and 'senior staff' of the decidedly informal and unofficial 'Political University of Robben Island' were segregated from the younger, more recently sentenced militants. This was in line with an earlier assessment by the former prisons minister Jimmy Kruger, who felt that, unlike the mainly younger militants, Mandela was someone with whom the government might 'do business'.

The visit by Van der Merwe evidently played a part in Mandela's decision to write to Kobie Coetsee at the end of 1984 to propose 'talks about talks' with P.W. Botha. (The award of that year's Nobel Peace Prize to Archbishop Desmond Tutu also seemed to signal that the world expected a change in attitude.) There was no reply. However, after Oliver Tambo broadcast a New Year message on 8 January that included the call to 'render South Africa ungovernable,' P.W. Botha publicly offered to free Mandela if the ANC leader 'renounced violence'. Mandela's response, read to a packed rally in Soweto on Sunday 10 February 1985 by his daughter Zindzi, was a masterpiece. It turned the tables on Botha, and pointed out that it was not he or the ANC that had begun the violence. To thunderous applause Zindzi, a powerful speaker in her own right, read:

> I am surprised at the conditions that the government wants to impose on me. I am not a violent man . . . [it was] only when all other forms of resistance were no longer open to us, that we turned to armed struggle. Let Botha show he is different to Malan, Strijdom and Verwoerd. Let him renounce violence. Let him say that he will dismantle apartheid. Let him unban the people's organisation, the African National Congress. Let him free all who have been imprisoned,

banished or exiled for their opposition to apartheid. Let him guarantee free
political activity so that people may decide who will govern them.

Botha was reportedly furious. This may have accounted for the level of
cold anger he displayed in February when he summoned Sampie Terreblanche
and Willie Esterhuyse to his 18th-floor office. He had heard of their intention
to visit the ANC in Lusaka and he made it clear that this would not be
tolerated. However, he was almost certainly aware at that stage not only of
the proposed meeting with the ANC, but also of 'tentative' and other contacts
that had already been made.

Among these were the talks between the big business-sponsored South African
Foundation and the ANC. Established to promote a 'positive image of South
Africa', the SA Foundation had initially been closely linked to the government,
but as the bulk of business swung behind a reforming position it had displayed
a more independent attitude. In January 1985 David Willers, the SA Foundation
representative in London, met two ANC officials in the British capital. One of
them, the ANC chief representative Solly Smith (Samuel Khunyeli), was a South
African intelligence agent. Certainly from 1984 he reported regularly and in
depth on all contacts. He was also, as a senior ANC member in the vital post
in London, privy to the thinking of the exiled leadership.

Willers assured the ANC duo that, for reasons of self-interest, South African
business was committed to fundamental reform, including unbanning the
ANC. Significantly, Willers remembered that Solly Smith warned that the task
of reconstruction would become much harder if the ANC were to be
'undermined by more radical elements'. While the bloodshed and brutality
reached new extremes at home and in the region, a common interest of
business, government and the ANC was defined.

Despite a Republican administration under Ronald Reagan in charge in
Washington, a bipartisan 'Free South Africa' movement was growing, and
congressional and business groups gave a warm reception to Oliver Tambo
when he visited the US in March 1985. This followed a visit to South Africa by
Senator Edward Kennedy at the invitation of the Nobel Laureate Desmond
Tutu and fellow cleric Alan Boesak. As the plight of the apartheid system
worsened, business began to find a place for the ANC in its calculations.

But with the situation on the ground in South Africa slipping out of
government control, there were some within the ANC leadership who began
to see for the first time a real possibility of the forceful seizure of power.
Among these individuals was political commissar Chris Hani of Umkhonto we
Sizwe (MK), the ANC's military wing. To some of the long-term political
prisoners in Pollsmoor and on Robben Island, this prospect also seemed
feasible, though a more sober assessment would have shown that no forces

MK could rally were any match for the repressive might of the apartheid state. Yet here was the threat of a popular and perhaps highly destructive revolution with an unpredictable, possibly very radical, final outcome.

Botha and his generals still sought a more advantageous way out of their impasse. To buy time, they attempted to re-establish a geographic cordon sanitaire by means of agreements such as those they had brokered with Swaziland and Mozambique. Botswana refused to comply and suffered a massive raid on its tiny capital, Gaborone, on 14 June 1985. Houses and office blocks were destroyed and twelve people killed, only four of them having any connection with the ANC. The TRC never clarified who planned, ordered and carried out this murderous raid.

Lesotho's prime minister, Chief Leabua Jonathan, who owed his position to the intervention of the apartheid state, continued to play for time as he contemplated biting the hand that had fed him. He was toppled in a military coup in January 1986. South Africa's hand was behind this, but no details have ever publicly emerged.

It was not as if Botha – like the more informed members of his cabinet, as well as his military chiefs – did not know that the ANC's long-standing policy favoured a negotiated settlement. They knew, but they also knew that the ANC interpreted this as a negotiated transfer of power to the majority. Neither government nor business was ready to countenance this. Gavin Relly, when he took over the chair of Anglo American from Harry Oppenheimer in 1982, had summed up the verdict of business on the idea of one person one vote. '[It] would be a formula for unadulterated chaos at this point in our history,' he said. Such racist notions permeated every level of South African business and persisted even after regular contacts were established with the ANC leadership. So business, while it pressed for reform, continued to play its part in maintaining – and milking – the system.

After the Van der Merwe visit to Lusaka, more and more business leaders openly considered, and in some cases promoted contact with the ANC. But it was the events of July and August of that year that focused business minds as never before on the need to do something – fast. On 31 July, under investor pressure and following the declaration of another state of emergency in South Africa, the Chase Manhattan Bank in the US stopped rolling over loans to the apartheid state. The bank would extend no further credit. It wanted back the money it had lent. Wounded by the bad publicity and the withdrawal of union, Church and other 'anti-apartheid' funds, Chase Manhattan decided to quit the very small market that was South Africa.

This simple and barely trumpeted business decision began a chain reaction. Britain's Barclays Bank, for example, found itself losing its lucrative British student market as anti-apartheid students picketed, protested and withdrew their accounts. South Africa, once such a profitable investment destination, was becoming a liability.

But the banks, like other investors that had battened on to apartheid, were loath to withdraw completely if there were profits still to be made. They pinned their hopes on a long-touted and supposedly ground-breaking speech that Botha promised to deliver at the National Party congress in Durban on 15 August 1985. In the preceding days and weeks a battle went on behind the scenes within the cabinet and the Broederbond. The modernisers urged Botha to use the opportunity to announce major concessions, the traditionalists, among them F.W. de Klerk, encouraged Botha's tendency to caution. Some also expressed resentment at South Africa being 'pushed around' by 'international financiers'.

The traditionalists argued that while concessions should be granted, to 'go too far' would be seen as weakness at a time when another miners' strike had erupted, the trade unions showed no inclination to be tamed, and whole townships were effective no-go areas for troops and police. The traditionalists advocated toughness, not timidity, and Botha was caught in the middle. So when he came to speak, he announced several probable concessions, but they were delivered – and drowned – amid bluster and bile. Broederbond modernisers such as reserve bank governor Gerhard de Kock and finance minister Barend du Plessis were horrified as Botha, who had little grasp of economics, railed against 'communist agitators' and the foreign media. 'I am not prepared to lead white South Africans and other minority groups on the road to abdication and suicide,' he declared. It was passages such as this that were remembered, rather than the commitment to 'a united South Africa, one citizenship and a universal franchise'. Most commentators saw the speech as a classic example of the finger-wagging belligerence and paranoia associated with Botha at his most obdurate.

Within weeks, the money markets gave their assessment: the rand collapsed. A debt moratorium and tight financial controls were imposed by the reserve bank. Business confidence evaporated. Botha, like a petulant schoolchild, felt misunderstood and hard done by. To the exasperation of the modernisers, he retreated from the reformist path he was being urged to take, especially by Niel Barnard, the National Intelligence Service chief who had emerged as one of the most powerful voices for pragmatism.

It was against this background that Tony Bloom, fourth-generation head of the Premier Group, Gavin Relly and Zac de Beer of Anglo American, together with newspaper editors Tertius Myburgh and Harald Pakendorf, flew to Lusaka in September. The delegation left, if not with the blessing, certainly with the knowledge of Botha. Myburgh enjoyed close contacts with military intelligence and Pakendorf was seen as a representative of the moderniser wing of Afrikanerdom whose most powerful members included Pieter de Lange and Niel Barnard.

The group sat with President Kenneth Kaunda, Oliver Tambo, Thabo Mbeki, Chris Hani and Mac Maharaj, and was widely reported to have been impressed by the ANC leaders. Bloom enthused that the ANC economic and political model appeared to be 'Sweden rather than Russia'. Tambo correctly assessed the attitude of the business group in a broadcast the following month. He saw them as potential allies who would switch sides and even join forces to destroy apartheid 'provided they are sure the system will not be replaced with something worse for their economy, for their pockets, for their profits'.

The doyen of Afrikaner capital, Anton Rupert, then weighed in with a comment apparently meant to smooth the way for further talks with the ANC. In an interview with the *Star* newspaper in Johannesburg on 29 September, he noted: 'Apartheid is dead, but the corpse stinks and must be buried and not embalmed.' Not that Rupert was in favour of universal franchise in a unitary state. He hedged his bets, and still talked of 'population groups' and 'co-existence'. Yet the signals were clear: business, even where it owed its position to Broederbond and government patronage, was prepared to forgo every aspect of apartheid. So long as capitalism survived, racism could be dispensed with.

As part of a campaign to prepare the apartheid constituency for change, Rupert arranged that leading Broederbond moderniser Willie Esterhuyse write a brief biographical volume about him. It appeared in 1986, and though flattering to an embarrassing degree, it gave a clear signal that the modernisers were prepared to sacrifice apartheid. Esterhuyse went on to lead talks with the ANC and to become a close friend of Thabo Mbeki, while also acting as the official conduit to Niel Barnard and the NIS.

Tambo read the signals correctly, and bore them in mind when he met with British business chiefs in London in October 1985. These were people who had ignored the ANC for all the years of exile. Now, with the townships in revolt and profits threatened, they were keen to talk. Even a few Conservative MPs broke ranks to speak to Tambo. The time of talking had dawned, and it became even more obvious at the Commonwealth Heads of Government meeting that month in the Bahamas.

Margaret Thatcher tried to hold the line for Botha and his policies by opposing proposals for sanctions. She was bolstered by assurances from people such as Chief Buthelezi, industrialist Harry Oppenheimer and PFP parliamentarian Helen Suzman that support for the ANC within South Africa tended to be 'greatly exaggerated'. However, the rest of the Commonwealth did not share Thatcher's chilliness towards the ANC. A split threatened. It was averted when a compromise established a Commonwealth Eminent Persons' Group (EPG). Co-chaired by former Australian prime minister Malcolm Fraser and by General Olusegun Obasanjo, the former Nigerian military ruler, who became that country's democratic president in 1999, the EPG would travel to South Africa 'in search of a settlement'.

This search would include discussions with Mandela in Pollsmoor prison. The South African government agreed, but before the EPG arrived Mandela had his first serious discussions with the apartheid state. They took place in the Volks Hospital in Cape Town where the ANC leader had been taken for a prostate operation in November. An entire floor of the hospital was sealed off and handpicked staff sworn to secrecy when Mandela arrived. After his operation, he received two visitors, prisons minister Kobie Coetsee and another Broederbonder, General Johan Willemse, the commissioner of prisons. If news of their visit leaked, they could maintain that they were merely discussing prison conditions and nothing more.

In the event, nothing of substance was discussed. But a process had begun. Mandela, probably correctly, assumed that one of the tactics of the apartheid state would be to try to drive a wedge between him and the exiled leadership. So when he returned to Pollsmoor to be given a separate cell in the prison hospital, he put in two requests: he wanted to speak to his fellow prisoners in Pollsmoor and to send a message to the exiled leadership through his lawyer, George Bizos. Both requests were granted and Coetsee personally gave the go-ahead to Bizos to travel to the ANC in Lusaka. There he informed Tambo about what had happened and that Mandela would not conclude any deals without the concurrence of the exiled leadership. It was agreed that the contacts between Lusaka, Mandela and the government would be kept secret.

Botha was kept fully briefed, but, concerned for his traditionalist support base and perhaps wishing to keep his options open, he insisted that he not be directly implicated. Coetsee was the ideal go-between as prisons minister. As with the first conversation in the hospital, should news of the meetings leak it could be said that it was prison conditions that were being discussed. In the meantime, the bloodshed and bluster continued. Even while the government committed itself to the visit by the EPG, an SSC meeting on 27 October, chaired by Botha, recommended 'offensive action' against the ANC in Lesotho, where Leabua Jonathan was still resisting his former masters. Defence minister Magnus Malan, a confidant of Botha, warned in December that the military would not hesitate to 'root out terrorists wherever they may be . . . events . . . demonstrate that we are dealing with textbook examples of communist-inspired terrorism . . .'

That month in Lesotho a Vlakplaas death squad working under the direct orders of police chief Johan van der Merwe and led by Eugene de Kock raided two homes in the capital, Maseru. Their faces hidden by balaclavas and carrying silenced weapons, they murdered nine people, including a young mother, Jackie Quinn, and the two top MK operatives in the region, Morris Siabelo and Joe Majose. Van der Merwe later applied for, and was refused, amnesty for this attack. He had failed to disclose full details of the operation. The ANC responded with a bomb at a shopping centre in the east coast town of Amanzimtoti.

But there were also developments of common concern to government, business and the ANC. One was the formation that December of a self-proclaimed 'giant of the labour movement'. More than 500,000 workers organised into thirty-two unions combined to form the Congress of South African Trade Unions (Cosatu). This came at first as a body blow to the ANC, and in particular the SACP. They had hoped that the unions, when they came together, would do so under the banner of the ANC-aligned and SACP-controlled SA Congress of Trade Unions (Sactu).

Although some of Cosatu's unions professed allegiance to the ANC and its Freedom Charter, the predominant trend was for independence. The major influence behind its formation had come from 'workerist' elements considered hostile, if not to the ANC, certainly to the SACP. The concern of business and government focused on the talk emanating from Cosatu of the need for a 'workers' charter' and for a revolution leading to 'workers' control'. But this was always within the context of the union movement itself. Talk of setting up a 'workers' party' came to nothing, leaving open the vacuum eventually occupied by the ANC and SACP.

In late 1985 it was also becoming obvious to the ANC that Mikhail Gorbachev's Soviet Union faced growing economic problems and was steering much closer to the United States. This had implications for both the ANC and the allied SACP, as well as for the apartheid government. One of the major sources of funding and certainly of military materiel for the ANC was starting to dry up. Increasing amounts of support, especially for the farming, educational and child-care projects in countries such as Zambia and Tanzania, were coming from the Scandinavian countries and from the Netherlands. The grip of the SACP on the purse strings of exile had been severely weakened.

Another factor, though not much mentioned, was the disillusion felt by
various senior figures about the economic performance of Eastern Europe and
the Soviet Union and the racism encountered there by a number of students.
Oliver Tambo was obviously more impressed with the Scandinavian countries,
and particularly Sweden. In a religious man who had at one time intended to
become an Anglican priest, this was not unexpected by the SACP radicals.
What worried them more was that Thabo Mbeki, one of the best and brightest
of the SACP's young stars, seemed 'rather too impressed with the Swedes'.

Against this background, the seven members of the EPG arrived in South
Africa on 3 February 1986. To begin with, the government saw the visit as an
opportunity to promote as the way forward the supposed 'gradualism' of
Botha. But it soon became obvious that there were other agendas in play.
Mandela, the prisoner, seemed to be exerting more influence than President
Botha.

When the EPG met the ANC leader he assured them of the ANC's
willingness to suspend violence and to seek a negotiated settlement. The
discussions in Pollsmoor prison provided the outline for the EPG proposals of
terms for negotiations, namely that talks could start once the ANC renounced
violence and the government released political prisoners, unbanned the ANC
and withdrew its troops from the black townships. This had only to be
confirmed by Lusaka. This proposal and Mandela's agreement to it found its
way to the cabinet via constitutional affairs minister and moderniser Chris
Heunis. His civil servant son, Jan, had sat in on the talks with Mandela. Kobie
Coetsee had declined Mandela's invitation to stay on for the discussions and
had left after introducing Mandela to his 'guests'.

While the prospect of a negotiated settlement brokered by the EPG caused
jubilation among some of the moderniser element, it caused a great deal of
resentment among the more traditionally minded. The idea of uitlanders,
foreigners, dictating to the government what it should do was anathema to
Botha and a number of the hardliners who surrounded him. The military too
felt it was not yet time to move towards talks. Both the Pentagon and the CIA
were still supporting their venture in Angola, where the bulk of the ANC army
was based. They argued for wiping out this element before starting any talks.
Only the military knew in detail that June had seen a highly destructive
seaborne assault on Angola's Port Namibe, and plans were well under way for
a drive, ostensibly by the rebel UNITA movement, to take the strategic town
of Cuito Cunevale.

The military smelled a major breakthrough coming, and what they knew
the SSC would know. In any case, it was the advice of the military that carried
the day with Botha. This was apparently the reason for launching air raids on

Gaborone, Lusaka and Harare on the day that the EPG arrived back in South Africa from talks with an exiled ANC leadership that had agreed to the preconditions for negotiations. General Magnus Malan confirmed to the TRC that Botha and himself ordered the raids, on 19 May 1986, without reference even to the State Security Council.

The closest Botha seems to have come to explaining himself was the remark made to journalist Patti Waldmeier that 'if Reagan can bomb Libya, I can bomb Zambia', implying that Botha saw himself in league with the US administration. As it was obviously intended to do, the bombing of three Commonwealth capitals scuppered the EPG mission. It was followed by an even more draconian crackdown on the home front, but Botha had over-reached himself. He had alienated many of his leading ministers by his unilateral decision in launching the raids.

However, there was no danger that the bombings would rule out further talks, and the Ford Foundation in the US was already finalising arrangements for a meeting between the ANC and the NP modernisers. In June, a month after the raids on the neighbouring capitals, the foundation brought together in New York an ANC delegation headed by Thabo Mbeki and an 'Afrikaner' group led by Broederbond chairman Pieter de Lange. The modernisers, including the NIS chief Niel Barnard, who had reportedly already made tentative contact with the ANC in Geneva in 1984, appeared to be gaining the upper hand. Invariably big business, which had benefited so hugely from apartheid, was the facilitator in the series of contacts.

While the Ford Foundation meeting was taking place, Gold Fields, the British-based mining company with a most reactionary image, agreed to sponsor talks in Britain. Overnight, the company that only a few years before was reputed to have patented its own rubber bullet for use against its workforce, became an apparent champion of peace and non-racism. They were backed in this move by the Anglo American Corporation.

Also in June 1986, Chris Ball, the chief executive of Barclays Bank in South Africa, who had missed out on the trip by a big business delegation to meet the ANC in Lusaka, turned up in London. He urgently wanted a meeting with Oliver Tambo. It happened that Tambo was in London at the time and a dinner was arranged. He and Thabo Mbeki met with Ball, who urged them to introduce a 'short sharp shock' of financial sanctions to 'bring the government to its senses'.

This displayed a remarkable political naiveté, but underlined the fact that negotiations were now part of the equation. With business roughly, if reluctantly, on side, Tambo decided that the next target for talks had to be the Afrikaner elite. So when Michael Young, the communications director of Gold

Fields, asked if he could help facilitate talks with anyone, Tambo at once suggested 'the Afrikaners'.

It had become clear by then that the twin tracks of the state-sponsored trek from apartheid would be more repression and bloodshed on the one hand and secret but closer contact and talks on the other. It was an obvious bid to gain as much dominance as possible before any open talks began. A similar logic motivated the exiled ANC, with much sabre-rattling rhetoric and an increase in sabotage and armed attacks accompanied by numerous formal and informal contacts and talks, mostly kept secret from all but a small group of the top leadership.

Mandela too engaged in further talks. With another state of emergency declared and the townships in growing turmoil, he met with Kobie Coetsee at Coetsee's official residence. As Mandela noted in his autobiography: 'I told him I wanted to see the state president and the foreign minister, Pik Botha.' Coetsee promised to see what he could do and Mandela returned to his cell. He waited as the weeks rolled into months and the state launched what was arguably the most brutal phase of a long campaign of terror.

Full details of government, military and police plans over this period are still unknown, but the more apartheid crumbled, the more the government ensured that it retained its superiority in terms of brute force. It also trained and equipped surrogate forces. Its various security arms bribed, blackmailed and otherwise recruited and compromised thousands of informers and part-time agents as they sought to keep control over what all agreed would be an inevitable transition towards at least greater democracy.

But only in 1987, after the ANC had been effectively driven out of the neighbouring states, did the serious business of talks and talks about talks get under way. By then, too, the tide had turned, within the major trade union federation, when the 'Charterists' finally triumphed over the 'workerists' and the federation adopted the ANC Freedom Charter. This was a great relief for the ANC leadership, which had come to realise over the previous year how fragile was their hold on the unfolding processes.

This was underlined by the international campaign organised in 1986 around the jailed 'workerist' trade union leader Moses Mayekiso and four of his comrades. The Friends of Moses Mayekiso was launched in London with the approval of Mayekiso's metalworkers' union, and of Cosatu as well as the International Metalworkers' Federation. Based in the offices of the National Union of Journalists, it was viciously opposed, particularly by the SACP-dominated SA Congress of Trade Unions. The Friends supplied funding directly to the union in South Africa rather than through the usual – and demanded – ANC and SACP channels and gained massive international trade union support.

Despite demands by Sactu that the campaign be boycotted, it won the support of trade union federations from Britain to Brazil and Japan, together representing more than 30 million workers.

In Britain, where Sactu claimed its greatest influence, only three trade union general secretaries, all considered close to the SACP, refused to endorse the campaign. But most of the branches and regions of the unions headed by Arthur Scargill, Ken Gill and Hector Mackenzie signed up as Friends of Moses Mayekiso. Warning bells rang for astute observers within the ANC and SACP. They could not take trade union support for granted. It might be available should a new political force emerge within South Africa. Despite the adoption of the Freedom Charter by Cosatu, there were still rumblings throughout the federation about the need for a 'workers' party'.

This was one consideration among many that increased the pressure toward a negotiated settlement. But the whole process was only to move into high gear after the South African Air Force lost control of the skies over Angola. At the same time, its troops were forced to retreat from south of Cuito Cunevale and, under pressure from the US and USSR, independence loomed for Namibia.

6

The Namibian dress rehearsal

From the point of view of the apartheid state, perhaps the most important meeting of 1986 did not involve any of the parties to the South African conflict. It was the coming together of Ronald Reagan and Mikhail Gorbachev in that unlikely venue, Reykjavik, Iceland. There the two superpower leaders, feeling the pinch of the arms race to different degrees, resolved to withdraw from the costly regional conflicts in which they were involved. Angola, which housed the armed wings of both the Namibian independence movement, SWAPO, and the ANC, was just such a conflict. South Africa, backed by the USA, occupied parts of southern Angola and provided military and logistical back-up to the rebel UNITA movement. Cuba, backed by the USSR, provided much of the sophisticated weaponry and skilled personnel and troops supporting the MPLA government.

But the details of such agreements take time to work out; their implementation even longer. The various allies on both sides also had to be consulted. While this process went on, both sides hurried to gain advantage by pouring additional assistance to their surrogates before the eventual ceasefire. The US was in an invidious position: its major oil companies were doing good business with the MPLA government. In one of the great ironies of the time, they relied on Cuban troops, which their government opposed, to protect their installations. So the US government was supporting UNITA in order to defeat Cubans who were protecting US oil interests in Angola.

The Soviet Union had no such dilemma and sent a massive amount of materiel into Angola. Most worrying for the South Africans and their UNITA allies was the inclusion of sophisticated anti-aircraft and radar equipment, along with MiG-23 fighter aircraft. These quickly ensured aerial supremacy for the Angolan government side. There were also increasing incursions into Namibia by the People's Liberation Army of Namibia (PLAN), the armed wing of SWAPO.

SWAPO came into being in 1959 to demand independence for the former German colony that South Africa treated as a fifth province and still referred to as South West Africa. Two-thirds the size of South Africa, mineral rich and largely desert, SWA/Namibia had been administered by successive South African governments ever since South African troops had seized it in 1915 in one of the campaigns of World War One. In 1920 the League of Nations awarded the territory to Britain. It would be administered by South Africa with a view to its eventual independence.

After World War Two and the formation of the UN the South African government maintained that, since the League of Nations no longer existed, SWA/Namibia belonged to it. South African prime minister Jan Christiaan Smuts asserted in 1947 that SWA was 'inextricably tied' to South Africa: 'Nothing but war can alter this association.'

Nearly twenty years later, as the apartheid government applied its 'home-land' policies to the territory, the UN General Assembly revoked the 1920 mandate. When South Africa flatly rejected the UN edict, SWAPO moved into a phase of 'armed struggle'. This had little effect except to incure a harsh security crackdown that sentenced leading SWAPO members such as Toivo ja Toivo to long terms on Robben Island. But SWA/Namibia was put firmly on the international agenda, and in 1973 the UN recognised SWAPO as 'the authentic representative of the Namibian people'.

The collapse of the Portuguese empire in 1974 dramatically changed the fortunes of SWAPO and its armed wing. For the first time, they had friendly territory, across the border in Angola, from which to operate. 'Hot pursuit' of PLAN units was the original excuse used by apartheid forces when they could not deny they had operated inside Angola. This began years of havoc in northern Namibia and into Angola. From the beginning, and with the certain support of the CIA and of elements within the Pentagon, the idea was for South African forces to provide full military back-up to the UNITA movement. This led to the steady escalation of the conflict until by June 1987 the largest conventional war in the world was being waged in Angola.

The focus at that time was the town of Cuito Cunevale, a government forward air base defended by Angolan government FAPLA forces and Cuban troops. It was besieged by UNITA and South African forces, but held out against tanks, artillery and numerous infantry assaults. By May 1988 a battered UNITA and South African force retreated. Arguments still swirl around the details of this battle, but the fact remains that South African troops withdrew and the skies belonged to the usually Cuban-piloted MiG-23 aircraft. It was a time when the hawks in Pretoria were arguing for a full-scale commitment of all of their military might and the Cubans, by then probably more than 50,000 strong, were talking of a drive south to liberate Namibia. So far as the superpowers and their détente policies were concerned, matters were clearly getting out of hand. They intervened decisively as the defending and retreating forces from Cuito Cunevale regrouped.

The deal the superpowers cobbled together called for both the South Africans and the Cubans to withdraw from Angola and for UN Resolution 435, demanding independence and democratic elections in Namibia, to be implemented. European support was assured, both East and West, so when the US and Soviet governments summoned a South African and Cuban delegation to a meeting in London on 3 and 4 May 1988, the surrogates were confronted with a fait accompli, one that pleased neither party, and left only details to be settled. One of the people in the South African delegation was Lukas Daniel Barnard, head of the NIS and the man directly involved in secret talks with Nelson Mandela as the South African state used increasingly desperate measures to crush resistance on the home front.

Neither the Angolan government and UNITA, nor the ANC and SWAPO were present at this meeting. It was only later, when the detail was agreed, that they were informed. Part of the deal was that 'all foreign troops' must withdraw from Angola. This meant, of course, the ANC armed wing, MK. In New York, in December 1988, with the continuity of US policy assured by the election of Republican George Bush, all parties to the Angolan conflict signed a comprehensive treaty. The more than 4,000 MK fighters began to withdraw, most of them to Uganda, which had offered sanctuary and training facilities. This put the MK fighters further away from South Africa than they had been in nearly thirty years' armed struggle.

The ANC was in no position to resist. Nor, essentially, was the South African government. Hardliners within the military argued that an all-out push could secure Angola, but this, from both a political and military perspective, was a dead end. So, reluctantly, the two sides of the South African conflict that had confronted one another in Angola, retreated. But both did so knowing that the implementation of UN Resolution 435 brought closer the prospect of democratic change within South Africa itself.

This held especially true because the situation on the ground within South

Africa remained volatile. Faced with continued mass resistance, fissures had opened up throughout the ruling elite. The consensus was that some accommodation must be sought with the devil it knew, rather than see the rise of some new incarnation that might not have compromise in mind.

The apartheid planners decided to make the best of a bad job: they would use the emerging Namibian situation as a dress rehearsal for the tactics they might use to orchestrate change within South Africa. They might yet be able to retain their grasp on the levers of power while making major political concessions. After all, there had already been considerable success with the MNR in Mozambique. There, by means of terror, bribery and the ability to capitalise on mistakes made by the Frelimo government, a tiny South African-backed force had grown into a substantial opposition. By 2002 it was in a position to challenge for parliamentary power. It was this thinking that swayed the decision that would cost the South African taxpayer between R185.5 million and R188.5 million in just nine months.

Various think tanks considered the prospects and drew up plans. The primary object, it was decided, was to ensure that the SWAPO liberation movement, which clearly had majority support in Namibia, failed to gain a two-thirds majority in the first independence poll. There were even hopes expressed that a coalition of South African-supported parties could win the election. This would pave the way to employ a similar tactic in South Africa.

The outlines of projects proposed by the various agencies operating in Namibia were drawn up toward the end of 1988, and by February of the next year the massive injection of government funding necessary was agreed in principle. Government ministers such as Roelf Meyer and Leon Wessels, as well as F.W. de Klerk, denied any knowledge of the expensive and complex plans to destabilise SWAPO and interfere in the Namibian election. Yet the entire South African cabinet appears to have been involved in okaying the additional secret budgets. Cabinet members were briefed, some at regular internals, by security police and military intelligence officers.

Significantly, one of the people regularly briefed, either on his own or in the company of government ministers such as Chris Fismer, was Pieter de Lange, chairman of the Broederbond. Given the history of that organisation, it is likely that its think tanks provided most if not all of the general guidelines for the various activities that seem to have fallen collectively under the umbrella of Operation 435.

But there were problems from the start, largely because an element of panic appears to have pervaded the adventure. Thugs, killers and assorted agents of the Civil Cooperation Bureau, for example, were drafted into Namibia from every sector where they were operating. As Colonel Christoffel Nel told an in camera hearing of the TRC: 'This was a recipe for disaster.' Competing agencies and operatives, all of them flush with cash, were turned loose on the territory with orders to destabilise SWAPO and to fix the coming election in favour of the other parties. One of the greatest blunders here was the killing of Anton Lubowski, a senior internal official of SWAPO and its most prominent white member. Evidence later emerged that while one agency was trying and failing to recruit Lubowski, others were planning to discredit him, while a CCB unit planned and carried out his assassination.

Also in Namibia from the start was the Koevoet (Crowbar) police unit whose members bumped up their salaries with bounties for the corpses of claimed SWAPO fighters. They kept records of their 'contacts with the enemy' and the number killed and captured, and their proclaimed kill-to-capture ratio reveals that Koevoet was nothing more than a death squad. Former Koevoet member John Deegan admitted in 1997: 'We were basically automatons. We would just kill. That's how we got our kicks. We were adrenalin junkies.' Several Koevoet members were reported to have worn T-shirts emblazoned with the legend: 'Killing is our business – and business is good.'

Because of the uncertainty and degree of secrecy that surrounded the talks about implementing Resolution 435, some police and military units were caught flat-footed. According to several reports, they still held sizeable numbers of detainees whom they felt they could not afford to release. Disposing of them apparently presented a problem until troops of the United Nations Transitional Assistance Group (UNTAG) arrived on 1 April 1989.

SWAPO fighters based until then in Angola maintain that they decided to move south to the UN bases in accordance with the agreement reached in New York. The South African military maintained that SWAPO invaded. South Africa's foreign minister Pik Botha, backed by British prime minister Margaret Thatcher, insisted that South African troops be redeployed in the north of Namibia. The UN gave permission. In the ensuing fighting, at least 300 Namibians died, a number by a single shot to the back of the head. The TRC examined this evidence and ruled that there was 'prima facie evidence that some of the dead may have been summarily executed'.

By the time the fighting erupted, most of the other schemes were already under way. The military had by far the biggest budget and dubbed its project Operation Heyday. The security police were deployed under the banner of Operation Victor, while the CCB carried out its plans as Operation Baptism Day (Doopdag). There was also Operation Agree. What it all amounted to was the South African government turning loose its dogs of war. On one level, there was only a broad decree to aid anti-SWAPO elements, sow confusion and otherwise hamper SWAPO in order to prevent a landslide victory in the elections scheduled for November. But since some of the surviving records circulated at the highest levels do refer in detail to various projects, it can be assumed that detailed knowledge of these operations was available to the SSC.

Copies of letters exist from then finance minister Barend du Plessis and law and order minister Adriaan Vlok which refer directly to the level of secret funding and to the operations. Most of the documentary evidence that has so far surfaced relates to the Security Branch's Operation Victor. However, overall political control fell to the minister of health and development, Willem van Niekerk, who had joined the Broederbond in 1967. He qualified for the job because he had formerly administered the territory on behalf of the government. His main task seems to have been to disburse funds.

These funds took time to agree because of bureaucratic delays along the government's secret channels. Months could elapse between issuing instructions and releasing the necessary funds. The reason the security police were able to mount their Operation Victor as early as February 1989 was apparently that the military, through the CCB, provided R250,000 in seed money. This then had to be repaid by the police. However, all of the funding for the various secret projects came eventually from central government, much of it paid through the ministry of health. So although this assortment of projects was run by different government agencies, it appears that Operation 435 was the first coordinated, central government-run operation.

Because the CCB did not admissibly exist, there is no mention of funding for this murderous entity. It received its funds through the military's R125 million budget – one reason why this budget was so high. The CCB was certainly very active. Its 'managing director', Colonel Joe Verster, seems to have run three separate operations in Namibia in the months leading up to the elections in November 1989. These involved everything from attempting – in Lubowski's case, succeeding – to assassinate SWAPO leaders, to sabotaging vehicles and introducing cholera bacteria into the drinking water of SWAPO refugee camps. Although Verster had a relatively free hand, he was directly answerable to the 'field commander' of Operation 435, South African army chief General Kat Liebenberg. However, the haste with which the various operations were put together, the secrecy required, together with inter-service rivalries, personal resentments and large sums of money, meant that control was extremely hard to establish or maintain.

This clearly raised concerns in the treasury. In a 'Top Secret' document, of which only ten copies were made, the auditor-general laid down strict rules of accountability for R185.5 million in secret funds. The army got R125 million, the police R26.5 million, the National Intelligence Service R3 million, the Department of Foreign Affairs and the Department of Information R15 million each. However, the auditor-general also noted: 'In the light of the percentage increase that the above amounts bring to bear on the accounts concerned, it is necessary that the Treasury gives further attention to this with the object of preventing any unnecessary public disclosure.' Much of the funding was channelled through the ministry of national health and population development, with the ministries of finance and law and order also directly involved. The State Security Council approved the budgets on 2 May 1989.

For a brief period, the military set up an international media agency in a Windhoek hotel. Army captain Nico Basson ran it. Later he publicly broke ranks and gave evidence about terror tactics in South Africa as well as some details about the Namibian operation. His claims about interference in the Namibian election process were subsequently supported and expanded, independently and anonymously, by another, more senior, officer. In terms of intelligence-gathering, it seems that provision was made to 'tap into' all media and diplomatic reports sent out of the country. However, Military Intelligence had been involved in the Namibian political scene for more than a decade. From at least 1977, MI had been involved at various levels with the Democratic Turnhalle Alliance (DTA), the attempt by the Namibian-based and Broeder-bond-linked National Party to put forward a non-racial face.

The South African military continued to back the DTA in the 1989 election, while the police, through Operation Victor, gave support to nine minority and largely rightwing and ethnically-based parties. Some efforts were made to link the nine smaller parties and the DTA, but nothing came of this. The minority parties were all supported through a phoney Namib Foundation (Namib Stiftung) set up by the South African security police under Brigadier Hein Olivier. Security police around South Africa were given various sums of money to feed into its account. The 'foundation' then funded the parties.

The funding was lavish. Each party received furnished offices, vehicles, and salaries for full-time officers and organisers. All were given access to professional media and training facilities. Journalists were recruited locally and drafted in from South Africa. A weekly tabloid newspaper, *N'Afrika*, was paid for by the Namib Foundation, which also employed several hundred Koevoet members, including many still paid by the police. A number of their wives and family members were also paid as functionaries of the foundation, some of them listed as members of a choir. A list provided by the anomymous senior officer, makes it clear that more than 6,700 individuals were paid by the Namib Foundation, among them members of both the security police and the military.

In certain cases, nepotism appears to have run riot. Jan de Wet, leader of

Aksie Christelik Nasionaal (ACN – Christian National Action), for example, received a salary and a car, as did his wife, daughter and son-in-law, all of them listed as party officials. In all, 450 vehicles were supplied, ranging from family sedans and minibuses to 4 x 4 cross-country trucks.

In an effort to guard against vehicles and equipment disappearing into private hands after the election, the police security planners registered a company, Bush Campers Ltd, in South Africa. It was from Bush Campers that the Namib Foundation leased vehicles and other equipment, including computers. Although the commander on the ground was Olivier, security police chief General J.J. 'Basie' Smit was in overall command of the police operation. After South Africa's democratic transition, Smit resigned in disgrace amid allegations of involvement in gun-running and corruption, but in 1999 he became the president of the International Police Association, which has observer status at the United Nations.

The budget agreed for Operation Victor and the infrastructure segment of Operation 435 was R67 million ($25 million). A building in Kaiser Strasse in the Namibian capital, Windhoek, was bought for R1.65 million for use as the head offices for the 'Namib Foundation parties', while thirty to forty other premises in the capital were also rented for use by the parties. Most of these premises appear to have been owned by politicians supported by the Namib Foundation, and this provided them with additional income. The same applied in other regions of the country.

Similar financial backing was given to the DTA by its military backers. T-shirts, stickers, flags and campaign literature were also produced. Four South African journalists – Johan Liebenberg and Koos Liebenberg from the apartheid-supporting *Die Transvaaler* newspaper and Arno Kotze and Bill Sharp from the South African Broadcasting Corporation – were imported to bolster the work of eight locally recruited journalists. Sharp returned to the SABC, and in 2002, was nearing retirement as programme manager of South Africa's national SAfm radio station. He claimed in an interview that he did not know 'who exactly had been behind' the Namib Foundation. It was 'something funny', but since he only ever had to translate speeches and give advice to local politicians on addressing the media, he did not concern himself with who ran the operation. In any event he had 'always wanted to visit Namibia'. He and Kotze had their own office and he insisted they had no idea that a number of the South Africans involved were members of the South Africa security police.

Nearly R3 million of the funding for Operation Victor was spent on a series of seminars and workshops for political parties and activists. These were arranged and run by Pretoria management consultant Leo van der Walt, in conjunction with R&W Communicor, a Johannesburg company run by Sjaas

Reyneke and André Walters. A political training programme that none too subtly portrayed SWAPO as a dangerous, dictatorial and terrorist organisation was drawn up in consultation with the Institute for Strategic Studies at the University of Pretoria and with an academic from the University of South Africa.

Over a three-month period starting on 6 March 1989 more than 1,000 party activists each underwent a week's intensive training at various upmarket holiday resorts. Its aims were listed as providing motivational, organising and managerial skills to the participants, as well as 'communication skills' to 'describe and speak about' human rights, ideologies, Resolution 435, SWAPO and the constitution of the emerging state. Having portrayed 'revolutionary' and 'socialist' ideologies as grossly undesirable, the courses defined SWAPO as a revolutionary and socialist organisation and concluded:

> Revolutionaries never lose their true colours. If they are forced to take part in free elections, and do and manage to win, they will eventually implement their ideas of dictatorship and socialism, even if it takes somewhat longer than if they had come to power as a result of military victory.

A combination of bribery and implied threats ensured large attendances at minority party meetings. Known Koevoet members would fetch and transport people to these meetings where free T-shirts and food were distributed. Most who attended were paid R10 apiece. These mass meetings gave the impression that the opposition to SWAPO was much larger than the election eventually showed. It was an illusion that took in many observers, but it also appears to have fooled the security forces: even at a senior level, they began to believe their own propaganda.

As the November election drew close there were increasingly confident predictions of a victory for the DTA and the minorities. These were apparently relayed to President F.W. de Klerk by a military and police delegation that included Brigadier Olivier. According to a report of the meeting given to senior security police officers, De Klerk was 'ecstatic' to hear it projected that the DTA and the Namib Foundation parties would win 70 per cent or more of the vote. He reportedly agreed to an additional R3 million for projects in the week running up to the election. So far, no documentary evidence of this additional amount has been uncovered.

In the event, the DTA garnered 27 per cent of the popular vote and the combined Namib Foundation parties 10 per cent. This denied SWAPO the two-thirds majority the party had seemed certain to win only months before.

In the subsequent open election in 1994, SWAPO's share of the poll soared from 57 per cent to 72 per cent. This bears out the assessment of the security forces: that without their intervention, SWAPO would easily have gained a two-thirds majority and the right to adopt a constitution written by itself. They certainly made this claim, and the South African government seems to have regarded Operation 435 as a success.

This judgement ensured that similar tactics would be employed in South Africa, but adapted to be even more effective. On its immediate home ground, the National Party was counting on support from various 'homeland' parties and ultimately, if indirectly, from the Inkatha movement and from the Democratic Party. The ANC, it was thought, could find itself only the largest of a multitude of smaller parties whose combined strength made it a minority.

As in Mozambique, where in just ten years a small group of state-sponsored terrorists had spawned a large rebel movement, so it was hoped that random terror, blamed on the advent of the ANC, might yield much the same result in South Africa. Here was the genesis of what became known as 'third force' violence, and of much of the 'black on black' violence that was used in the propaganda efforts of the apartheid government at home and abroad as it attempted to edge itself onto some moral high ground.

But underlying these plans were the talks that had begun in earnest even as the conflict in Angola threatened to erupt into a war that might engulf the whole region.

7

Serious talking begins

In early 1987, Nelson Mandela was again taken from his cell in Pollsmoor prison to the official residence of prisons minister Kobie Coetsee. It was the first of several informal talks between the two men over the year before Coetsee proposed a meeting with a four-strong 'working group' that would comprise himself, General Willemse, who had met Mandela at the earlier hospital meeting, Fanie van der Merwe, the director-general of prisons and Niel Barnard, head of the National Intelligence Service. Although Mandela did not know it, all were members of the Broederbond.

Mandela was wary of the inclusion of Barnard, but this was a chance to open serious negotiations, so he accepted the proposal. In May 1988, shortly after Barnard had returned from the meeting in London with the Russians, Americans and Cubans, he and the government's secret working group met with Mandela. The meeting was held in the officers' club inside Pollsmoor prison and was the first of a series of weekly meetings.

While these were going on, Michael Young, with funding from the rightwing chairman of Gold Fields, Rudolf Agnew, began to arrange the first of a series of talks between 'Afrikaners' and the exiled ANC leadership. These would amount to informal contact between the government and the ANC, but through individuals who could deny they were in any sense connected to the government – in this case, senior Broederbonders who were not part of the state apparatus. Young approached Fleur de Villiers, a South African journalist working with Gold Fields in London, who was close to senior figures in the Botha administration. Whom should he contact to invite for such talks, specifically with Thabo Mbeki? She recommended Willie Esterhuyse, who had already met Mbeki at several international gatherings, and Sampie Terreblanche. They were the Stellenbosch academics and leading Broederbond modernisers who had originally been invited by the Quaker H.W. van der Merwe to meet the ANC.

Both men agreed to the meetings. Unbeknown to Terreblanche, Esterhuyse was also reporting to Niel Barnard on all the contacts. (By this stage, in any event, Terreblanche was on his way out of the Broederbond, having come to the conclusion that everything that had been done in the name of apartheid was morally indefensible.) Barnard agreed that Esterhuyse should inform Thabo Mbeki that such reporting would take place. Esterhuyse says this was because he did not wish to act as a spy and requested this provision. However, his informing Mbeki that he was reporting to the effective managing director of the apartheid system, and Botha's closest adviser, put a different complexion on the talks. They were no longer informal discussions with a group of individuals, but in effect an indirect set of negotiations between the upper echelons of the ANC and the power brokers of the apartheid state.

These talks began in earnest in London in December 1987. Then Sampie Terreblanche and Willie Esterhuyse arrived in Britain for Terreblanche to deliver a lecture at the Royal Commonwealth Society comparing the problems of Gorbachev's perestroika – the Russian shift towards a more liberal system – with the reforms proposed by Botha in South Africa. This highlighted the similarities of two authoritarian systems attempting to come to terms with a transition to democracy. Terreblanche, a political economist, made a strong plea for a 'mini Marshall Plan' – a massive injection of development aid – to enable southern Africa to achieve this goal. He received little practical support. He had also expected to meet privately with Thabo Mbeki, but there was a delay. While he and Esterhuyse waited, they were housed in Anglo American private accommodation in a secluded square off London's Charterhouse Street.

In the event, it was Esterhuyse alone who met with Mbeki. It was a time of shadow boxing, as both Esterhuyse and Mbeki subsequently indicated and supporting interviews confirmed. Barnard and the NIS were still looking for ways to open a gap between what they perceived to be the 'moderates' and the 'radicals' within the ANC. In particular, they wanted to promote a split between the ANC and the SACP. This was almost ironic, since Thabo Mbeki, although frequently criticised within the SACP, was at that time still a leading member of the Communist Party.

By then, it was obvious to anyone not blinkered by ideological prejudice that the Soviet Union faced growing economic problems and was less than enthusiastic about promoting revolution in South Africa. The message even appears to have got through to that most dedicated supporter of Moscow, the SACP general secretary Joe Slovo. He noted in March 1987: 'I believe the transition in South Africa is going to come through negotiation.' For some of the veterans of the 1964 mutiny within the ANC, this was vindication at last: they had maintained at the time that the Russians were pursuing their own interests, which did not include sponsoring a serious mass uprising within South Africa. The SACP and the ANC, they complained, were being held in reserve as surrogates in the global game of the superpowers. This paralleled the way the US supported, but did not seriously encourage, UNITA and the FNLA to fight the Portuguese during the days of colonial rule in Angola.

This assessment of the MK mutineers was based on the fact that the Russians provided orthodox military training to MK fighters. 'We had tank commanders, artillery specialists and that sort of thing. Not what you need for a guerrilla war, especially not an urban guerrilla war,' one of the 1964 survivors noted. Only four of their number – 'perhaps by accident' – were trained by former Czech urban guerrillas in 'fighting from the kitchen sink'. The training more usually provided tended to keep the MK fighters stranded in the frontline states, their skills of little use in an urban underground environment.

That the 'guerrilla option' of a 'liberation army' sweeping in from outside to seize victory was romantic nonsense was accepted by many within the ANC by the time the talks began. But there were others who saw the leadership of the internal uprising being assumed by the external force. MK, lionised within the townships, could step into a commanding position as an internal revolution swept the old order from power. This was a variation on romantic notions, derived from the Cuban revolution, that enjoyed wide currency both within the MK and among leading MK figures like Chris Hani. However, it amounted to an admission that it was the mass uprising within South Africa rather than any guerrilla activity that had forced the apartheid state into concessions. Most MK leaders were not in favour of compromise, deals and a negotiated settlement. For them, the fact that Cosatu in July 1987 had adopted the Freedom Charter meant that the bulk of the organised working class – the spearhead of the revolution – had swung away from the vague 'workerist' position and was prepared to accept ANC/SACP leadership.

For this reason, Oliver Tambo and Thabo Mbeki kept secret from some of their very senior comrades the extent – or even the fact – of the talks in progress. The Botha government and its successor under De Klerk were similarly reticent. But while talks held with individual 'Afrikaners' were deniable, Botha and the SSC were kept fully informed by Barnard, whose unofficial presence in the negotiations was ensured by Willie Esterhuyse. For the government it was a time of probing and finding out, of negotiating without the risk of commitment. On both sides it was a case of leaderships seeking common ground while still unsure that they could carry their constituencies with them onto that ground.

It was not only Barnard who received full reports. Another of the Broederbond modernisers involved was the theologian turned newspaper editor Wimpie de Klerk, brother of the man who would succeed Botha as president. As one of the regulars at the meetings, he admitted that he filed regular reports to his brother, then the leader of the Transvaal NP, and a prominent member of the AB's traditionalist wing.

The fact that Mbeki, and apparently the ANC, was much more 'flexible' and 'pragmatic' than had been assumed was relayed both by Esterhuyse to his handlers and by Wimpie de Klerk to his brother. This was confirmation of the assessment made the year before by Tony Bloom of the Premier Group after the first business contact with the ANC. Several of these reports related to the series of more than ten meetings held in the two years until May 1990 at Mells Park House, a stately mansion set in parklands near the English city of Bath. In these affluent surroundings, paid for by the mining houses, the surrogates of the apartheid state met in secret with the leading lights of the ANC. After each of these encounters, Willie Esterhuyse admits he was debriefed by NIS officials at various safe houses around South Africa.

Symbolically, Esterhuyse and Mbeki toasted the televised release of Nelson Mandela on 11 February 1990 in the opulence of Mells Park, and with champagne drawn from the cellars of Consolidated Goldfields. But that was towards the end of a remarkable series of meetings, both within South Africa and at various venues abroad. Some of these were high-profile gatherings such as the one held in Dakar, Senegal, in August 1987 between an ANC delegation led by Thabo Mbeki and fifty 'Afrikaner intellectuals'. Most were clandestine get-togethers involving small groups. Nelson Mandela, by his own calculations, had more than forty meetings between 1988 and 1990 with the government's 'working group', all of them involving Niel Barnard. Barnard would also inform Mandela of the meetings between Esterhuyse and Mbeki, as well as other 'outside contacts'. Mandela's reponses would be relayed to Tambo in Lusaka, initially via the lawyer George Bizos.

By the end of 1988, the decision had already been made: Mandela would be released. But there is a problem with people who have been incarcerated for decades. They struggled at first to operate in a normal open environment. Even to open a door may come hard to people who for years have had every door barred and locked, opened only by their guards. So Nelson Mandela, after hospital treatment for tuberculosis late in 1988, was moved in December of that year to a cottage in the grounds of the Victor Verster prison outside the town of Paarl, east of Cape Town. The cottage had a garden and swimming pool, a spacious living and dining area and three bedrooms. A prisons department chef was on hand to prepare meals both for Mandela and, over the coming months, for his steady stream of visitors. As Mandela himself remarked, it gave the illusion of freedom, but he 'never forgot that it was a gilded cage'.

The first visitor to the cage arrived the day after Mandela moved in. It was Kobie Coetsee. As Mandela recalled in his autobiography, Coetsee informed him that the cottage would be his last home 'before becoming a free man'. A telephone line and fax – assumed to be monitored by the NIS – were later introduced to enable Mandela to communicate with Tambo and the exiled leadership in Lusaka.

There was no magnanimity here. Massive bloodshed and repression in South Africa had failed to bring resistance under control. The United Democratic Front, the basically ANC-oriented collection of more than 600 organisations, had continued to grow, undeterred by mass arrests and detentions of its leading members. Instead, in 1989 Cosatu joined in an informal alliance with the UDF, known as the Mass Democratic Movement (MDM). Having no formal structure, it could not be banned, but it provided an example of growing grassroots democracy. The interpretation of the Freedom Charter within militant sectors of the MDM also tended to be more radical than in the mainstream of the ANC. Stress fell on the nationalisation of mines, banks and 'monopoly industry'. The spectre loomed again of a major social and economic upheaval.

Regular visitors to Mandela were the members of the 'working group'. Finally came the meeting with Botha himself and then, after Botha's stroke and eventual resignation, talks with F.W. de Klerk. But while these discussions proceeded, the world outside the gates of Victor Verster was changing fast. The security clampdown might have brought many deaths and cowed much overt resistance, but apartheid was effectively at an end. Segregationist laws, from separate buses to residential areas, were simply being ignored. Banned organisations and individuals began to 'unban' themselves. It was no longer possible to enforce the myriad petty apartheid laws without which the system began to unravel.

In September 1989, only a month after Botha's departure, political detainees around the country started hunger strikes that caused many to be released. Gaining confidence from the growing defiance around the country, banned and house-arrested activists began to discuss the possibility of a mass refusal to obey their restrictions. In Cape Town twenty-two banned and house-arrested people, including the future finance minister Trevor Manuel and the chair of the first regional UDF meeting, Amy Thornton, publicly decided to defy the orders restricting them. Thousands of activists and the diplomats of twelve foreign countries turned up to support them. The twenty-two were also in the forefront of the first legally permitted mass protest march in Cape Town on 13 September. It had been called to protest against police brutality. Archbishop Desmond Tutu, sensing the feeling on the ground, knew that many thousands would turn out. He approached the Dutch Reformed Church theologian Johan Heyns to intervene with De Klerk. Heyns, one of the most liberal of the Broederbond modernisers, who was assassinated in his own home in October 1994, prevailed on De Klerk to authorise the march.

For Mandela, watching events from his cottage at Victor Verster prison, this was proof of De Klerk's good faith and commitment to reform. But what motivated De Klerk was a series of events unfolding outside Africa. According to Gerrit Viljoen, the constitutional affairs minister and De Klerk's closest adviser at the time, the new president authorised the march with his eyes very much on events in Eastern Europe.

The Broederbond and the government were fully aware of the parallels that existed between the authoritarian regimes and largely state-centred economies of South Africa and Eastern Europe. It was this parallel that Sampie Terreblanche had highlighted in Britain when he lectured on 'Gorbachev's perestroika versus Botha's reform'. Just like Botha, so too had Gorbachev discovered that to restructure the economy called for greater political freedoms (the process the Russians called Glasnost). But the relaxation of some authoritarian controls merely led to demands for more.

De Klerk was not seen among his peers as an intellectual, but he did have a warranted reputation for applying cold logic. If the genie of revolution was out of the bottle, he reasoned, it would probably be impossible to put it back. Better to allow it room so that its fiery essence might dissipate. In other words, learn from Gorbachev's mistakes.

So it was that perhaps the biggest-ever protest march in Cape Town's history got under way, led by the clerics Desmond Tutu and Allan Boesak, with the twenty-two 'restrictees' to the fore, openly flouting the laws of the land. Viljoen, De Klerk and a group of other senior NP members watched the television coverage as anywhere between 30,000 and 60,000 chanting, cheering and dancing people took over the centre of the city. Several of those at the presidential residence were horrified by what they saw; it was too reminiscent of the scenes shown of recent events in Eastern Europe. De Klerk, however, pointed out that such marches could not be stopped; better to have 30,000 or more marching to a meeting at the city hall and the open expanse of Cape Town's Grand Parade outside it, than have many more marching on parliament with revolutionary intent.

Versions of these exchanges tend to agree. The size of the march and its peaceful nature seemed to give confidence to De Klerk. On the ground, activists also noticed a major change: not only were the police absent, but suddenly there were many new faces vying to get to the front of the march, among them a whole detachment from the Democratic Party. The mayor of Cape Town and several leading businessmen, apparently having heard that the march would be permitted, also emerged in new roles as anti-apartheid activists.

8

From the Berlin wall to Codesa

By the middle of 1989, perhaps the only group that had not realised that the Soviet Union was crumbling was the SACP. There remained an almost naive faith that, somehow 'the Soviet' would provide a way forward; that revolutionary change in South Africa, under the SACP, was still on the cards. This belief was encapsulated in the documents from the seventh SACP congress, held in Havana, Cuba, in July. That congress and the circumstances surrounding it probably give the best example of the duplicity and secrecy of the manoeuvrings that led to the 'new South Africa'. It was chaired by Thabo Mbeki, who also helped to pen the fundamentally insurrectionist 'Path to Power' programme of the party. Yet Mbeki had flown to Cuba via Bermuda, where he had secret meetings with senior NP and Broederbond members. Discussions were coming to a head, and it was already agreed by those involved in the talks about talks that a move toward a negotiated settlement was only a matter of time.

As Mbeki later told journalist Mark Gevisser: 'There were some people who were not only sceptical, but hostile to the idea [of a negotiated settlement]. They saw it as selling out, treachery ... You couldn't convince them about the fact that, in reality, the struggle was moving away from an insurrectionary path.' On this basis, Mbeki decided to 'run these parallel paths'. And, as he saw it, 'the insurrectionary one would lose.'

But it was the insurrectionary one that emerged publicly, in documents such as *The Path to Power*. This stated, in flagrant disregard of reality, that:

World socialism accounts for more than one-third of the world's population, in dozens of countries advancing along a path that reveals the intellectual and moral potential of humanity. A new way of life is taking shape in which there are neither oppressors nor the oppressed, neither exploiters nor the exploited, in which power belongs to the people.

This was only months before the Berlin Wall fell and the people of Romania and other tyrannies of Eastern Europe overthrew the masters who ruled under a Communist Party banner. It made nonsense of the claims of *The Path to Power* and critically undermined the SACP. Put against the realities of the fall of the Berlin Wall and the collapse of the Soviet bloc, a negotiated settlement – a compromise between a racist regime and its anti-racist opposition – emerged as the only alternative. In January of 1990, Joe Slovo penned his pamphlet asking: 'Has socialism failed?'

The scene was set for the first visits to South Africa by members of the exiled ANC and for the release of Nelson Mandela. On 10 October 1989, De Klerk had given a further pointer to the government's intention by releasing eight leading 'Robben Islanders'. Walter Sisulu, Raymond Mhlaba, Ahmed Kathrada, Andrew Mlangeni, Elias Motsoaledi, Wilton Mkwayi, Oscar Mpetha and Jafta Masemola of the PAC were given their freedom at the same time that De Klerk gave legal authority to an already widespread reality, the desegregation of beaches. In November he also announced the dissolution of the National Security Management System, although not of the SSC and the various spy agencies and death squads. The harassment of activists, and the killings, continued.

De Klerk was also under heavy pressure from within the security establishment, especially the police. Butana Nofemela had spoken out from death row about the existence of the Vlakplaas death squad, and the former death squad commander Dirk Coetzee had defected to the ANC. There was a danger of too much of the state apparatus coming unglued, and mounting disquiet among the hardliners within the political and security elites. They had supported the De Klerk who had stated earlier that year that 'one person, one vote would be a catastrophe'. Now the same man was emerging as the proponent of some form of non-racial democracy. Ever the wily politician, De Klerk was able to maintain his control over the political and security apparatus by pledging a variation on democratic norms that would protect 'white interests'.

His arguments were reinforced after 14 November with the election results from Namibia. These revealed that, though over-optimistic in their projections, the security forces had certainly been able to curtail the potential SWAPO vote. In South Africa, with its established and dependent homelands and a longer lead-in period to any elections, an even better result should be relatively simple to achieve. De Klerk also agreed to ensure that any constitutional arrangement would guarantee 'group rights' and would amount to a white veto on legislation.

At this time, the NIS chief Niel Barnard and his deputy, Mike Louw, assumed more direct control over the talks process. Early in 1989 Barnard instructed Willie Esterhuyse to set up a formal meeting between the NIS and the ANC. Esterhuyse and Mbeki initially met in the offices of British American Tobacco in London – a meeting arranged in utmost secrecy. Neither side was sure that it could carry its own leadership, let alone its constituencies.

But there were many hitches and, with the last racial election looming on 6 September, it was decided that Mike Louw and his director of operations, Maritz Spaarwater, posing as Michael James and Jacobus Maritz, should meet Thabo Mbeki and Jacob Zuma (John and Jack Simelane) at the Palace Hotel in Lucerne, Switzerland, on 12 September. It was the first formal, official contact between the two sides, and the culmination of a series of clandestine contacts around the world. The game of talking while appearing not to talk was at an end.

It is perhaps significant that this meeting took place against the express wishes of Mandela and without informing De Klerk in advance. 'We had to do something to get the other side on board,' Louw said later. In common with Barnard and other senior NIS personnel, he felt it was essential to 'keep the ANC together' to have an acceptable negotiating partner; and that the government had to move fast 'while we still have the power'.

What the apartheid camp feared was fragmentation. The disparate elements of the white right seemed to share only a vaguely articulated desire to establish a segregationist 'Afrikaner homeland'. Economic reality dictated that most supporters of the various rightwing currents would not wish to live in such a segregated region, but fragmentation would weaken the government's negotiating position.

There were similar fears of fragmentation within the ANC, and felt more acutely because the negotiators were acting from a much weaker position. The ANC's mass base of support lay within the country, and could readily be swung behind a more radical programme than the compromises now being struck at the highest level.

This was the background that kept the negotiations, both between Mandela and the 'working group' and Mbeki and the NIS, on track. It also underlay De Klerk's decision to use the opening of parliament on 2 February 1990 as the platform to announce the release of Mandela and the unbanning of the ANC, PAC and SACP. Four days after that, Louw and Spaarwater were back in Switzerland to meet with Mbeki and Aziz Pahad. This time it was to work out the details for the return of some of the exiled ANC leadership.

There was certainly a degree of confidence among the NIS negotiators and De Klerk. They were saving their own skins, but in doing so, they were also smoothing the way for the ANC as a partner with whom they could do business. Against this background it should have come as no surprise that the ANC and the renamed New National Party could form an alliance in 2001. Several leading commentators, not least Sampie Terreblanche, maintain that at the time of the early negotiations the NP hierarchy was convinced that it could 'outnegotiate' the ANC – that a grateful Mandela would concede the demands for 'power sharing' among ethnic groups. A strong element of racism pervaded this thinking, an arrogance born of a lifetime of playing the masters in a master-and-servant environment.

However, once serious negotiations got going, with internal and external pressures all coming into play, Mandela would not give way. Negotiators such as Cyril Ramaphosa, Mac Maharaj, Thabo Mbeki and the communist bête rouge, Joe Slovo, also proved more than a match for their opposite numbers. Power sharing and ethnicity fell off the agenda, to the horror of Kobie Coetsee, who had been one of the main driving forces behind negotiations. Like several of the planners of the transition, he feared a backlash from the traditionalists. He need not have worried, even though by 1993 the fragmented Right had come together. But unease was heightened when, on 10 April 1993, the charismatic SACP leader Chris Hani was assassinated. Because a neighbour memorised the registration number of the killer's car and immediately tele-phoned the police, the murderer was stopped and arrested before he had disposed of the murder weapon. The arrest of Janusz Walus, and later of Clive Derby-Lewis, helped to take much of the heat out of the nationwide protests.

In the face of the move toward a united liberal democracy in South Africa the white Right had united as the Volksfront (People's Front). Led by former army chief General Constand Viljoen, the Volksfront had also forged an alliance with three homelands. The Concerned South Africans Group (Cosag) linked the Volksfront and KwaZulu-Natal (KZN), Bophuthatswana ('Bop') and Ciskei. This might have provided a serious challenge to the geographic unity of the country but for the fact that the Bop leader, Lucas Mangope, had very little popular support and Ciskei's Oupa Gqoza even less. The leader of the Inkatha Freedom Party in KZN, Chief Mangosuthu Buthelezi, had considerable support and was deeply involved with the security forces, but in the event he swung to the ANC.

Although Viljoen subsequently claimed that he had more than 50,000 armed and trained men ready to answer his call to arms, this seems unlikely. When the opportunity arose to show his hand, he marshalled just 1,500. That was when Mangope precipitated a crisis in March 1994 by announcing that he would not accept the reincorporation of his territory into South Africa. The homeland civil service promptly went on strike and the people of Bophutha-tswana rebelled and were joined by the local police. The main shopping complex in the capital, Mmabatho, most of it owned by the Mangope family, was looted. Men, women and children streamed through the stores, helping themselves to everything from refrigerators to beds, chairs, tables and crockery; it was a festival of the oppressed.

Mangope called for the Volksfront militia to restore order. This was the one and only chance that apartheid traditionalists and their surrogates had to reverse the process that culminated in agreement at the final Convention for a Democratic South Africa (Codesa) talks. Codesa had completely eschewed the idea of ethnicity or federalism. In one of the many ironies that abound, the resolution to the final impasse at these talks was credited to Joe Slovo. The SACP leader, aptly referred to by Allister Sparks in Britain's *Observer* newspaper as 'a sheep in wolf's clothing', put forward the 'sunset clauses' that clinched the final deal. These guaranteed a five-year transition period, a government of national unity, and the jobs and pensions of the apartheid civil service and military; they amounted, in effect, to the proposals advanced by Mandela in his earlier, secret, talks.

It was the rejection of this deal by Mangope that triggered an uprising and brought Mmabatho to a standstill. But when Mangope called in the Volksfront, the Bophuthatswana army mutinied. The Volksfront militia and their wild fringe, the Afrikaner Weerstandsbeweging, beat an ignominious retreat. However Viljoen, a consummate military strategist, had a contingency plan in place. Even before Mangope had launched his futile defiance, Viljoen had, without informing the constituent elements of the Volksfront, registered to take part in the country's first non-racial election, agreed by Codesa. He had agreed with Thabo Mbeki that the Volksfront vote could be taken as a measure of support for an Afrikaner homeland. The vote was minuscule, but Viljoen entered parliament.

Before the transition, the apartheid regime was able to increase the salaries of a wide range of officials. Pensions and redundancy payments were set at much higher levels than they might have been. This ensured the loyalty to the NP of much of its traditional constituency. The core of the modernising Broeder-bond was also able to hold together. But despite bloodshed, including letter bombs and random killings, the ANC scored an overwhelming victory at the polls.

The new dispensation was presented to the world as some form of modern miracle. It was in fact a cobbled-together compromise resulting largely from the bad miscalculation of the NP planners about the chances they had to manipulate the ANC leadership, and in particular Nelson Mandela. Their best-laid plans had gone awry. But the agreement that was struck affected every aspect of the transformation. It also contained plans that aimed to ensure that the illusions necessary to sustain this compromise would be first created and then preserved.

9

The genesis of the TRC

Out of the compromise of the Codesa talks at Kempton Park emerged the Government of National Unity. It drew together, on the basis of equal responsibility and apparent joint culpability, the authors and administrators of apartheid and the leaders of the anti-racist opposition. For such a compromise to work required a bridge between the bloody and oppressive past and a more hopeful, and humane, future. It needed a link between perpetrators and victims, between those responsible for a crime against humanity and those who had resisted it.

In such circumstances, the truth could never out. On the one hand were the representatives of a deeply corrupt and brutal regime; on the other, those representing the mass of the wounded and oppressed majority. The constituency of one side wished silence, secrecy, or failing these an automatic route to absolution; the majority constituency wanted to rip aside the lies, deceits and obscurantism of the past. One side wanted to forget, the other to know.

Within the upper echelons of both sides, there was much to hide, many private agendas were working to deflect, blur or stymie demands for full and frank disclosure. Unity became the watchword, reconciliation the means. There was broad agreement that too much of the truth would be a dangerous thing, although this tended to be dressed up in demands and assurances to rule out 'witch hunts'.

Besides, the outline of the TRC was already in place – even before the

Codesa talks had reached their conclusion and the delegates had agreed the tacked-on addendum that led to the vague promise of reconciliation and reconstruction. Alex Boraine, former president of the Methodist Church, Anglo American Corporation executive and Progressive Federal Party member of parliament, played the leading role. In 1986 he and fellow PFP parliamentarian Frederik van Zyl Slabbert resigned from parliament and founded the Institute for a Democratic Alternative for South Africa (Idasa), whose stated aim was to seek a way to the politics of negotiation. The following years were spent considering how such a transition could and should be managed. Contacts were made with like-minded groups and with potential funders. By 1993 Boraine and his group, like the ANC executive, had come to the conclusion that some form of truth commission with an amnesty provision would be necessary to cement the concept of national unity.

Without some public reconciliation of the racist past with a hoped-for non-racial future, the compromises of negotiation might not hold. The ANC had soon realised that its original demand to prosecute the apartheid criminals would be as politically impossible as the blanket amnesty demanded by the NP. The one was simply unworkable when trying to take over the apartheid state machine; the other would be unacceptable to a mass constituency, which had only recently fought and forced the concessions that produced negotiations.

These were conditions almost tailor-made for those beneficiaries on the liberal fringe of the system. They had always ignored the material basis of apartheid. For them it was a sin, an aberration manifest as white power. The issue was not seen as racism versus anti-racism. As Boraine was to state on more than one occasion, 'white power' was the thesis, 'black power' the antithesis. This was the basic conflict. What was needed was a synthesis, a middle road between what were classed as unacceptable extremes. This analysis effectively opened the way for those beneficiaries nominally opposed to apartheid and who had, until then, been condemned for their hypocrisy by both pro- and anti-apartheid activists. Leading the charge was big business, which, in the wake of the mass uprisings of 1984 and 1985 and the slump in the economy, had become remarkably outspoken about the need for some kind of democratic change.

The underlying liberal premise – that all violence should be equally abhorred – cut the moral high ground from under the liberation forces, equating the violence of resistance with the violence of oppression. In so doing, it elevated to undisputed moral superiority those few individuals such as Archbishop Desmond Tutu who had non-violently resisted apartheid and had survived. It also made room on the alleged moral high ground for all who could claim not to have been directly involved in the tortures and killings. They had merely to declare a previous anti-racist conviction. Many did.

Critical, factual, analysis of the past gave way to amnesia and smug self-righteousness. National Party parliamentarians with histories of adherence to far right – and frankly fascist – ideology suddenly emerged as self-proclaimed champions of a non-racist future. The great turning point from which to claim support for change was 1986. This was the year when continuing and growing mass resistance turned the tide. Fear coursed through the white establishment and triggered thoughts of compromise and racial cohabitation at almost every level.

The credo of the liberal beneficiaries of apartheid had always been evolution, not revolution. Anti-apartheid activists had for years seen this belief as both facile and self-serving. Suddenly it emerged as a bridge, a means to transform the system without any fundamental alteration. The case of big business as the core of a stable society no longer had to be argued: it was accepted. Here was the genesis of the Truth and Reconciliation Commission. It was a development that attracted criticism even from people who later supported or joined the TRC. Nobel laureate Archbishop Desmond Tutu, later to gain even greater international renown as the TRC chairman, was initially sceptical. Reconciliation was 'a theological concept', he told the author. Politicians would do well to 'leave it alone'.

But several politicians were hard at work devising a means to realise the vague pronouncements about the need for a commission that would deal with both truth and reconciliation. None put in more effort than Alex Boraine. In February 1994 he was the driving force behind the Idasa international conference at Somerset West, east of Cape Town. Entitled Dealing with the Past, it involved leading national and international human rights campaigners and provided a number of ideas that fleshed out the 'post-amble' tacked onto the interim constitution (Act 200 of 1993). This stated:

> This Constitution provides a historic bridge between the past of a deeply divided society characterised by strife, conflict, untold suffering and injustice, and a future founded on the recognition of human rights, democracy and peaceful co-existence and development opportunities for all South Africans, irrespective of colour, race, class, belief or sex.
>
> The pursuit of national unity, the well-being of all South African citizens and peace require reconciliation between the people of South Africa and the reconstruction of society . . .
>
> . . . These can now be addressed on the basis that there is a need for understanding but not for vengeance, a need for reparation but not for retaliation, a need for ubuntu but not for victimisation.

In order to advance such reconciliation and reconstruction, amnesty shall be granted in respect of acts, omissions and offences associated with political objectives and committed in the course of the conflicts of the past . . .

As the idea of the TRC took clearer shape, the religious undercurrent persisted. A cardinal element, the right to amnesty, was based on the concept of confession leading to absolution. The systemic nature of apartheid was also clearly not at issue. Apartheid was to be regarded rather as a sin, with its roots in frail human nature. Individual victims and confessing perpetrators would be the focus. It seemed inevitable that churchmen would lead the TRC when its final composition was decided.

After the Somerset West conference, Boraine took on the central role in moving the process forward. He resigned from Idasa and set up Justice in Transition as a non-governmental organisation to provide government with 'the best possible advice' as it considered the legislation necessary to establish a TRC. Funding for Justice in Transition came from billionaire philanthropist George Soros via Aryeh Neier, who headed the Open Society Institute in New York. Boraine was executive director and Paddy Clark his assistant. It was they who sent a detailed proposal to then President Nelson Mandela describing how a TRC structure might operate.

Other groups that had been collecting and collating information about human rights abuses by the apartheid state were persuaded to withdraw in favour of the proposed new structure. Among them was the Independent Board of Inquiry, which comprised leading campaigners such as lawyer Brian Currin and Sheena Duncan of the Black Sash. They and others decided that it would be best to have a single body that would unearth the horrors of the past. However, some of these early investigators thought that the proposed TRC would focus on the systemic abuses of apartheid itself. They were to be disappointed.

The decision by Boraine to approach Mandela came after discussions with two of the leading lawyers in the ANC, Kader Asmal and Albie Sachs. Justice in Transition also began immediately to organise a 'Truth and Reconciliation' conference to be held in Cape Town in July, where leading participants, notably the then ANC justice minister, Dullah Omar, went out of their way to assure the NP and the more extreme rightwing elements that a TRC would not 'result in a witch hunt'. The object would be reconciliation. A TRC would provide 'a morally acceptable basis' to advance this cause.

Boraine in particular stressed that 'moral order and economic justice' were two sides of the same coin. He added his weight, and effectively the weight of the conference, to the liberal macro-economic line championed by big business. To deal with the poverty and socio-economic problems of apartheid 'disciplined commitment to economic growth' was necessary, he said. This concept of redistribution through growth – the 'trickle-down' economics usually associated with Thatcher and Reagan – was later adopted by the ANC-led government in its Growth Economy and Redistribution (Gear) macro-economic framework.

After the conference, papers were published and seminars held. Boraine was later to note in his book on the TRC experience: 'The stage was set. We had learnt from other countries, we had consulted widely, the commitment of the government was clear. Now the hard and detailed work of drafting the Bill had to be tackled.'

In this too, Boraine played a major role. Together with a high-powered team, comprising mainly lawyers, he served on the committee whose recommended legislation created the TRC. It was obvious that he would have to play a leading part in the envisaged structure.

There was some lobbying for Boraine himself to head the TRC, but this was clearly out of the question. Given the politics of South Africa, it seemed essential that the figurehead in this international shopfront for democratic transition should stand for the exploited and oppressed. Because the violence of oppression and the violence of resistance to it had been equated, members of the liberation movements were precluded. Yet the person chosen to head the TRC should have impeccable anti-apartheid credentials. Desmond Tutu was clearly the only choice. He agreed to take on the chairmanship. In the political context, Boraine made the ideal deputy. He had a consistent record of opposition to apartheid, but from within the system. As such, and as a member of the apartheid parliament, he had also been a member of a 'loyal opposition' that had supported some of the murderous cross-border raids launched by the government. From the side of the beneficiaries, he was clearly the first choice as deputy to Tutu.

The final choice of the chairman, his deputy and fifteen other commissioners rested with Nelson Mandela. The president was presented with a shortlist of twenty-five names selected by a multi-party committee that had interviewed forty-five of the 299 people nominated by various groups and individuals. There was considerable lobbying and horse trading throughout the selection process. The apartheid establishment, having adopted the rhetorical garb of champions of fairness and equality, demanded equal representation on the TRC. Its media noted that there were far too many 'struggle types' nominated. The demand for a blanket amnesty also continued to be voiced by the NP as it came under increasing pressure from its own constituency.

Now that the NP had failed to win agreement on a parliamentary minority veto, the 'sharp end' of the apartheid machine – the police and the military –

fearing that they would end up the scapegoats, began to point publicly to the 'collective responsibility' of the political establishment. Individuals should not be blamed for carrying out their orders, even if only under 'implied authority'. The naming of names was a particular concern.

General Constand Viljoen, known in anti-apartheid circles as the butcher of Cassinga, raged against 'moralists' and 'sentimentalists' whom he blamed for demanding full disclosure of deeds and the names of perpetrators. When he addressed the parliamentary portfolio committee considering the Promotion of National Unity and Reconciliation Act that established the TRC, he called for a general amnesty. There should be no names named, merely the acceptance by the various leaderships of collective responsibility for human rights violations of the past.

The police took a similar line. The force had more to fear from the naming of names, since they were to the forefront of the individualised brute maintenance of the system. They handled the everyday domestic torture, most of which did not result in death. Most of those tortured by the military, mainly in Angola and Namibia, did not live to tell the tale. The bodies of hundreds were dumped far out in the Atlantic. But the CCB was a military formation that had carried out murders such as that of the academic David Webster. Under pressure from their underlings, the generals of both the military and the police sought to squeeze their political masters. They hinted in their submissions that they might really be forced to tell all; to disclose who had given which orders and when.

The police even mentioned to the portfolio committee the now notorious Simonstown Council and the existence of parts of the command structure. It was the main outward sign of the argument raging backstage between the politicians and generals of the old order, driven by pressure from the lower ranks. This resulted in demands for big concessions from the transitional authority. Some were won.

The extent of the compromise was reflected in the composition of the TRC announced by President Nelson Mandela on 15 December 1995. Fifteen of the seventeen names had come from the final shortlist. Mandela added two: a Methodist Church leader from KwaZulu-Natal and a lawyer. There were no direct challenges to the list, and certainly not to the names added by Mandela. But De Klerk expressed his unhappiness with the final choice, and in particular with that of the chair and the deputy. The IFP, through its leader, Chief Buthelezi, lodged a blanket objection to the commission. Yet one of the IFP parliamentarians, Harriet Ngubane, had served on the committee that drew up the shortlist. It was proof that the jockeying for influence continued.

De Klerk was concerned that both Tutu and Boraine had histories of opposing the NP government. This he saw as a form of bias. Like Viljoen and other rightwingers, he also baulked at a parliamentary statement by justice minister Dullah Omar. After stating that the TRC legislation would apply equally to all human rights violations, Omar stressed that the struggle for liberation was rooted in the principle of human rights, whereas the quest of the apartheid state to sustain itself through repression was 'an affront to humanity itself'.

De Klerk rejected this analysis. He was backed by the generals. But Omar's distinction was academic. The comparison – the equalising – had already been accepted. The commotion from the Right was, therefore, more in the form of threats that reneging would result in confrontation. This they saw as possible because, while two of the seventeen commissioners were Broederbonders, Wynand Malan representing the moderniser wing and Chris de Jager the traditionalists, the majority had credentials as campaigners for human rights. As such, in Viljoen's view, they were 'idealists', incapable of understanding the practicalities of politics and security.

There were also anti-apartheid opponents of the TRC. They tended not to be interested in the specifics and condemned the whole exercise as futile or worse. The main fear from these quarters was that the TRC would mount a whitewash of the recent past, or at any rate would disguise and sanitise more than it might reveal. Opposition came from leading anti-apartheid families such as Mxenge, Biko and Ribeiro.

Dumisa Ntsebeza appreciated their arguments. They were, after all, also made by many of his friends and political confreres. He too had wrestled with the implications of this product of the Codesa compromise. His conclusion was that it was deeply flawed. But it was also the only chance on offer to gain any real new insight into the apartheid past and how it had operated. He had no illusions that it would rip apart the protective screens thrown around the political and security elites, or reveal the full extent of the horrors of the past, who planned and who carried them out, by whose command. But it could start a process which, once in motion, would be difficult, if not impossible, to stop. On the way, victims would be identified and reparations offered for the damage done to them, their families and communities. On balance, therefore, he felt that involvement in the TRC was an opportunity not to be missed.

On this basis, Dumisa Buhle Ntsebeza, revolutionary socialist, former death row inmate, human rights lawyer and internationalist, accepted nomination as a commissioner. Like most of the others on the final shortlist, he had no detailed idea of what being a commissioner might entail. In any event, he did not seriously consider, given his radical background, that he would be appointed. But as the December vacation drew near a phone call informed him that he had been selected. He had hardly had time to come to terms with this news, almost half disbelieving it, when on 15 December President Nelson Mandela announced on national radio the names of the seventeen individuals, including Dumisa Ntsebeza, who would comprise the country's Truth and Reconciliation Commission. It was official.

The Umtata lawyer was still sitting behind his laden desk wondering what the appointment might mean when the telephone rang. It was Paddy Clark, Boraine's assistant at Justice in Transition. The first meeting of the commission was to be held next day at Bishopscourt, official residence of the Anglican archbishop, Desmond Tutu. He should be there. An airline ticket to Cape Town would be waiting for him at the East London airport.

So began a hectic and, for most commissioners, often bewildering rush of events. The legislation establishing the TRC was in place and the commissioners had been appointed. That was as far as it went. There had been no official notification, only the publication of the fact in the *Government Gazette* and the radio announcement. There was no office, telephone or budget. The commissioners did not know where they would be working, what they might be doing or how much they would be paid. Justice in Transition – effectively Boraine and Paddy Clark – filled the gap. Together with Tutu, Boraine arranged the first meeting and notified the relevant authorities. He also saw to it that the travel arrangements were made. Even at such short notice, sixteen of the seventeen commissioners promised their attendance. Only Khoza Mgojo, the Methodist cleric from KwaZulu-Natal, could not make it to that first meeting.

On the morning of 16 December, the normally informal security at Bishopscourt was transformed. Security guards were everywhere and the newly appointed commissioners had to undergo a search before being admitted into the archbishop's residence. They were a diverse grouping: seven women and nine men of different ages, professions, and ethnic and political backgrounds. Eight were lawyers by training and four, including the chair and his deputy, were Christian ministers of religion. There was at least one atheist, a couple of agnostics, a Hindu and a Muslim, but most were Christians and a majority had displayed commitment to or been active in human rights campaigns. Demographically, the commission was unbalanced, since 35 per cent – six members

– were drawn from the ranks of apartheid's 'white' beneficiaries who comprised just 17 per cent of the population. Only seven commissioners – 41 per cent – came from the black African community that made up 70 per cent of the population. From the start there was an undercurrent of concern that carried a racial essence.

There were also, from the start, suspicions about hidden agendas. Although nobody mentioned the Broederbond, or perhaps even thought about it, some fingers pointed at Wynand Malan. Boraine considered that Malan had a watching brief for some group outside the commission. He mentioned as much in his book about the TRC experience. However, in a remarkable lapse, he failed to mention that Malan had also been a co-leader of the party to which he had himself belonged. Nor was it ever mentioned by anyone, including Malan himself, that a decade ago he and the Progressive Federal Party spokesperson on police, Tian van der Merwe, had been briefed about the murderous activities of Vlakplaas and had held their tongues.

Malan, who reputedly had a major fall-out with P.W. Botha, joined the Democratic Party – successor to the PFP – after it was formed in 1988, and became one of its triumvirate of leaders. The modernising leadership of the Afrikaner Broederbond, under chairman Pieter de Lange, had by then authorised Broeders to join other political formations in preparation for future change. Malan resigned from his DP leadership position in 1990 after being challenged about his AB membership. The challenge came at a closed DP conference and was mounted by veteran journalist, Broederbond investigator and then DP city councillor, Hans Strydom.

Malan admitted at the time that he had retained his AB membership when he left the NP. In justification, he stated that there were many other Broeders within the ranks of the DP. Strydom maintained that membership of the AB was incompatible with membership of the DP. He forced the matter to a vote and narrowly lost. So Hans Strydom resigned from the Democratic Party and refused to rejoin when told that Malan had resigned his leadership position.

There was also concern among commissioners with more activist backgrounds about the inclusion of Chris de Jager. The Broederbond lawyer hailed from the far right of the political spectrum and had a reputation as a diehard racist. Although he did not stay the course as a commissioner, he served throughout on the committee that granted amnesty, where he worked closely with lawyer Sisi Khampepe. In 2001 it was Khampepe who recommended De Jager for appointment as a judge.

There was evidence of tension when the sixteen commissioners assembled on 16 December 1995, so there was ready agreement to the suggestion that they should go on a retreat to get to know one another better and come to grips with the task ahead. For several the retreat, held at the Anglican centre of Faure in the Western Cape, was an eye-opening, interesting and, on balance, worthwhile experience. It certainly laid the ground for what was to follow, even to the emphasis on a fundamentally Christian outlook. As Boraine described it, the priest who led the retreat 'helped us to distinguish between grievances and grief and to hold together a passion for justice and a compassion for the perpetrators'.

But time was short. Whereas the initial eighteen months allotted for the commission to complete its business had begun with the publication of the appointments, these new commissioners still had to reorganise their schedules, complete their existing work and tie up their affairs. Then there was the question of setting up the basic infrastructure. Premises had to be found, furniture and stationery ordered, telephone and data lines arranged, before matters such as job descriptions could be agreed and responsibilities assigned. Alex Boraine was clearly the only commissioner in a position to take on such tasks. He was also one of the commissioners who felt strongly that the TRC should hasten its findings. In a matter of weeks, with the aid of Manie Steyn, an official seconded from the Justice department, not only was the TRC headquarters in Cape Town established, but so too were regional offices in East London, Durban and Johannesburg.

It was necessary now to agree tasks for the various commissioners and to appoint the staff to tackle a wide range and massive load of work. Tutu and Boraine met to discuss which commissioners should assume which roles. There were two committees and an investigative unit, each to be chaired by a commissioner. Two more commissioners had to be appointed to the Amnesty Committee, where it was the president's prerogative to appoint the chairperson and most of the members. Tutu proposed that he announce his choices to the commission for their approval rather than open up the matter to debate. This caused some resentment, but there were no objections to Tutu's nominations, although the KwaZulu-Natal lawyer Richard Lyster declined his invitation to head the investigations unit.

Tutu took charge of the Human Rights Violations Committee, with Yasmin Sooka and Wynand Malan as his deputies. Hlengiwe Mkhize agreed to chair the Reparation and Rehabilitation Committee, with Wendy Orr as her deputy, while Sisi Khampepe and Chris de Jager accepted appointments to the Amnesty Committee. Richard Lyster felt that he should not head the investigative unit because he had antagonised the IFP in KwaZulu-Natal, an area where much investigation would obviously take place. What was needed, he argued, was a rather less controversial appointment in so important a political post. Nobody seems too sure who first mentioned Dumisa Ntsebeza.

Within the context of the IFP and KZN, the Umtata lawyer was not controversial. He said himself that he had little experience of investigations outside of legal matters, but he had a good sense of what should be done, and besides, as other commissioners pointed out, the unit would hire investigative staff. So Dumisa Buhle Ntsebeza took over as the political head of the still-to-be established TRC investigative unit. This made him, effectively, third in seniority in a TRC structure that had to be built in a hurry.

The commissioners then left to settle their own affairs and to clear the decks for the months ahead. By January, when the commission came together again in the offices found and furnished by Boraine, the question of staff had grown critical. Tutu announced that he wanted to bring with him into the TRC his personal assistant, Lavinia Crawford-Browne. He also proposed that his existing media officer, John Allen, be appointed TRC communications director. Some of the commissioners, including Ntsebeza, were taken aback. These were the first – and prominent – staff appointments, and they had been made without advertising the posts or conducting interviews. Both appointees were also white. As with most decisions in those very early days, however, they 'went through on the nod'. Boraine then announced that he too wished to bring in his existing assistant, Paddy Clark. He also recommended a young lawyer, Paul van Zyl, who had worked closely with him during the lead-up to the TRC. The hard-working and able Van Zyl eventually became the commission's executive secretary.

Ntsebeza's expressed judgement that these early high-profile appointments were a bad political mistake helped to strengthen the misapprehension among some commissioners that he was a black nationalist. (Just as the concept of atheism seems never to have entered the mind of most commissioners, so too were the subtleties of anti-racist politics ignored.) His stress that the TRC should try to ensure an ethnic and gender balance reinforced the misunderstanding about his political views, and his insistence that the chief executive of the TRC had to be a black African, a representative of the majority of the country's population, seemed to confirm his supposed 'black power' orientation.

In that inaugural period of what one insider called 'barely controlled chaos', opinions were formed and resentments took root. Boraine took full responsibility as he rode roughshod over regulations and the niceties of bureaucratic procedure. 'I knew that we had to move, and move fast, and I think we got off the ground in record time; that was all I was concerned about. I was strongly of the view that a truth commission should not last too long, and therefore we had no time to waste,' he wrote later.

This hasty and autocratic process, let alone the thinking behind it, left a legacy of anger within the TRC. Boraine was accused of flouting democracy. At times, especially in the hectic early months, there were also clashes at meetings of the commission. They usually came when Ntsebeza challenged the use by Boraine of the collective 'we' in referring to decisions which had not involved all the commissioners. Any support for such objections tended to come from black commissioners and this polarised the tension between the representatives of apartheid's beneficiary and victim communities who served on the TRC. To many eyes, it also confirmed the opinion that Ntsebeza belonged in what was seen as the black nationalist camp.

That his first choice for the national director to head the investigative unit was not only white, but a South African policeman, failed to dent this quite widely held perception. Ntsebeza wanted Frank Dutton, the most prominent of the few policemen who had decisively broken with the old regime and had investigated and prosecuted human rights violators. Dutton agreed to assist in vetting applications to join the unit, but he turned down the top job. He had been offered a post with the United Nations war crimes tribunal in former Yugoslavia. It provided as great an investigative challenge without the strain of working alongside police force and military personnel who tended to detest him. But he gave advice. Going through the job applications, he dismissed one out of hand: Johan Breytenbach. 'Don't touch,' Dutton warned. Ntsebeza was to remember that curt warning months later when Breytenbach, former station head in both Washington and London for Hendrik van den Bergh's BOSS, emerged in the TRC headquarters, employed as an investigator.

With Dutton unavailable, Dumisa Ntsebeza was under pressure to find an alternative fast. The unit was critical to the TRC. There would be police seconded to it who might well carry baggage from the past, and even be pursuing other agendas. It was essential that the effective managing director of the unit be an astute and independent investigator, hopefully with knowledge of the police. Dutton had mentioned one name: Wilson Magadla, a long-serving murder and robbery detective. He had worked with Dutton for several years. Magadla was ready to come out of retirement, but he did not feel he could handle the top job. As a black policeman, he had never been given administrative training or experience. He was a basic hands-on investigator, not a manager. But he had a wide knowledge of police personnel, what they were and how they operated. As such, he seemed the ideal appointment as a deputy to a director who might have investigative skills, but lack the police experience and contacts. Magadla accepted the post.

Various commissioners formed and reformed interview panels, discussed and debated appointments as they flew from one centre to the next. Many appointments were made literally on the run between airports. There were occasional disagreements, but nothing serious. Speed, as Boraine kept stressing, was of the essence. There was also no time to assess possible personal bias in interviewing panels. Ntsebeza suggested, for example, that he step down from the panel interviewing applicants for the post of research director. He did so because Stellenbosch academic André du Toit was an applicant. Du Toit had played a major role twenty years earlier in saving Ntsebeza from a possible death sentence. He might be biased in his favour. The suggestion was turned down.

In the event, Du Toit could not start immediately as research director. Another applicant, Charles Villa-Vicencio, a professor of religion and friend of Boraine, could. He was appointed by the panel, which included Boraine. 'There was nothing untoward in this,' Ntsebeza stressed later, but it provided more fuel to simmering race-based resentments that were to grow within the TRC staff. Even in the early months, several of the black staff referred disparagingly to the white executives as 'the NUSAS old boys' club'. Many of the executives had been active in the liberal National Union of SA Students.

These resentments were given an additional boost when the Port Elizabeth lawyer and advocate Glenn Goosen was appointed as national director of the investigative unit. This happened after the second of two senior journalists offered an interview for the post had declined. It was, on one level, an awkward appointment for Dumisa Ntsebeza to make. He had sat on an interview panel which had earlier rejected Goosen for the less senior post of national legal officer. It went to another lawyer, Hanif Vally. There had been some tension at that earlier interview when Ntsebeza jokingly asked Goosen if he was related to the notorious police torturer Piet Goosen, who came from the same area. After that interview Goosen continued to work closely with several of the senior TRC staff, including lawyer Howard Varney, a consultant assisting the TRC. Varney had been involved with the special investigative task unit that prepared the case against former defence minister Magnus Malan and a clutch of generals. He recommended Goosen as national director.

Time was passing. Crucially, there were no other candidates in immediate prospect. An interview was scheduled. At it, Goosen reminded Commissioner Ntsebeza of his query about Piet Goosen, who was no relation. 'I am still not related to him,' Goosen remarked sharply. The query had clearly rankled. But he had briefed himself well, and seemed to have an excellent grasp of the needs of the investigative unit. Ntsebeza had no hesitation in endorsing the appointment. Besides, the first hearings were scheduled for April. Already the flood of statements from victims had begun. Each one would have to be investigated in an atmosphere where Left and Right, for differing reasons, opposed the process.

What was also obvious, even at that early stage, was that a large number of the key personnel involved in sustaining the system, as well as in committing some of its worst abuses, would not be coming forward. The guarantees about 'witch hunts' ensured that most of apartheid's architects and directors would never shed light on the past. Many would remain in positions of power and authority, having literally got away with mass murder and worse.

10

A tale of three survivors

What the TRC hearings made clear was the fact that the centralised organ of state repression, with its many blood-stained tentacles, continued to function for years after the supposed first steps towards a democratic transition – that key accessories, including named murderers, were quietly absorbed into the new order after 1994. Some of their names flitted briefly before the TRC, others were never mentioned. Most were never summoned to a hearing and were never questioned.

Of the thousands of agents, operatives and part-time informers compromised by what they did to maintain apartheid, most remain buried within the new dispensation. A few, with material or academic resources or marketable skills, migrated, mainly to Britain, Australia, New Zealand and Canada. One such person was implicated in some of the more horrific acts condoned by the apartheid state and the medical establishment of the military. His name and activities were mentioned in the health sector hearings of the TRC. But by then he was ensconced in his new position, practising as a psychiatrist in Canada.

Another served with zeal for fifteen years from 1982 and received a single passing mention in the first five volumes of the TRC report. Yet his career gave a penetrating insight into the workings of Military Intelligence outside South Africa, and is linked by accusation and suspicion to the assassination in 1986 of Sweden's prime minister, Olof Palme. Even more intriguing than the career of this agent is that of the man who was his handler both before and after South Africa's democratic transition in 1994. His name never featured in TRC hearings and he did not apply for amnesty or explain his role as a foot soldier and administrator for more than thirty years of brutal repression.

The following are only three examples of the thousands of individuals who never appeared before the TRC and who continued to survive and, in many cases, to thrive in the 'new' South Africa.

1   H.W. Doncaster, personal file as at 15.09.2002

Horace William Doncaster, Major-General, Military Intelligence (rtd)

Date of birth: 09.02.1950; military number: 66339243E

Career soldier, 33 years service; promoted brigadier, 1993; major-general, 2000; given 'employer-induced retrenchment package', November 2001; retired, April 2002.

Senior positions in and eventual director of MI 'dirty tricks' unit, Directorate of Covert Collection (DCC); handler of agents and operatives, commended for 'intelligence' work 'in the bush' in Namibia and Zimbabwe, for liaison work with police Special Branch and for the 'development of a target policy on the ANC'.

Involved in planning and ordering cross-border raids. Never appeared before TRC. Never made amnesty application. Never gave any information. Retained Military Intelligence position under ANC government. Awarded good service medal 28 January 1998.

Horace William Doncaster is one of the great survivors from the 'sharp end' of the repressive machinery of apartheid. His name is not widely known even within the military, for much of his career was spent in the twilight world of military intelligence. In the year 2000 he was promoted from brigadier to general. Two years earlier he was presented with a long-service medal by the then deputy defence minister, Ronnie Kasrils, a central committee member of the Communist Party. Kasrils remarked privately about Doncaster: 'He is a professional. Before, he worked for them. Now, he works for us.'

Perhaps Horace William Doncaster is the epitome of the soldier-patriot motivated only by blind and dedicated service to whichever government is in power. Or he may be the classic mercenary, interested only in ensuring his job and his pay. But he was centrally involved in the bloodletting and terror of the apartheid years, including 'service on the border'. As such, he was given the opportunity to make a submission to the TRC, to clear away some of the murk of the past, and to apologise for the slaughter and brutality he inflicted. Like so many others in the upper echelons, he chose silence. He also chose to destroy and order the destruction of documentary evidence of that past.

The disappearance of files, computer disks and equipment from the Directorate of Covert Collection was largely his responsibility. The evidence of most of the military's dirty tricks over the years vanished after Judge Richard Goldstone's investigators blundered into the DCC headquarters near Pretoria in November 1992. In March of the following year, F.W. de Klerk ordered the early retirement of twenty-three senior officers who were too grossly compromised by so-called 'third force' actions. Goldstone's inquiry had struck a significant blow, even though the forced retirements were also moves to cover up the past. Significantly, the Military Intelligence chief, General Stoffel van der Merwe, retained his post. Brigadier Doncaster took another career move upward: he became the director of DCC.

Doncaster was one of the relatively few 'English' conscripts who chose a career in the army. Less than three weeks after his nineteenth birthday, he was appointed a second lieutenant in the infantry corps. After further training he was sent in December 1969 for the first of several stints 'on the border'. Between then and March 1973, he spent a total of nearly a year based either in Rundu, on the Namibia/Angola border, at Katima Mulilo, across the Zambezi river from Zambia, or at Chirundu, near the eastern Zimbabwe/Zambia border. In those days the South African military and police, often acting at cross-purposes, were trying to destabilise Zambia, launching cross-border attacks and planting the landmines that were still causing havoc thirty years later.

What Doncaster did during those border operations is not known, but whatever it was commended him to his superiors. He was later to be awarded the Pro Patria medal for this period, and in March 1971 was promoted to full lieutenant. In June of that year he and another young infantry officer, W.E. Basson, were sent for 'special duty' at army headquarters. Both men emerged as part of the Department of Military Intelligence (DMI). Nearly two weeks after this apparent graduation, Doncaster was posted to Chirundu in Zimbabwe, where he spent eighty-five days and won more praise.

In March 1973, after returning from operations apparently in the Caprivi Strip of Namibia, Doncaster was reclassified as an intelligence officer and joined the Intelligence Corps. The following year is a blank, but it must have been impressive, as he was promoted to captain in May 1974. Shortly after, he took up a post as an instructor at the Military Intelligence college. Sometime in 1975, he was given at least one foreign posting, perhaps to an embassy, for additional training, or to conduct a clandestine operation. In any case his star rose higher: by January 1978 he was a major and had been awarded the military bronze medal for good service, a military commendation certificate, and the Pro Patria medal.

In 1979 Major Doncaster was awarded the military commendation medal, and on New Year's Day 1981 he attained the rank of Commandant. His hands-on experience in Namibia must have stood him in good stead: he was appointed at the same time as second in command of the DMI 'West Front' at the highly secretive DCC. This meant helping to organise information-gathering, agents and operatives in Namibia and Angola, deciding on targets in the region and planning the operations to eliminate, neutralise or otherwise deal with targets. This appears to have been his real forte. His citation for the Southern Cross medal, awarded in 1983, makes it clear that he was a key figure in a total strategy that included the mass murder of suspected members of the Namibian independence movement, SWAPO, and the disposal of their bodies at sea. By this time, Doncaster had become the senior staff officer in charge of the Department of Military Intelligence (DMI) 'Home Front' at the DCC.

Two operations that enhanced his prestige were Skerwe and Vine, attacks mounted on Maputo in Mozambique. Skerwe (Splinter) was a series of air strikes launched against what were assumed to be ANC houses in the Matola and Liberdade districts of the Mozambican capital. Doncaster and his unit collated the information sent in by agents in Maputo, selected the targets and orchestrated the operation. According to their information, the only real threat to low-flying Impala aircraft was an anti-aircraft missile battery on the outskirts of the city. It became a primary target.

Full details of the raid and its consequences were never released. It seems that between ten and fourteen aircraft, armed with rockets, hit their targets shortly after dawn on 23 May 1983. Estimates of those killed ranged from three to sixty-four, but were probably closer to the higher figure. Several houses used by ANC members were certainly demolished with a still unknown number of casualties. A local crèche and a jam factory were also destroyed.

Operation Vine involved a 'Recce' seaborne landing in October 1983 on a beach outside Maputo. The target defined by Doncaster and his DCC 'desks' was an office converted from former servants' quarters on the roof of a four-storey apartment block near Maputo's diplomatic sector. It was an administration centre that processed ANC members travelling in and out of South Africa. Spies reported that scrupulous records were kept in locked filing cabinets in the rooftop eyrie. In the apartment immediately beneath the office lived six ANC members who worked in the building or elsewhere in Maputo. Mozambican officials occupied the other apartments.

The security establishment wanted the files stored in the cabinets. Doncaster's office took on the task and developed an operational outline. The aim was to burgle the penthouse, escape with as many files as possible, and leave behind incendiary charges that would destroy the remaining documentation. In addition, Doncaster proposed developing special charges that could blast downwards through the reinforced concrete floor of the apartment block to kill the ANC members asleep below.

A team of eleven Recces, led by a captain, trained for six weeks using mock-ups of the rooftop office and experimented with explosives on concrete pipes of the same estimated thickness and consistency as the apartment building floor in Maputo. In the event, the squad could not get into the office. As compensation they placed their explosive charges on the roof and detonated them by remote control as they headed back to the beach and their rendezvous with a ship lying offshore. The explosives tore three holes in the concrete roof and ripped apart the rooms below, killing and injuring the several occupants.

The security establishment praised Doncaster for his 'competent leadership', which had enabled 'the expertise, capacity and product of the Home Front desks' to render 'one of the most important contributions to the combating of the enemies of the RSA'. But Doncaster was singled out in particular for his ability to work with the security police. This was seen as vital in the post-Simonstown Council period. To make the total strategy as effective as possible required maximum cooperation and coordination between police and military units. Doncaster was a liaison officer with the police and this work, noted in his Southern Cross medal citation, 'contributed to a better understanding between the two forces which, in turn, leads to greater effectiveness'.

Next came a promotion to colonel, in 1985, and the post of 'Senior Staff Officer, Covert Collection, Division 1'. There was talk of perhaps a posting as a military attaché. He certainly spent time in countries like Namibia, but seems to have retained his DCC post as the bloodshed and terror reached its peak. An internal appraisal in 1989 noted that he was responsible for building up the terrorism section of Military Intelligence. He was also apparently central to planning and developing an effective disinformation division. How far he was involved in the massive combined military and police operation in Namibia in the run-up to the October 1989 election is still not known.

That month also saw the first cracks emerge in the wall of secrecy surrounding the police death squads as Butana Nofemela spoke out from his death row cell. This made the military 'dirty tricks' units all the more important; they might have to carry the day. Doncaster's career continued to prosper. In 1991 he became chief of staff at 'Central Collections'. At the same time, the former head of DCC, J.J. 'Tolletjie' Botha, became chief of the 'Central Collections Bureau'. In April 1993, Horace William Doncaster became a brigadier and the 'Director of Covert Collection'. It was at this time that the greatest destruction of records, files and other documentation took place.

At this time too, Doncaster took over the handling of one of the DCC's top spies and operatives, the military's man in Maputo, the supposed shipping company agent Nigel Barnett. Doncaster remained his handler until Barnett was arrested in Mozambique in March 1997. Military Intelligence had continued to pay this long-term spy up to February of that year. What he was doing, why he was doing it, and how an apartheid-era operation continued to function in a friendly country after South Africa's democratic transition remains a puzzle. Equally puzzling is how this trained killer and spy could walk free, apparently on bail for a serious offence that has never been scheduled to come to court.

2 Nigel Barnett

In the world of espionage where deception is a way of life, Nigel Barnett is an acknowledged master. To the tiny group aware of his existence he was 'Mr 200 per cent', one of that rare kind who excel as both agents – spies – and operatives or 'men of action'. Within Interpol, the international police agency, his names and background are known. The Swedish police keep a file on the person whose last formal identity was Nigel Barnett. For Nigel Barnett (South African identity number 500630 5202006) remains a suspect in the murder in 1986 of Swedish prime minister Olof Palme.

Today he may have shed 'Nigel Barnett' and dyed his dark brown hair, always parted on the left. There are two identity card photographs of Barnett, taken only two years apart, in 1990 and 1992, and even they reveal totally different hairstyles and hair lengths and could, at first sight, be different people. In another identity document, issued in 1981 in the name of Henry William Bacon, the spy who was born Leon van der Westhuizen sports a heavy dark beard and moustache. In October 1983, as Nicho Esslin, he was clean-shaven and wore a rather shorter hairstyle than either of his Barnett variants.

All of the documents are genuine, three of them issued in South Africa and one by the South African trade mission in Mozambique. All of them were found in Barnett's apartment in Maputo in 1997 by police investigating a personal feud between what they thought were two businessmen. After fifteen years living undetected as the top South African Military Intelligence agent in Mozambique, Nigel Barnett had grown careless or conceited. He embroiled himself in a public, personal, row, and attempted to settle it by paying some street urchins to set fire to his adversary's yacht. The urchins were caught and gave him up. When police raided his apartment they discovered enough material to reveal that Nigel Barnett was, at the very least, a spy.

During the short spell he spent in prison before his release pending trial for attempted arson, Mozambican, South African and Swedish authorities interviewed Barnett. He could hardly deny his spying activities and quite readily confessed, but only to gathering routine information about the port and its traffic. He was even less forthcoming about the rest of his life and his background. He sketched a pedestrian existence, a consistently passive background role. The general outline does appear to have been fairly accurate, the detail not.

For the life of Nigel Barnett/H.W. Otto/Henry Bacon/Nicho Esslin was anything but mundane. He was far from being the passive observer or harmless traffic cop and navy diver he claimed once to have been. Born in Queenstown in the Eastern Cape province on 29 May 1949, he was named Leon van der Westhuizen by his mother, who put him up for adoption. A local couple, British-born Jeffrey Harold Walker Bacon and his Swedish missionary wife, Aina Amanda Eriksson, completed the formalities and adopted the child as a younger brother for their son Olaf, the survivor of twin boys born to Amanda Eriksson two years earlier. The addition to the family was registered as Henry William Bacon and, as such, went into the world.

He was a tall, strong and athletic boy who seems to have protected his older brother from 'bacon and eggs' teasing in their youth. School for them both was the prestigious Dale College in King William's Town, where Henry Bacon shone brighter on the sports field than in the classroom. When he was a lanky fifteen, the woman he thought of as his biological mother died. He was very close to her, and it was from her that he learned the Swedish he still speaks. Her death was a severe blow. An even bigger one was the discovery that Amanda Eriksson was not his mother; that he was adopted. When and how he found out is not known, but he seems to have broken off almost all contact with his brother and father while still in his teens.

Certainly he seems to have moved as far away from home as he could once he completed his schooling in 1967. Like other white youths of his age, he was conscripted into the army, and in June 1969 he joined the navy where he became a diver. A motorcycle accident in suburban Cape Town in 1971 put paid to this part of his career, but he had developed a taste for the armed services and a liking for danger. Rhodesia promised both, with a bush war under way and a demand for trained soldiers. Henry William Bacon headed north and joined the British South African Police, the paramilitary regiment that proudly boasted the British Queen Mother as its colonel-in-chief.

Henry Bacon excelled. Drafted into the Special Branch, the unit that specialised in information gathering, interrogation and 'pseudo operations', he became accustomed to the use of disguise and false identity. Like others in the unit, he 'blacked up' at times to get closer to guerrilla groups or to terrorise villagers in their name. The BSAP Special Branch pioneered these operations in the Zimbabwe bush before the most brutal of the special forces, the Selous Scouts, made such practices their own. Literate, quick-witted and athletic, Bacon received training and practical experience as an agent and operator. He extracted information by casual means and cruel; he eavesdropped, debriefed sources, wrote reports and killed. It was a time of secret cross-border raids and often wholesale slaughter; a time when the social misfits who hacked off, dried and wore the ears of the killed as necklaces, were regarded merely as 'hard men'. In this milieu, Henry Bacon thrived. A citation for 'gallantry' issued on 5 October 1979 commends him for his conduct 'whilst engaged in anti-terrorist operations'.

The actions referred to took place in the Lumgundi district near the northern town of Sinoia in late 1978 and, in particular, on 8 and 9 January 1979. Bacon's commanding officer recommended him for the award, not just for the 'specialised operations' but also for his conspicuous dedication to duty. The twenty-nine-year-old Detective Section Officer not only built up a network of informers when he ran the Special Branch office at Sipolilo; he also took part in regular 'clandestine operations'.

Also operating in Rhodesia/Zimbabwe at the time as part of a joint BOSS and South African National Intelligence Service unit was Att Nel. As a colonel in charge of 'East Front' at the DCC, he was to become Bacon's operational handler for the best part of a decade until 1994. Given the small numbers and the closeness of the cooperation between the South African spy unit in Zimbabwe and the BSAP Special Branch, it is most likely that Nel and Bacon met in Rhodesia/Zimbabwe as minority rule crumbled. Bacon was one of the bitter-enders who saw the last vicious fights to stave off the inevitable transition to democratic elections. Like thousands of his kind, he headed south as independence dawned. A trained spy and killer, he was a gift to apartheid South Africa. He had also picked up some knowledge of Portuguese, possibly as a result of cross-border operations into Mozambique.

Although Bacon claimed not to have left Zimbabwe till 1981, it seems most probable that he returned to South Africa early in 1980, together with the special forces members who went to make up the apartheid state's 6 Recce battalion. It is also possible that he was recruited just before Zimbabwe's independence elections by Major Neil Kriel, the Selous Scout who founded what became known as the Civil Cooperation Bureau, the military's dirty tricks, assassination and mass murder squad. Kriel was sent into newly independent Zimbabwe by Brigadier 'Tolletjie' Botha to sign up all the 'hard men' he could. Some were to remain behind in Zimbabwe to provide information and, in some cases, to carry out assignments. Most were to come south, either to be absorbed into the 'Recce' groups or to serve in the CCB.

However he was recruited, Bacon's range of skills got him attached directly to the Military Intelligence directorate – the Directorate of Covert Collection – as an agent and operative. He reported ultimately to Att Nel as the head of the East Front desk that ran actions in and information out of Mozambique. But he was also available for service elsewhere, both in Africa and Europe. His very first operation appears to have been within months of returning to South Africa. He was sent into the Mozambique capital to pinpoint, probably with the aid of established 'Rhodesian' informers in the Frelimo government's security forces, the houses used by South African ANC personnel.

This led to 'Operation Beanbag', when an attack column drove into Maputo and attacked and destroyed three houses used by the ANC. SB Colonel Jac Buchner and Major Callie Steijn of Military Intelligence were responsible for overall planning. A former Rhodesian Special Air Services officer, Garth Barrett, was in command of the column. A DCC operative from Maputo, apparently Bacon, drove into South Africa to give the final briefing to Barrett before the column set out. In Maputo they attacked and destroyed the target houses. Sixteen ANC members, a Portuguese electrical company engineer, Jose Ramos, who happened to be driving by, and three Recces died in the raid. Two of the Recces, Robert Hutchinson and Ian Suttill, were British. They were SAS members who had fled independent Zimbabwe.

According to Nigel Barnett's account, at that time he was leading a quiet life in the Wankie district of Zimbabwe. It was only in the middle of 1981 that he left Zimbabwe and reapplied to join the South African Navy in Cape Town. He certainly did spend time in the Navy in 1981, but it seems to have been a period of reorientation, both to reaccustom him to the workings of a port and to provide additional training. At the Simonstown naval base near Cape Town he appears to have worked with 'Com Nav', the naval communications division, and to have been attached to security. His official designation was as an officer in the personnel section. However, he may have been able to travel abroad as part of the deep cover prepared for him by Colonel Att Nel. As Nigel Barnett, shipping agent, he did require some knowledge of several overseas ports, in particular Hong Kong.

What he did and where he went is not known. All that is clear is that in December 1982 he changed his surname from Bacon to Esslin, having applied through the home affairs department under the Aliens Act. This name change was gazetted on 10 December, and Bacon promptly resigned from the Navy.

The ensuing sequence of name and job changes seems to have been coordinated by Colonel Nel as part of creating a 'legend' for the man once known as Henry William Bacon.

Naval personnel officer Bacon left Cape Town in December 1982. Nicho Esslin arrived in Durban in January 1983, having applied to join the Durban-based Polaris Shipping Company. This was one of the many front companies set up by the security establishment over the years. They conducted legitimate business, often made sizeable profits, but were essentially security operations, providing everything from cover for spies and assassins to channels for smuggling arms, laundering money and financing bribes and destabilisation measures.

But Nicho Esslin was not given a job when he reported for duty to the Polaris office in Durban's Cowey Road. Instead, as Nigel Barnett, a name and identity selected by Att Nel, he became a director of another front company, Lesotho Mountain Carriers (LMS), with offices in Maseru and Maputo. LMS was a subsidiary of Polaris. The shipping company was, in turn, owned by the main DCC front company, Pan African Investment Corporation (PAIC), and acted as an agent for the Gold Star Shipping Line, itself a front for one of the Israeli security agencies. Bacon/Esslin/Barnett was obviously being prepared for an important posting with the collaboration of Israeli intelligence.

Apart from a name on a single bank account in Durban, into which the DCC paid regular sums, Henry William Bacon had vanished. Anyone checking on him might discover that he had legally changed his surname to Esslin. A dedicated researcher with contacts inside the home affairs department might also be able to discover that Bacon had become Nicho Esslin, with the same South African identity number: 490529 5115 00 6. That Nicho Esslin's identity book bearing this number had only been issued in October 1983 would indicate that Esslin still existed then.

Only Nicho Esslin ceased to exist within two months of Bacon's name change, although a bank safe deposit box was maintained under this name. From February 1983 there was only Nigel Barnett, allegedly born in the then nominally independent 'homeland' of Transkei one day, one month and one year later than Bacon/Esslin and bearing the identity number 500630 5202 00 6. All contact ceased with family and former friends. Nigel Barnett, a director of Lesotho Mountain Carriers, with no military history and a career in transport, was on his way to becoming the deep cover agent in Maputo. He also had, perhaps then and certainly subsequently, another identity as H.W. Otto.

According to Nigel Barnett's CV, in 1982 he emigrated from South Africa to Hong Kong, where he worked for the Gold Star Line and was stationed in

Kobe, Japan, Bangkok and Colombo. His permanent residence was Hong Kong and he had visited Beira and Maputo aboard a Gold Star ship in 1983. Since such a story could be checked, it is probable that Barnett did in fact spend time in the various Gold Star offices and did visit Mozambique. In prison in Mozambique in 1997, he admitted that he had travelled to Hong Kong in early 1984 to familiarise himself with the harbour and the Gold Star office. He had also spent ten days visiting other ports such as Kobe and Bangkok before being appointed as the agent for Gold Star in Maputo. At no time, he said, did he receive any training as a spy.

This was one of the many lies of a man whose whole life was a lie. Apart from his Rhodesia/Zimbabwe experiences, evidence exists that he attended an eight-week theoretical and practical intelligence course at DCC headquarters in Pretoria between January and March 1984, shortly before his long-term posting to Maputo. His brother thought he had been attached to naval security after his return from Zimbabwe and before he broke off all contact.

Given only what is known of the man who became Nigel Barnett, it seems obvious that he was a highly trained spy and killer. He had a fascination with weapons and held at least four licensed firearms at the time of his arrest in 1997. These were a 10 mm Glock pistol, a .22 calibre Astra pistol, a .308 Spandau Mauser rifle, and his apparently favoured weapon, a .357 Magnum revolver. The latter was the calibre and type of weapon that ended the life of Olof Palme in a Stockholm street shortly before midnight on 28 February 1986. The weapon that killed Palme has never been found.

However, in Maputo, throughout the bloody years of destabilisation, Nigel Barnett appears to have operated mainly collecting, collating and sending information to his masters. Most of it concerned the ANC – on members, houses where they stayed, vehicles they used, who visited them and when. He provided 'target' information, including photographs and building plans, in line with the demands of KIK. Operations he was involved in outside Mozambique may well have been in another guise, such as H.W. Otto, so as not to endanger his work in Mozambique.

Barnett named two spies in the ANC office, 'Francis' and 'Monde', who passed on information via a Mozambican citizen, Carlos Pinto, to Antonio Pombo, a former military liaison officer at the South African trade mission in Maputo who was based in the Swazi capital, Mbabane. Subsequent investigations established that Francis was Francis Malaya, who later became an askari. Pinto carried envelopes to and from Maputo and Swaziland. This was at the time when South African hit squads were bombing, killing and kidnapping real and imagined anti-apartheid activists in Swaziland. These actions, the TRC ruled, led to gross violations of human rights.

These facts alone – and most of them were made available to the TRC – should have ensured serious attempts to bring Nigel Barnett before the TRC for questioning. No such attempt was made, although he was interviewed in prison by a Swedish investigator attached to the TRC. Nor was there any move to subpoena Colonel Att Nel, or any of Barnett's other named handlers. One of these was Jack Widowson, allegedly a member of Hendrik van den Bergh's 'Z' squad and the police special task team. His name was also linked to the 1977 murders of Robert and Jean-Cora Smit. The TRC found that these had been committed by members of the security forces. The deaths constituted a 'gross violation of human rights' for which there had been no amnesty applications. Widowson's name appeared in the 1992 Steyn report as having been connected with 'third force activities'. In the post-apartheid dispensation, he became a member of the ANC government's National Intelligence Agency (NIA).

But it is Nigel Barnett who remains of particular interest to the Swedish authorities. They know that elements in the apartheid security services had talked about killing Olof Palme. The Swedish prime minister was seen as a dangerous enemy. He had been instrumental in steering Sweden's Social Democratic government into solid support for the ANC, and in the week before he died had granted virtual diplomatic recognition to the liberation movement. There is plenty of circumstantial evidence that links South African security forces with at least plotting, and perhaps committing, Palme's murder. South African security, for example, gathered regular reports on Palme's activities from a Swedish agent, a medical doctor and academic who was recruited while working in South Africa.

The Swedish police also know that Barnett failed a polygraph (lie detector) test. This is no positive proof of any wrongdoing. However, in his interviews with Mozambican, South African and Swedish authorities he gave details of his various visits to Sweden. None of these coincided with the death of Olof Palme. But he did mention that on one visit he walked through Stockholm at a time when there was a light dusting of snow on the ground. The Swedish police checked on the weather at the times Barnett admitted to having been in Sweden. On none of these occasions was there any snow on the ground. But on the night that Olof Palme was shot, the description of the weather and the streets of Stockholm matched.

Once again, this was not proof positive that Bacon/Esslin/Barnett had been in any way connected with the murder of the Swedish prime minister. But he had almost certainly been in Sweden on at least one other occasion that none of his various passports reflected. Interestingly, at the time of the assassination a new man had just taken over the Ander Lande (other countries) desk at the

DCC. This was the unit responsible for clandestine activities across the world, and its new commander was a long-distance assassin with a reputation for trying to prove himself. However, Craig Michael Williamson, the letter-bomb killer and London bomber, denied knowing anything about the killing of Olof Palme or about the existence of Nigel Barnett. The latter claim, at least, seems highly improbable.

The only link that emerged came from Eugene de Kock. He recalled being told by former security police 'analyst' and gun-runner to Inkatha, Philip Powell, that two of Williamson's close associates, Jonty and Cindy Leontsinis, knew who had carried out the Palme assassination. Jonty Leontsinis, a Johannesburg horticulturist who operated within security police and Military Intelligence fronts, was another friend from Williamson's school days. Neither Jonty nor Cindy Leontsinis, who in 2002 were living on their farm in KwaZulu-Natal and running a national seed company, were ever investigated or interviewed by the TRC. Powell, although implicated in gun-running, left for England to study for an MA degree in conflict resolution in London.

In early 2003 Bacon/Esslin/Barnett/Otto was still in Cape Town, although he had apparently gone to ground. He was still, technically, on bail, awaiting trial in Mozambique. Reports that he was working for the National Intelligence Agency could not be confirmed.

3   Aubrey Levin

The name of Aubrey Levin emerged during the health and human rights submission to the TRC. This dealt primarily with the complicity of members of the medical profession in supporting and disguising the often nakedly brutish application of apartheid within the military and police. The most widely known case was that of the doctors – Ivor Lang and Benjamin Tucker – who conspired with security police torturers in the case of the torture and murder of Steve Bantu Biko.

But there were many others, especially those medical practitioners who worked as district surgeons, and in some cases as active members of reservist security units. Some had retired by 2000, others were still in practice, and one, involved in chemical and biological warfare research, had been appointed a professor at the University of Pretoria.

The medical professionals enjoyed high status under apartheid and continued to do so after the transition, although many had been active and often enthusiastic collaborators or were horribly compromised. One such specialist was Jan Adriaan Plomp, professor of psychiatry. When the trade unionist and radical medical practitioner Neil Aggett died in detention in 1982, the police decided to have it demonstrated that Aggett had committed suicide. According to testimony given to the TRC, Lieutenant S.P. Whitehead was ordered by a Brigadier Muller to gather evidence to confirm the opinion that Aggett had suicidal tendencies.

The state's trump card was Professor Plomp. He had never met Neil Aggett or his family or friends, and did not interview the police who had interrogated and tortured the anti-apartheid activist, but he had no problem with the brigadier's diagnosis. He told the inquest into the death of Aggett:

> Although Dr Aggett was brought up as an Anglican, there are indications that he did not keep to the church or religious connections from his early adult years. His journal shows that he was disillusioned with religion and, in his declaration to the security police, he mentions that he adheres to Marxism, an ideology which excludes religion. It must be mentioned here that loss of religious conviction and religious participation is one of the aspects of social isolation which is regarded by experts as one of the most significant in suicide.

Such was the level of insight put at the service of a murderous state and accepted as expert evidence by a compliant judiciary. But there were some practitioners who dwelled within the belly of the beast. These were the medical personnel, especially attached to the military, who misused their expertise in distorted and damaging ways.

It was in this milieu that Aubrey Levin thrived. He commanded the major psychiatric wing of the military hospital at Voortrekkerhoogte in Pretoria, and rose to become the government's head of mental health. But by the time the TRC came into being Levin was long gone, like a number of collaborator colleagues. He had migrated to Canada, to the city of Calgary in Alberta. Canada was also the destination of two medical practitioners who had worked with Wouter Basson, the man in charge of chemical and biological warfare experiments. Levin was not connected with these. His field was psychiatry, and his name emerged in relation to the 'treatment' and 'cures' offered to homosexual conscripts in the military. It was here that the homophobic and proudly proclaimed extreme rightwinger made his mark.

Hints of these surfaced at hearings of the TRC, but the commission chose not to pursue them or to subpoena Levin. It was left to a group of activists to follow up the allegations and to delve into the background, particularly into psychiatric and surgical practices in the military. This included 'gender reassignment' surgery that had sometimes caused horrific mutilations.

With backing from the Rowntree Trust, Mikki van Zyl, Jeanelle de Gruchy, Sheila Lapinsky, Simon Lewin and Graeme Reid started a major investigation.

Their Aversion Project, which looked into the human rights abuses of gays and lesbians in the apartheid military, triggered further investigations by journalist Paul Kirk. When these were published in August 2000 the tactic Levin had employed when his name emerged at the TRC was used again: he threatened legal action.

Levin denied that he had taken part in gender reassignment surgery – the surgical alteration of the genders of individuals. But he had never been accused of this. The allegation was that he had referred military conscripts whom he could not 'cure' of homosexuality to surgeons and the knife. That several of these dangerous operations were botched and others left uncompleted cannot be blamed directly on Levin. Possible knowledge of these practices certainly can be.

But there were many other accusations levelled at this nephew of the first Jewish member of the National Party. His family were perhaps unique as Jews who attempted to assimilate completely the Afrikaner nationalist ethos. Unlike other Jewish collaborators such as Percy Yutar, the state prosecutor of Nelson Mandela and the Rivonia trialists, the Levins did not align themselves primarily with the Jewish community or Zionism. An uncle was the first Jewish NP member of parliament, and young Aubrey grew up as a perpetual outsider, pretending to be an insider in a party and regime riddled with anti-semitism.

Academic, and nothing like the macho figure that he aspired to be, Aubrey Levin played a prominent role in his local NP branch. He tried to start a conservative student organisation while at university, and even before he qualified as a psychiatrist he betrayed the homophobia that would make him notorious. In 1968, as a GP studying psychiatry, he wrote to parliament asking to be invited to speak on possible changes to the laws on homosexuality being contemplated at the time, and claiming to have 'treated many homosexuals and lesbians and enjoyed some measure of success in therapy'. The therapy referred to was the now widely discredited aversion method using electric shocks. Some colleagues called him 'Dr Shock'.

On qualifying, he joined the army as a colonel – a fact that raised eyebrows, and suggestions of political favouritism. At the Voortrekkerhoogte military hospital near Pretoria he began practising in Ward 22, set aside for treating those classified as 'deviant'. (This category in apartheid South Africa's white military included not only male and female homosexuals but also heterosexual men who for pacifist or political reasons refused to undergo military training.) Levin has admitted that while in charge at Voortrekkerhoogte he adminstered aversion therapy, including 'mild electric shocks'.

Individuals he treated tell a different tale. Only one of the people who, for a brief spell, worked with him has given evidence. A young psychologist intern, who adopted the name Trudi Grobler for her testimony, was so horrified by what she had seen that she reported what seemed to be blatant cases of abuse to her superiors and the University of Pretoria. She referred specifically to the case of a woman being 'treated' for lesbianism who had been so severely shocked that her shoes 'flew off her feet'. The result was that Trudi Grobler was excluded from the psychiatric wing of the military hospital run by Aubrey Levin.

Levin's 'treatment' of homosexuals, both male and female, comprised attaching electrodes to his subjects' arms. These were connected to a machine operated by a dial calibrated from 1 to 10. Suspected gay men were shown black and white pictures of naked men and encouraged to fantasise about the pictures. They then received increasingly painful shocks. The next stage was to show the 'patient' Playboy centrefolds, described in glowing terms by the psychiatrist, with no shocks administered. Levin employed the same farcical process, using pictures of women counterposed with naked men, with those women deemed to have lesbian tendencies.

But it was not only homosexual 'deviance' that Levin and his unit treated. Also affected were various individuals who displayed their deviance in refusing to take up arms or to serve in the apartheid military. Those who made a public stand at the time of conscription were immediately designated unstable, and many were referred to Aubrey Levin. These were obviously not candidates for simple aversion therapy: they qualified for narco-analysis. This meant administering drugs such as sodium pentathol – the so-called 'truth' drug – which totally lowered the subject's inhibitions.

Levin admits to using narco-analysis, but only sparingly, and in cases where patients suffered severe post-traumatic stress. He implied that he had never used this therapy on people who were not severely disturbed. However, a military conscript referred to Levin after refusing to undergo military training has given a starkly different story. He was a normal young man when he reported for military training and declared that, on principle, he could not serve in the apartheid forces. The authorities referred him to the psychiatric unit and Aubrey Levin.

In an interview with the author, he told how Levin strapped him down and drip-fed him some kind of drug that made him feel drowsy and lose consciousness. It was only next day, again strapped down and with Levin standing over him, that he found out what had happened. Levin played back to him tape recordings of his uninhibited ravings, prompted by goading and questioning from the psychiatrist. His innermost thoughts, fantasies and fears were laid bare to be mocked and teased by Levin. He heard himself eventually 'howling like an animal'.

This process was repeated on several occasions. The victim was eighteen at the time, and neither his nor his parents' consent was sought for the treatment he underwent. When he finally emerged from what he still describes as a nightmare, he suffered the same disorientation mentioned by other Ward 22 patients. Years of therapy followed before he felt he had regained some degree of stability. But although he went on to complete a doctorate at university and became a newspaper editor, the nightmare never disappeared.

These serious allegations cried out to be scrutinised in depth. They never were. Just as equally serious charges of Levin's misconduct at the Fort England hospital near Grahamstown were not investigated. In many cases these accounts of gross human rights abuse amounted to the word of a patient, allegedly mentally unstable, against the word of a psychiatrist. But there were other staff present, people such as Trudi Grobler, whose evidence adds to a picture of depravity and barbarity, even torture, that betrays the Hippocratic oath.

The TRC never took advantage of the powers it had to delve into these allegations of abuse and gross impropriety. But then there were many areas that were opened up and, for one reason or another, were never examined by the TRC. Individuals, from lowly spies to assassins, blackmailers and the blackmailed, compromised teachers, judges, lawyers and civil servants, lie hidden within the fabric of a society where many of those who manipulated them, and know and can use their secrets, also remain at large.

This was a reality that would come back to haunt the TRC, almost disabling this creature of compromise that, for all its faults, at least revealed something of the horrors of the hidden past.

11

The poisonous past reaches into the TRC

The first year of the TRC was probably the most hectic in the lives of most commissioners and staff, more so because the internal tensions had not eased, with accusations of incompetence and racism endemic. It could scarcely be otherwise in such a pressured environment, peopled by individuals ranging from downright racist officials from the old order to resentful black nationalists, with every shade of attitude in between.

But work was being done at a surprising pace, despite the many obvious shortcomings. Information gleaned from the thousands of victims' statements was augmented by a variety of leads and insights from sometimes frightened, occasionally contrite and often cynically hostile amnesty applicants. While several important investigation reports were simply disregarded, other leads were followed up. As a result, more perpetrators stepped forward to apply for amnesty. Many of the initial leads came from Eugene de Kock, the last head of the death squad based at Vlakplaas. De Kock, probably correctly, saw himself as being set up as the patsy, the sacrificial lamb for all the evils of apartheid. He is still widely regarded as probably the only perpetrator to have 'come clean'.

Investigators took advantage of their status to delve into what was left of the documentary evidence of the past. By the end of the first year there were vast bundles of documents and scraps of paper to sort through. The sheer volume of material almost swamped the available facilities. There was too little control, and too many demands on the time of most officials. There were also the territorial battles and all the subterfuges used to hide errors and inadequacies that are found in any large corporation under pressure. In such an atmosphere, unconscious slights could run riot and assume political and racial connotations. Constant sniping from the National Party and other rightwing elements accused the TRC of bias and distortion.

Eager investigators took at face value the powers of search and seizure vested in the TRC. When they used a search warrant issued by a magistrate to raid the Youngsfield military base outside Cape Town, the outraged military lodged a strong protest with the TRC. This led to what investigations head Dumisa Ntsebeza later admitted was 'perhaps my biggest single mistake in the TRC'. He did not oppose the suggestion by the military – supported by his senior colleagues – that a 'nodal point' be established through which all military information would be channelled. This amounted to establishing a censor who would filter all information pertaining to the military and its activities. Only approved material would surface.

Early in the process, some international investigators left, privately expressing frustration at what they perceived as the blundering and amateurism around them. There were also allegations of corruption from one of the regional offices. One of the Gauteng investigators walked out when an attempt to establish a nationally coordinated but regionally based investigative framework was blocked by the national director. Because of the nature of the work, and of those who did it, much of the friction and distrust occurred within the investigative unit.

The fact that former senior BOSS agent Johan Breytenbach was employed as a head office investigator caused more than raised eyebrows. Dumisa Ntsebeza was horrified. He called Breytenbach into his office and spelled out his position. If Breytenbach so much as 'stepped an inch out of line', he would be out. They talked behind closed doors, since Ntsebeza did not want to be seen to be undermining Glenn Goosen, the national director who had made the appointment. But he also made it clear to Goosen that he thought the appointment was not wise.

In other quarters in the TRC and beyond, the hiring of Breytenbach was seen as confirmation that sinister forces were loose in the TRC. It was widely known that Breytenbach's CV proclaimed his security background. A cursory check would have revealed that he had been one of the senior apartheid operatives from the days of the notorious BOSS. He had resigned from the post-apartheid National Intelligence Agency the year before the establishment of the TRC, and set up a private security company in Pretoria. Within a year, at the time when it became clear that the TRC would be based in Cape Town, he moved to the city, apparently to establish a branch of his company, and applied to join the TRC as an investigator. His wife, Dumisa Ntsebeza learned, was based in the Cape Town offices of the NIA. The connection of his move and his background made him singularly inappropriate as a TRC investigator. Small wonder Frank Dutton had simply said: 'Don't touch.'

This appointment fanned the fires of suspicion that smouldered at all levels of the commission. In the seventh- and eighth-floor offices of the Cape Town block that housed the TRC, little remained secret for long. There were also racial overtones to many of the rumours and suspicions. Breytenbach was white and the man who had hired him was white. For many staff on the TRC, this was proof positive that foul forces were at play.

Paul van Zyl, who sat on the interview panel that appointed Breytenbach, justified the appointment as a 'calculated risk'. Glenn Goosen refused to discuss the matter when Piers Pigou, an investigator who had formerly served with the Independent Board of Inquiry, raised it in Gauteng. Pigou's argument was that Breytenbach could only be acceptable to the TRC 'if he brought something to the table'. Breytenbach had held such senior positions in the old security order that he had to have a mass of information about human rights abuses and who had committed them. 'I felt that unless he was going to come clean about his past, he shouldn't be with the TRC,' Pigou recalled later.

The Breytenbach appointment added to the legitimate fears that there were powerful elements that wished the TRC discredited, wound up or destroyed. The process was going too deep. There had been investigations initiated around the Trojan Horse incident, where police hidden in a crate on the back of a truck had shot and killed youths in Cape Town's Athlone. Wilson Magadla had opened inquiries into the March 1986 massacre of the 'Gugulethu seven'. Both had flushed out further amnesty applications. The National Party, the police and military were all claiming bias, and there were calls for the TRC to be shut down.

All of this increased the tensions within the commission, which were further boosted when a vital statement relating to the murder of the seven young activists in the township of Gugulethu disappeared. Information seemingly drawn from it, and which could have jeopardised the investigation, was then published in a Sunday newspaper. One of the people named as being involved was Johan Breytenbach; another was a Dutch investigator, Cees Koojmans. An inquiry was instituted and Breytenbach was suspended pending its outcome. The issue of his security clearance or lack of it then became a focal point.

Because of the kind of work they would be required to undertake, Dumisa Ntsebeza stated at the start of the recruitment process that the appointment of all members of the investigative unit should be subject to security clearance.

But, in another of the many omissions that were to plague the TRC, no formal process for vetting was put in place. Glenn Goosen disputed its validity. In a memorandum dated 8 January 1997 he noted: 'There is, as I understand it, some dispute as to whether it is a prerequisite that a security clearance be obtained by investigators.'

He went on to state that, as the 'nodal point in dealings with the NIA', he had been required to obtain 'Top Secret' clearance from the agency. He had 'identified' four other members of the unit, including Johan Breytenbach, as needing to apply for this classification. Although he had interviewed Breyten-bach, he could not 'recall whether the issue [of security clearance] was raised with him or not', but he remained supportive: 'Johan Breytenbach is a key member of the unit and I would prefer that he be at work.' In the event, the post-apartheid NIA did not grant Breytenbach a clearance and he left the employ of the TRC.

It was against this background that a time bomb landed on Dumisa Ntsebeza's desk in the form of an 'information note' (Inligtingsnota) delivered on 10 May 1997 by a very serious-looking John Lubbe, a captain seconded to the TRC from the police service. Lubbe said he had found the note in a police file while investigating the amnesty applications of three young men sentenced for the 30 December 1993 Heidelberg Tavern massacre in Cape Town. The attack, by a group of Apla gunmen on a bar mistakenly thought to be used by security personnel, had resulted in the deaths of four people, with five others badly injured. If Ntsebeza owned a white Audi sedan, then the note definitely implicated him. Dumisa Ntsebeza did own and drive such a car, and admitted as much as a stony-faced Lubbe handed over a document marked GEHEIM (Secret).

Ntsebeza picked it up, noting the date, 7 January 1994. He read it slowly, and with mounting disbelief. It claimed that on the night of the Heidelberg attack an eyewitness had identified his white Audi car, driven by a man answering his description, parked in a street in the Gugulethu township outside Cape Town. Young men had carried rifles wrapped in blue overalls from one car, identified as having been used in the attack, to the Audi. The clincher was the registration number of the white sedan: XA 12848. It was the number of Dumisa Ntsebeza's Umtata-registered car.

Ntsebeza dropped the papers on the desk, shook his head and, characteristically, burst out laughing. 'This is bullshit,' he exclaimed. Lubbe bridled. To him, this was no joke. In an attempt to explain, Ntsebeza pointed out that the document, compiled by a 'Captain J.J. Louw', was endorsed by General N.S.

Snyman. 'This is the man I sued on behalf of General Holomisa,' he said. 'So I am not surprised to see this.' General Snyman had given a statement to the Afrikaans-language newspaper *Rapport* in which he accused Holomisa of sheltering murderers. The Heidelberg killers were 'sitting and laughing' at the police because they enjoyed the protection of 'the Transkei military dictator, General Bantu Holomisa'. Holomisa had promptly summoned Ntsebeza and instructed him to launch an action for defamation against Snyman and *Rapport*.

There was no time to spell out the details. Ntsebeza saw no point in explaining that this was not the first occasion when his name had cropped up in similar official documents that were, effectively, licences to kill. What he did not realise was that Lubbe had already decided that he was guilty of involvement in the Heidelberg massacre.

When Ntsebeza, after copying the note, ordered Lubbe to pursue his investigations, he did not realise that the apartheid-era policeman would set out – as he later confessed – only to confirm the allegations against the TRC investigations head. Evidence to the contrary would simply be shelved. So Ntsebeza, with his copy of the information note in hand, called to see Tutu and Boraine. He knew that the mere existence of such a document, however ludicrous it might seem, could still prove an embarrassment. He wanted their guidance, and besides it was best that they were aware of the note and its contents.

'It's something that could come up,' he noted, 'and I wouldn't like a situation where that happened and you hadn't seen it.' The three men perused the document. It bore little resemblance to the facts that had emerged in the trial of three Apla members found guilty of the massacre and who had applied for amnesty to the TRC. The evidence had been that they dumped their stolen car in Gugulethu after disposing of the weapons they had used. Tutu concurred that it was nonsense; that since the note was written in 1994, it had obviously been an attempt to frame Ntsebeza. No action had been taken then or since.

At the very least, by not even questioning the lawyer, the police were guilty of negligence. Had there been any substance to the claim, they would have acted. It was not as if Ntsebeza had been in hiding. He had been very prominent, travelling between Cape Town and Umtata in his named white Audi sedan on legal business. At the time the note was dated, he was in Cape Town. That February he had returned to the city to attend Boraine's Dealing with the Past conference and to visit clients in the local Pollsmoor prison who had, coincidentally, been detained for questioning in relation to the Heidelberg attack. (They were subsequently released). Tutu agreed that it seemed suspicious for the note to turn up at a time when the TRC was under concerted attack from the NP and the security establishment, but none of the three senior commissioners thought any more about the matter. It was a single jolt in a bumpy ride. The vital armed forces hearings lay ahead, and there was much work to be done.

Another problem suddenly appeared when Tutu was diagnosed with prostate cancer. His trip to the United States for treatment would keep him out of South Africa for six to eight weeks. In his absence, Boraine took over, with Ntsebeza as deputy, but one important cog was now missing from a fragile machine.

During the weeks that followed, Lubbe made no attempt to inquire into the allegations made in the information note. According to his subsequent reports, he only tried – unsuccessfully – to interview the three Apla members imprisoned for the Heidelberg attack. On 24 July, one of the applicants for amnesty, Brian Madasi, finally agreed to speak to Lubbe. He confessed no knowledge of any white Audi or of the involvement of Dumisa Ntsebeza.

This information would only emerge some time after the TRC was thrown into turmoil next day. Dumisa Ntsebeza recalled later how an agitated Glenn Goosen burst into his office. The Johannesburg radio station, 702, was broadcasting the fact of Ntsebeza's involvement in the Heidelberg attack, he said. What should be done? The whole thing was 'getting out of hand'. Ntsebeza agreed, but he remembered later that he had insisted: 'Look, it's just one of those dirty tricks.' As it turned out, copies of the information note had been leaked not only to the radio station but to other media outlets and to the Johannesburg TRC office.

Ntsebeza realised that Alex Boraine was going to have to field a deluge of media queries. He and Goosen sought out the acting chairperson, and the three of them agreed a press release. In it, Boraine stated that the allegation about a car owned by Dumisa Ntsebeza being involved in the Heidelberg attack had surfaced on 10 May. Although Ntsebeza denied the allegation, and none of the amnesty applicants had mentioned his car, he had instructed that the inquiry should continue. He had also immediately informed both Tutu and Boraine and had 'recused himself entirely from the investigation'. This, they hoped, would put paid to the rumour and speculation. With hindsight, the hope was naive.

Boraine arranged for Lubbe to continue the investigation. Lubbe should report directly to Goosen, who would report to Boraine. None of the other commissioners were involved in this arrangement. There were no consultations and no official word. But, within the hothouse environment of the TRC a wave of facts and rumours quickly spread. The staff, as Tutu was later to note with regret, tended to be split along racial lines. White staff either thought Ntsebeza guilty or had strong doubts about him; black staff were virtually unanimous in their support for the embattled investigations unit head.

Several of the black TRC staff expressed deep concern that a white investigator – a policeman from the apartheid era – was investigating Ntsebeza. Not only that, but the investigator was reporting to a white director who in turn reported to a white deputy chairperson. The opposite side believed that there was no smoke without fire, insisted on the need for 'objectivity', and made several false assumptions about Ntsebeza's political views and background. In broad terms, the media reflected a similar divide.

The TRC chief executive, Biki Minyuku, only got to hear of the allegations after the radio broadcast on 25 July. When Glenn Goosen briefed him about the decisions taken, he objected to the idea of Goosen investigating his superior, and proposed that a small group of commissioners be appointed to evaluate the investigation. Goosen agreed, and in early September he relayed this proposal to both Tutu and Boraine, but nothing was done and the investigation went ahead without any additional oversight.

For Dumisa Ntsebeza it was the start of a nightmare. He felt himself trapped in a world where paranoia lurked at every turn. He had supplied an affidavit on 25 July explaining exactly where he had been during the time of the Heidelberg attack and who had been with him. He knew his car had not been taken by anyone, the police had not so much as mentioned any allegations to him, yet the whispers and the rumours persisted, and were not at all alleviated by the fierce support he also received. It merely showed that logic was not at issue. For example, no investigator from either the police or the TRC had checked with his partner, Nana Makaula, or with his host, the medical doctor Nandi Mbawu, under whose roof he had spent the night of 30 December 1993 when the Heidelberg attack took place.

He soon got to hear that Lubbe had traced Bennett Sibaya, the source of the claimed eyewitness statement that implicated him in the attack. Sibaya had stuck to his story. Confusion persists as to how Lubbe came to interview Sibaya by himself. Goosen told the subsequent inquiry, chaired by Judge Richard Goldstone, that he had instructed Lubbe to go with Wilson Magadla to interview Sibaya. Magadla remembered that he had asked to do the interview and had been told by Goosen to leave it to Lubbe. At any rate, Lubbe conducted the first interview with Sibaya on his own. Fellow policeman Deon Peterson kept watch in a car parked some distance away.

This was in clear breach of TRC practice, which endeavoured always to pair seconded police with other investigators. What is not in dispute is that Lubbe took with him to the interview a photograph of Dumisa Ntsebeza. Contrary to elementary investigative routine, he showed both the photograph and the original statement to Sibaya, asking him if he could recall the statement and identify the person in the photograph. Back at the office, Lubbe reported to Goosen and Magadla that Sibaya had not recognised the photograph, but had said he was sure he would recognise the Audi driver if he saw him face to face. Furthermore, not only had he confirmed his original statement; he had given more detail.

Magadla was astonished. What Lubbe had done was a gross breach of procedure. The veteran detective recalled later that he had protested about the way the investigation had been conducted. Goosen, however, seemed satisfied. 'Leave it to Lubbe,' he instructed. Magadla did not know that Boraine had instructed Lubbe to handle the matter and to report only to Goosen, who would report only to the deputy chairperson. Deeply concerned, not only about Lubbe's behaviour in effectively prompting a witness, but also about the embellishments to a statement added more than three years after the event, he decided, unofficially, to do some checking of his own.

Lubbe meanwhile noted the further evidence that to him proved Dumisa Ntsebeza had a case to answer. The first new point Sibaya recalled was that he had overheard one of the young men carrying weapons on the night of the Heidelberg attack mention that a cap had been left in the stolen car when the weapons were being transferred. But this evidence had emerged publicly during the trial of the Apla members sentenced for the Heidelberg massacre. Lubbe never checked this fact. Nor did he ask where Sibaya was at the time of the trial. Had he done so, he might have discovered that Bennett Sibaya had sat in the public gallery of the court while that evidence was being given.

The clincher for Lubbe, and for the growing horde baying for Ntsebeza's blood, was the map. Sibaya had apparently forgotten to mention it at the time, but he now recalled that he had picked up a piece of paper after witnessing the night-time transfer of arms. After the Audi had sped off, its brake lights illuminating the number plate, he had noticed a slip of paper lying on the ground. It had been dropped by one of the young men. He picked it up and saw that it was a roughly drawn map that included the names Hartleyvale stadium – which marks the turn-off to the Heidelberg Tavern – and Heidelberg.

The following day, Wilson Magadla interviewed Sibaya in isiXhosa. He found him to be a 'remarkably intelligent man' for someone professing to be a humble gardener with hardly any formal education. But Sibaya stuck to his story and seemed 'coherent'. Magadla reported as much to Goosen. However, he felt even more concerned, and not only about the embellishments, though these seemed strange to say the least. What particularly puzzled Magadla was Sibaya's insistence that he had seen and memorised the registration number of the car when the number plate was illuminated by the brake lights. Magadla found a similar Audi vehicle and tested Sibaya's claim. It was impossible. The brake lights simply did not illuminate the number plate. It was not proof positive that Sibaya was lying, but it raised more questions. Other black investigators fumed. Word leaked of the discrepancies between two statements made more than three years apart: how the later statement gave much more specific detail than did the first. This was a set-up, the black investigators muttered.

Goosen, in the meantime, was kept briefed by Lubbe. He saw nothing untoward in the additions to the original statement. Later he claimed that he was deeply involved at the time, in 'other pressing and time-consuming TRC matters'. The idea that one of the country's most prominent human rights lawyers would be openly involved in the transport of weapons, using his own quite distinctive car, did not strike him as incongruous. To black TRC staffers, the fact that the president of the Black Lawyers Association and council member of the Law Society in the Western Cape could be thought to be so stupid smacked of racism. As an advocate, Goosen had represented a military agent at the inquest into the murders of the 'Cradock Four'. At the very least, he should be aware of the dirty tricks perpetrated by the security forces. The fragile unity of the TRC was coming apart at the racial seams.

12

Accusations and fightbacks

Two weeks into August 1997, Dumisa Ntsebeza began to feel that unless he did something, he might be swamped. 'Drowned in bullshit,' as he put it later. A supposed investigation had set off a spate of rumour and conjecture, yet he had not been interviewed. Nor had Nana Makaula or Nandi Mbawu. If a genuine investigation was taking place, why had there not been even an elementary check on his whereabouts at the time of the Heidelberg massacre? That would surely put paid to much of the speculation.

He decided that he had better appoint a lawyer to act for him while he stuck it out at the TRC. The entire organisation was in flux. If the intention in planting the allegations had been to derail the commission, it seemed to be succeeding. On 11 August he penned a memo to Glenn Goosen mentioning that he had been troubled by the publicity relating to the alleged involvement of his car in the Heidelberg attack. He was keen not to interfere with the investigation, but felt that 'I do not want to prejudice my own rights'. He asked if he could have copies of the report that implicated him in the Heidelberg attack and Snyman's note that repeated the allegation, plus a transcript of the radio broadcast stating that his car was used.

Glenn Goosen was on holiday at the time. When he returned seven days later, his reply was coldly official. Although he addressed it 'Dear Dumisa', using the first name Ntsebeza had signed off with, he eschewed the casual 'Regards' used by his boss in favour of a formal, Yours faithfully, Adv.

(Advocate) Glenn Goosen. His memo noted that he was 'pleased to be advised' that Ntsebeza had decided to retain counsel. 'As you are aware,' he went on, 'we generally do not provide information relating to our investigations to persons implicated until we are in a position to do so without compromising either our investigations or the sources of our information.' Ntsebeza's 'legal advisors' should communicate with the legal officer.

'Persons implicated.' Ntsebeza was furious. He might have been 'implicated' in a scurrilous report from a dubious source in very strange circumstances. But here was the man in charge of investigating the matter referring to him as a 'person implicated', having failed to check elementary facts. Perhaps it was time to call it a day and resign. But to do that would lend credibility to the accusations. Already the TRC had been damaged. No, he decided: he would stay and fight.

It was no easy decision. Senior people within the TRC were viewing his presence as disruptive in itself. There were murmurings that perhaps, if he left, the TRC could return to normal; that it could survive his resignation. But other voices argued that his departure would spell the success of the exercise to derail the TRC.

In late September Dumisa Ntsebeza and research head Charles Villa-Vincencio were scheduled to travel to Britain to attend a Burying the Past conference in Oxford. On 26 September, shortly before he was due to leave, Ntsebeza was unofficially informed that Glenn Goosen had completed his investigations. A summary of his findings had been submitted to Tutu, along with a recommendation that outside authorities – which Ntsebeza took to mean the police – should further investigate the matter. He had still not been interviewed, either by Goosen or Lubbe, his alibi had not been checked, and yet it was assumed he had a prima facie case to answer. To cap it all, he received a telephone call from a reporter on the Afrikaans-language newspaper *Die Burger*, which had heard that Goosen's recommendation was that he resign from the TRC.

Ntsebeza was outraged. He wrote at once to his lawyer, Christine Qunta, with whom he had shared a legal partnership before entering the TRC, instructing her to demand a copy of the full investigative report. He had been defamed and insulted. Now he would fight back. At least, he reassured himself, he had the support of Tutu and Boraine. They had never retracted their statement of May in which they agreed that the allegations were nonsense. What rang false was that Lubbe had resigned after handing in his report. When he went, he took with him all the documentation relating to his investigation. It was never returned.

But Dumisa Ntsebeza was exhausted. The pressure was starting to tell. He sometimes felt he was merely going through the motions, pushing paper. In this state he made a mistake. At a commission meeting, various topics in an agenda were placed on the table for discussion. Many went through on the nod. One that did so was a proposal from Glenn Goosen that the investigative unit be closed down – even though the life of the TRC had just been extended by the government. Dumisa Ntsebeza did not notice the motion; did not even recall it being put. When he realised what had happened, he immediately called a halt to the process.

This was to result in some of the most bitter arguments inside the TRC. Perhaps with justification, Ntsebeza saw the move to shut down the investigative unit, whatever the rationale, as an attempt to sideline and remove him, to amputate a troublesome limb. In any event, closing down the unit when it could still take on new cases until December meant that many investigations would be curtailed. The investigative function would be left to the amnesty committee, and would relate only to amnesty applications. He could not allow this. He instructed Goosen to canvass the opinions of the heads of the investigative unit in the various regions and to open up discussion on the issue. He would deal with the matter when he returned from his overseas trip.

When he got back he was pitched headfirst into controversy. The closure proposal had gone ahead in his absence. He had not been consulted and nor had Wilson Magadla. The regional heads had been presented with a fait accompli. 'Their views have not accounted for anything,' he thundered in a memo copied to virtually anyone who mattered within the TRC hierarchy. This was 'an unacceptable method of consultation', he said. It was 'sinister and very manipulative'. He highlighted the words 'unacceptable' and 'sinister'. With hindsight, he felt he should have taken a more measured approach, but at the time he was angry and frustrated. He had just received a formal notification that he, 'as a person implicated in the [amnesty] application' of the Heidelberg gunmen, could be present at the hearing.

What Ntsebeza did not know was that the evidence leader of the amnesty committee, another lawyer, Paddy Prior, had that day requested further investigation. The request, as Goosen later remarked, was 'not through the usual channels'. But there was nothing sinister in this. Prior had merely asked one of his assistants, who asked Zenariah Barends, the head of the Western Cape unit. She assigned Mark Killian. What specially concerned Prior was that R250,000 in reward money had been paid out. Had Sibaya received any of this? On 13 October, investigator Killian began checking the evidence collected by Lubbe. The police would not tell him who had been paid reward money – most of it was in fact paid to two informants, listed in confidential records as James Dlamini and Nicollas Phongolo of Sterkspruit in the Eastern Cape. But in less than ten days Killian was able to show that Sibaya's statements did not hold water. Even the streets in Gugulethu that he mentioned did not tally with reality. Lubbe had simply never checked.

Dumisa Ntsebeza did not know about Killian's investigation. He only became aware of its general conclusions when several of the black investigators hurriedly whispered what they knew about it to Qunta during the Heidelberg amnesty hearing. The notice to him, signed by fellow commissioner Mary Burton, duly informed him that he had the right to be present at the hearing and to be 'represented by a legal representative'. He could also 'testify, adduce evidence and submit any article to be taken into consideration'. He urged Christine Qunta to 'get cracking'. She did. In just three days she learned a lot about Bennett Sibaya. He spoke fluent English and several other languages, had travelled widely, owned valuable property, and was negotiating to buy still more. Whatever he was, he was not the simple, ill-educated gardener he affected to be.

Dumisa Ntsebeza scarcely had time to think about such matters. The battle over restructuring the investigative function of the TRC had become increasingly bitter. Goosen had taken especial umbrage at the use of the word 'sinister' in Ntsebeza's memo. He noted that the restructuring proposal had the support of TRC chief executive Biki Minyuku. Ntsebeza would still not countenance the closure of the unit. Goosen announced his resignation.

This added grist to the media mill. Alex Boraine attempted to mediate. He brought Goosen and Ntsebeza together and Ntsebeza apologised profusely for having overreacted. In his own terms, he grovelled, because he felt that the TRC would be harmed if the resignation went ahead. On 17 October Goosen responded to the overtures by way of a memo to Minyuku. He acknowledged Ntsebeza's expressions of regret, but maintained that the memorandum he objected to was 'a culmination of similar actions'. 'Unfortunately his regret does not remove the very real consequences of the memo and as such my position as national director remains untenable.'

The media were having a field day reporting on the scene in the TRC in the run-up to the 'Heidelberg hearings'. These began calmly on 27 October 1997, with Dumisa Ntsebeza in attendance. Also in the room were the surviving victims and their families, along with hovering photographers, television cameras and journalists, and the Democratic Party's Dene Smuts. The tragedy and heartbreak that emerged were by then standard media fare. What the pack was waiting for was the evidence of an apparently humble gardener that was likely to topple Dumisa Ntsebeza and perhaps even the TRC.

*

The event, when it came, did not disappoint the media. The drama would dominate public consciousness. It would also edge out disturbing evidence given by one of the victims, Roland Palm. Palm was in the Heidelberg Tavern on the fateful night of 30 December 1993 – ironically to discuss another case of a probable police frame-up, another of the countless routine injustices, reeking of racism and corruption, that still litter the penal system. His son Brandon had been sentenced in 1992 to twelve years' imprisonment for robbery and assault. Brandon protested his innocence, but the court held that if he was innocent then the police must be lying. This the judiciary would not accept. The word of a policeman with eighteen years' service carried a lot more weight than that of an eighteen-year-old security guard, even if some of the evidence appeared contradictory. That the policeman was white in what was still effectively an apartheid court, and the security guard was not, played a definite if unquantifiable role.

Roland Palm was bitter after the TRC hearing into the Heidelberg massacre. He had given his evidence, laid open his ongoing hurt, and made just one request for reparation: that the case against his son be investigated. Brandon's jailing had split asunder a family already under strain. Roland Palm had grown obsessed with seeking justice. A humble working man, he had petitioned the high and the mighty, demanding and pleading, all to no avail. The TRC seemed his last chance, but his plea was drowned in the media frenzy surrounding Dumisa Ntsebeza.

Palm's main supporter in the battle to free his son and clear his name had been his daughter Rolanda. Twenty-two years old, a recently qualified primary school teacher, she had died in the hail of bullets that tore through the tavern on the night of 30 December. He and his daughter had walked to the Heidelberg from the family home nearby to discuss what else they could do about Brandon's case.

Some of the evidence in Brandon's case indicates that he may have been the victim of a particularly cynical attempt to extort R500,000 from the security company for which he worked. He was accused of brutally beating a woman and stealing her gold wedding ring. According to forensic evidence, the woman had fought back against her attacker or attackers and must have scratched them badly, since there were traces of skin beneath her fingernails. Brandon bore no scratches and the skin under the woman's fingernails was not his. His only possible link to the crime was the fact that he had a gold ring wrapped in a sock in his bag. He had bought it for his sister's twenty-first birthday, and was keeping it with him until the end of the month when he could afford to have it engraved.

By the time it was clear that the ring was not the one stolen, Brandon was already under arrest and had been asked to sign documents. It was apparently assumed that he could not read and he was told merely to sign, but he noticed that the documents appeared to be some form of admission of guilt and a claim against the company for which he had worked. He refused to sign. And so he went to court, was sentenced, and was unlikely to gain remission because he refused to admit guilt and express remorse. It was this desperate problem that father and daughter were discussing when the Apla gunmen opened fire. 'Get down,' Roland yelled and he saw Rolanda fall. Under the table he reached out and pressed her down as a grenade clattered across the floor. He counted to ten, waiting for the explosion. When nothing happened, he looked up. There was blood on Rolanda's shoulder.

Enraged, Roland leapt up and ran to the door, determined to see who had done this. There was no sign of the gunmen, but just around the corner he noticed a van – a 'mellow yellow', a police vehicle. Thinking the police had already arrived, he ran back to check on his daughter. She was lying very still, and only then did it dawn on him that she might not be alive. He knelt beside her, lifted her head and desperately felt for her pulse. There was no pulse. In his grief he rushed from the tavern. He had to get home to tell his wife. As he turned right at the corner he was aware of the van parked across the road. Behind the wheel was a person in a white shirt. Something white. He did not pay attention. It was only when he was a block away that the thought struck him, briefly, that it was strange that the police had not stopped him. It was, he recalled years later, only a fleeting thought. He raced to his home and sobbed out the story to his wife.

Several days later, a still shaken Roland Palm received a visit from Superintendent Des Segal, investigating officer for the Heidelberg attack. He came to take a statement, but when Roland Palm mentioned having seen a police van close to the Heidelberg just after the attack, Segal told him that he must have been mistaken. When Palm insisted on what he had seen, Segal at first put forward the possibility that the van had been in the vicinity and had been radioed to attend. 'Then why didn't they go in to the tavern?' Palm remembered asking. Segal blurted something about the police perhaps having been told there was a bomb in the building. This was odd. 'If they thought there was a bomb, why didn't they stop me when I came out?' Palm demanded. Segal looked uneasy. 'You were drunk,' he said. 'You must have been drunk. You were seeing things.' But he completed the statement, got Palm to sign it – and left telling Myra Palm that her husband must have been very drunk on the night of the attack.

The Apla trial came and went and Roland Palm was not called to give evidence. Once again Segal informed Myra that Roland had obviously been drunk. Besides, he could not be used as a witness because if he gave evidence he would 'let the suspects walk'. Rage at his helplessness soon gave way to depression. Both Roland and Myra Palm – she blamed him for both the jailing of their son and the death of their daughter – suffered bouts of acute anxiety. Despite intensive therapy, he was unable to shake off feelings of rage and guilt that still stalked him years later.

He followed the Apla trial closely and what he learned intensified his anger and frustration. He noted that only three men stood trial, when the police admitted that six had taken part in the attack. This fact and the circumstances surrounding it were to puzzle TRC investigators nearly three years later. Like Roland Palm, they too noted with interest that Des Segal, the investigating officer in the Heidelberg case, and another policeman, Mike Huysamer, had died in a car accident on 9 May 1997. In the car were found an RPG rocket launcher, an AK47 rifle and other illegal weaponry and ammunition. Evidence so far unpublished indicates that Segal and Huysamer were ferrying weapons and ammunition from a cache on a farm near the town of Worcester to a new secret depot in the Ceres area when they died. Their orders came from a senior police officer who feared that word of the cache had leaked to investigators associated with the TRC.

What Palm did not know and the TRC investigators did was that Segal had been involved in at least one controversial killing of a suspected 'terrorist'. They also knew that although the fatal accident had occurred in the rural area outside Ceres, the controversial Western Cape police chief Leonard Knipe had attended it. Knipe, who saw the new century in as national head of criminal investigations, played a controversial role in the initial investigations of cases like that of the 'Gugulethu Seven' killings. His findings in favour of the police gave him a reputation as the 'sweeper' for official acts of murder and mayhem. In 2002, having retired on a pension from the police force, Knipe was an 'associate' of the private investigations agency Fivaz and Associates, set up by former police commissioner General George Fivaz.

Such matters beyond the ken or interest of Roland Palm. All that concerned him was that the media clamour that had erupted, especially on the last day of the Heidelberg hearings, had apparently drowned out his own voice. 'All I know is that my daughter is dead. My son is alive, but he sits in jail for something he didn't do. I don't want money. I just want justice,' he said as Brandon entered his tenth year behind bars.

There was considerable criticism later that the cross-examination and the drama of the Sibaya evidence swamped what was supposed to be the focus of the event, the victims and their suffering. Boraine was one of those who expressed their sorrow at what some observers more bluntly categorised as a 'media circus'. Dumisa Ntsebeza, much against his will, stood at its centre. It could not have been otherwise. The future of the whole TRC process was at stake, let alone his own character and career. Christine Qunta came into the hearings bristling with anger. She had discovered a great deal about Bennett Sibaya, and she wanted to expose the man who had become a tool for the possible demolition of the TRC. If Dumisa Ntsebeza fell on the basis of Sibaya's claims, the National Party and the securocrats would have won. The pain and public anguish of thousands would come to nothing.

When Sibaya took his seat, his head was bowed and his eyes downcast. He listened patiently to the interpreted questions and responded softly in isiXhosa. He was the epitome of the humble servant, and was accepted as such by most of the white observers. When Christine Qunta rose to question Sibaya, liberal sensitivities were shredded.

Qunta tore into Sibaya. None of the journalists had bothered to check the truth of the Sibaya claims, although information was not hard to find. Qunta had the information and she used it. As journalist and author Antjie Krog was later to admit, the white staff, together with the white journalists, were dumbfounded. Krog noted later how Qunta, 'climbs into Sibaya in a way that leaves most of us speechless'. The reason, she told her readers, was that 'Through the Truth Commission we have come to accept that poor people seldom have reason to lie, whereas the well dressed rich often have every reason you can think of.'

Blind to the background and echoing her cohorts, Krog criticised Qunta for her use of 'sophisticated English' when addressing Sibaya. Throughout, Sibaya did not falter. He listened through his headphones and responded only to the isiXhosa translations. He remembered clearly, he said, the number of the car he had seen: 'XA twelve-eight, four-eight.' Ntsebeza's Audi.

Essentially patronising sympathy rallied to Sibaya. Angry gut feeling fell behind Ntsebeza and Qunta. The argument was deeply emotional. When the lawyer produced evidence that the gardener owned upmarket property, that he was negotiating to buy more, and that his original statement to the police had been in flawless English, she was simply disbelieved or wholly supported. Almost without exception the matter was seen in black and white, in terms both of fact and pigmentation.

Sitting among the mainly white TRC staffers at the time was Pumla Gobodo-Madikizela, a woman from Cala whom Dumisa Ntsebeza had recommended to the TRC. She grew more and more dismayed as she listened to those around her. All seemed convinced that Dumisa was implicated. Perhaps he might have been, she thought, but not in the way they supposed. She realised that these white staffers had no experience of the other side of the apartheid divide. They did not understand what it was like; that one did not question a known comrade who asked for a room for the night, or the loan of a car. And Dumisa Ntsebeza was an activist and a firm friend of those fighting the system. Perhaps he had become involved in this way; had lent his car without knowing how it might be used.

As a 'homegirl', Gobodo-Madikizela decided to take preventive action on behalf of her beleaguered 'homeboy'. She sought out Archbishop Desmond Tutu and pointed out what he must surely know: that comrades might lend their cars to others without knowing how they were used. Perhaps the archbishop should speak to Dumisa Ntsebeza. Tutu listened impassively, but turned down the suggestion. 'Dumisa must live with the consequences of his own choices,' he said.

It was a disconcerted Pumla Gobodo-Madikizela who telephoned Dumisa Ntsebeza at home that evening to tell him what she had done. He listened, speechless, until fury overwhelmed him and he told her through half-clenched teeth: 'I said I was not involved and I was not involved. There are better ways that I would have found to be involved, but that is not the level at which I operate.' There was silence at the other end as he put down the telephone.

Even Pumla Gobodo-Madikizela apparently felt he had a case to answer, and Tutu, with his comment about living with one's choices, might think so too. Only minutes before, reviewing in his mind the first day of the hearing, he had felt that, on balance, it had gone well. Sibaya was still playing whatever role it was he had chosen, but the evidence had mounted that he was not what he seemed at first sight. With Pumla's call his spirits declined again. Worse was to come.

Next morning the newspapers were full of the news that a humble gardener had identified the car owned by Truth Commissioner Ntsebeza as being involved in the transportation of weapons used in the Heidelberg killings. The spotlight, which had never been far from Ntsebeza, now shone fully on the commissioner – on what was perceived as his probable downfall, and with it perhaps the downfall of the TRC process.

When the hearing broke for lunch, Dumisa Ntsebeza made his way back to his office. There was a message from the man who had appointed him, President Nelson Mandela. He had returned from Scotland and wanted Ntsebeza to telephone him. With fearful anticipation, Ntsebeza punched in the number. The voice at the other end informed him politely that the president was resting from his journey and could not be disturbed. Ntsebeza should telephone again later. It was an even more anxious Dumisa Ntsebeza who made his way back to the hearing that afternoon, but there was some good news waiting. Mark Killian's investigation had exonerated him. It showed Lubbe's investigation to be, at the very least, shoddy and biased. This information would eventually come into the open. In the meantime the hearing continued.

Lubbe had also omitted to mention to the amnesty committee that he had shown a photograph of Dumisa Ntsebeza to Sibaya and that Sibaya had failed to recognise it. Had this fact been known, the farce that followed might have been avoided. As it was, Sibaya was asked if he recognised the driver of the white Audi he claimed to have seen on the night of 30 December 1993.

Sibaya shuffled to his feet and moved across the room towards the desk where the amnesty committee members sat. 'Looks like him,' he muttered, indicating committee member Ntsiki Sandi. Titters of relieved and nervous laughter coursed around the room as Sibaya, nodding thoughtfully, shuffled towards the back of the hearing room to where Dumisa Ntsebeza sat. Some paces from the TRC commissioner he stopped, wagged his finger at Ntsebeza, and murmured: 'It's him.' There was uproar. In breathless prose, Antjie Krog remembered the incident in her personal account of the TRC: 'An excited babble reverberates around the room; every journalist knows this is drama at its best.'

Which was just what the display amounted to. It was pure theatrical titillation. Given the evidence, even to that point, there was no fact to confirm Sibaya's performance. But it was the drama that focused journalistic minds. The media pack leapt on the story and discarded sense. Several of their number did not even wait until the hearing was completed. Those who did, apparently failed to understand the importance of the ruling that Dumisa Ntsebeza's affidavit about his whereabouts on the night of 30 December 1993 was admitted on an exculpatory basis. What this meant in simple terms was that the two judges, Hassan Mall and Andrew Wilson, and the advocate, Ntsiki Sandi, who made up the amnesty committee for the hearing, accepted Ntsebeza's statement about where he had been. So too did the evidence leader, Advocate Paddy Prior, representing the interests of the victims. Sibaya's evidence was dismissed.

Dene Smuts, the Democratic Party MP, had stayed the course, but when she left the hearing she promptly issued a press statement calling for the resignation of Dumisa Ntsebeza. Mud had been flung and it stuck. Ntsebeza had been pointed out in a highly dramatic fashion. Mundane facts could not compete with such excitement. Against the advice of some colleagues, Dumisa Ntsebeza called a press conference. He spelled out the facts and announced: 'I will not walk. This is nonsense. I have work to do and I am not going anywhere.' It was a bold performance. By then anger had replaced the shock of having Sibaya point him out.

Ntsebeza got home in time to see his defiant performance on the main television news. For better or worse, he had made his stand. He picked up the telephone, punched in Mandela's number, and the call was quickly answered. The deep, slightly gravelly tones were unmistakable. Ntsebeza introduced himself, but before he could say any more, Mandela spoke. 'Sewundiphendule [You have already given your answer] Dumisa,' he said. 'I saw you now on TV. I was worried that you would get angry and resign.' He felt 'that gardener' was clearly lying and was glad the commissioner was not going. As to those who demanded his resignation, Mandela was concise: 'They can go to hell.'

Dumisa Ntsebeza was elated. He had been legally vindicated, the president had supported him and, with Boraine in Denmark and Tutu on his way to Lesotho, he was about to become acting chair of the TRC once again – on his forty-eighth birthday. The tide, he felt, was turning. But the first telephone call that next morning was not to wish him happy birthday or to pledge support or congratulate him. A businesslike Archbishop Tutu called from Lesotho. He was disinterested in what Mandela had said and reminded a suddenly deflated Ntsebeza that he, Tutu, was still the chair of the TRC.

Tutu was alarmed by what was happening. His media director, John Allen, had informed him about the growing acrimony among the staff. This was the 'OJ Simpson syndrome', white against black. It was tearing the TRC apart. Given Ntsebeza's position, it might be best if the head of the investigations unit stepped down and took leave until the amnesty committee had 'cleared up the matter'. Allen had drafted a press release. It would be sent to Dumisa for approval.

Ntsebeza was dumbstruck. Then he asked: 'What about the others?' He felt the other commissioners should also be involved. After all, the TRC was a collective. But Tutu was adamant that the agreement should be between the two of them. If Ntsebeza refused to take leave, Tutu would have to call an emergency meeting of the commission. This would look bad and it would mean 'more of us telling you to take leave'. Tutu's decision stood. Ntsebeza must go until things were resolved. In the meantime, the archbishop said, he would not be contactable in Lesotho.

Ntsebeza suddenly felt very tired and, as he later explained, 'sick of the whole business'. But he got no chance to even think of throwing in the towel. His partner Nana had heard his side of the conversation, and when he tried to explain that perhaps, on balance, he should consider Tutu's suggestion, she exploded. 'No way,' she snapped. 'You are not stepping down.' In the ensuing shouting match she pointed out that Tutu had no authority just to ask him to go on leave 'like you are his little boy'. Her husband was stung by the remark, but he conceded that to go on leave would be a tacit admission of guilt, and portrayed as such in the media. He agreed that he would not take up the archbishop's suggestions; that he would 'fight this thing all the way'. But he still wanted to consult with his brother Lungisile, whom he regarded as extremely level-headed and a political colleague to boot.

Lungisile refused even to discuss any pros and cons. His answer was a firm no to taking leave. Let there be an emergency meeting of the commission and let the whole matter be aired. Dumisa was relieved, but still felt he should sound out one of the other commissioners who was also a man of the cloth, Bongani Finca. The cleric from the Eastern Cape was sympathetic. 'We have been embarrassed this whole week,' he said. 'But what are we if we cannot function as a collective?'

Dumisa Ntsebeza felt confusion and doubt evaporate. He was in a fighting mood. He telephoned Christine Qunta to update her. She was furious. 'I am your legal representative,' she almost shouted down the line. 'If they want to make suggestions and proposals, they should speak to me. If they carry on, we'll see them in court'.

While Ntsebeza waited for the promised draft press release to be delivered, the telephone rang again. It was Pippa Green, a journalist with the *Sunday Independent*, whom he knew and respected. She came straight to the point: 'Look Dumisa, if you were involved, just tell me.' Dumisa invited her round to discuss the issue. While he was waiting for her the press release arrived from John Allen. There was also a telephone call from Alex Boraine in Denmark. Because of the serious situation, he intended to cut short his stay and come back. He implied that he had not spoken to Tutu. He would contact Ntsebeza as soon as he arrived, and over the weekend they could 'get our ducks in a row'. Ntsebeza agreed to the meeting.

He turned his attention to the press release, which took the form of an official statement from the chairperson of the TRC. It stated that Tutu believed all the correct procedures had been followed in dealing with the allegations against Dumisa Ntsebeza. It concluded:

> Out of consideration to the sensitivities of the victims and survivors of this particular attack, I have today asked Dumisa to take leave until the matter of the allegations which have been levelled at him have been resolved. I want to repeat, and emphasise very strongly, that this does not constitute a judgement or opinion on the allegations, but is a step taken out of respect for the feelings of the people at the centre of this process – the victims and survivors. And it is a mark of

Dumisa's dedication and commitment to the process that he has accepted my advice.

Calmly, Ntsebeza picked up the telephone and called John Allen. 'Tear it up,' he said. All copies of the press release should be destroyed. 'I am not going to resign or take leave,' he added. Within an hour, Tutu was on the line from Lesotho. A special meeting of the TRC would be called for Monday morning. Dumisa Ntsebeza should be present.

Had she known of the chain of events that morning, Pippa Green might have been surprised at how controlled Dumisa Ntsebeza seemed. She spent most of the day with him, going over various aspects of his life and the strange circumstances of the Sibaya allegations. He then settled down to a relatively quiet weekend. Boraine did not contact him again, so he lined up his ducks by himself, running through his mind what he should say when – as he must – he came to address his fellow commissioners.

13

Vindication and afterthoughts

When Dumisa Ntsebeza arrived for the special TRC meeting on the Monday morning, most of the commissioners were already there. Tutu began the proceedings. He said he had first heard of the accusation against Dumisa Ntsebeza when he had returned from the United States in August. He had recommended that Dumisa take leave of absence. Under the circumstances, this was the only course.

Dumisa Ntsebeza remembers that he felt remarkably calm as he began his response. He would simply speak his mind. He did, for two hours. He started by pointing out that both Tutu and Boraine had been informed of the allegations in May. 'These men knew in May that there was this note. Who brought it to them? I brought it to them. I said I need your guidance. I could not call a TRC meeting and I do not blame them for not calling a meeting. They saw it as the nonsense that it is.' The tragedy was that 'we are doing in November what we should have been doing in May'. He took up the issue point by point, admitted his own mistakes, but maintained that Tutu and Boraine had the responsibility to bring the matter before the commission. 'Even then they took the position that the police should have done something about it . . . I can't understand that you must sit here while the archbishop and Boraine take the position that I am guilty.' All of them had seen, in case after case, how dirty tricks had ruined people. What would happen to the TRC if he were to go? 'You will be deader than a doornail.' It would be said that there was no smoke without fire: it would be all that the remnants of the old regime would need.

What particularly riled Ntsebeza was the fact that the TRC was usurping the role of its own amnesty committee. Two judges and an advocate were evaluating the evidence and would be presenting their finding in due course. 'So what is the hurry?' he asked. He could not resist a parting shot. Noting that 'the two leaders here are men of the cloth', he ventured that there might be a similarity between what was happening and the biblical story of Abraham being willing to sacrifice his own son in order to atone. For Isaac there had been divine intervention, and Abraham had been led to a bush behind which was a lamb to be sacrificed. 'I hope there is a bush here – and a lamb as well,' he said.

Tutu was businesslike. 'I stand by what I said, but give us time to discuss the matter.' Dumisa Ntsebeza acknowledged the instruction, left the room, and he took the elevator to the eighth floor. As he walked down the corridor to his office he passed knots of people, whispering, glancing. He didn't pause, strode into the office, closed the door and slumped into the chair behind the desk. He felt strangely elated. He had acquitted himself well in an arena in which he had often felt alien and uncomfortable. He had fought a good round, and if the fight continued he would take it on to the courts. It was not just a matter of personal vindication. He had been targeted to sink the TRC and discredit its all too few disclosures.

What Dumisa Ntsebeza did not know as he slumped into his chair, was that another leading anti-apartheid figure, the poet and performance artist, Mzwakhe Mbuli, was facing a similar, although much more serious dilemma. In the same week that Ntsebeza had so dramatically been pointed out by Sibaya, Mzwakhe Mbuli had been arrested for robbery. Four years later he was, as Ntsebeza had been twenty years earlier, still in prison awaiting an appeal. This was eventually rejected and, in 2003, he was about to enter his seventh year of a thirteen-year sentence.

Mbuli, known as the 'peoples' poet' had, like Ntsebeza, been on a security police 'hit list' in the 1980s. A Vlakplaas operative, Kobus Klopper, who appeared before the TRC, admitted this. He also admitted to having planted explosives and hand grenades in Mbuli's home. Klopper was a friend of the policeman who arrested Mbuli on a charge of having robbed a bank in broad daylight on 28 October 1997.

The circumstances of that arrest and the subsequent trial, including refusals of bail, triggered a campaign for the release of Mbuli. Started by Mbuli's

London-based music agent, Gill Lloyd, it gained the support of a number of prominent individuals, including the Democratic Party veteran Helen Suzman and Dumisa Ntsebeza.

Mbuli and two friends were sentenced to thirteen years in prison by Judge Piet van der Walt who also turned down Mbuli's appeal against conviction. He did admit that the police investigation was 'shoddy'. But he also found that, if he were to believe Mbuli's evidence, then he would have to come to the conclusion that the police had been involved in fabricating the case. This, Judge van der Walt felt, was 'unlikely'.

How shoddy the investigation had been was very clear. There was no forensic evidence and the sole witness who identified Mbuli admitted that she had done so on the basis of having seen his photograph in a newspaper and had not seen him at the scene of the crime. The whole affair was a farce. Mbuli, a political activist, and the target of an apparent assassination attempt in 1996 also had a perfectly reasonable explanation for what had happened.

He had agreed to work with the Swaziland police to try to establish who was behind obvious drug smuggling and gun running from Swaziland. Shortly before his arrest, he relayed this information, and his suspicion that high-ranking South African police officers and government officials were involved, to an official he felt he could trust. He was seeking more solid facts when he received an anonymous telephone call. The caller said he had some very important information and instructed Mbuli to drive to the Waverley shopping centre in Pretoria. The caller would make himself known in the parking lot of the shopping centre.

Mbuli and two friends duly drove to the parking lot where a man approached the car and thrust a paper bag through the window before running off. Mbuli tried to follow and, while driving around the shopping centre looking for his contact, was stopped by the police. In the car they found the bag and, inside it, a pistol and R13,000, apparently the proceeds of a bank robbery.

Neither Mbuli's nor his friends' fingerprints were found on the bag, the pistol or the money. None of the staff at the bank that had been robbed identified any of the three men as having been involved. In the case of Mbuli, a tall, well-built man whose face was known throughout the country, this was particularly odd. The video surveillance camera usually in use at the bank had also not been functioning on that day.

It all added up, as Ntsebeza was later to comment, to being remarkably similar to so many cases that had passed before the TRC. It also had echoes of the nearly successful attempt in 1976 to 'frame' the anti-apartheid activist Peter Hain. Hain, who went on to become a minister in Britain's Labour government, was also arrested on a charge of bank robbery. On that occasion, the South African security police used a look-alike to stage the robbery in the London suburb of Putney after ensuring that Hain was in the area. A South African agent anonymously tipped off the police that Hain had snatched £490 from the bank and fled. What the South Africans had failed to check was that Hain had changed his hairstyle. The look-alike therefore looked very much like Peter Hain had looked only weeks earlier. But within two hours, Peter Hain was arrested and charged. He was acquitted in the Old Bailey in April of 1976 and went on to write of the experience in the book, *A Putney Plot?*

Dumisa Ntsebeza's brief reverie was interrupted only minutes after he returned to his office when Wilson Magadla burst in. The old detective was grinning from ear to ear as he slapped both palms onto the desk. 'I can't believe what's happened,' he said. 'Sibaya! Sibaya has been trying to get hold of the archbishop all morning. He wants to come in. To apologise. To clear your name.' Right at that moment, three investigators were on their way in to the office with Bennett Sibaya.

Dumisa Ntsebeza sat bolt upright, his mouth open. Then he began to smile. Magadla had no time to say more before the summons came to return to the emergency meeting. The same groups of staff were still hovering and whispering, but most were smiling too. They had seen Magadla race into Ntsebeza's office, and the word had soon spread, both that the commissioners had reached a decision and that Sibaya was on his way in.

Ntsebeza took the stairs to the seventh floor and resumed his seat in the commission meeting. Tutu had the floor. To the applause of the commissioners, he stated that the TRC felt it would be improper for Dumisa to step down. But an independent inquiry would be necessary.

Just at that point, Lavinia Crawford-Browne sidled up to Tutu and whispered in his ear. Tutu thanked her and turned back to the commissioners. Bennett Sibaya, he said, was in his office. 'I don't know what he has to say, but it appears he wants to clear Dumisa's name.'

That was indeed Sibaya's purpose. He said he had tried to indicate at the amnesty hearing that he was under pressure to lie. That was why he had first pointed out Ntsiki Sandi. But it was only after learning that the security policeman Des Segal was dead – killed in an accident with a load of illegal weapons in his car – that he knew it was safe to tell the truth. Segal was a brutal man with a reputation as a killer. According to Sibaya, it was Segal who had beaten him and then coached him in the evidence he might have to give in order to implicate Dumisa Ntsebeza in the Heidelberg massacre.

Sibaya apologised to Tutu and Ntsebeza. The story he told had a ring of truth, but it was also confused and confusing. He appeared reluctant to implicate anyone other than Desmond Segal, who was dead, in any questionable activity. Significantly, he failed to mention that Captain John Lubbe had shown him a picture of Ntsebeza. Nor did Sibaya offer any clue about his background or where he had learned the smatterings of various languages, including Russian, he had displayed on different occasions.

He claimed that he was merely a gardener, but that he had made a lot of money poaching crayfish. It was when he was caught poaching on 4 January 1994 that he was taken to Desmond Segal. He had expected simply to pay the usual bribe of R100 or R200 and be set free, but Segal arrested him and his companion, a taxi-driver known as Mazibuko.

According to Sibaya's sworn statement, he and Mazibuko were taken to the Bellville South police station, where Segal severely assaulted both of them. They were then given photographs of a black man and told his name was Ntsebeza and that they should remember his face. Segal also wrote down a Transkei car registration number that they had to learn by heart. Detective Johannes Machiel Etsebeth, whose name Sibaya claimed not to remember, later took down a statement by Sibaya.

Etsebeth's name emerged in a TRC hearing relating to the fatal shooting of Cape Town political activist Welile 'Deks' Dakuse on a piece of waste ground in January 1989. Dakuse, his wrists handcuffed in front of him, was shot twice by Etsebeth. The incident was seen by anti-apartheid groups as another summary execution. Etsebeth claimed self-defence. He and Segal said that Dakuse was showing them an arms cache when he produced a grenade and was about to pull the pin. His killing was simply accepted by the authorities.

Sibaya did, however, state that only he had made a statement. His friend Mazibuko had failed to turn up at the police station as Segal had demanded. Later it was discovered that Mazibuko had been shot dead. These events may have accounted for the fear Sibaya expressed about white people.

Pieces of jigsaw turned up, but too few to make a complete picture. Sibaya was seen at various times in the company of a group of white men who would drop him off at the local horse-racing track. His knowledge of Russian and ability to quote at length and in fluent English from the writings of Karl Marx and Lenin seemed to indicate that he might have been an early ANC or SACP recruit sent to the Soviet Union for training. In the 1970s he had been seen in Ghana by Mxolisi Mgxashe, a South African journalist then in exile. Mgxashe remembered that Sibaya was a member of a ship's crew. It was suspected that he could have been one of the security agents placed routinely on all South African-crewed ships.

Whatever he was or had been, Sibaya was not saying. When he was arrested in August 2000 and charged with perjury, he lapsed into his role of humble monolingual gardener, insisting on an isiXhosa interpreter. He also asked to be kept in prison, with an initial trial date set for November 2001, as he said he feared for his safety, though from whom he would not say. He continued to delay the legal proceedings and to remain in Pollsmoor prison until his case was finally heard in September 2002 and he was sentenced to three years in prison for perjury. The past, whose instrument he had been, seemed to be haunting him, but he still would not elaborate on any of his statements.

As Judge Richard Goldstone, who chaired the later commission of inquiry into the allegations against Dumisa Ntsebeza, remarked: 'The evidence does not sufficiently establish the identity of any person or persons who might have conspired with Mr Sibaya . . .' It was yet another example of unfinished business. An individual case, but with ties to a system controlled from the centre of political power. So it had been with much of the TRC story. Sibaya had been able to set back its already flawed and highly selective process by many months. Yet instead of this and other setbacks being seen in the media as amounting to a faulty start to examining the recent past, the TRC was already being widely hailed and promoted as a model for exposing the truth and bringing about reconciliation. The myth-makers were busy, weaving illusions based on moral equivalence, selective amnesia and religious atonement.

For Dumisa Ntsebeza, this rankled. But he was also personally angered by the fact that, although he had been advised to take up his right to legal assistance, the TRC refused to pay his legal bill. Yet this was a body which had given R1.6 million to P.W. Botha to prepare a submission to the TRC, which he then refused to deliver. It also took place within a system that had paid out more than R8 million to help former defence minister General Magnus Malan and others through a criminal trial that had, in the eyes of many legal practitioners, been farcical.

Such petty slights, like petty apartheid, tended to cause immediate anger and hurt. But they were nothing compared to the real hurt caused by a system that the TRC had barely begun to address when, with great fanfare, it abruptly wound up its proceedings. Even in terms of the narrow, personalised focus – which had effectively treated a few symptomatic boils on a totally diseased body politic – it had fallen abysmally short.

How was it, for example, that Joe Mamasela, confessed mass murderer and torturer, who publicly refused to apply for amnesty, was still employed by the state and faced no prosecution, four years after the TRC closed down? This was a man who, among his many crimes, had abducted ten young men in 1986 from Mamelodi near Pretoria, drugged them, and then burned them to death in a minibus. Was it because he had publicly announced that he knew, but would not name, five ministers in the first post-apartheid cabinet who were apartheid agents? Such rumours and insinuations will continue to circulate until the matter is resolved once and for all.

What about Joe Verster, the managing director of the CCB, and his band of murderous thugs? How was it that Henry William Bacon, aka Nico Esslin aka Nigel Barnett aka H.W. Otto, suspect in the killing of Swedish Prime Minister Olof Palme and on bail on an arson charge in Mozambique, could quietly settle in Cape Town in 2001? And above all, why turn a blind eye to those senior figures in the security establishment and their political masters who ordered and authorised so many of the proven cases of gross human rights abuse?

The fact that General Johan Coetzee, having made hardly any disclosures, was practising law in his hometown of Graaff-Reinet at the turn of the century was another source of anger. Even more flagrant was the conversion of another police general, Johan van der Merwe, involved in bombings and in ordering a murderous cross-border raid, into a leading figure in the Association for Equality before the Law, established to defend apartheid era human rights offenders. The list of such leading figures, directly involved in the commissioning and execution of everything from murders to blackmail, bombings and torture in the apartheid cause, is lengthy: the number runs into thousands. These are people who have – often literally – got away with murder.

Once again, of course, the price of this unfinished business is paid by those who have already suffered horribly. Many relatives of the missing and the murdered, prominent among them the Biko, Ribeiro, Mxenge, Slovo, Schoon, Asvat and Madaka families, are still seeking, if not justice, at least an approach to the truth. There has been no closure for them.

The UN declared apartheid a crime against humanity. It robbed generations of people not only of the dreams, but of the ability to dream. Apartheid was a complex system in which social engineers and planners set out deliberately to cripple the majority of the population at every possible level, from economic and occupational to educational and emotional. In pursuit of this goal, with a total and callous disregard for any human rights, they condemned millions of people to a slow death through malnutrition and preventable disease.

To police this system, another section of the population was infused with the poison of racism. This was systematically done through formal schooling that purposely manipulated history. Its aim – and broad achievement – was to provide the managerial and supervisory ranks on the one hand and the fodder for the factories, mines and farms on the other.

Here lies some of the world of unfinished business left unexplored by the TRC. It is not a healthy legacy. The agenda may have been aided by South Africa's transition to liberal democracy, but by not digging too deep the TRC has, in the long run, bequeathed a poisoned chalice. Until this tainted past is faced head-on, there will be no real transformation.

The TRC process went some of the way towards uncovering the truth, but it baulked at exposing the horrifying extent of the apartheid system and at bringing to book the most senior perpetrators of the human rights abuses it promoted: the politicians and the generals. The TRC deputy chairman, Alex Boraine, claimed that there was neither 'the time nor the resources to sniff out informers'. The truth is that there was not the political will to do so, or to probe too deeply into the system itself, let alone how the transition came about. The time exists; the resources could be found. The guilty are still there, many still in positions of enormous power. This book has shown that there is still a huge amount of evidence to be uncovered. Some of the documentation is still hoarded – as a form of insurance or even of blackmail – by a number of apartheid criminals, across the political spectrum, who escaped scot-free.

The fact that these issues have not been faced has enabled the myth of a 'fairytale' transition in South Africa to be widely disseminated across the world. Yet how long will this last? If the past is not dealt with, it will return to haunt us.

14

Endnote

by Dumisa Buhle Ntsebeza

Terry Bell and I have collaborated since 1993, when he visited me in Umtata at the time that I was handling the case of five youths who were murdered in their sleep by South African security forces. We shared a concern then that many of the horrors of the apartheid past might be buried, with potentially damaging consequences for the future. This concern was the genesis of the Understanding Our Past project and of this book.

Some readers may wish that *Unfinished Business* was specifically a book about the TRC. But it obviously is not. Others might have wished that it had focused on the history and activities of the Afrikaner Broederbond, since it deals in some detail with the AB. Some others might have wished that Terry had concentrated on the Transkei and/or my life and times in that context.

But in the many discussions throughout a lengthy literary gestation, I had to agree that there was already a plethora of books about the TRC. The important aspect missing from them was the detail of the attempt to frame me and so derail the process. As to the Transkei, there are already a number of general books on the subject, as the bibliography attests. But there were shards and fragments of fact – to use Terry's term – which had not yet surfaced at all or which provided insufficient detail. The AB is, indeed, a vital area of exploration. That it was the true brain of apartheid, and how, in general terms, it functioned, was what this book set out to explain. Obviously the AB is in need of much deeper examination. That would be another project entirely.

What *Unfinished Business* does do, and with great effect, is provide a wake-up call to all of us to start looking critically at what we have achieved since 1994. It is a clarion call to ask us what is the real legacy of the TRC and whether it is sustainable. It challenges us to question whether it is not a necessary requirement for us to critically appraise where we are and where we should be going if we are to sustain the achievements of the TRC.

As I became more involved in this project, I began to appreciate – and I would hope that you, the reader, can comfortably reach the same conclusion – that far from this book being an attack on the TRC, it is in fact a critical eulogy to its achievements. It acknowledges what the TRC achieved, given the time and capacity constraints, and given the breadth of its mandate. Despite an often brutally frank and harshly critical assessment of those who were the players in its struggle, the fundamental assumption is that the TRC played a tremendous role in the history of South Africa. The fundamental judgement is that it is amazing that it did so, considering the fundamental flaws with which the process was encumbered almost from the start.

For me, having served in the TRC, this is not a comfortable book to be part of, because it is not flattering of the manner in which I ran the investigative unit. It is not complimentary of a number of things that we did in the TRC, or rather did not do. I collaborated in the writing of *Unfinished Business*, however, because I am of the firm view that it says things that need to be said, now that the honeymoon is over – the time when we tried to believe that the TRC was the panacea for all our country's evils.

The first, South African, edition of this book was completed as South Africa prepared to host the World Conference Against Racism in August 2001. It emerged at a time when the United States of America, the self-styled policeman of the world, was attempting blatantly to dictate the agenda of that conference. The United States, using the threat of boycott, sought to prescribe that the conference should not deal with slavery and reparations and the Zionism/racism debate.

In this book, you will have read of the involvement of South African intelligence services as well as South African security forces, in one way or the other, with the United States and other countries of the West. In this period of transformation, it is necessary for South Africa to refuse to allow the United States to dictate a transformation agenda. An apartheid-free and independent

South Africa must be prepared to take its place among the free nations of the world that need now to fight the battle for economic emancipation. That too is the unfinished business of South Africans in their endeavour to deal with the evils of apartheid capitalism.

In the context of the Truth and Reconciliation Commission, the question of reparations reached a sticking point because our government seemed to prevaricate on the need for it to meet the recommendations of the TRC. It was a sad state of affairs: a democratic government that was behind the establishment of the TRC in the first place being unwilling to make reparations pursuant to the TRC's recommendations. The TRC recommended that those victims identified by the process be compensated to a maximum amount of R3 billion. This has not been done. The Mbeki government opted instead to give the victims a one-off payment of R30,000 and refused to impose a wealth tax on multinational corporations, as was recommended by the TRC. Yet the same government has been prepared to mortgage our country's future for what now appears to be a R50 billion-plus arms deal – the cost of which seems forever increasing – to foreign institutions for what clearly appear to be dubious gains.

It is a sad reflection of our times that while our government continues to blow hot and cold as to whether those identified victims of apartheid are to receive adequate and meaningful reparations, the TRC process has granted amnesty to a number of applicants, some of whom were guilty of the most heinous crimes. At the same time, prominent businessmen have been in denial as to their duty to pay reparations. One of them noted that such payments would be 'a waste of time'. As a consequence, the impression has been created that the TRC process was actually lenient towards perpetrators and has been disrespectful and unkind to victims and survivors.

Indeed, the victims of gross human rights violations identified by the TRC process have had to suffer the humiliation and ignominy of having to wait and hope for a government pay day which is still going to be subject to a lot of bureaucratic red tape.

The finalisation of the TRC process was stalled because Chief Mangosuthu Buthelezi and the Inkatha Freedom Party obtained a High Court injunction to halt the handover of the final report, and suggested that the TRC alter its finding relating to the IFP and its role in human rights abuses to one with which the party and Buthelezi would be more comfortable. The finding, published in 1998, was that the IFP was the non-governmental entity most responsible for the perpetration of gross human rights violations in the mandate period of the TRC. This standoff between the TRC and the IFP was overcome by a settlement that gave the IFP space in the final volumes of the TRC report to put in an appendix. This pours invective on the TRC process.

Another aspect of the unfinished business of the TRC is the extent to which it failed to seize the moment to promote reconciliation not only between perpetrator and victim, but also between beneficiaries (mostly white people) and victims (mostly black people).

Although the TRC held institutional hearings, we failed, it seems to me, to interrogate the role of big business, of the transnational companies, for their part in sustaining and perpetuating the apartheid order. We did not set out to find the evidence that would have supported a recommendation that the transnational companies, and the imperialist countries from whence they come, owe to the victims of South Africa (mostly black people) a duty to give reparations. It should not have been a duty of government alone to provide reparations, even if this is what the statute provided.

I think a case can be made that those who created an environment of 'gross human rights abuses' in South Africa, among them internally and externally based transnational companies, and the countries that supported them, are liable for the reconstruction of South African society. In a programme of reconstruction and development, reparations should include amounts that should be paid by big business both in and outside of South Africa. It is also essential to uncover the level of complicity of these corporate entities in the crime of apartheid. That also continues to remain the unfinished business of the TRC process.

It is, however, one aspect that is now being dealt with through the launching of what is expected to be a protracted series of class action lawsuits in the United States. These claims take advantage of the Alien Tort Claims Act of 1789, which grants jurisdiction to US federal courts over any civil action by an alien for a tort committed in violation of, among other things, the law of nations. I am privileged to have been appointed South African lead counsel in the cases which, if necessary, will be presented right up to the highest court in the US and possibly beyond.

The cases seek to chart new waters in an area of the law that is, admittedly, both imprecise and developmental. But they could also create a revolutionary legal precedent in international human rights law. Handled professionally and correctly, they could pave the way for similar cases elsewhere; international human rights law could develop in future to a degree where all those who do business in countries that have no regard for human rights must realise they do so at their peril.

The most ironic development with regard to these claims is the almost violent language with which they have been publicly rejected by the democratic government. Leading the charge, President Thabo Mbeki said his government found it 'unacceptable that matters that are central to the future of our country should be adjudicated in foreign courts'. The minister of trade and industry went so far as to suggest that, even if the victims of apartheid were successful in the foreign courts, the South African government would not enforce the judgements of those courts.

So, in a matter in which the victimised poor seek to get the beneficiaries of apartheid to be held to account for their unjust enrichment through apartheid, a crime against humanity, it is the leadership of a democratic government that seeks to protect the partners in the crime of apartheid from their day of reckoning.

While this book is not calling for a witch hunt (in the sense of relentless prosecutions), it opposes any form of blanket amnesty for perpetrators of the most heinous crimes in South Africa.

To grant such individuals amnesty – and it is reported that among these are army and police generals of the apartheid order and leading figures from KwaZulu-Natal – would be more than a travesty of justice. It would be a complete mockery of the achievements of the TRC process. It was therefore reassuring that President Mbeki told parliament in April: 'There shall be no general amnesty'. Amnesty yes, reconciliation yes, but amnesia, no!

Another worrying aspect of our quest for the truth has been the disappearance of thirty-four archive boxes and two folders of documents from the TRC archive. One of the files contained in that collection relates to the incomplete investigation into the 1988 murder in Paris of Dulcie September, the ANC's chief representative in France. We cannot afford to lose any more of the evidence of our past.

I agree with James Baldwin, quoted at the very beginning of the first file of this book:

> Not everything that is faced can be changed, but nothing can be changed until it is faced.

A second quotation used in this book, this time from Mac Maharaj, also bears repetition:

> To hide the horrors of the past in a collective amnesia would leave posterity with a legacy of festering guilt and unrelieved pain.

This book has been as much of a learning curve for me as it has been a wonderful experience to be involved in its creation. I trust that you too have found it as instructive and challenging as I have in rereading it. I would also hope that you will join me in committing yourself to ensuring that the truth about South Africa and apartheid – in a global and national context – is never buried nor distorted.

I rest my case.

Cape Town
May, 2003

Notes on sources

File 1: A crime against humanity

1

Major sources were the Goldstone Commission report, Harms Commission of Enquiry, TRC documents, especially the draft report entitled 'The Destruction of Records', as well as interviews with TRC officials, with Judge Richard Goldstone and taken from contemporary newspaper reports, especially from *Vrye Weekblad*. Other useful sources were *Reconstruction through Truth* (Asmal, Asmal & Suresh-Roberts), *In the Heart of the Whore* and *Into the Heart of Darkness* (Pauw) and De Kock and Gordin's *A Long Night's Damage*.

2

Author's own experience, including witnessing the 1960 shooting of Hendrik Verwoerd and research by the author for his *South Africa – a Modern Studies Handbook*, together with interviews with Paul Heylen (in New Zealand) and Sampie Terreblanche, provided material for this chapter. This was reinforced with material from the Hans Strydom archive, from relevant Hansard reports, and from contemporary newspaper reports. Additional sources were J.J. Human's *South Africa 1960*, Deborah Posel's *The Making of Apartheid 1948 to 1961*, Tom Lodge's *Black Politics in South Africa since 1948*, and Davenport and Saunders' *South Africa – a Modern History*.

3

The primary source for this chapter was the Hans Strydom archive, as well as discussions with Hans and Gertie Strydom, Sampie Terreblanche and the late Charles Bloomberg. Newspaper exposés by Bloomberg, Strydom, Ivor Wilkens and Hennie Serfontein, together with their books, *The Super Afrikaners* (Strydom and Wilkens), *Brotherhood of*

Power (Serfontein) and *The Afrikaner Broederbond* (Bloomberg), filled in detail, as did *Volkskapitalisme* by Dan O'Meara. Also invaluable was an interview with a senior Military Intelligence officer regarding reports on Namibia. *The Discarded People* (Desmond) provided the background to forced removals.

4

Details of the Kommunikasie Navorsingskomitee (Communication Research Committee) came from a series of interviews in New Zealand with Paul Heylen and documents from the author's archive. This was reinforced by the Pirsa archive at the University of Cape Town and by TRC documents and evidence which emerged in the trial of Wouter Basson. Details of the methods of recruitment for the early undercover agents came from an interview with a former policeman and now minister of religion and interviews with and an investigation into Anthony Roland Hitchcock, one of the early 'R' section recruits. These confirmed much of the material on the subject contained in Gordon Winter's *Inside BOSS*. The statements regarding Solwandle Ngudle's death were made to the author during interrogation at Compol security HQ, while John Harris managed to speak briefly to the author while both were held in nearby solitary cells in Pretoria Local prison. The woman who admitted telephoning the bomb warning was interviewed in Zambia in 1965 by the author. The material relating to John Lloyd and personal detail regarding Harris and the station bomb is from the archive of Ann and David Wolfe and interviews with Hugh Lewin. Information on journalist agents came from interviews with TRC investigators, from the confidential 1994 Security Branch head office list of 'media contacts', as well as interviews with, among others, Aida Parker, Chris Olckers and the late Tony Stirling. Additional sources included the Erasmus commission, author's personal knowledge of Gerhard Ludi ('QO18') – a 1964 interview with 'QO43', Klaus Schroeder and a 1963 interview with B.J. Vorster, as well as John D'Oliveira's *Vorster the Man*.

5

Interviews with a former parliamentary messenger and workmate of Dimitri Tsafendas, together with the transcript of the police interrogation of Tsafendas, bore out the findings about the probable mental condition of Tsafendas as reported by Peter Lambley in *The Psychology of Apartheid*. Interviews with Paul Heylen and Helen Suzman's *In No Uncertain Terms* provided useful background on the stabbing and subsequent events. Background to the political, military and media manoeuvring came mainly from interviews with journalists, including the late Tony Stirling, political commentators such as Sampie Terreblanche, and an interview with a senior Military Intelligence officer. Contemporary newspaper reports, and books such as *Vorster the Man* by John D'Oliveira, *They Live by the Sword* by Jan Breytenbach, and Peter Stiff's *The Silent War* were useful. Information on the emergence of the modern trade union movement came from interviews with trade unionists and books such as *Building Tomorrow Today* (Friedman), and on the economic background from *Black and Gold* (Sampson). The Africa Analysis archive and the author's archive provided information on Mozambique and Angola, as did the research by Anders Nilsson published as *Unmasking the Bandits*. Published references on the Smit murders and on 'Muldergate' and its background included *The Paper Curtain* and *The Real*

Information Scandal (Rhoodie), *South Africa – A Skunk among Nations* (De Villiers), *Mulder-gate* (Rees & Day), *Inside BOSS* (Winter) and TRC reports.

6

Information on Botha's plotting relies on reported private conversations with former cabinet minister Chris Heunis confirmed in interviews with Sampie Terreblanche; on contemporary newspaper reports and on TRC documents. Useful published information on the development of the Department of National Security came from *Rand Daily Mail* investigations. Britain's *Private Eye* archive provided useful background on the involvement of the Thatcher family in South Africa. Documents collected by TRC investigators gave a clear picture of the structure and operation of the National Security Management System. TRC hearings also gave an insight into the atrocities committed in neighbouring states. These were reinforced, together with more general background, in two separate interviews with Lieutenant Frederich 'Rich' Verster. Information on activities in Chile came from the author's experience in Chile in the immediate aftermath of the 1973 coup.

7, 8, 9

TRC documents and investigations by the author, including a series of interviews with contemporaries, contacts and ex-colleagues of Craig Williamson and Zac Edwards, together with a 64-page police report filed by Williamson in 1975, formed the basis for these chapters. Interviewees included Cedric de Beer, Glenn Moss, Rick de Satge, Laura Schultz, Eric Abraham, Ray and Jack Simons, Hugh Lewin, Horst Kleinschmidt, André Proctor, Geoff and Debbie Budlender, Sheila Lapinsky and the late Marius Schoon. Research undertaken by the Environmental and Developmental Agency (EDA) for the unpublished 'EDA Story' compiled by Verle Dieltiens from interviews by Robert Berold was also drawn on. Interviews with Neville Rubin regarding the IUEF years and with Rory Doepel regarding Fabio Barraclough added background. An interview with Barraclough confirmed the profile built largely from University of Witwatersrand files and the Trust Deeds of the ERT and PST. This was further corroborated in correspondence with the British Royal Society of Sculptors. The official IUEF Commission of Inquiry report into the Williamson affair, together with IUEF documents (author's archive), and contemporary newspaper reports ranging from the British *Guardian* (23 January 1980) to South African newspapers such as the *Rand Daily Mail*, *Daily Despatch*, *Sunday Times*, *Sunday Tribune* and *Sunday Post* over the same period, provided information and confirmation of data accumulated during investigations and discussions in various areas including the Hertford Inn. Useful information was also gleaned in telephone interviews with members of the Spanish anti-apartheid groups and with Mike Terry, former secretary of the Anti-Apartheid Movement in Britain.

File 2: End of the apartheid road

Much of the general information for the chapters in this file came from the 1956 report of the Tomlinson Commission, from *South Africa – the Peasants' Revolt* (Mbeki), *Black Politics in South Africa since 1945* (Lodge), *South Africa's Transkei – the Political Economy of an Independent*

Bantustan (Carter, Karris & Stultz), *South Africa's Transkei – the Politics of Domestic Colonialism* (Southall), *Transkei's Half Loaf* (Stultz) and *Tomorrow's Sun* (Joseph), as well as interviews with Paul Heylen in New Zealand. Apart from already listed published sources, TRC hearings into the Pondoland revolt provided useful information about the rebellion and the government's reaction. Material relating to traditional rule and to the Ntsebeza family came mainly from interviews with the Ntsebeza brothers and from discussions with their sister, Matuse. Additional information on the 1968 'Catwalk' incident came from former Rhodes University student Bryan Rostron. Detail on the Puflsa trial was obtained from the court record and from interviews with the Ntsebeza brothers. The personal archives of the brothers and contemporary reports such as that written by Andrew Nash provided much of the insight into the killing and subsequent events surrounding Bathandwa Ndondo. Letters, banishment orders and other documents from the archives of the Ntsebeza brothers, together with an interview with Winnie Mandela recorded by journalist Vernon Wright and *Tomorrow's Sun* (Joseph), as well as TRC hearings and documents provided the information on banishment. Information on the murders of Dumisa Ntsebeza's clients, the assault on Joseph Miso and the North Crest massacre is largely from the personal archives of the Ntsebeza brothers and from interviews with them supported by pathology reports, court records, some TRC documentation, and an interview with, and documentation supplied by, General Bantubonke Holomisa.

File 3: From cul-de-sac to compromise

1

TRC hearings and documents, contemporary newspaper reports and Hansard together with a 1982 NUSAS report *Total War in South Africa – Militarisation and the Apartheid State* and interviews with a former Civic Action draftee provided the background for this chapter. Other published sources included *Black and Gold* and *Mandela* (Sampson), *A Crime Against Humanity* (ed. Coleman) and *Who's Who in South African Politics*, vol. 3 (Gastrow).

2

Interviews with the late Rowley Arenstein, and confidential discussions with three senior ANC members, together with the Sue Rabkin affidavit and correspondence relating to the disappearance of Iggy Mathebula, a list of security police undercover agents (author's archive) and information provided to the author by Eugene de Kock, together with TRC documents, were the main sources of information for this chapter. Additional information was provided by a former colleague of the three spies Olivia Forsyth, Joy Harnden and Gordon Brookbanks.

3, 4

Details of the structure and operation of the State Security Council and its adjuncts was pieced together from disparate documents (author's archive and TRC), interviews with responsible TRC investigators, and TRC hearings. Material on the rugby tour came mainly from New Zealand anti-apartheid sources and in particular from Tom Newnham, author of

By Batons and Barbed Wire. It included interviews in New Zealand with Precious McKenzie. Information on possible informants in the ANC, and the separate intelligence organisation came from discussions held between the author and Joe Gqabi shortly before Gqabi was assassinated. Much of the detail about the 1964 mutiny in the ANC came as a result of interviews, primarily with Ameen Cajee, while information on the 1984 mutiny was gleaned from interviews with Bandile Ketelo and five other mutineers, and with a 'loyalist' MK commander, and was influenced by discussions with Andrew Masondo. Some information on the background and consequences of the 1984 mutiny came from two senior ANC sources. Piers Pigou provided invaluable help with information regarding TRC proposals and investigations, while Stanford University student research provided detail on the involvement of IBM. *The Right to Learn* (Christie), South African Research Services' material and *Power!* (MacShane *et al.*) contributed to the background on student and worker militancy. Other useful sources included *Black and Gold* (Sampson), *A Crime against Humanity* (ed. Coleman), *Searchlight South Africa* (vol. 5), *Comrades against Apartheid* (Ellis & Sechaba), *The Mind of South Africa* (Sparks), *Detention and Torture in South Africa* (Foster) and *Reconciliation through Truth* (Asmal *et al.*).

5

Brief discussions between the author and Willie Esterhuyse and Sampie Terreblanche in London in 1987, and several subsequent interviews with Terreblanche, together with numerous earlier discussions with Moses Mayekiso, Geoff Schreiner and other unionists in the mid-1980s, gave a good indication of the viewpoints at the time of the AB modernisers and of the trade union 'workerists'. The author, as international coordinator of the Friends of Moses Mayekiso campaign, was also in a good position to observe the tensions and stresses then. Interviews over the past three years with two senior members of the SACP, one of whom had served on the central committee, provided information on the SACP and Thabo Mbeki. Additional and confirmatory data came from the newspaper series 'The Thabo Mbeki Story' (Mark Gevisser, *Sunday Times*) and *The Life and Times of Thabo Mbeki* (Hadland & Rantao). Additional information on union activity came from sources such as *Breaking the Chains* (Kraak) and Friedman's *Building Tomorrow Today*. Also useful were *Long Walk to Freedom* (Mandela), *Mandela* and *Black and Gold* (Sampson), *Tomorrow Is Another Country* (Sparks), and discussions with Ronald Segal in 2001 and Olusegun Obasanjo in 1999.

6

Confidential information passed on to Africa Analysis in London in 1988 by a European presidential aide provided the background for the early part of this chapter. Much of the information was confirmed by subsequent TRC investigations and hearings. Various documents, including copies of letters from government ministers – available to the TRC – paint a clear picture of the destabilisation programme, the amounts spent and the extent of responsibility. Included in this is the official audit report of secret funds dated 12/8/91 and marked 'Top Secret'. Interviews with a senior Military Intelligence officer provided information on the reports to Pieter de Lange and to F.W. de Klerk. Additional information and confirmation came from interviews with journalists Bill Sharp, Jim Freeman and Gwen Lister. *Comrades against Apartheid* (Ellis & Sechaba), *Namibia – the Last Colony* (Green *et al.*), *South*

West Africa/Namibia (Tötemeyer) and UN documents, including *A Principle in Torment* and *A Trust Betrayed – Namibia*, were also useful sources.

7

Interviews between 1980 and 1982 in Tanzania and in London with Ameen Cajee and several early MK recruits, together with interviews between 1999 and 2001 with Sampie Terreblanche, Amy Thornton and several senior MK and ANC members now in government service, provided the core of this chapter. Various published sources used included *Mandela* (Sampson), *Anatomy of a Miracle* (Waldmeir), *The Life and Times of Thabo Mbeki* (Hadland & Rantao), *Tomorrow Is Another Country* (Sparks) and Gevisser's *The Thabo Mbeki Story*.

8

A number of long-serving members of the SACP, including Ray Simons, Jeremy Cronin and the late Chris Hani and Jack Simons, provided perspectives on much of the material in this chapter. So too did commentaries in *Searchlight South Africa* and other published sources such as *The Path to Power* (SACP), *The Last Trek* (De Klerk), *Reconciliation through Truth* (Asmal et al.), *Country of my Skull* (Krog), and *Looking Back, Reaching Forward* (ed. Villa-Vicencio & Verwoerd), together with TRC and Codesa documents.

9

Interviews with Dumisa Ntsebeza, documents from his personal archive and discussions with various members of the TRC form the basis of this chapter, together with, in particular, *A Country Unmasked* (Boraine). Background and additional information came from discussions with various participants at the Codesa I talks, and from a pre-TRC interview with Archbishop Tutu.

10

Interviews with TRC investigator Jan-Ake Kjellenberg and the reports he submitted to the TRC were the sources for much of the information relating to Horace Doncaster and his long-serving Mozambique agent, Henry Bacon etc. As deputy defence minister, Ronnie Kasrils confirmed some of the information gathered, while a senior Military Intelligence officer and another former officer, Henri van der Westhuizen, provided additional data on Doncaster and Bacon/Esslin/Barnett. Investigative journalist Debora Patta provided some of the current information relating to Bacon. The primary source of information about Aubrey Levin came from *The Aversion Project* compiled by Mikki van Zyl, Jeannelle de Gruchy, Sheila Lapinsky, Simon Lewin and Graeme Reid. This was supported by the final submission to the TRC of the Health and Human Rights Project, by an interview with a former inmate of Ward 22, discussion with Prof. Leslie London and by reports in the *Mail and Guardian*.

11, 12, 13

Dumisa Ntsebeza supplied most of the background for these chapters and made available
relevant letters and documents from his personal archive. Interviews with Wilson Magadla
and other TRC investigators, together with the report of the commission of inquiry headed
by Judge Richard Goldstone, filled in detail and provided confirmation of events. Different
perspectives on these events were gained mainly from books by Alex Boraine (*A Country
Unmasked*), Desmond Tutu (*No Future without Forgiveness*) and Anjic Krog (*Country of My
Skull*). Information about and impressions of Bennett Sibaya were gained from the author's
observations, from a detailed assessment made by the man who acted as Sibaya's financial
consultant, and the assessments of estate agent Mike Levy, lawyer Martin Sheard and
journalist Mxolisi Mgxashe. Roland Palm provided the information, including documentation,
regarding the arrest and jailing of his son.

Select bibliography

Alden, Chris: *Apartheid's Last Stand – the Rise and Fall of the South African Security Forces* (Macmillan, London 1996)

Allighan, Garry: *Verwoerd – the End* (Purnell & Sons, Cape Town 1961)

Arnold, Guy: *South Africa – Crossing the Rubicon* (Macmillan, London 1992)

Asmal, Kader, Louise Asmal and Ronald Suresh-Roberts: *Reconciliation through Truth: A Reckoning of Apartheid's Criminal Governance* (David Philip, Cape Town 1996)

Bell, Terry: *South Africa – a Modern Studies Handbook* (Observer, London 1987)

Benson, Mary: *Nelson Mandela – the Man and the Movement* (Penguin, London 1994)

Bloomberg, Charles: *Christian Nationalism and the Rise of the Afrikaner Broederbond in South Africa 1918 to 1948* (Macmillan, London 1990)

Boraine, Alex: *A Country Unmasked – inside South Africa's Truth and Reconciliation Commission* (OUP, Oxford 2000)

Botha, P.W. (compiled by J.J.J. Scholtz): *Fighter and Reformer – Extracts from the Speeches of P.W. Botha* (Bureau of Information, Pretoria 1989)

Breytenbach, Jan: *They Live by the Sword* (Lemur, 1990)

Carter, Gwendolyn M., Thomas Karris & Newell M. Stultz: *South Africa's Transkei – the Political Economy of an Independent Bantustan* (N-W University Press, Evanston, 1967)

Cawthra, Gavin: *Brutal Force – the Apartheid War Machine* (IDAF, London 1986)

Christie, Pam: *The Right to Learn – the Struggle for Education in South Africa* (Raven, Johannesburg 1985)

Coleman, Max (ed.): *A Crime against Humanity – Analysing the Repression of the Apartheid State* (HRC, Johannesburg 1998)

Davenport, Rodney & Christopher Saunders: *South Africa – a Modern History* (Macmillan, London 2000)

Davies, Rob, Dan O'Meara & Sipho Dlamini: *The Struggle for South Africa – a Reference Guide to Movements, Organisations and Institutions* (vol. 2) (Zed, London 1984)

De Klerk, F.W.: *The Last Trek – a New Beginning* (Macmillan, London 1998)

De Kock, Eugene (as told to Jeremy Gordin): *A Long Night's Damage – Working for the Apartheid State* (Contra, Johannesburg 1998)

De Villiers, Les: *Secret Information* (Tafelberg, Cape Town 1980); *South Africa – a Skunk among Nations* (International Books, London 1975)

Desmond, Cosmos: *The Discarded People – an Account of South African Resettlement* (Christian Institute, Johannesburg 1970)

D'Oliveira, John: *Vorster the Man* (Ernest Stanton, Johannesburg 1977)

Du Pisanie, J.A. (ed.): *Divided or United Power – Views on the New Constitutional Dispensation* (Lex Patria, Johannesburg 1986)

Ellis, Stephen & Tsepho Sechaba: *Comrades against Apartheid – the ANC and the SACP in Exile* (James Currey, London 1992)

Els, Paul: *We Fear Naught But God – the Story of the SA Special Forces (the Recces)* (Covos Day, Johannesburg 2000)

Esterhuyse, Willie & Philip Nel (ed.): *The ANC and Its Leaders* (Tafelberg, Cape Town 1990)

Esterhuyse, Willie: *Anton Rupert – Advocate of Hope* (Tafelberg, Cape Town 1986)

Foster, Don: *Detention and Torture in South Africa – Psychological, Legal and Historical Studies* (David Philip, Cape Town 1987)

Frederickse, Julie: *The Unbreakable Thread* (Zed Books, London 1990)

Friedman, Steven: *Building Tomorrow Today – African Workers in Trade Unions 1970 to 1984* (Raven, Johannesburg 1987)

Gastrow, Sheila: *Who's Who in South African Politics* (vol. 3) (Hans Zell, London 1990)

Green, Reginald, Marja-Liisa Kiljunen & Kimmo Kiljunen (ed.): *Namibia – the Last Colony* (Longman, London 1981)

Hachten W.A. & C.A. Giffard: *Total Onslaught – the South African Press under Attack* (Macmillan, Johannesburg 1984)

Hadland, Adrian & Jovial Rantao: *The Life and Times of Thabo Mbeki* (Zebra, Johannesburg 1999)

Health & Human Rights Project: *Final TRC Submission* (Cape Town 1997)

Human, J.J.: *South Africa 1960 – a Chronicle* (Tafelberg, Cape Town 1961)

Johnson, R.W.: *How Long Will South Africa Survive?* (Macmillan, London 1977)

Joseph, Helen: *If This Be Treason – Diary of the Treason Trial 1956 to 1961* (André Deutsch, London 1963); *Tomorrow's Sun* (Hutchinson, London 1966); *Side by Side* (Zed, London 1986)

Kraak, Gerald: *Breaking the Chains – Labour in South Africa in the 1970s and 1980s* (Pluto, London 1993)

Krog Antjie: *Country of My Skull* (Random House, Johannesburg 1998)

Lambley, Peter: *The Psychology of Apartheid* (Secker & Warburg, London 1980)

Lipton, Merle: *Capitalism and Apartheid – South Africa 1910 to 1986* (David Philip, Cape Town 1989)

Lodge, Tom: *Black Politics in South Africa since 1945* (Longman, London 1983)

Ludi, Gerhard & Blaar Grobbelaar: *The Amazing Mr Fischer* (Nasionale Boekhandel, Cape Town 1966)

Ludi, Gerhard: *Operation Q018* (Nasionale Boekhandel, Cape Town 1969)

MacShane, Denis, Martin Plaut & David Ward: *Power – Black Workers, Their Unions and the Struggle for Freedom in South Africa* (Spokesman, Nottingham 1984)

Mandela, Nelson: *Long Walk to Freedom* (Little Brown, London 1994)

Mbeki, Govan: *South Africa – the Peasants' Revolt* (Penguin, London 1964)

McKinley, Dale T.: *The ANC and the Liberation Struggle – a Critical Political Biography* (Pluto, London 1997)

Meli, Francis: *South Africa Belongs to Us – a History of the ANC* (Zimbabwe Publishing, Harare 1988)

Newnham, Tom: *By Batons and Barbed Wire* (Real Pictures, Auckland 1980)

Nilsson, Anders: *Unmasking the Bandits – the True Face of the MNR* (ECASAAMA, London 1990)

NUSAS 82: *Total War in South Africa – Militarisation and the Apartheid State* (Allies Press, Cape Town 1982)

O'Meara, Dan: *Volkskapitalisme – Class, Capital and Ideology in the Development of Afrikaner Nationalism 1934 to 1948* (Raven, Johannesburg 1983)

Pampallis, John: *Foundations of a New South Africa* (Zed, London 1991)

Pauw, Jacques: *Into the Heart of Darkness – Confessions of Apartheid Assassins* (Jonathan Ball, Johannesburg 1997); *In the Heart of the Whore – the Story of Apartheid's Death Squads* (Southern, Johannesburg 1991)

Posel, Deborah: *The Making of Apartheid 1948 to 1961 – Conflict and Compromise* (OUP, Oxford 1991)

Rees, Mervyn & Chris Day: *Muldergate – the Story of the Information Scandal* (Macmillan, Johannesburg 1980)

Rhoodie, Eschel: *The Paper Curtain* (Voortrekkerpers, Johannesburg 1969); *The Real Information Scandal* (Orbis, Pretoria 1983)

Rhoodie, N.J. (ed.): *South African Dialogue – Contrasts in South African Thinking on Basic Race Issues* (McGraw-Hill, South Africa 1972); *Apartheid and Racial Partnership in Southern Africa* (Academia, Pretoria 1969)

Rupert, Anton: *Progress through Partnership* (Nasionale Boekhandel, Cape Town 1967)

SACP: *The Path to Power* (SACP, 1989)

Sampson, Anthony: *Black and Gold – Tycoons, Revolutionaries and Apartheid* (Hodder & Stoughton, London 1987); *Mandela – the Authorised Biography* (Harper Collins, London 1999)

Sanders, James: *South Africa and the International Media 1972 to 1979 – a Struggle for Representation* (Frank Cass, London 2000)

Saul, John S. & Stephen Gelb: *The Crisis in South Africa* (Zed, 1986)

Schrire, Robert (ed.): *Leadership and the Apartheid State from Malan to De Klerk* (OUP, Oxford 1994)

Scott, John: *Venture to the Exterior – through Europe with P.W. Botha* (Acme, Port Elizabeth 1984)

Serfontein, J.I I.P.: *Brotherhood of Power – an Exposé of the Secret Afrikaner Broederbond* (Rex Collings, London 1978)

Shubin, Vladimir: *ANC – A View from Moscow* (Mayibuye, Cape Town 1999)

Simons, Jack & Ray: *Class & Colour in South Africa 1850–1950* (IDAF, London 1983)

Slovo, Gillian: *Every Secret Thing* (Little Brown, London 1997)

Southall, Roger: *South Africa's Transkei – the Politics of Domestic Colonialism* (Heinemann, London 1982)

Sparks, Allister: *The Mind of South Africa* (Heinemann, London 1990); *Tomorrow Is Another Country – the Inside Story of South Africa's Negotiated Settlement* (Heinemann, London 1995)

Stiff, Peter: *The Silent War – South African Recce Operations 1969–1994* (Galago, Johannesburg 1997); *Selous Scouts – Top-Secret War* (with Ron Reid-Daly, Galago, Johannesburg 1982)

Strydom, Hans & Ivor Wilkens: *The Super Afrikaners – inside the Afrikaner Broederbond* (Jonathan Ball, Johannesburg 1978)

Stultz, Newell M.: *Transkei's Half Loaf – Race Separation in South Africa* (David Philip, Cape Town 1980)

Suzman, Helen: *In No Uncertain Terms – Memoirs* (Sinclair-Stevenson, London 1993)

Tambo, Oliver (compiled by Adelaide Tambo): *Preparing for Power – Oliver Tambo Speaks* (Heinemann, London 1987)

TRC: *TRC Reports*, vols 1–5 (Juta, Cape Town 2000)

Tötemeyer, G.: *South West Africa/Namibia* (Fokus-Suid, Pretoria 1977)

Tutu, Desmond: *No Future without Forgiveness* (Random House, London 1999)

Van der Merwe, Hendrik W. & David Welsh: *NUSAS, ASB, NAFSAS, SASO – Student Perspectives of South Africa* (David Philip, Cape Town 1972)

Van Zyl, De Gruchy, Lapinsky, Lewin & Reid: *The Aversion Project* (GALA, Johannesburg 1999)

Various editors: *SA Review* nos 3, 4 & 5 (Raven, Johannesburg 1986, 87, 89)

Villa-Vicencio, Charles & Wilhelm Verwoerd (ed.): *Looking Back, Reaching Forward – Reflections on the Truth and Reconciliation Commission of South Africa* (University of Cape Town, Cape Town 2000)

Waldmeir, Patti: *Anatomy of a Miracle* (Penguin, London 1997)

Webster, Eddie (ed.): *Essays in Southern African Labour History* (Ravan, Johannesburg 1978)

Williams, Gwyneth & Brian Hockland: *The Dictionary of Contemporary Politics of Southern Africa* (Routledge, London 1988)

Winter, Gordon: *Inside BOSS – South Africa's Secret Police* (Penguin, London 1981)

Wolpe, Harold: *Race, Class and the Apartheid State* (Unesco, Paris 1988)

Index

DATE DUE

GAYLORD · PRINTED IN U.S.A.